AMERICA & ISLAM

OTHER BOOKS BY THE AUTHOR

The New Arab Journalist: Mission & Identity in a Time of Turmoil
Reflections in a Bloodshot Lens: America, Islam & the War of Ideas
Seeds of Hate: How America's Flawed Middle East Policy Ignited the Jihad
Co-edited with Stephen Franklin
Islam for Journalists (and Everyone Else)

For my children: Annya, Shantara and Justin

*"[T]he arc of a child's life only appears for a while to match
the arc of a parent's,*

in reality one sits atop the other."

Exit West, Mohsin Hamid

And for my wife, Indira:

Who gave me the gift of our family and so much more.

CONTENTS

REVIEWS

About *The New Arab Journalist*

"Lawrence Pintak remains the foremost chronicler of the interaction between the Arab and Western media worlds ... There is no better starting point for defusing the clash of nationalisms and worldviews than absorbing the kind of factual understanding that emanates from this book."
RAMI KHOURI, COLUMNIST AND FORMER DIRECTOR
Issam Fares Institute for Public Policy and International Affairs.

"Many Western journalists have been fascinated by the Middle East, but very few are capable of telling you just how it works."
YOSRI FOUDA, FORMER CHIEF INVESTIGATIVE
CORRESPONDENT, AL JAZEERA

About *Reflections in a Bloodshot Lens: America, Islam & the War of Ideas*

"An acute, informed and timely insight into colliding worlds of perception which dominate the global agenda."
JIM MUIR, MIDDLE EAST CORRESPONDENT
FOR THE BBC AND OTHERS

"Pintak combines the keen eye of a journalist with [a] sharp intellect. [He] is not afraid to demolish entrenched mythologies."
HISHAM MELHEM, WASHINGTON CORRESPONDENT,
***AN-NAHAR* NEWSPAPER (LEBANON) AND HOST,**
AL-ARABIYA TV'S *ACROSS THE OCEAN*

About *Seeds of Hate: How America's Flawed Middle East Policy Ignited the Jihad*

"One of the most perceptive accounts of the nightmare in Lebanon."
THE WASHINGTON POST

"A tour d'force."
ANTHONY LEWIS, FOREIGN AFFAIRS COLUMNIST,
THE NEW YORK TIMES

"Reminiscent of early Hemingway."
JOHN COOLEY, *MIDDLE EAST JOURNAL*

ABOUT THE AUTHOR

"A historian is often only a journalist facing backwards."

KARL KRAUS

Lawrence Pintak is an award-winning journalist and scholar who has written about America's complex relationship with Islam since 1980. A former CBS News Middle East correspondent, he was the founding dean of The Edward R. Murrow College of Communication at Washington State University (2009–16) and was named a Fellow of the Society of Professional Journalists in 2017 for "outstanding service to the profession of journalism" around the world.

Pintak reported on the birth of modern suicide bombing and the rise of Hezbollah, the Iran-Iraq War, the Israeli invasion of Lebanon and a variety of other stories across the Middle East. His career extends from the Carter White House to the Indonesian revolution, Armenia to Zimbabwe. He won two Overseas Press Club awards and was twice nominated for international Emmys.

Pintak hosted *American Fault/Lines*, a ten-part, one-hour radio series examining divisive issues in the U.S. following the 2016 U.S. presidential election, and *The Murrow Interview*, a series of broadcast conversations with leading figures in international affairs and global journalism. He was founding publisher of the online journal *Arab Media & Society*. His work has appeared in *The New York Times*, ForeignPolicy.com, CNN. com, the *International Herald Tribune*, *The Daily Beast*, *The Seattle Times* and a variety of other publications and he is frequently interviewed by NPR, CNN, Al Jazeera English, BBC and news organizations around the world.

Prior to WSU, Pintak served as director of the Kamal Adham Center for Journalism Training and Research at The American University in Cairo, where he headed what was then the only graduate journalism degree in the Arab world, and he has helped modernize curricula at journalism schools in the Arab world, the Caucasus and Pakistan. He is a member of the board of advisers of the Center for Excellence in Journalism in Pakistan, the Content Advisory Committee for the Media Majlis in Qatar, and has been an adviser to the U.S. State Department on journalism in Pakistan. He holds a PhD in Islamic Studies from the University of Wales, Trinity Saint David.

AUTHOR'S NOTE

I n the fall of 2015, as I listened to the increasingly vitriolic anti-Muslim rhetoric of the GOP primary, I decided it was time for another book. My previous works had all dealt in some way with the intersection of media, perception and policy in America's relationship with the world's Muslims. Now that intersection was playing out right here at home.

I thought it would be important to write a forward-looking book: 'Where do we go from here?' What damage had the GOP primary done to America's relationship with our Muslim allies abroad and our Muslim citizens at home? What steps were being taken to repair that damage and move forward?

And then Donald Trump won the election. For several months, I struggled to identify a new vision. Did I wait four years and chronicle how his presidency affected America's relationship with the world's Muslims? And what if he won a second term? Should I wait eight years? Neither was an option; my attention span is too short.

In the end, I settled on the approach taken in the following pages. It is certainly not the last word on America and Islam in the Trump era, but I would like to think this book frames the conversation and gives a baseline of facts in a time when they are becoming an endangered species.

The campaign showed us—and the world's Muslims—who Trump is and what he thinks of them; his first year in office gave us a sense of how that rhetoric is transformed into policy toward Muslims at home and abroad. I have tried to chronicle all of this against the backdrop of America's long and complex relationship with Islam.

A word on citations: The overwhelming majority of the notations in this book provide references for comments by Trump, members of his administration and the candidates he defeated in the primary. Since most of these have been widely reported, my preference would have been to dispense with specific citations. However, in an era when politicians reject as "fake news" their own words if they are no longer convenient, I thought it important to carefully source each quote.

While researching this book, I interviewed hundreds of people on three continents, many of them on multiple occasions. Given all the references I mention above, I have opted not to include citations listing the specific time and place of the interviews. In most cases, it is clear from the text that these quotes come from conversations with me. I think I am safe in saying that anytime you see a quote that does not include a citation for another source, it is from an interview I conducted.

INTRODUCTION

All those who have any religion are against the emigration of people from the eastern hemisphere.
PRESBYTERIAN MINISTER DAVID CALDWELL (D. 1824)

"Islam hates us."

Those three words helped propel Donald Trump to the White House. They provoked jeers from his supporters, fear within the American Muslim body politic and anger across the Muslim world. And they won him enough votes to capture the Electoral College.

That declaration—"Islam hates us"[1]—demonized an entire religion, reshaped the image of America as a nation of tolerance and refuge and did more damage to the country's long-term interests than the death of a thousand civilians in drone strikes.

Trump's words reflected a simplistic and distorted worldview, but the fault did not lie with him alone. Donald Trump was the almost-inevitable product of a long history of misguided policies and misleading assumptions about Islam.

The reality TV star and master media manipulator deftly tapped a primal fear among those who subscribed to the near-religious conviction that Islam and the West were destined for a "clash of civilizations."[2] The theory, which posited as ineluctable a confrontation along the "bloody borders" between the Islamic and non-Islamic worlds, was based on false assumptions, but the words and actions of at least six U.S. presidents would make it a self-fulfilling prophecy.

From Jimmy Carter's early funding of those who would become the Taliban to Ronald Reagan's disastrous military foray in Lebanon, which gave birth to Hezbollah; from George H. W. Bush's double-cross of Iraq's Shi'a to his son's ill-fated invasion of that country; from Bill Clinton's dithering on Bosnia to Barack Obama's empty promise of a "new beginning" in relations between the United States and the world's

Muslims, American administrations had simultaneously fueled the radicalization of Muslim extremists, angered America's natural allies in the Muslim world and created the circumstances that facilitated the demonization of the world's 1.6 billion Muslims.

The logical culmination came in 2016. Donald Trump and ISIS; it was the perfect storm. The rise of the blood-soaked Islamic State, the first acts of terrorism by American Muslims on American soil and the take-no-prisoners rhetoric of the U.S. presidential campaign meant conditions had ripened for the arrival of a modern-day crusader, ready to cast asunder the moral conventions that—at some level—had constrained his predecessors, in order to "eradicate" the "evil" of Islamist extremism from "the face of the earth."[3]

He was hailed by a subset of Americans in search of someone—or something—to blame for their economic plight, and urged on by a cadre of true believers, led by advisers who were convinced, "We're in a world war against a messianic mass movement of evil people."[4]

Donald Trump's rise inspired not only his legions of supporters but also his sworn enemies as well. For Trump's rhetoric, and later actions, were, as Iran's foreign minister put it, "a great gift to extremists."[5]

"The natural relationship between Islam and the United States is one of friendship," President Jimmy Carter had declared in a February 1980 speech in Morocco, three months after the U.S. embassy in Tehran was stormed and fifty-two American diplomats were taken hostage. The embassy siege enraged the American people, but Carter made clear he would not be provoked: "I can assure you that this just anger will not be twisted into a false resentment against Islam or its faithful."[6]

Four decades later, those comments seemed almost quaint. We were living in a very different world.

"Why?" No Longer

In the wake of the U.S. invasion of Iraq, I published a book about the fundamental disconnect between the U.S. and the Muslim world.[7] As I wrote at the time,

The essence of this worldview disconnect was encapsulated in the question that rose like a collective moan from the U.S. body politic after 9/11, "Why do they hate us?" and was mirrored by an equally bewildered, "Why can't they see?"[8]

A decade later, an alliance of cynical politicians, Islamophobes and white nationalists jettisoned the "why?" and transformed a plaintive question into an angry statement: "Islam hates us." The result was a toxic cocktail of vitriol that fed fear and anger at home and resentment abroad.

Muslims were "terrorist savages" and "mongrels," part of the "rubbish from the desperate and criminal populations of the Third World" who had "backfilled" America.[9] Those comments, from the owner of a Washington state aerospace manufacturing company, were emblematic of how the name-calling and innuendo of the primary gave permission for grassroots Islamophobes to openly say what they had so long whispered among themselves.

Terrorist atrocities in Paris and Brussels, the killing of fourteen people by a Pakistani-American and his Pakistani wife in San Bernardino, California, and the unspeakable slaughter of forty-nine at an Orlando nightclub by Omar Mateen, the mentally unstable and homophobic U.S.-born son of Afghan immigrants, were just a few of the incidents that became campaign fodder, inevitably fueling Islamophobia within a portion of the electorate and resonating outward across the media and the minds of other Americans.

In previous elections, it was common for candidates on both sides of the aisle to compete over who was more supportive of Israel. At times in the 2016 presidential primary, it appeared that the goal was to see who could prove themselves the more committed enemy of Islam.

Moors and Devils

Anti-Muslim xenophobia was nothing new; America's fear of Islam was older than the republic itself. Even before Paul Revere rode through Massachusetts warning, "The British are coming," his compatriots were effectively saying the same thing about Muslims.[10]

In the 1600s, Cotton Mather, minister of Boston's Old North Church, fulminated against "Mahometan Turks and Moors, and Devils" when news trickled back to the colonies that Americans were being taken hostage in North Africa, a precursor to today's Middle East kidnappings.

Mather reassured his congregants that "we are afar off, in a Land, which never had (that I ever heard of) one Mahometan breathing in it."[11]

But just because Mather hadn't heard about them didn't mean they weren't there. It is believed the first Muslim arrived in the New World around 1527 with the conquistadors and the first documented Muslim settler in the U.S. was recorded in the Dutch province of New Netherland—we now know the area as the mid-Atlantic states—around 1630. In fact, according to scholar Kambiz Ghaneabassiri's book *A History of Islam in America*, you could almost say America owed its existence to Muslims in a backhanded kind of way, since Europeans were, in part, looking for a trading route that avoided the Muslim empires of North Africa and the Middle East when they "discovered" America.[12]

Many of the slaves dragged ashore in irons were Muslims, prisoners captured during West African jihads against those considered insufficiently pure by tribes that adhered to a fundamentalist interpretation of Islam—not unlike modern extremists from the so-called Islamic State and its offshoots. In fact, Islam was introduced to the North American continent by the Spanish long before Protestantism, though even then, according to historian Sylviane A. Diouf, it was viewed with fear and suspicion: "[T]he fight against the possible spread of Islam had been an intense preoccupation in the Spanish colonies."[13] The first revolt by Muslim African slaves, on the island of Hispaniola in 1522

> prompted the newly crowned Charles V of Spain to exclude from the Americas "slaves suspected of Islamic leanings." He blamed the revolt on their radical ideology rather than the harsh realities of living a life of slavery.[14]

But there was money to be made, so slavers largely ignored Charles. It is likely there were more Muslims in America in the years after independence than Catholics or Jews.[15] African-American abolitionist and statesman Frederick Douglass was believed to have been descended from Muslims.[16] (It's worth noting that as he marked Black History Month shortly after taking office, Donald Trump would seemingly reincarnate Douglass, who died in 1895, telling his audience, "Frederick Douglass is an example of somebody who's done an amazing job and is getting recognized more and more, I notice."[17])

George Washington listed on his 1784 property records two slaves named "Fatimer" and "Little Fatimer," almost certainly named for

Fatima, the daughter of the Prophet Muhammad.[18] Colonial-era slave documentation frequently mentioned Muslim names like Mustapha, Bilali, Moosa (from Moses) and Bubacar (from Abu Bakr, who became the leader of Islam on the death of the Prophet Muhammad).[19] But most slave owners were likely unaware of the religion of their human property, both because of the language barrier and the fact that many slaves submitted to pseudo-conversions to Christianity for their own protection.

Scholars believe that some African-American plantation traditions can be traced back to Islam. An example is the "ring shout," a dance in which participants turned counterclockwise around a church or altar, likely a New World re-enactment of worship at the Ka'aba in Mecca, Islam's holiest site, one circumambulation of which is known as a *sha'wt*.[20] Copies of the Qur'an arrived with early European settlers and would soon be printed in America. Mather himself is said to have read the Muslim holy book regularly; "know thine enemy" and all that. But Mather was far from being a lone voice of intolerance. As historian Thomas Kidd documented in his book *American Christians and Islam*, gentle Roger Williams, the Quaker founder of a refuge for religious minorities in what became Rhode Island, prayed that "the Pope and Mahomet" would be "flung in to the Lake that burns with Fire and Brimstone," while Aaron Burr wrote of the "Rise of that false Prophet and great Impostor Mahomet."[21]

That notion of a "false Prophet" traced its lineage back to the Crusades and was woven into Western literature and lore, from Dante, who consigned Muhammad to the ninth circle of Hell, to Thomas Aquinas, who wrote,

Muhammad ... perverts almost all the testimonies of the Old and New Testaments by making them into fabrications of his own.[22]

Medieval troubadours riled up the masses with "searing images of Christ being hit in the face by an Arab and a mounted Saracen [Muslim soldier] above the Holy Sepulchre, his horse urinating on the sacred site,"[23] firmly imprinting a visceral revulsion of Muslims on the Christian European mind.

The Life of Mahomet, a popular anti-Muslim tract published in 1802, demanded "the conquest of Mahometan countries," arguing,

The monstrous blasphemy and absurdities of Mahomet must fall ... The contest is between barbarity and benevolence, between Jehovah and a monster in the shape of a man.[24]

Hatred of Islam and Muhammad was even exploited by Voltaire, who used it as cover for a political commentary on French tyranny in his play *Mahomet the Imposter*:

The sword of Alcoran [the Qur'an] in my bloody hands
Will impose silence on the rest of humanity.[25]

The play was later adapted by the American revolutionaries and staged in Baltimore, with King George III replacing the French king as the analogy to Muhammad as the imposter.[26]

Former president Barack Obama may have laughed off claims he was a Muslim, but from the earliest days, Islam has been an epithet in American politics. Thomas Jefferson was the first leader accused of being a secret Muslim, the ultimate slur in eighteenth-century America.[27] John Adams was labeled the "new Muhammad,"[28] and John Quincy Adams disparagingly compared Jefferson to "the Arabian prophet."[29]

Muslims were the first enemies of the new republic. The U.S. Navy was created to battle them. In the years after independence, the Barbary pirates were ravaging American shipping along the North African coast, prompting Thomas Jefferson to order a navy be built to mount what would be the first of many U.S. military interventions in the Middle East. In a nineteenth-century version of "shock and awe," the Navy and the Marines brought the Pasha of Tripoli to his knees. That's the "shores of Tripoli" part of the Marine Corps hymn.[30]

Francis Scott Key's 1805 poem "When the Warrior Returns from the Battle Afar," sung to the melody later reused in the "Star-Spangled Banner," celebrated the U.S. defeat of the Barbary pirates, when "the turbaned heads bowed" and the Islamic crescent flag was "obscured by the light of the star-spangled flag of our nation."[31]

Like today's anti-Muslim conspiracy theorists, early Americans feared more than just the swords of Muslim marauders. The Ottoman Caliphate had pioneered the use of vaccinations to fight smallpox, so naturally some colonialists considered them "the work of the Devil."[32] No surprise, since many early Americans, such as Congregational pastor Jonathan Edwards, equated Muhammad with the Antichrist and believed the war against Islam would bring about Armageddon and Judgment Day,[33] echoing Protestant reformer Martin Luther who, centuries before, had declared, "The person of the Antichrist is at the same time the pope and the Turk," the era's common term for Muslims.[34] Those notions were still alive in twenty-first-century America, with both Christian[35] and Muslim[36] anti-vaccine zealots using that same "work of the Devil" line, while born-again preachers like Pat Robertson and Franklin Graham were still tying Muslims to the end times.[37]

As Jack Shaheen so effectively documented in his books *Reel Bad Arab* and *The TV Arab*, Hollywood has fed the anti-Muslim/Arab narrative since Rudolph Valentino donned headgear in *The Sheikh* in 1921. But the 2016 Republican primary legitimized anti-Muslim rhetoric in ways we had never seen before.

Enter Donald Trump

"There is tremendous hate," Trump said of Muslims around the world in the March 2016 GOP debate. "Large portions want to use very, very harsh means" against Americans.[38]

His campaign trail speeches, and those of senators Marco Rubio and Ted Cruz, the opponents he would eventually vanquish, were no less incendiary than the sermons of clergy who had preached religious hatred 350 years before. They repeatedly erased the line between extremists who acted in the name of Islam and the vast majority of the world's—and America's—Muslims.

"You rely on the promotion of fear and Internet lies to fuel the flames of hate and divisiveness across our country," the Muslim Public Affairs Council (MPAC) charged in a February 2016 letter to Trump, challenging him to a debate. "Well, we have news for you: We will no longer be bullied. We will no longer be your punching bag."

But they were. And it had the potential to shape America's relationship with a quarter of the world's population for decades to come.

On an Emirates Airline flight from Washington, DC, to Dubai in early 2016, one of my fellow passengers, a Kenyan-American Muslim, asked permission to use the exit space in front of me to perform his prayers. If this was a U.S. carrier, I wondered, would he have still felt comfortable about such a public profession of faith? And after another eight months of harsh election rhetoric, would he and his co-religionists think twice before even going to a mosque in America?

PART ONE

POLITICS—THE MUSLIM BOGEYMAN

1 MEDIA CODEPENDENCE

[I]f thought corrupts language, language can also corrupt thought.
GEORGE ORWELL
Politics and the English Language

The president of the United States might be a secret Muslim supporting the Islamic State. That was the gist of Donald Trump's comments to an American television interviewer in June 2016, after the worst mass shooting in American history.

"Look, we're led by a man that either is not tough, not smart or he's got something else in mind," the presumptive Republican nominee told *Fox & Friends*. "He doesn't get it, or he gets it better than anybody understands. It's one or the other."[1]

Then he added a four-word rejoinder encapsulating all the anti-Muslim innuendo of the 2016 presidential campaign. "There's something going on," Trump said. "It's inconceivable. There's something going on."[2] In that loaded phrase lived all the latent fears buried in the DNA of Americans of European descent since our distant ancestors took up swords in the first Crusade.

Something's Going On

Stoking anger against the external enemy is a tried and true tactic of rulers throughout history. The 2016 presidential campaign proved it also works well for candidates willing to exploit the basest of human emotions. It began early in the GOP primary campaign when Trump lobbed one of his first anti-Muslim bombs: an incendiary and widely discredited claim that he saw "thousands and thousands of people ... where you have large Arab populations" cheering as the World Trade Center collapsed.

"Hey, I watched when the World Trade Center came tumbling down. And I watched in Jersey City, N.J., where thousands and thousands of people were cheering as that building was coming down. Thousands of people were cheering. So something's going on. We've got to find out what it is."[3]

Something's going on. We're not sure exactly, but there's something. Not saying what it is, not making any accusations . . .

The idea that there was *something going on* among Muslims and Arabs was the theme to which he kept returning throughout the campaign.

- *"We don't know what's happening,"* Trump said when announcing that he was running for the GOP nomination, referring to Mexican and Middle Eastern immigration.[4]

- *"There's something going on,"* he said in the primary debate after the San Bernardino shootings.[5]

- "You know, *there's something definitely going on,"* he confided to an interviewer, referring to the reaction of Muslims to the Paris attacks in November 2015. "There's something nasty coming out of there."[6]

- *"There's something going on* in the mosques," he told a North Carolina rally in November 2016.[7]

It was a strategy of innuendo to which it was difficult to respond, casting suspicion without an overt accusation. It left its targets off balance and his political rivals scrambling to show they were *even more* concerned.

"Radical Islam is on the rise," Senator Ted Cruz proclaimed in the first Republican primary debate in August of 2015, "Global jihadists" are "an existential threat to our nation." The next time they met, Ben Carson warned that, "[O]ur children will have no future if we put our heads in the sand." Wisconsin governor Scott Walker also seized on the next generation card: "We need to live in a world where our children are free, free from the threats of radical Islamic terrorism." Governor Bobby Jindal said America was being threatened by an "invasion" of Muslims who threatened to "colonize" the U.S., adding that American Muslims "want to use our freedoms to undermine that freedom in the first place."[8]

"You feel safe right now?" Trump asked in the September California debate. "I don't feel so safe."

When they gathered in Milwaukee in November 2015, former governor Jeb Bush raised the specter of the Muslim enemy within. "We have a caliphate the size of Indiana that gains energy each and every day to recruit Americans in our own country," he warned, calling "Islamic terrorism" the biggest threat facing the U.S. Yet Bush would be, in relative terms, an outlier as the campaign progressed, occasionally speaking out *for* Muslims. He gave an early indication of that later in the same debate, pointing out that just as Christians in Syria, Iraq and Lebanon were under threat from the so-called Islamic State, "if you're a moderate Islamist, you're not going to be able to survive either," seemingly conflating the terms "Islamist" and "Muslim."

Bobby Jindal was more concerned about the threat to his own co-religionists. Asked in the September debate about a fourteen-year-old Muslim boy who had been arrested in Texas for bringing a clock to school, he replied, "I'm glad that police are careful. I'm glad they are worried about security and safety issues. Look, in America we don't tolerate them. The biggest discrimination that's going on is against Christian business owners and individuals who believe in traditional forms of marriage."

That was news to American Muslims, who were experiencing record levels of hate crimes, many of which went unreported by the FBI and thus by the national media.[9]

Feeding Frenzy

Liberal commentators might have expressed outrage at each new incendiary comment, but controversy meant ratings and so the media—particularly cable TV—eagerly fanned the rhetorical flames. The issue of mosque closings was a vivid example of the synergistic relationship between the candidates and American news organizations. In October, Fox Business anchor Stuart Varney asked Trump whether he would follow the example of Great Britain, which had revoked the passports of suspected militants and closed some mosques. When Trump responded, "I would do that, I think it's great," apparently referring to canceling the passports of Americans fighting for ISIS rather than mosque closings, Varney took it another step, seemingly putting words in the candidate's mouth: "Can you close a mosque? I mean, we *do* have religious freedom."

When ISIS killed more than 100 people in a series of suicide bombings and shootings in central Paris the following month, the anti-Muslim tenor of the campaign—and the synergistic media coverage—ratcheted up another notch. On MSNBC's *Morning Joe*, host Joe Scarborough trolled for the day's juiciest sound bite. The French interior minister had called for shutting down mosques in central Paris. What did Trump think of the idea of doing the same in the U.S.? "I would hate to do it, but it would be something that you're going to have strongly consider," the future president replied. "Some of the ideas, some of the hatred, absolute hatred, is coming from these areas," adding, "We're going to have to watch and study the mosques because a lot of talk is going on at the mosques."

Over the coming days, the media seemed to egg on the candidates with increasingly provocative questions, eagerly seized on by the political rivals as they battled to bag the most headline-grabbing sound bite. Muslim databases. ID cards listing religion. Watch lists.

"I want surveillance of certain mosques, okay? If that's *okay*?" Trump sarcastically asked the cheering crowd at one rally. "I want surveillance. And you know what? We've had it before, and we'll have it again."[10]

"We have no idea who's being sent in here," he later told ABC's George Stephanopoulos, referring to Muslim refugees. "This could be the—it's probably not, but it could be the great Trojan Horse of all time, where they come in."[11]

Rubio wasn't about to let Trump have all the airtime. "It's not about closing down mosques," he told Fox. "It's about closing down any place—whether it's a cafe, a diner, an internet site—*any place* where radicals are being inspired."[12] That's "just wrong," Jeb Bush responded. But the frenzy of anti-Muslim election rhetoric kept pushing things to the extreme. By the Fox News-moderated debate in January 2016, Bush was also warning of the threat at home. "[I]f we allow this to fester, we're going to have Islamic terrorism, multi-generations of it all across this country," he told Chris Wallace.

Co-moderator Megan Kelly seemed to try to push them even further, pointing out that the Supreme Court had ruled the First Amendment effectively protected hate speech. "In other words," she provocatively explained to Senator Marco Rubio, "radical Muslims have the right to be radical Muslims, unless they turn to terror." Rubio readily took the bait. "Megyn, that's the problem, 'radical Muslims' and 'radical Islam' is not just hate talk. It's hate action. They blow people up. Look at what they did in San Bernardino."

The media fever generated by those serial provocations was nothing compared to the feeding frenzy of the so-called "Muslim ban" as Trump

[handwritten margin note: not really constitutional]

called for "a total and complete shutdown of Muslims entering the United States until our country's representatives can figure out what the *Hell* is going on!"[13] The ban would stop "the extraordinary influx of hatred and danger coming into our country," the future president tweeted.[14]

It was a seminal moment in the campaign, and for the country.

"We don't have to have refugees come to our country, but *all Muslims*, seriously?" Bush asked when the candidates gathered a week later, adding that Trump's comments were "unhinged." Ted Cruz wanted to split the difference. He had just introduced legislation to ban refugees from nations where ISIS or Al Qaeda "controls significant territory" (He also wanted to "carpet-bomb" Syria to eliminate ISIS).

New Jersey governor Chris Christie was on record as opposing the profiling of Muslims. But it sounded very much like he was advocating exactly that when Kelly asked him about the neighbors of the San Bernardino killers, "They saw Muslims, and they did not think that was enough to call the cops. Do you?"

"I think what people should do is use their common sense," explained the former prosecutor.

You see something that's suspicious, you call law enforcement.... What that is, is just common sense. They thought something was wrong.

Kelly then asked Ben Carson, "Do you think the GOP messaging on Muslims has stoked the flames of bias on this as the Democrats suggest?"

"Well, I don't know about the GOP messaging, but I can tell you about my messaging," Carson replied in his understated style. "You know, [we] need to stop allowing political correctness to dictate our policies, because it's going to kill us if we don't."

Political correctness. It was quickly becoming code for skirting civil rights in the name of expediency when it came to Muslims.

Carly Fiorina was a case study in the way Islam and American Muslims were used as a political football during the campaign. Shortly after 9/11, Fiorina, then the CEO of Hewlett-Packard, spoke admiringly of Islamic civilization, saying that "we could learn a lesson" from Muslim rulers of the past.[15] Fiorina took a very different tone as she prepared to announce her candidacy for the GOP nomination. After a series of ISIS attacks in Paris that claimed seventeen lives, Fiorina appeared on comedian Bill Maher's HBO program and laid the blame firmly on Islam. "No one's doing this in the name of Christianity, of Judaism," she said.

Maher uncharacteristically seemed to defend Muslims: "There are crazy Christians, there are crazy Jewish settlers right now." "There is no moral equivalence!" Fiorina snapped in response.[16]

Nothing it seemed, was too bizarre for the primary campaign. Marco Rubio told an interviewer that he bought a gun because "if ISIS were to visit us or our communities at any moment, the last line of defense between ISIS and my family is the ability I have to protect my family from them or from a criminal or anyone else who seeks to do us harm. Millions of Americans feel that way."[17]

Rating and Profits

No matter how hard they tried, the other GOP candidates' exposure paled in comparison to that of Donald Trump. The real estate magnate was ubiquitous across the media landscape from the day he announced his campaign. In the twelve months leading up to the election, he generated a jaw-dropping $5.69 billion in free media (650 million media mentions), twice as much as Hillary Clinton and 3.5 times more media value than Obama in 2012.[18] It was "the most media-focused election spectacle this country has ever witnessed."[19]

CNN may have become Trump's putative nemesis after the election, but it was his bully pulpit during the campaign. For the media in general, Trump was a cash cow, but no media outlet benefited more than CNN. Trump and CNN chief Jeff Zucker had forged a successful partnership when Zucker was the head of NBC Entertainment and Trump's show *The Apprentice* was his biggest reality hit. Now they were turning politics into a reality show. The relationship was mutually profitable. CNN gave Trump 24/7 exposure, Trump increased CNN's prime-time audience by 70 percent, generating $1 billion in revenue, making 2016 the most profitable year in CNN's history.[20]

No wonder then that Trump was the center of attention when CNN hosted the second GOP primary debate. With eleven candidates crowded on the stage, Trump was the fulcrum point. Anchor Jake Tapper started off by asking Carly Fiorina whether she would be comfortable "with Donald Trump's finger on the nuclear codes." When Fiorina said that was up to the voters, Tapper turned and asked Trump for his response. For much of the debate, each time one of the other candidates made a comment, Tapper turned and asked, "Mr. Trump?"

[handwritten margin note: Trump had CNN under his finger so he had...]

One exchange summed up the debate. Former Wisconsin governor Scott Walker, who had not had a chance to say a word, broke in:

WALKER: But Jake, Jake, Jake, Jake . . .

TAPPER: I want to—I want to give Mr. Trump . . .

WALKER: But Jake, this –this is—this . . .

TAPPER: . . . Mr. Trump, I want to give you a chance to respond to something that your rival to your left, Governor Bush, said.

After Trump's long monologue, Tapper turned to Jeb Bush.

TAPPER: Governor Bush, would you feel comfortable with Donald Trump's finger on the nuclear codes?

BUSH: I think the voters will make that determination.

WALKER: Jake, this is—this is—this is . . .

TRUMP: But I have to say . . .

And so it went. Trump tallied more speaking time than anyone else on the stage, more than twice as much as Walker and Mike Huckabee,[21] just as he had done in the previous Fox-hosted debate.[22]

CNN's "debates have been embarrassing, its primary-night coverage consistently unwatchable, and its fawning treatment of Donald Trump pathetic," *Slate* media critic Isaac Chotiner wrote after Anderson Cooper's softball interview with Trump following his win in the March 15 primary.[23] "Had Trump lost the election, CNN would probably have returned to its previously scheduled struggle for survival," *The New York Times Magazine* wrote in a scathing article about the relationship between Trump and the network.[24]

CNN wasn't alone in benefiting from—or facilitating—the Trump ratings bump. The media industry was in deep trouble before candidate Trump came along, but the campaign meant the "money's rolling in," CBS chief Les Moonves boasted at an investment conference. Trump's candidacy "may not be good for America, but it's damn good for CBS."[25] Fox had record profits and what Trump kept calling "the failing *New York Times*" saw subscriptions skyrocket. It was also good for media personalities. Fox anchor Megan Kelly became a "brand" with her made-for-TV tiff with Trump, MSNBC's *Morning Joe* leapt from obscurity as its co-hosts' relationship with Trump shifted from coddling to faux combative, and while other candidates complained they couldn't get airtime, Trump literally phoned it in to TV shows across the dial, all eager for the ratings.

Make no mistake, there was plenty of criticism of Trump on the op-ed pages, and the talking head galleries on most TV shows scrupulously balanced the respective candidates' surrogates, but it didn't matter. Truth-telling was lost in the torrent of inflammatory sound bites and tweets. Trump dominated the conversation, proving the axiom that all publicity is good publicity.

It wasn't until after he clinched the nomination—and particularly, after he won the election—that the media seemed to recognize its role in facilitating his rise and began to adopt a more confrontational tone.

"America has just lived through another presidential campaign week dominated by Donald Trump's racist lies," *The New York Times* wrote in a 24 November 2015 editorial. The article called the candidate to task for his distortions of the number of refugees entering the country, false statistics about whites murdered by African Americans, and for repeating his spurious claim about Arab Americans celebrating on 9/11. The paper compared Trump's fearmongering with the communist-baiting of Senator Joseph McCarthy and the racism of George Wallace.[26] The Times followed up with an editorial titled "Truth and Lies in the Age of Trump," one month after the election.[27]

But to America's shell-shocked Muslims, it was all too late.

Between the Lines

Beyond the rote repetition of the often-anti-Muslim sound bite-of-the-day was the more implicit bias woven through the American media.

"MUSLIM KILLERS" screamed the headline the *New York Post* superimposed on a picture of one of the San Bernardino massacre victims lying dead. The headline was factually accurate, but it was also self-consciously inflammatory. Not "*JIHADI* KILLERS." Not "*ISLAMIST* KILLERS." Not "*MUSLIM EXTREMIST* KILLERS." Just *MUSLIM KILLERS.*

Columbia University professor Edward Said once wrote that "covering Islam is a one-sided activity that obscures what 'we' do, and highlights instead what Muslims and Arabs by their very flawed nature *are*."[28] In other words, "we"—non-Muslim Americans—sometimes do terrible things. But when an individual Muslim does that same terrible thing, it is a manifestation of something built into his/her DNA. Never was it more evident than in that *Post* headline.

A few days later, there was an example of more subtle bias in *The New York Times*. At the center of the front page was a set of three photos taken inside the apartment of the shooters, Pakistani immigrant Tashfeen Malik and her U.S.-born husband, Syed Rizwan Farook. The caption read, "A Home Revealed." The centerpiece was a photo of a small kitchen table above which hung a tapestry with the 99 names of Allah in Arabic script. On the surface, it was innocuous, but in it many American Muslims saw an insidious form of stereotyping.

"These are things that all Muslims have in their house," said Linda Sarsour, an outspoken Arab-American leader. "There's nothing about that that tells you a story about what terrorism looks like. So you're telling me that when my friends who are not Muslim come into my home and see a Qur'an and see frames on the wall with a scripture from my religion, is that supposed to tell you something? I mean, it's absolutely outrageous."[29]

The *New York Post*'s editors, famous for inflammatory and outrageous headlines and a history of Islamophobia, probably knew exactly what they were doing. Their counterparts at the *Times* were likely oblivious to the unspoken message of the photo.

I had personal experience with this unconscious cultural—academics would call it "Orientalist"—bias. In 2011, *The Times' Week in Review* section published an article I wrote on a major survey of Pakistani journalists. It was part of a series of such surveys I conducted in the Middle East, South Asia and Indonesia examining how perceptions of reporters and editors in these Muslim-majority countries varied on a range of issues such as relations with the U.S., terrorism, domestic politics and religion.

I could not have asked for better exposure. The entire back page of the Sunday section was devoted to the results, with color charts and my analysis. However, that was all undermined by the headline, written by the editor: "Inside the (Muslim) Journalist's Mind."[30] It was a classic Orientalist framing. If the article had been about a survey of *New York Times* reporters, would the editor have used the headline, "Inside the (Christian) Journalist's Mind" or "Inside the (Jewish) Journalist's Mind"? The answer is obvious, but he saw nothing wrong with making Pakistani journalists a proxy for all Muslim journalists around the world, framing Islam as a monolith, and portending that a Western researcher had the godlike power to get "inside" a Muslim's mind.

There was nothing new about any of this. As I reported in my 2005 book, *Reflections in a Bloodshot Lens*:

> [T]he U.S. media has had a long and inglorious relationship with the world's Muslims, characterized by stereotype, distortion and oversimplification. That cliché-ridden portrayal would create the frame through which Americans viewed Islam and those who practiced it in the wake of 9/11: dehumanizing Muslims, creating the cultural ground for violence and fueling the subsequent polarization of attitudes between the U.S. and the Muslim world.[31]

Little changed in subsequent years. A study of U.S. media coverage between 2007 and 2013 by the British media watchdog group Media Tenor reported that at least 75 percent of U.S. reporting about Muslims in that period was negative. Even as the quantity of coverage of Muslims in the U.S. media dropped after 2010, "the tonality continued to deteriorate."[32]

By 2015, with the launch of the U.S. presidential campaign and the wave of terrorist attacks in Europe, a study of reporting in *The New York Times* found that Islam received more negative coverage than cancer. Only 8 percent of *The Times'* headlines about Islam or Muslims during that entire year was classified as positive.[33] As the Institute for Social Policy Research (ISPR) put it, "The rise and constant media coverage of the so-called Islamic State is often conflated with discussions about Islam itself, creating an environment of fear of Muslims among some Americans."[34]

A Harvard study of three major television newscasts—the *CBS Evening News*, Fox's *Special Report* and the *NBC Nightly News*—found that over a two-year period beginning in April 2015, "there was not a single month where TV news stories with Muslims as the protagonist was more positive than negative," and in 40 percent of those months, negative stories outnumbered positive stories more than four to one. "The media's shortcoming is more in what they don't do than what they do," wrote author Meighan Stone. "What journalists underplay are positive developments in the Muslim community."[35]

Such coverage had an impact not only on the American body politic but also on Muslims themselves. Almost one-third of Muslims agree that their co-religionists are "more prone to negative behavior than other people," far higher than any other religious group.[36] The result was an identity crisis among Muslim youth. Half of those questioned in another

bad media coverage fucks w/ non-Muslim americans but also Muslims

survey said they were not sure they could be both Muslim and American, and only one-third of them were willing to tell their friends they were Muslim.[37]

Along with the negative framing of Islam was the inevitable reminder of the link between terrorism and the religion itself. The photo of the accused San Bernardino terrorists' home in *The New York Times* was emblematic of a phenomenon familiar to Muslims: stories about terrorism were frequently illustrated with generic images of Islam. "[N]o matter the article, anything about Islam includes publishing the same photo: praying Muslims," Libyan-American activist Hend Amry tweeted in 2016 with a montage of images from news articles.[38]

But that photo also underlined another reality: as Islam moved from an international story to one found on Main Street, USA, responsibility shifted from foreign correspondents, who were likely to have at least some glancing knowledge of the topic, to local general assignment reporters in places like Poughkeepsie and Peoria who were used to covering city hall or chasing fires. *Sending unqualified reporters*

As *BuzzFeed* reporter Hanna Alam wrote of the San Bernardino coverage: "When that cluster of reporters went into the shooter's home and they were marveling over ordinary items of a Muslim household, as if they were evidence of extremism … I just thought about how little the reporters knew about Islam to point to those things as, you know, 'ooh look here's evidence.'"[39]

But, she argued, the conscious effort on the part of some news organizations to show the "positive" side of Islam could be almost as bad: "Anti-Muslim hostility has led to a well-meaning but sad genre of corrective journalism that says, 'Look at this Muslim doing a normal thing!'"

Allam, who previously covered the Arab Spring revolution in the Middle East, was part of a small cadre of former foreign correspondents who gained their knowledge of Islam and Muslims abroad and brought those insights into their coverage of the American Muslim community and U.S. policy toward Islam. Allam also happened to be Muslim, an even tinier subset of reporters covering the topic. She and her colleagues were swimming against the tide.

With the U.S. presidential primary, the dominant media narrative framed Islam and Muslims in an ever-more negative light, not least because of the media's tendency to endlessly echo the inflammatory comments of the candidates. Among the more responsible news organizations, care was taken to "balance" claims with counterviews, but such an approach served only to ensure that the accusations themselves were given the same degree of credibility as the counterarguments in the false equivalence of what is known as "he-said, she-said journalism," as in, "He said the sky is green, she said the sky is blue. It is up to the public to decide who is right." In the process of such coverage, the idea that the sky may be green begins to take root among some in the audience.

Not everyone was swayed. A Pew survey in the spring of 2017 found that half the U.S. public said media coverage of Islam was unfair. However, the other half said Islam was not "part of mainstream U.S. society." In other words, Muslim-Americans were not *real* Americans.[40]

As researchers Brian J. Bowe and Tajj W. Makki noted in a study of coverage of mosque-building controversies,

> As Muslim-Americans work to carve out a hybrid identity, a key part of their struggle will be challenging the dominant media discourse that insists on the incompatibility of the two parts of that hyphenated identity. It's not enough to say coverage of Islam is too negative and should be more positive.... [E]ven ostensibly positively valenced frames may perpetuate reductive stereotypes.[41]

Fragmented Media

Until CNN, the first cable news channel, went on the air in 1980, each night some 80 million Americans tuned to one of the three major network newscasts, the *CBS Evening News*, NBC's *Nightly News*, and *World News Tonight* on ABC. As a result, Americans back then had a shared world view. They may have disagreed whether the U.S. *should be* in Vietnam or whether Richard Nixon *should be* impeached, but they all acknowledged American troops *were* in Vietnam and Richard Nixon *was* president. There was a factual baseline for the national debate.

By the 2016 election, the media landscape had splintered. Fox News and conservative talk radio held the right flank; MSNBC, *The Nation*, *Slate* and a handful of other online publications protected the Left, and the "mainstream media"—*The New York Times*, *The Washington Post*, *The Wall Street Journal*, CNN, NPR and the major networks—roughly straddled the center. But the GOP primary also brought to the fore a set of hard-right—in some cases obscure, conspiratorial and/or outright racist—web publications, such as *Breitbart* and *InfoWars*.

Many of Trump's words and ideas about Muslims, Hispanics and other minority groups had originally percolated within this fringe mediascape. As the anti-Muslim, anti-immigrant rhetoric of the campaign heated up, these ideas were being repeated daily in the "mainstream" media and slowly normalized.

This splintering meant that by the time Trump faced Hillary Clinton in the general election, Democrats and Republicans had largely retreated into their respective media silos. By the end of the campaign, Americans could barely agree the sky was blue or that gravity held us all in place. Facts no longer existed. Orwell's Newspeak had become reality. If we didn't agree with what the media said, it was "fake news."

The June 2016 attack on an Orlando, Florida, nightclub that left 50 dead could not have been better timed for Trump, who had just sewn up the Republican presidential nomination.

"What has happened in Orlando is just the beginning. Our leadership is weak and ineffective. I called it and asked for the ban. Must be tough," Donald Trump declared in one of a series of tweets after the tragedy, conveniently ignoring the fact that the killer was born in the same New York borough as Trump himself.[42]

> Appreciate the congrats for being right on radical Islamic terrorism, I don't want congrats, I want toughness & vigilance. We must be smart![43]

With each terrorist outrage, American Muslims raised their voices in a chorus of denunciation. "On behalf of the American Muslim community, we, the undersigned … unequivocally say that such an act of hate-fueled violence has no place in any faith, including Islam," read a statement signed by almost 500 leaders of the American Muslim community after the Orlando massacre.[44]

Despite that, there was a constant drumbeat of claims that American Muslims did not denounce terrorism. One proponent of that myth was "Judge" Jeanine Pirro, a Muslim-bashing Fox host who regularly pilloried Muslim guests naive enough to go on her program. Michigan Imam Muhammad Ali Elahi was just such an unsuspecting victim. Pirro paired him with anti-Muslim campaigner Brigitte Gabriel after the San Bernardino tragedy:

Pirro:	The Muslim community is not coming forward ... Imam, I'm going to give you another chance ... Should the family of the San Bernardino attackers, who saw the weapons, who saw all of the instruments that they used, should they have said something, and why didn't they?
Elahi:	We have to condemn terrorism, but you have to do something about it. President Trump must do something about it. Let us deprive them the resources, and they would die—
Pirro:	Imam, do you agree that we've got to prevent the radical Islamic extremists from coming into this country and killing us, and killing Muslims, too? Yes or no?
Elahi:	We are absolutely against any radicals, Islamic, Christians, any of them.
Pirro:	I'm going to tell the court stenographer you said, "yes." Now to Brigitte. Brigitte, why can't he say yes?
Gabriel:	He's beating around the bush and does not want to answer the question.[45]

Pirro's performance would likely have received high marks from her boss, Fox Chairman Rupert Murdoch, who once tweeted, "Maybe most Moslems peaceful, but until they recognize and destroy their growing jihadist cancer they must be held responsible."[46]

The theme of Muslims failing to speak up was in keeping with the standard set by other Fox hosts, such as Greta Van Susteren, who issued an open challenge in 2014: "I will give any Muslim leader of national or international stature the platform right here, On the Record, to condemn Islamic extremism and to make a call to arms of every Muslim leader of every mosque to do the same."[47]

The Council on American-Islamic Relations (CAIR) wasted no time taking up the challenge, but Van Susteren and her producers weren't interested. CAIR issued a statement saying that every time a terrorist outrage took place, they sent condemnations to 170 Fox e-mail addresses, but those denunciations—which upset the Fox narrative—never made air. "Time after time, we hear Fox hosts and commentators calling for Muslim leaders to speak out, asking where the Muslim condemnations of terrorism and religious extremism are," said CAIR executive director Nihad Awad. "That's a good question. Where are those condemnations? Those condemnations are in the in-boxes of Fox staffers."[48]

[handwritten margin note: just pushing their narrative]

Islamophobia had been integral to the Fox News franchise since its earliest days, but the channel didn't have a monopoly on anti-Muslim bias. "Fox News is only the most obvious offender; the channel's supposed rivals on the left and on mainstream CNN are in fact active and crucial partners in the effort to vilify Muslims. In many ways, they are worse," journalist Max Fisher charged in a *Vox* article.[49]

Fisher cited examples like CNN's Don Lemon cutting off a noted Muslim-American human rights lawyer to ask him, with no apparent context, whether he supported ISIS; CNN host Chris Cuomo arguing that Muslims "are unusually violent. They're unusually barbaric"; and CNN co-host Alisyn Camerota repeatedly badgering religious scholar Reza Aslan to defend widely debunked accusations about Islam that had been broadcast by comedian Bill Maher. The latter segment was the epitome of false equivalence: the claims of someone with no expertise in a field given equal weight with those of a highly credentialed subject-matter expert.

Maher, meanwhile, proudly wore his anti-Muslim views on his sleeve, once boasting that when he first made negative comments about Muslims—such as, Islam is "the only religion that acts like the mafia, that will fucking kill you if you say the wrong thing"—he was greeted with stony silence by his studio audience, but more recently "they have really come around" and now stand up and cheer.

As Fisher wrote, *public getting less tolerant*

That bears repeating: the audiences used to sit quietly or boo when Maher espoused his hateful and factually incorrect views on Islam. Now they stand up and cheer. That is the power of the American media, and it's a power that is increasingly directed toward prejudice, hate, and fear.

One topic to which Maher—like Fox's Pirro—consistently returned was the demand that Muslims denounce terrorism. With each new terrorist outrage, cable news was crowded with commentators insisting that American Muslims condemn such violence, ignoring the fact that with each such atrocity countless Muslim leaders did just that. A nineteen-year-old Muslim American college student in Colorado was so frustrated by the ritual that she compiled a 712-page dossier of all the times Muslims condemned violence, which was then transformed into a website, muslimscondemn.com.

The irony was that many of those Muslim leaders being attacked by anti-Muslim crusaders for their alleged silence or extremist sympathies also found themselves on the hit list of the extremists themselves. One set of death threats came in an article in *Dabiq*, the Islamic State's glossy magazine, titled, "Kill the Imams of *Kufr* in the West," using an Islamic term that means "one who denies the truth."

The magazine, part of a media operation that had been called "the special forces" of the militant group, labeled Suhaib Webb, a white convert and leading American imam, "a clown" who uses "thug life vocabulary ... for taming Muslim youth in the West"; it called Hamza Yusuf, the founder of a leading Islamic university in the U.S., "a crusader" against Islam using "semantic oratory more akin to sorcery"; and said Yasir Qadhi, the head of another Islamic university in the U.S., "emphasizes his love for the United States and his disavowal of anything and anyone who is against American ideals" and urges Americans "cooperate with *kafir* [unbeliever] law enforcement." They and a dozen others in the West were "venomous imams" and "evil scholars [who] take and twist the statements of the early *ulema* [clerics] ... to fit their apostatical version of the religion."

Also included on the hit list were Congressman Keith Ellison; Hillary Clinton aide Huma Abedin; and several Muslims working behind the scenes in the U.S. government, many of whom had earlier been accused by the right of being Muslim Brotherhood infiltrators. "Kill the crusaders and other disbelievers and apostates," the article ordered, "to make an example of them, as all of them are valid—rather obligatory—targets."[50]

Gold Star Pride

By the summer of 2017, American Muslims were exhausted. For more than a year, it seemed they couldn't turn on a television set without coming under attack. And then the parents of a fallen American Muslim soldier took the podium at the Democratic National Convention and directly challenged the GOP nominee in front of a worldwide audience.

American Muslims were jubilant. For the previous week, they had been grappling with the reality that Trump had been confirmed as the Republican nominee for president after telling themselves—and everyone else—it could never happen. Now they proudly watched and rewatched the video of Khizr Khan, his wife Ghazala standing at his side, before an audience of tens of millions, publicly calling Trump on the carpet for what they saw as his campaign of hate. Their son, U.S. Army Capt. Humayun Khan, died in Iraq trying to protect his men from a suicide bomb. "If it was up to Donald Trump, he never would have been in America," the Pakistani-American lawyer told the crowd. "Donald Trump consistently smears the character of Muslims. He vows to build walls and ban us from this country." Then he spoke directly to Trump:

> *Have you ever been to Arlington Cemetery? Go look at the graves of brave patriots who died defending the United States of America. You will see all faiths, genders and ethnicities. You have sacrificed nothing and no one.*[51]

It was an electrifying moment. American Muslims were filled with pride, but it was quickly replaced by shock and anger.

"Who wrote that? Did Hillary's scriptwriters write it?" Trump asked in an interview with ABC News' George Stephanopoulos. "If you look at his wife, she was standing there, she had nothing to say, she probably—maybe she wasn't allowed to have anything to say, you tell me," adding, "I think I've made a lot of sacrifices. I work very, very hard."[52]

The backlash against Trump was immediate, much of it from within his own party. "I hope Americans understand that the remarks do not represent the views of our Republican Party, its officers, or candidates," said Senator John McCain.[53] The chairman of the House Armed Services Committee issued a statement saying he was appalled. Republican senator Lindsey Graham said, "There used to be some things that were sacred in American politics—that you don't do—like criticizing the parents of a fallen soldier even if they criticize you."[54]

Surely, many American Muslims thought, this would be Trump's final undoing? Anyone who had ever served in the military would certainly turn on him. They watched. They waited. But in the end, like every other word and deed that would have derailed another candidate, the controversy just washed over the GOP nominee. Despite the predictions of so many at the time, he would win the vote of enlisted servicemen and women by a landslide, with numbers even higher than those of former Vietnam POW and military hero John McCain.[55]

The Politics of Expediency

Plenty of politicians across the political spectrum did raise their voices against the anti-Muslim bigotry of the campaign. In his final State of the Union address, President Obama told the nation, "[W]e need to reject any politics—*any* politics—that targets people because of race or religion.... This is not a matter of political correctness. This is a matter of understanding just what it is that makes us strong." He continued:

> When politicians insult Muslims, whether abroad or our fellow citizens, when a mosque is vandalized, or a kid is called names, that doesn't make us safer. That's not telling it like it is. It's just wrong. It diminishes us in the eyes of the world. It makes it harder to achieve our goals. It betrays who we are as a country.

However, Muslims noted that it wasn't until late in his presidency, when there was no political risk, that Obama first visited a mosque. Hillary Clinton regularly challenged her rival's racist views; however, at times her defense of Muslims came across to them as self-serving. At the town hall-style second presidential debate, Clinton responded to an American Muslim who asked a question on the minds of many of his co-religionists: "How will you help people like me deal with the consequences of being labelled as a threat to the country after the election is over?"

"[U]nfortunately, there's been a lot of very divisive, dark things said about Muslims," Clinton replied, facing the young man. "It's also very short-sighted and even dangerous to be engaging in the kind of demagogic rhetoric that Donald has about Muslims. We need American Muslims to be part of our eyes and ears, on our front lines." What most American Muslims wanted to hear was that they were *wanted* because they were *Americans*, not that they were *needed* only to weed out terrorists in their ranks.

It wasn't only Democrats who were, in their own patronizing way, coming to the defense of America's Muslims. There were also plenty of Republicans who spoke up. South Carolina governor Nikki Haley said of Trump's proposal for a ban on Muslim immigration, "It defies everything that this country was based on and it's just wrong" ... "absolutely un-American" and "unconstitutional."[56]

"What was proposed yesterday is not what this party stands for, and more importantly, it's not what this country stands for," Speaker of the House Paul Ryan, one of the top Republicans in Congress, told reporters the day after Trump called for the Muslim ban.[57] "We need to aggressively take on radical Islamic terrorism but not at the expense of our American values," insisted Republican National Committee Chair Reince Priebus.[58]

But by Election Day, the critics on the Republican side had largely fallen silent. Priebus would become Trump's first chief of staff, Haley would accept the post of UN ambassador in the Trump administration, and when Trump announced his ban on the entry of citizens of seven Muslim countries one week into his presidency, Ryan told reporters, "What is happening is something we support."[59]

Political expediency had Trumped American values.

2 PRISONERS OF THE LONG WAR

The enemy is within the gates; it is with our own luxury, our own folly, our own criminality that we have to contend.

MARCUS TULLIUS CICERO

Guilt by association. It was the centerpiece of the GOP campaign. And it was something Muslims in Portland, Oregon, a bastion of Pacific Northwest liberalism, knew a lot about. They had faced innuendo, stereotyping and mistrust since 9/11.[1]

"We have people living in our country that want to do great harm to our country," Donald Trump told CBS News after the March 2016 suicide bombings in Brussels that killed more than 30 people and injured hundreds more. Asked whether Americans should profile their neighbors, he replied, "Everybody should watch out."

Portland's Muslims felt like that had been the U.S. government's approach to them for almost two decades.

Just ask Brandon Mayfield. A Portland lawyer and military veteran who converted to Islam when he married his Egyptian-American wife, Mayfield was accused of being involved in the 2004 Madrid train bombings that killed 200 and injured more than 2,000.

The evidence seemed pretty damning: a fingerprint on an unexploded bomb in Spain that was a "100 percent" match to Mayfield, according to the FBI. Except that it wasn't. The Spanish, who never thought the fingerprint belonged to Mayfield, eventually arrested an Algerian who *was* a match.

"Being Muslim was the circumstantial evidence of my guilt," Mayfield, who was eventually freed and quietly paid $2 million in compensation, told me when we met in a coffee shop in a strip mall outside the city.

He was not alone. Portland had been a hot spot for the prosecution of Muslims by the local FBI anti-terrorism task force. Even when the accused was found guilty, the cases were surrounded by complaints of entrapment, use of undercover informants and, as in the Kevin Bacon parlor game, six degrees of separation from Osama bin Laden.

"This is a tax fraud case that was transformed into a trial on terrorism," the Ninth U.S. Court of Appeals ruled in the case of an Iranian-American who ran an Oregon-based Muslim charity that was a branch of a controversial Saudi Foundation. "The appeal illustrates the fine line between the government's use of relevant evidence to document motive for a cover up and its use of inflammatory, unrelated evidence about Osama Bin Laden and terrorist activity that prejudices the jury."

That was under Bush and Obama. Now there was Trump and Cruz. "We need to empower law enforcement to patrol and secure Muslim neighborhoods before they become radicalized," Cruz said in response to Brussels. Such a directive struck a chord in Portland.

"The Muslim community here understands what he is proposing because we have been under surveillance for many years," said Kayse Jama, the Somalia-born executive director of Portland's Center for Intercultural Organizing. "Pitting neighbor against neighbor and ordering law enforcement to focus on Muslims and not others is dangerous and against American values."

"It's plainly unconstitutional, boorish, base and counterproductive," playing into the narrative that "ISIS and their fellow travelers want to advance," Sarah Eltantawi, a professor of comparative religion at Evergreen College in neighboring Washington state, told me.

The obvious question Muslims in Portland and across the country were asking: did Cruz want to "secure" Muslims *from* some*thing* or "secure" them *in* some*where*?

"It's a recipe for a police state to have neighborhoods patrolled based on religion," Ibrahim Hooper, spokesman for the Council on American-Islamic Relations (CAIR), said when I reached him by phone in Washington, DC. "What constitutes a Muslim community? Is it a Muslim couple? Ten Muslims? 100? Is it going to be 'show us your papers'? Checkpoints? Midnight raids? It is reminiscent of the Stasi in [East] Germany, not the American government in 2016."

History is replete with examples of the power of words among zealots—including, sometimes, those who wore a badge. "If you're a true believer, you ignore facts because you believe so strongly in your mission and start to believe in your own infallibility," said Steven Wax, referring to the phenomenon known as "confirmation bias." Wax had headed the Federal Public Defender's Office in Portland for thirty-one years and defended Mayfield and others accused of terrorism, including several Guantanamo detainees. "Some of these people are such true believers—not religious ideologues—and that belief distorts their judgment and they take everything that fits their theory as fact," Wax explained. Another factor, he said, was the law enforcement atmosphere under Attorney General John Ashcroft. "Fear fomented at the top trickles down and drives so many of the actions of the individuals."

Ron Silver, a former U.S. attorney in Portland, agreed that confirmation bias was one of the factors in the issue of Mayfield's alleged fingerprint. "Having worked with the FBI, I think it was very hard for them to accept that they could be wrong, and Spain could be right," he said.

Many immigrants in Portland's Muslim community of roughly 50,000, a mix of ethnicities from Pakistanis, Arabs and Turks to Uighurs, had already experienced the consequences of what happens when true believers are inflamed by the magniloquence of a charismatic leader; none more so than the city's 500 Bosniak Muslim families, refugees of the Serbian pogrom against them in the 1990s. "Everything started with hate speech, with inflammatory rhetoric. And then genocide," Imam Abdullah Polovina, a refugee of the war, recalled as we sat in the office of his mosque, his voice dropping to a whisper. "Not just one city, all over."

Mayfield was subject to surveillance, including eavesdropping devices in his home, for almost a year. The affidavit for his arrest made much of the fact he was a Muslim: he had done the legal work to arrange custody for the son of a local Muslim convicted of terrorism; he ran ads for his immigration and family law practice in a local Muslim community newspaper; he was seen driving past his mosque "several times a day." And so it went. A review of the case by the Department of Justice inspector general concluded that all this influenced the technicians at the FBI's fingerprint lab.

One of the examiners candidly admitted that if the person identified had been someone without these characteristics, like the "Maytag Repairman," the Laboratory might have revisited the identification with more skepticism and caught the error.[2]

The FBI's use of undercover operatives in the Mayfield case and several other Portland investigations created a climate of suspicion. Such tactics, among other things, led the city of Portland to withdraw from the Joint Terrorism Task Force (JTTF) with the FBI in 2005. As a result, in the first decade of the 2000s, the local Muslim community had a good relationship with the local police but not the feds. "The first time I met with the FBI, I told them, FBI equals fear in the Muslim community. Police department and the sheriff equals compassion, trust," said Salma Ahmad, president of the Islamic Society of Greater Portland.

Portland Muslims were not alone in the suspicions of the FBI. The circumstances that led to such lack of trust had been experienced by Muslims across the country. One example was Minneapolis-St. Paul. When twenty-two young Somali men joined the militant group al Shabab in the late 2000s, the FBI organized a Specialized Community Outreach Team (SCOT), ostensibly to build relations with the city's Somalis. It quickly became clear "SCOT intentionally commingled community outreach with intelligence gathering and investigative activity," even though members of the Somali community were the ones who came to law enforcement about the rise of extremism in their ranks, according to a study.[3] The local FBI office pushed back on the DC-mandated program, which was also being rolled out in five other cities. It was revised, but civil liberties groups claimed the link between outreach and intelligence gathering remained close in Minneapolis and elsewhere.[4]

In the aftermath of the Mayfield case, the Portland FBI office, under new leadership locally and in Washington, had worked hard to build bridges with the Muslim community. It was one reason that despite a deep-seated suspicion about Trump and his ilk, in the spring of 2016 Portland's Muslims were still clinging—almost desperately—to a conviction that the America they loved would not abandon them.

"Deep down in our hearts as Muslims, we believe that this noise from Trump is no more than a McCarthyism 2.0 going on, and in my humble opinion this too shall pass, like any other storm," insisted Mohammad Saeed Rahman, the Pakistan-born head of a financial advisory firm who also happened to be among the 5 percent of Muslims who identified as Republican. Khalid Khan, a professor at the University of Portland, agreed. "Every society has its Taliban," he said of Trump and like-minded anti-Muslim campaigners. "But we have confidence the American people are smart enough not to elect him."

After Trump's call to ban Muslims from entering the U.S., the Portland city council passed a resolution denouncing the idea. "Presidential candidates have the right to say dumb things, and we have the right to censor them for it," Commissioner Nick Fish said at the time.[5] Not long after, the city council in Beaverton, a Portland suburb that is home to Nike, passed a similar motion to "declare support for the Muslim community and reaffirm Beaverton as a welcoming city" for immigrants.[6]

For Salma Ahmad, the resolutions only confirmed her belief in the country that had been her home for fifty years. "I treasure in my heart the Constitution, because it is my protection," said the Philippines-born Ahmad, who had been a guest at President Obama's final State of the Union address and had served as a liaison between the FBI and Portland's Muslims.

But, as elsewhere, the comments further exacerbated tensions in the Portland Muslim community. "You have a good number of people who cannot deal with the pressure and they just isolate themselves," said Imam Polovina, the Bosniak imam. A poll by the Institute for Social Policy and Understanding during the primary found that 58 percent of American Muslims said they had suffered religious discrimination in the past year. Portlanders had not been spared.[7] The only confirmed incident of hate crime was the 2005 arson of a mosque in Corvallis, Oregon. But Portland Muslims said rude comments—particularly to women wearing hijab head coverings—were all too common. When Dana Ghazi, the president of the student's association at Portland State University, ran for office on an anti-racist, anti-homophobic platform, she "received emails and tweets that aimed at attacking my identity as a Middle Eastern Muslim immigrant rather than discussing my politics," she told me.

Embarrassment

Mayfield's was among a series of cases that had rocked the Portland Muslim community in the decade after 9/11. One of the most sensational was the conviction of the so-called Portland Seven, the nation's first major terrorism case after 9/11. It involved a group of Portland Muslims who set out to join the anti-American jihad in Afghanistan. Only one made it as far as Pakistan, where he was killed; the rest were arrested on a tip from an FBI informant when they returned home after failing to get to Afghanistan. Among them was Intel engineer Mike Hawash, who was picked up a year after traveling to China, where the group attempted to enter Afghanistan. The local Muslim community and Intel leaped to his defense. There were rallies, outraged statements to the media and fundraisers. When he pleaded guilty of conspiring to aid the Taliban, it was a huge embarrassment for the city's Muslims.

Rahman said it was "the stupidity" of the Portland Seven that put Portland's Muslim community "on the map" for federal law enforcement agencies. "They paid the price, but they took the rest of the community with them," he told me, shaking his head angrily. Others believed that targeting of the community was part of a "crusade" by overzealous members of the FBI's Joint Terrorism Task Force. Either way, the drama—or trauma—wasn't over.

Another high-profile case involved Mohamed Osman Mohamud, who was given a thirty-year sentence for attempting to set off an explosive device at the city's 2010 Christmas tree lighting. Mohamud, a student at Oregon State University, was a case study in the fine line between foiling and fostering a terrorist plot. The basic fact that the young man, who emigrated from Somalia as a child, was flirting with extremism was indisputable. He was in email contact with Amro Alali, a Saudi Arabian fugitive with suspected links to terrorism, and to Samir Khan, a Saudi-born American al Qaeda propagandist who would later be killed in the U.S. drone strike that assassinated Anwar al-Awlaki, an American alleged to have coordinated numerous terrorist plots from his base in Yemen. Beginning in high school, Mohamud wrote articles for an al Qaeda propaganda magazine published by Khan.

Mohamud's slide toward extremism did not escape notice. A local imam tried to counsel him, as did others. His lawyers and federal prosecutors disagree on when he first came on the FBI's radar screen, but what is confirmed is that his father reached out to the FBI with concerns his son was being radicalized. Mohamud received help, but it wasn't the kind his father had in mind. That call either sparked or ramped up a sting operation rather than an effort to deter him from terrorism. Long-time law enforcement officers say the culture of government encourages arrest over intervention. "There is no upside to trying to turn a kid who is going bad in another direction," a top Department of Homeland Security (DHS) official based in the field told me. "If it works, no one notices. But if you don't arrest him or choose not to launch a sting operation to give you the evidence to do that, and the kid does commit an act of terror, your career is over."

When the FBI began investigating Mahmud, even its own agents didn't think the then-nineteen-year-old Somali American was capable of planning and executing the bombing on his own. By that point, he had graduated high school and was at college. Mohamud "left behind his radical thinking" and was a "pretty manipula[ble], conflicted kid," an agent wrote after his initial evaluation of the youth. Even after an undercover agent posing as an isolated Muslim in Eastern Idaho carried on an email conversation with him over several months asking how to join "the fight" for Islam, Mohamud never suggested violence. But the FBI was not done. Months later, it reached out to him again. This time, an undercover agent posed as a representative of a religious council recruiting volunteers for "a project." According to the appeals court ruling,

> When offered five ways to be a good Muslim—(1) pray five times a day; (2) go to school to learn something that would help the brothers overseas, such as engineering or medicine; (3) raise money for the brothers; (4) become operational; or (5) become a martyr—Mohamud almost immediately picked "become operational." Mohamud explained "operational" meant "doing like the other brothers do when they get a car, fill it with explosives, park it near a target location, and detonate the vehicle."[8]

The agent told him he had a "brother that could help him with explosives." At the next meeting, the agent brought along a second undercover operative posing as an explosives expert. After a short discussion, Mohamud said he wanted to set off a car packed with explosives, with himself inside, at the Christmas tree lighting ceremony in downtown Portland. The agents pointed out that many women and children would die. Mohamud was enthusiastic.

> Yeah, I mean that's what I'm looking for ... You know what I like to see? Is when I see the enemy of Allah then, you know, their bodies are torn everywhere.[9]

To test whether he was serious, the agents gave him $2,800 to "purchase a list of bomb components, decide where to park the van with the bomb, and rent his own apartment," according to court documents.[10]

Several times through the process, the undercover agents reminded Mohamud that he did not have to go through with the bombing. FBI reports say he never wavered. Before the fateful day, he recorded a martyr video in case he did not survive.

Carry on oh brothers, and march on ahead to meet your creator and lie on silk beds, and the martyrs don't die, so don't say they're dead. Explode on these *kuffar* [unbelievers]. Alleviate our pain. Assassinate their leaders, commanders, and chiefs.[11]

After his arrest, Mohamud cried and told the jail's psychiatric nurse he didn't understand "how he had gotten from just being a student to being labeled a terrorist in jail."[12]

The "bomb" Mohamud tried twice to set off was a fake supplied by the FBI undercover agents. That was not unusual. Nationally, in two-thirds of cases involving a perpetrator believed to be Muslim, undercover operatives or informants provided the means—such as bombs or firearms—to carry out the attack. That was true in only two out of twelve cases that did not involve Muslims.[13] One such case involved a mentally ill panhandler who was arrested for plotting to commit terrorism after an FBI informant gave him $40 to buy a knife, some duct tape and a machete at Walmart.

The other issue in the Mohamud case was his lawyer's claim that the FBI surveillance of him prior to the sting operation was illegal. The agency had obtained a warrant from the Foreign Intelligence Surveillance (FISA) court on the grounds that his emails were picked up "incidentally" in monitoring suspected terrorists overseas. The FISA court issues surveillance warrants for Americans when there is probable cause to believe they are agents or targets of a foreign power and "are or may be" engaged in or abetting espionage, sabotage or terrorism. Documents released by Wikileaks in 2014 revealed that the 7,485 e-mail accounts the FISA court approved for monitoring between 2002 and 2008 included those of numerous high-profile American Muslims, including university professors, the head of CAIR and a Republican Party operative who served in DHS during the Bush administration.[14]

Loren "Renn" Cannon, the FBI agent in charge in Portland in 2018, defended the use of undercover agents, informers and sting operations. "If we're going to try to prevent things, then you can't do it without these techniques," he told me, insisting that they were now used sparingly and with layers of oversight, "because when you're trying to prevent, on the intelligence side, that ethic of preserving the rights that we all cherish is absolutely critical."

Former FBI agent Michael German said there were many good agents in the FBI like Cannon who were deeply concerned about civil liberties, "but there are others who buy into these Islamophobic themes." Those views were reinforced by FBI training courses riddled with anti-Muslim stereotypes and disinformation. A 2012 internal FBI investigation reported that one trainer told agents, "A Muslim employee's loyalties will always lie first and foremost with Islam and therefore, you should not trust a Muslim coworker."[15] A primer instructing FBI agents how to justify FISA requests, released as part of the Wikileaks archive, had this placeholder filled in where the surveillance subject's name should be written: "Mohammad Raghead."[16]

The appeals court in the Mohamud case rejected both of his lawyers' arguments, essentially ruling that the FBI tiptoed right down the fine line between a lawful investigation and a violation of the nineteen-year-old's constitutional rights. The court observed that "the most troubling aspect of this 'incidental' collection [of emails] is not whether such collection was anticipated, but rather its volume, which is vast."[17] Nevertheless, the court said procedures were followed and the surveillance was constitutional. Likewise, on entrapment, the court ruled that "while the government's conduct was quite aggressive at times, it fell short of a due process violation."[18]

The ruling worried civil rights lawyers and Muslim activists. In their view, the Mohamud case was just one among many examples of agents pushing the envelope on racially motivated surveillance and tempting individuals to turn words into action in order to arrest them. "Tear up Texas," an undercover FBI agent texted to the subject of one investigation a few days before he attacked a "Draw Muhammad" cartoon contest organized by anti-Islam campaigner Pam Geller in 2015. "U know what happened in Paris," the shooter replied, referring to the ISIS attack there. "So that goes without saying."[19]

"do [sic] you think you can kill?" another undercover agent texted Justin Sullivan, a nineteen-year-old in North Carolina, before providing a silencer for an automatic weapon he was to use in a mass shooting to announce his "Islamic State of North America." Sullivan was given a life sentence.[20] That sentence, like the 30 years given to Mohamed Osman Mohamud, reflected another national pattern: prosecutors sought three times the sentence length for Muslims than non-Muslims in similar cases.[21]

Mohamud and Sullivan had something else in common: parents in both cases alerted the authorities, imploring them to help prevent their sons from turning radical ideas into radical acts, only to find their child ultimately convicted of terrorism-related offenses. It was part of a national pattern.

A local imam and a former Taliban recruiter who focused on preventing extremism tried to intervene with former Virginia honor student Ali Shukri Amin when he began to show signs of becoming radicalized. But their infrequent interactions were no match for the ISIS recruiter who spend endless hours online with the Amin and became his best friend. Ultimately, the imam advised Amin's mother it was time to alert the FBI in order to protect her son from the Islamic State. "We followed this advice and that decision contributed to Ali being investigated and prosecuted," his mother told the judge in his terrorism trial. "While we are glad that Ali did not go abroad, we also feel very confused and conflicted about having played a role in him being arrested."[22] He was sentenced to eleven years in prison for radicalizing a friend and helping him join ISIS in Syria.

Equally disillusioned was the father of Adam Shafi, a twenty-two-year-old Fremont, California, man. The father first approached the FBI when his son abruptly left for Turkey while on a family visit to Cairo. The son later claimed he was visiting refugee camps. Back home, the FBI taped phone calls on which Shafi said he hoped Allah would not let him die before spilling "a couple of gallons of blood for him." As he tried to leave the country again for Turkey, his father alerted authorities. He was arrested and eventually sentenced to twenty years in prison for attempting to support a terrorist organization. "Every minute, I just imagine him in that solitary confinement, facing twenty years, because I cooperated with the government," said Adam Shafi's father. "It's a horrible feeling. I can't get rid of it."[23]

After the guilty verdict, Mohamed Osman Mohamud's tearful mother told reporters the government "put ideas into his mind" and the undercover agents told him not to speak with his parents. His father regretted having called the FBI. "He is very sad, he feels like he betrayed his son," someone who knows him well told me.

The Muslim Kevin Bacon Effect

Then there was the issue of trial-by-innuendo, as in the ongoing case of the imam of Portland's largest mosque.

"Portland imam had ties to Osama bin Laden, 4 terrorist groups years ago, government alleges," read a headline in *The Oregonian* in the summer of 2016. The story reported that the government had initiated proceedings to have the cleric's citizenship stripped.

The gist of the government filing—a civil immigration suit, not a criminal indictment—focused on the fact that Sheikh Mohamed Kariye fought in the Afghan jihad and had a glancing encounter with bin Laden and his Palestinian mentor, Sheikh Abdullah Azzam. But the government's lawyers downplayed one inconvenient detail: All this happened in the mid-1980s, when both bin Laden and the U.S. government were supporting the anti-Soviet mujahideen militias. As *The Oregonian* pointed out, "They also don't say that bin Laden established al-Qaida in 1989 . . . after Kariye parted ways with the *mujahideen*."

Other supposed evidence against Kariye: a "prominent member" of al-Shabab, an al Qaeda affiliated terrorist group, witnessed his marriage in Somalia. But the wedding took place sixteen years before al-Shabab was formed. Another "damning" fact: in the 1990s, Kariye was associated with two charities that were later designated terrorist organizations by the U.S. The list went on.

The government had been after Kariye, a conservative Salafi cleric, for a long time. In 2002, he was arrested at the Portland airport "amid much fanfare," as *The Oregonian* reported, when traces of explosives were allegedly detected on his suitcases. There were so many police on hand that local reporters had a hard time believing the arrest wasn't planned in advance. Kariye spent five weeks in jail before the government decided that there *was* no residue.

In 2010, Kariye learned he was on the government's no-fly list, which prevented him from boarding a commercial aircraft. He joined others on the list in suing the government, demanding reasons for the listing and the opportunity to appeal. They won an initial victory in court. Not long after, the government filed a suit to "denaturalize" Kariye—strip him of his U.S. citizenship. Despite all the innuendo about terrorism, the actual legal case boiled down to an allegation he lied on his immigration form.

Use of such tangential charges was common in terrorism-related prosecutions. A 2010 Department of Justice report cited 399 "terrorism-related" convictions. In fact, only 107 were based on terrorism statutes. The rest involved immigration-related offenses or other unrelated charges. One example involved three men who an informant told the FBI tried to buy a rocket-propelled grenade launcher. After an extensive investigation, agents came up empty on any evidence of terrorism, but they did convict them of receiving two truckloads of stolen cereal.[24]

In Kariye's case, to anyone buying into the 2016 election year rhetoric, the circumstantial evidence was compelling: he was a Muslim Somali; he was a jihadi in Afghanistan; the Portland Seven came from his mosque, and so did two others convicted on terrorism-related charges and a third man, who been in regular contact with an American al Qaeda member convicted for involvement in the 1998 U.S. embassy bombings in East Africa. Kariye knew people who knew people who were bad guys. He preached a conservative brand of Islam. Surely, he must be guilty of *something*. After all, as Trump told CNN, "[i]t's very hard to separate" the militants from other Muslims "because you don't know who's who." Especially when you were dealing with, as Cruz said of Europe, "a toxic mix of migrants who have been infiltrated by terrorists."

To many Muslims, the federal government's unrelenting campaign of trial-by-innuendo wasn't much different from the FBI's surveillance of Martin Luther King Jr. in the 1960s on the pretext that he was, as a declassified FBI document alleged, "a whole-hearted Marxist" because he had occasional interactions with others the Bureau thought were communists. King's denials, FBI director J. Edgar Hoover said, were just evidence that he was the "most notorious liar in the country."[25]

"You're on a mission. You're a zealot and have this guy from Somalia who was a mujahideen and you get intelligence that he's still doing bad stuff, so you go berserk," said lawyer Stephen Wax, who advised Kariye's legal team.

From the law enforcement perspective, Kariye represented one of the most difficult challenges in balancing counterterrorism and civil liberties. "He's a bad guy," a national security official told me off the record. "He's a vector for so much, from the Portland Seven on up. But he's a careful guy." Undercover operations had come up dry. The U.S. government had plenty of tape of him saying things they didn't like, but nothing he said was illegal. They even had an undercover operative offer to sell him weapons. "They did it in the mosque," said Wax, with a tone of disbelief. The cleric was reportedly shocked at that bold attempt at what his lawyers claimed was clear entrapment.

There were similarities between Kariye and French Salafist Imam El Hadi Doudi, whose "patient and insistent proselytizing" was responsible for the spread of the ultraconservative strain of Salafism across Europe.[26] As with Kariye, authorities had no smoking gun with which to convict

Doudi, but in the spring of 2018 the French government began the process of expelling him from the country after thirty-seven years. In the U.S., it wasn't as simple as that. There was the Constitution. Speech was not illegal—which was why the government had been tied up in court with Kariye for years.

Another Oregon Muslim, Pete Seda, had it worse. He was jailed for almost three years before an appeals court ruled the government had conflated possible tax evasion with support for terror. That nexus came about because of another example of six degrees of separation from bin Laden. Seda ran the Oregon branch of the al-Haramain Islamic Foundation. "CIA, Treasury, and FBI officials have all expressed their concern about the al-Haramain Foundation's ties to both the Saudi Government and terrorist activity," according to a 2002 Senate report.[27]

There was significant evidence that al-Haramain's parent organization did have ties to bin Laden, but national security sources told me that there was never any direct evidence of involvement on the part of the Oregon office. "This is a big organization that is highly decentralized," one counterterrorism source in Washington told me. "There were definitely people in Saudi funneling money to terrorists, but that did not mean institutionally al-Haramain was a branch of al Qaeda, as some would make you believe."

"Al-Haramain opened a U.S. office in Oregon and received about $700,000 from its parent organization in Saudi Arabia," the conservative *Washington Times* reported, referencing Seda's conviction, when the "missing" twenty-eight pages of the 9/11 Commission report were released in July 2016.[28] What the paper did not mention was that counterterrorism officials knew that the terrorism ties were confined to certain branches of the foundation, that there was no evidence the Oregon office was involved in terrorism, and that Seda had been cleared of terrorism charges and freed three years before.

The process of unraveling a web of contacts and following a trail of money was a fundamental tool of law enforcement. But the Seda case was an example of how, when it came to terrorism and American Muslims, some investigators turned tenuous ties into evidence of guilt.

Al-Haramain wasn't the only example. The 9/11 report contained discussion of implied terrorist connections between several U.S. mosques and al Qaeda. The post-9/11 mindset of some in the national security establishment was evident in various passages of the 9/11 Commission report. Documenting alleged ties between two of the 9/11 hijackers who did their flight training in San Diego and a Saudi diplomat based in Los Angeles, the Commission reported:

> According to FBI documents and a CIA memorandum, al-Hazmi and al-Mihdhar may have been in contact with Shaykh al-Thumairy, an accredited diplomat at the Saudi Consulate in Los Angeles and one of the "imams" at the King Fahd mosque in Culver City, California. Also, according to FBI documents, the mosque was built in 1998 from funding provided by Saudi Arabia's Crown Prince Abdulaziz. The mosque is reportedly attended by members of the Saudi consulate in Los Angeles, and is widely-recognized for its anti-Western views.[29]

On the surface, those were fairly damning connections. But they were also wildly circumstantial. The Saudi government had funded hundreds of mosques across the U.S. in the previous decades in an effort to spread its austere branch of Islam. It was not surprising that Saudi diplomats living nearby would regularly attend a mosque built with money from the Saudi government. Two of the Saudi 9/11 hijackers who lived an hour or two away "*may*" have been in contact with a diplomat at the Saudi consulate who also happened to be an imam at that mosque. But was there any evidence to transform *may* into *did*? And, if so, in what context? The Saudi community in southern California was small. It was probably a good guess that any of the individual Saudis "may" have crossed paths at the mosque or on a visit to the consulate. And the mosque was "widely-recognized" for its anti-Western views by whom?

It was certainly the job of the FBI to pursue all suspicious connections as they tried to dig to the roots of the 9/11 plot and potential future threats inside the U.S. However, the way in which supposition played a factor was evident in the Commission's discussion of unverified suspicions that the Ibn Tamiyah Mosque in Los Angeles and the Islamic Center of San Diego were involved in money laundering:

> According to the former FBI agent in San Diego who was involved in this investigation, this scheme may allow the Saudi Government to provide al-Qai'da with funding through covert or indirect means. In his October 9, 2002 testimony the former agent commented on the possible money laundering:
>
> My guess Saudi—it's connected somehow with the Saudis. And knowing that probably 70–80 percent of the population of Saudi Arabia support Usama Bin Ladin, it might be an indication.[30]

In fact, most leading Saudi clerics had joined the chorus of condemnation of al Qaeda after 9/11, and a 2003 poll found that nine out of ten Saudis rejected bin Laden's actions. The vast majority of Saudis surveyed said al Qaeda's actions were not consistent with Islam or their own values.[31] Later in the report, that retired agent's "guess" morphed into:

The CIA and FBI have identified Ibn Tamiyah mosque in Culver City as a site of extremists-related activity. Several subjects of FBI investigations prior to September 11 had close connections to the mosque and are believed to have laundered money through this mosque to non-profit organizations overseas affiliated with Usama bin Landin. In an interview, an FBI agent said he believed that Saudi Government money was being laundered through the mosque.[32]

More evidence appearing to implicate al-Thumairy was uncovered in later years. A 2012 FBI report alleged that after two of the 9/11 hijackers arrived in Los Angeles, al-Thumairy "provided (or directed others to provide) the hijackers with assistance in daily activities, including procuring living quarters, financial assistance, and assistance in obtaining flight lessons and driver's licenses."[33] That was a decade after the first FBI allegations about al-Thumairy's possible involvement. As former senator and 9/11 Commission member Bob Kerry asked when news of the memo was reported in 2012, "If the decision was not to proceed, why? And if it was to proceed, what's the status?"[34]

The Saudis asked much the same in their 2017 response to the lawsuit by the families of the 9/11 victims:

A statement that an investigator "seeks to prove" a legal conclusion is neither an appropriate allegation nor competent evidence. That is especially so here because the investigator's attempt failed: the 9/11 Review Commission later found as of March 2015 that new evidence available to the FBI was "not sufficient" to support the conclusion that plaintiffs advocate.[35]

Such investigation-by-innuendo had major implications. Pete Seda may have been cleared, but as his lawyer Stephen Wax said, "He's tarred. He's Pete the Terrorist."

3 THE AMERICAN TALIBAN

The best jihad is to say a word of truth before a tyrannical ruler.

THE PROPHET MUHAMMAD

Book of Battles (Kitab al-Malahim), Sunan Abu Dawud 4344

In the strongholds of hardline Pakistani Islamist thought, they were talking about Donald Trump and laughing. Then they shook their heads with concern. "He doesn't belong in the White House, he belongs in a mental hospital," forty-six-year-old Hafez Tahrir Ashrafi, a Muslim cleric who was head of the country's Ulema Council, told me with a throaty roar. An obese man with a wild dark beard, Ashrafi was an adviser to the Pakistani government and a former jihadi who fought in Afghanistan as a youth.[1] He had been quoted in the Pakistani media endorsing suicide bombing against U.S. troops in Afghanistan.[2]

"We not believe the Americans will elect a man like that with his very dirty statements," Ashrafi continued when we spoke in early 2016, "but if that happens, then he creates the problem not for the Muslims, but for the Americans and for himself."

Ashrafi was not alone in that view. Senator Ted Cruz may have won Iowa, but it was Trump who had Pakistan's elite simultaneously amused and concerned. Dozens of interviews with a broad cross section of Pakistani intelligentsia—Islamists, liberals, policymakers and bloggers—could be summed up in a single sentence: in their view, Trump was a clown, but he was a dangerous clown who could cause long-term damage to U.S. relations with the Muslim world.

Pakistan's relationship with the United States was complex. It had been a vital ally in the Afghan war, but its intelligence services had played both ends against the middle, supporting some extremists for its own geopolitical aims, while battling others. The country was in a virtual state of civil war, and there were deep divisions between the civilian and military leadership. The Army had been locked in a major offensive against militants in the tribal areas and a simultaneous operation to wrest back control of Karachi, the commercial capital, from militias and criminal gangs, but there were ongoing rebellions in several parts of the country, jihadis of various stripes were active in every corner of the country, and the chief cleric of the so-called "Red Mosque," located less than a mile from Pakistan's Parliament building, had reportedly declared his support for the Islamic State. "Soon ISIS will unfurl the flag of victory on the whole world," Maulauna Abdul Aziz was quoted as saying.[3]

But Pakistan's importance to U.S. foreign policy was seen in its role as a supply line for U.S. troops in Afghanistan, and its efforts to help broker a deal in Afghanistan and mediate between Saudi Arabia and Iran—which made the impact America's campaign rhetoric problematic in the extreme.

"When people who are not sophisticated hear his comments and see Americans voting for him, that translates into anti-U.S. sentiment," said Dr. Ishrat Husain, a former central bank governor under the regime of Gen. Pevez Musharraf, said of support for Trump. "We can only hope he doesn't get the nomination. That would be a disaster."

But many Pakistanis who *were* "sophisticated" also questioned what Trump's success up to that point said about the direction of American society. They feared they were getting a glimpse into the dark side of the American psyche—and seeing it reflected back in their own. More than 4,600 people had died in sectarian violence in Pakistan in 2015, according to the country's Centre for Research and Security Studies (CRSS). "We're living in a world where we seem to be competing for the space from which you can preach or promote intolerance of the other," said Zohra Yusuf, chairperson of the nonprofit Human Rights Commission of Pakistan, with exhaustion in her voice.

Inside the heavily fortified walls of the Lahore University of Management Sciences, some of the country's best and brightest studied business, computer science and engineering, with images of careers in the U.S. dancing in their heads. "Social media is full of posts about Trump," a graduate student, who wouldn't give her name, told me when I asked if Pakistanis were paying attention to the primary campaign. "Positive or negative?" I teased, just to see the reaction. She and her friends erupted in laughter. "Negative, of course!"

America's Dark Side

In Pakistan, one heard much talk of visas denied and dreams quashed. One young woman with a newly minted medical degree had just returned home to Lahore after three months looking for opportunities in the U.S. where she had always dreamed of being a doctor. Now she was having second thoughts. It appeared that an Australian or New Zealand accent might be in her future. "She just didn't feel comfortable with all she was hearing and seeing on television," her father told me, referring to the anti-Muslim rhetoric. "She felt like people were judging her wherever she went."

Trump might have been a fixture on the social media feeds of educated Pakistani youth, but he was largely AWOL from the mainstream media. Ditto the U.S. primaries as a whole. "It barely comes up in our editorial meetings," Fahd Husain, executive director of Express News TV, one of dozens of often-sensational competing news channels, told me, sitting in his Lahore newsroom.

At the Karachi headquarters of Geo TV, one of the country's largest networks, I heard much the same. Geo had aired most of the GOP and Democratic debates with Urdu translations, but the broadcasts elicited relatively little comment. "People are more concentrated on what's happening in Pakistan," said Azhar Abbas, Geo's news chief. Not surprising given that the nation was still reeling from the deaths of more than twenty people, most of them students, in a January attack on a university. Schools had been off-limits; this attack had changed the rules of the daily carnage.

Badr Alam, the self-effacing editor of the *Herald*, an English-language newsweekly, sheepishly noted that another reason for the lack of coverage of Trump—and the campaign in general—was that many Pakistanis, including editors, simply didn't understand the U.S. primary system. "In the media I think there will be ten to fifteen people who would really know how the election happens."

Hameed Haroon, Pakistan's most influential publisher—and Badr's boss—said there was also a conscious decision on the part of some editors not to stir the international relations pot. The Pakistani media did not normally hesitate to publish anti-American rants, but Haroon, whose family owned the Dawn media group, said those opinions were usually tied to specific U.S. policy actions and included "a retreat mechanism," by which he meant that when policies or policymakers changed, the framing of the U.S. in the media also changed. Trump, said Haroon, endangered that failsafe "retreat mechanism" in U.S.-Pakistani relations. "It's not a conscious censorship as such, [but] to enshrine Trump as an example of how bad America is would open up darker perspectives and disbalance the possibility of any positive perception of America in this region," he told me.

Not everyone was so grim. "The Europeans have become more tolerant [toward Islam], but tolerance can be condescending," explained Muneer Kamal, chairman of both the Karachi Stock Exchange and the National Bank of Pakistan, who thought Trump was an aberration. "The Americans have moved to a completely different place—acceptance" of Muslims.

Still, Trump and Hillary Clinton were upending Pakistan's policy worldview about relations with Washington: since Dwight D. Eisenhower, according to the well-worn trope, Democrats tilted toward India, Republicans tilted toward Pakistan (and more problematically, Pakistani military dictatorships). But Democrat Clinton was a proven commodity, someone Islamabad could deal with. The battle of inflammatory sound bites on the Republican side had Pakistani heads spinning. "This time around," according to retired ambassador Ali Sarwar, head of the Center for International Strategic Studies think tank, "we can't make sense of the Republican party."

"You need a dose of Hillary to clean out a dose of Trump," said Haroon of Dawn. But he and others worried that a Clinton victory would not be enough; that something more fundamental was taking place in American society that would reshape U.S. foreign policy.

There was that theme again: the dark side. Economist Kaiser Bengali, an adviser to the governor of the state of Baluchistan, called it "the rise of the American Taliban," which he said began in the Reagan administration and was now hitting critical mass with the Trumpites. "This [rhetoric is] against the democratic values," warned Dr. Farid Ahmed Piracha, number two in Jemaah Islamiyah, Pakistan's largest Islamist group. "If there is such mindset, then there will be more difficulties for the United States and more terrorism."

But as every foreign correspondent knew, there was one ultimate go-to source for the real ground truth in every country: the taxi driver.

Heading to the airport in the military capital Rawalpindi through the deserted, early morning streets, fending off hawkers and beggars at each red light, my driver Syed and I talked American politics. On the other side of the world, Iowans were donning boots and parkas as they headed toward—well, wherever it was Iowans went in that bizarre quadrennial ritual known as the caucus.

"How many days lasts American election?" asked Syed.

"Ten months," I replied, wondering how I was going to explain this.

There was a long, pregnant pause.

"Hillary is a nice lady," he said.

And we drove on.

4 COGNITIVE DISSONANCE

If you're not confused, you're not paying attention.

TOM PETERS
Thriving on Chaos

Maybe it was jet lag. But the scene seemed surreal: the African-American hawker selling "Donald 'Fucking' Trump" buttons, the young Hispanic guy with the "Build a Wall" T-shirt, the grinning Asian-American fellow strategically placed behind the podium.[1]

I had stepped off a direct flight from the Middle East to Seattle just twelve hours earlier. Now, improbably, I found myself at a Donald Trump rally in the Seattle suburb of Everett. I had expected the crowd to be thick with camo, Confederate flags and NRA logos, and overtly hostile to those of us down in the media pen. The Trump supporters around me were polite, well dressed, and largely middle class.

But as soon as Trump entered the arena, the disorientation kicked back in. I had spent the past two weeks in Pakistan and the Middle East, steeped in the geopolitical complexities of the region, a place painted in shades of grey. Now I was back in Trump's world of black and white. "We are going to stop the Syrian refugees from entering the United States," Trump proclaimed to a thundering, foot-stamping ovation. "Did you see where they announced today tens of thousands of people coming in?" In fact, the administration had reported the arrival of the ten-thousandth refugee, meeting the target for the year. But as Trump continued to rile up the crowd, I was soon reminded that facts didn't always have a place in his world order. "We allow people to pour into our country, we don't know who they are but it's only a matter of time before bad, bad things are going to happen."

I thought about my conversation with a hardline Muslim cleric a few days before. He had the solution to Trump's concerns about

Syrian refugees: "America should go in and stop the fighting," Mufti Muhammad Naeem told me as we sat sprawled against pillows on the pristine white carpet of his air-conditioned office. Naeem was the head of Jamia Binoria Alimiyah, a madrassa considered the most important center of the fundamentalist Deobandi school of Sunni Islam in Pakistan. In the dusty, flyblown fifteen-acre complex outside his oasis-like office, more than 5,000 students—from young Pakistani children to PhD students from the United States, Europe and across the Muslim world—were studying an extremely conservative interpretation of Islam.

Naeem was no shrinking violet. The previous year, he had issued a fatwa against a government minister accusing him of apostasy, a virtual death sentence in Pakistan.[2] Given that his fundamentalist colleagues were inflamed by the U.S. presence in Afghanistan and Iraq and the ongoing drone strikes in Pakistan itself, I asked why he would want the U.S. to intervene in Syria. "America is powerful, it can do anything it wants. It can solve these things if it wants to," he confidently replied.

This from a man who was banned from entering the U.S. because of his alleged support for attacks on Pakistani Shi'ites. That antipathy for the Shi'a was exactly why he wanted the U.S. in Syria: to oust Shi'a Iran's ally Bashar al-Assad, drive out the hated Shi'ite militia Hezbollah and pave the way for a Sunni regime. The conversation was a reminder that nothing in what George W. Bush once dubbed "the Greater Middle East" was straightforward.

You would never know that listening to Donald Trump. Back at the rally, the candidate was now reciting lyrics to an Al Wilson song, "The Snake," which Trump said was the perfect allegory to the threat posed by Syrian refugees. In the song, a sympathetic woman rescues a half-frozen snake, only to be bitten by it in the end. When she asks why, the snake tells her she shouldn't be surprised because, "You knew damn well I was a snake before you took me in."

"It represents the truth," Trump told the cheering and laughing crowd. The "tidal wave" of Muslim immigrants, he said, repeating a common theme of the campaign, "could be the great Trojan Horse of all time." And naturally, it was all "Crooked Hillary's" fault. "Look at the world before and after she became secretary of state," Trump continued. "Pre-Hillary, in early 2009, Iraq was seeing a reduction in violence, Libya was stable, Syria was under control, the group we now know as ISIS was close to being extinguished, Iran was being choked by sanctions."

There was a seed of truth in there somewhere. Clinton certainly bore much responsibility for the chaos in Libya, pressing for the U.S. intervention, which was launched with no serious plan for what came next. But that intervention also prevented the slaughter of countless Libyans by dictator Mu'ammar Gaddafi and ultimately led to his demise. Sanctions against Iran were actually tightened in 2012, costing Iran $160 billion in lost oil revenue alone.[3]

Trump's account of a pre-Clintonian Middle East utopia left out the seminal events that shaped the region today: the Bush administration's invasion of Iraq and the Arab Spring. The Bush administration's overthrow of Saddam Hussein tore Iraq asunder and made Iran the dominant regional power. The 2011 Arab uprising, which the U.S. could not have stopped even if it had wanted to, unseated two dictatorships and sparked an authoritarian counterstrike from the Gulf to North Africa. The brief Arab flirtation with democracy gave way to a violent Arab Winter and the rise of the Islamic State.

That got me thinking about the Jordanian investment banker I had been drinking with at the in-pool bar of a luxury Dubai hotel a scant thirty-six hours before Trump took the stage. Between shots of tequila and bottles of Corona, he confided that while he didn't really like Trump, he thought the real estate tycoon was the only one who could save the world economy because "he won't mess around, he'll just order people to do things and they'll get done."

With that he waxed nostalgic about "the good old days" of Arab dictators. Saddam and Hafez knew how to run a country, the former Citibank executive recalled wistfully, referring to the late dictators of Iraq and Syria. "Democracy doesn't work in our culture," he continued, warming to his subject. "We're used to authority. No matter how old you are, when your father tells you to do something, you do it." Fathers held Arab families together and dictators held Arab countries together and, in his view, kept people safe. Except, I interjected, for the political dissidents having their genitals electrocuted.

But he did have a point. From the pool in Dubai, the glittering, mega-rich business capital of the Arab world, no matter which direction you looked there was chaos. In Yemen, the Saudis and Emiratis were locked in a bloody proxy war with Iran. Iraq had been a sectarian basket case ever since the U.S. ousted dictator Saddam. Syria was likely to be a failed state for the next generation. Afghanistan was living up to its history of consuming all invaders.

Immersed in the sound-bite culture of a presidential election campaign, it was easy to forget that the world was a very complicated place. To be fair, in one of his more trenchant foreign policy pronouncements, Trump once proclaimed, "The Middle East is one big, fat quagmire," and he blamed Bush for wrecking Iraq.[4] He was right on both counts. But then he said the U.S. needed to send upward of 30,000 troops to the region to fight the Islamic State,[5] only to announce a few months later that rather than direct intervention, he wanted to set up refugee safe zones, paid for by the Gulf emirates.[6]

In the region itself, the overarching confrontation between key Sunni Arab states and Shi'ite Iran, which played out in all the region's conflicts, dominated the narrative. There was genuine fear in the palaces of the Gulf that some inadvertent incident would spark a direct military confrontation. But what really kept Gulf leaders awake at night was the existential threat posed by the Islamic State, known there by the pejorative, Daesh.

"Iran is tangible and external," Nabil Khatib, then head of news at the Saudi-owned satellite channel al-Arabiya, told me. "Daesh is *of* them," he said, referring to the Gulf Arabs. "It's right here in the sand. It can appear from anywhere." The anti-ISIS strategy promised by Trump during the campaign, "bomb the shit out of 'em,"[7] was problematic, to say the least, since some of those extremists—and their supporters—were ensconced amid the glistening skyscrapers and ornate palaces of the Gulf royals.

Complicating future Middle East strategies even further was the fact that the twin threats of Iran and the Islamic State had shuffled the deck of regional power alliances. Israel—once so reviled in the Arab world that it was referred to only as "the Zionist entity"—now regularly met secretly with Saudi Arabia and the other Sunni states to share intelligence on their common enemies: Iran and the Islamic State.

Just across the Gulf of Oman in Pakistan, which Trump once called "the most dangerous country in the world,"[8] the government was trying hard to avoid getting caught in the middle of the confrontation between the Gulf states and Iran, which bordered Pakistan to the West. The Islamabad government had enough problems in its own neighborhood: the endless confrontation with India (which Trump said he expected to be "helping us out" in securing Pakistan's nuclear weapons if the country became unstable,[9] an invitation to regional chaos), civil war with domestic militant groups (while cynically supporting others), a revolt in Baluchistan, the Kashmir conflict, open hostility from the Afghan regime, and a military operation against the political party-cum-criminal gang that ran the commercial capital of Karachi.

The complexity of it all was enough to make your head spin.

Back in the Seattle suburb of Everett, the crowd was chanting "Trump! Trump! Trump!" Maybe the GOP nominee was right, I thought, longing to catch up on my sleep. Just build a wall.

5 THE MORNING AFTER

Of all the things you choose in life, you don't get to choose what your nightmares are.

JOHN IRVING
The World According to Irving

Back in the spring of 2016, when a Muslim American on an Emirates flight to the Middle East asked to pray in the space in front of my seat, I had wondered if, after another eight months of harsh election rhetoric, he and his co-religionists would think twice before even going to a mosque in America. I seemed to have my answer on the morning of November 9, 2016. American Muslims and Arab Americans woke up in shock and fear.

"The U.S. we knew yesterday is no longer the same U.S.," Khaled Jahshah, executive director of the Arab Center, told me as the final votes were tallied in the early morning hours. "To me this is an unprecedented white insurgency. We're in for some frightening surprises."[1]

America was suddenly a nation in which Muslims and other immigrants feared they were no longer welcome. After all, Trump had promised "a total and complete shutdown of Muslims entering the United States until our country's representatives can figure out what is going on."[2]

"I'm lost for words. I'm completely, completely shell-shocked. I was never expecting this in my wildest dreams. I really thought deep down inside that, 'Yep, it's just a phase. It's a fad. It'll pass,'" Yasir Qadhi, an influential imam with more than one million followers on social media, said when I reached him the next morning. "We need to hope and bank on the fact that the majority of Trump voters were disenfranchised, rural class, working-class, blue-collar workers, and not bigoted racists," because if they were racists "there's not much hope in the equation."

"For Muslim Americans, 11/9 feels like 9/11 all over again. The aftermath is frightening," tweeted law professor Khaled A. Beydoun. Most Muslims don't consume alcohol, but "[t]he last thing I said before going to bed was, 'This may be the first day I actually take a drink,'" former U.S. ambassador Asif Chaudhry texted me, with gallows humor. Anti-Muslim hate crimes were already at record levels. As the Southern Poverty Law Center reported:

> The days surrounding the 15th anniversary of the attacks of Sept. 11, 2001, have seen a stunning increase in what may be anti-Muslim hate crimes in the United States, ranging from arson to murder. In one case, a semi-truck driver appeared to deliberately drive his big rig into a Maryland mosque.[3]

Many Muslims now worried that Trump's victory would be seen by the fringe as a license for violence. After all, Trump had said of the distinction between violent extremists and other Muslims: "It's very hard to define. It's very hard to separate. Because you don't know who's who."[4]

"I'm genuinely scared for my wife, who wears a hijab. I told her don't go out shopping at night alone. I told my kids as well 'just be careful,'" said Qadhi, who lived in Memphis, Tennessee, where he was imam of the local mosque. "I am pretty sure they're going to get taunted today in school, but if it's just taunts, then at least it's better than anything more than that."

What would happen next, said Sohaib Sultan, the imam at Princeton University, depended on Trump himself. "If he tries to put water to some of the fires that he started then hopefully it won't result in violence. This is a very, very volatile position for America right now."

"The genie is out of the bottle," several people told me, using an ironic turn of phrase.

In his victory speech on election night, Trump promised to be a "president for all Americans" and to "unify our great country."[5] Many Muslim Americans wanted to believe he was sincere. Yet even if he was, they worried he might not be able to control his more violent supporters. "What concerns me is that this now gives people license to hate and to act on that discrimination and for it to be okay because of that, towards anyone," said Cherrefe Kadri, a lawyer from Toledo, Ohio. "Forget being a Muslim, forget being an Arab, but just, you know, that human portion just as a person. Where is that okay?"

Former ambassador Chaudhry, who was born in rural Pakistan and rose to serve as foreign policy adviser to the chief of U.S. Naval Operations, knew from experience the danger of hatred unleashed: "I've seen in Afghanistan and the Middle East [that] once these kinds of genies get out of the bottle, it becomes very, very difficult and it's a long process to put them back in."

It was not only Arabs and Muslims who feared they would be impacted. As we watched the final returns on Tuesday night, my adult daughter read a series of texts from friends in liberal Seattle. One friend had just passed a group of men striding through a key intersection in camouflage and brandishing Bowie knives. Another reported that as her boyfriend, an African immigrant, tried to help a drunk woman get into a police car, a passing driver shouted, "Careful, he's with Black Lives Matter!"

"I'm frightened," my daughter, who inherited her cinnamon-hued skin from my Indonesian wife, said with genuine distress on her face. She was not alone. "I'm scared for us," Karen Higuera of Boston tweeted. "I'm scared for my fellow latinos, muslims, women, people of color, the disabled, & mostly for my son."

Immigration bans. Police patrols of Muslim neighborhoods. Muslim registries. All promises made during the GOP campaign. The specter of internment camps no longer seemed quite so unthinkable. As Wednesday blurred into Thursday, social media was alive with incidents of anti-Muslim abuse. Maha Abdul Gawad tweeted:

As I am at Walmart today a woman came up to me and pulled my Hijab off and said, "this is not allowed anymore so go hang yourself with it around your neck not on your head." I am traumatized.[6]

The cloying fear was fed by celebratory social media posts, such as one from Georgia businesswoman Gabrielle Seunagal, who tweeted as @ classySnobbb: "No Islam in America. ISIS dies. No refugees. Thank God."[7]

Late on election night, journalism professor Shaheen Pasha, a Muslim American, posted on Facebook, "I'm going to bed now. In the morning, I'll check the news and wake my kids up and depending on what happens overnight, I'll talk to them. But for now, I want to go to sleep still believing in the country I was born in." The following morning, I asked Pasha, whose parents had emigrated from Pakistan, if she still clung to that belief. "I do, actually," she replied, despite the fact that she had been viciously trolled during the campaign by Trump supporters after she wrote an opinion piece in *USA Today* saying Trump's rhetoric was frightening her eight-year old son.[8] Like many Muslims I spoke with in the aftermath of the vote, Pasha believed Trump's victory would force America to hold a mirror up to itself and acknowledge that racism was not just confined to the political fringe. "Once you have it in your face for the world to see, you have to do something about it. I think that that's actually what's going to happen in the end," she said.

Pakistani-American Mohammad Saeed Rahman was equally determined to cling to faith in his adopted country. Back in the spring, he had told me that the American people would never give the nomination to someone like Donald Trump. Then, after Trump won the nomination, Rahman said they would never elect him. Now, he was trying to sound hopeful—but the goalposts had moved again. "My faith in America is in our Constitution," said the Portland, Oregon, businessman and philanthropist. "I believe the forefathers of our nation did a great job creating the constitution and if anybody's going to go out and mess around with one group of people, there will be a price to be paid." But he was trying to convince himself as much as he was me. A few weeks later, he texted me this telling note: "Sleepless in America."

For many Muslim leaders, Trump's triumph was a call to action. "I'm not going to despair. We are gonna wake up tomorrow and organize like we never organized before regardless," tweeted Muslim activist Linda Sarsour, who would later emerge as one of the coordinators of the women's march on Washington the day after Trump's inauguration and become a lead plaintiff in a lawsuit to overturn Trump's January 2016 immigration ban.[9]

"Muslims should reach out and understand the plight of white, poor uneducated people who came out in droves to vote for Trump," said Sohaib Sultan, the Princeton imam. "And instead of calling them names and casting suspicions on these people, we should try to understand what's going on in this country beyond our own interests."

"American Muslims: I need to see more of us man up. It's ok to be worried, but cowardice is not our way," tweeted Dawud Walid, executive director of the Michigan chapter of CAIR.

After 9/11, Daisy Khan had been a lightning rod for anti-Muslim sentiment when she and her husband spearheaded what came to be denigrated as the "Ground Zero Mosque," an Islamic community center in lower Manhattan. After Trump won the GOP nomination, she became convinced that Muslims had contributed to the rise of Trumpism by failing to grasp the impact of 9/11 on "the psyche of Americans." With Trump's election victory, she told me: "It's clear to us what the challenge is. It's clear to us what is the concern. As Muslims, we have a choice on how we engage with these people; having the kinds of conversations that we really haven't had in the past, face-to-face and alleviating the fears of people. That's the work that Muslims have to do."

Shaheen Pasha agreed. "We are going to have to put our narratives out there, and we're going to have to force people to listen to us. I think a countermovement is going to come out of this and I think it's going to be stronger because it's going to be led by the very people that have felt disenfranchised to begin with."

It was a message of hope in a climate of fear.

Ominous Clouds

Within a week of taking office, Donald Trump signed an executive order temporarily banning the entry of citizens of seven Muslim-majority countries and revoking more than 100,000 visas.[10] It was the first step in making good on his campaign promise to strike against Islam at home and abroad. The move played to his political base, but it also seemed to fulfill the 2003 prediction of American al Qaeda propagandist and recruiter Anwar al-Awlaki, who had warned that one day the U.S. would turn against its Muslim citizens.

> Muslims of the West, take heed and learn from the lessons of history: There are ominous clouds gathering in your horizon. Yesterday, America was a land of slavery, segregation, lynching, and [the] Ku Klux Klan, and tomorrow it will be a land of religious discrimination and concentration camps ... the war between Muslims and the West is escalating.[11]

As the administration insisted the immigration freeze was not a "Muslim ban," Trump adviser and former New York mayor Rudy Giuliani offered a behind-the-scenes take, explaining on Fox News:

> I'll tell you the whole history of it: When he first announced it, he said "Muslim ban" ... He called me up, he said, "Put a commission together, show me the right way to do it legally."[12]

The president himself chimed in with a tweet that once more blurred the lines between radicals and all other Muslims. "Everybody is arguing whether or not it is a BAN," Trump wrote. "Call it what you want, it is about keeping bad people (with bad intentions) out of the country!"[13] Those bad people, he said in another tweet, were "pouring in" and if there was another terrorist attack,[14] it would be the fault of the "so-called judge" who temporarily lifted the immigration freeze.[15]

The ban and the tweets only underlined the concerns of Muslims and other Americans who were worried about the future of civil liberties in America. They had already been put on notice when news broke that the First Family had taken part in a private service on Inauguration morning conducted by a Southern Baptist preacher who was on record as calling Islam an "evil religion" that "promotes pedophilia" and emerged "from the pit of Hell."[16]

They were made even more nervous when they heard comments by Trump's press secretary, Sean Spicer, who was asked about plans to overturn federal regulations to prevent discrimination on the grounds of religion, such as refusing to serve gays. "People should be able to practice their religion, express their religion, express areas of their faith without reprisal," he said without a hint of irony. "And I think that pendulum sometimes swings the other way, in the name of political correctness."[17] Muslims could only shake their heads when Spicer described the shooting at a mosque in Canada where six people were killed as "a terrible reminder of why we must remain vigilant and why the president is taking steps to be proactive instead of reactive when it comes to our nation's safety and security."[18]

The president, meanwhile, made no mention of that mosque attack or one a few days later at a Texas mosque, which was burned to the ground. All this made Trump's subsequent claim that the media was ignoring terrorist attacks that much more bizarre. "You've seen what happened in Paris, and Nice. All over Europe, it's happening," he told soldiers in a speech at the U.S. Central Command. "It's gotten to a point where it's not even being reported. And in many cases, the very, very dishonest press doesn't want to report it. They have their reasons and you understand that."[19]

"That's ludicrous," tweeted former Swedish foreign minister Carl Bildt.[20]

"It has been a busy day for presidential statements divorced from reality," anchor Scott Pelley reported on that night's CBS Evening News.[21]

Trump's unsubstantiated allegation came on the heels of repeated claims from aide Kelly Ann Conway that the media had failed to report on what she called "the Bowling Green massacre," an alleged terrorist attack that never happened.

What the media *was* ignoring was the trial of a white pastor accused of plotting to attack a small community of African-American Muslims in upstate New York. The only outlet that reported on the story was the local newspaper in the Tennessee town where the trial was taking place. "If he were Muslim, we would of course have heard of his sinister plot," wrote columnist and radio host Dean Obeidallah in *The Daily Beast*. "But as we have seen time and time again, terrorist plots by non-Muslims are met with a collective yawn by most in our media."[22]

That was because news editors and producers in New York and Washington, DC, knew their audiences: "Islamic" terrorism generated headlines and ratings; short of blowing up the Oklahoma City Federal Building, the actions of white racists rarely produced many eyes on the screen.

It was the same phenomena that meant Israel dominated foreign news coverage in the U.S. media while crises in places like Southeast Asia and Latin America were largely ignored. There had long been a deeply cynical trope circulating in American newsrooms about war and famine in Africa: "It's just more flies on black faces," meaning that in the eyes of the audience, it all just blurred together, so there was no point covering the continent.

"News is what I say it is," David Brinkley, the NBC Nightly News co-anchor in the 1960s, once famously pronounced.[23] To a large extent, that was still the case of the editors and producers concentrated in New York and Washington, DC. Back when Brinkley was anchor, there were three major newscasts and a handful of national newspapers. The Internet age meant they had been joined by an array of cable channels and a plethora of online news sites, blogs and Twitter feeds. They each had their own ideological agenda that shaped coverage, but they also shared a need to play to the interests of their respective audiences. Left, right or middle-of-the-road, they generally adhered to a common news agenda when it came to terrorism.

An examination of reporting in *The New York Times* and *The Washington Post* by the Institute for Social Policy and Understanding (ISPU) found that Muslims carrying out acts of violence received twice as much media coverage as non-Muslims accused of similar crimes, and in the case of foiled plots, Muslims received seven-and-a-half times the coverage.[24]

One example cited in the study was the Boston Marathon bombing, which killed three people and was carried out by a pair of brothers who were Muslim. It garnered 20 percent of all coverage related to terrorism in the period of the study. In contrast, a 2012 massacre of six people at a Sikh temple in Wisconsin by a white man constituted just 3.8 percent of the coverage; the mass shooting of nine parishioners at a Charleston, South Carolina, church by a twenty-four-year-old white nationalist accounted for 7.4 percent of the coverage; and a 2014 attack on a Kansas synagogue by another white man that left three dead accounted for 3.3 percent of the reporting.

A University of Georgia study found a similar result. "[A] perpetrator who is not Muslim would have to kill on average about seven more people to receive the same amount of coverage as a perpetrator who's Muslim," researcher Erin Kearns explained.[25]

The ISPU study found that the disproportionate coverage was also reflected in sentencing. In cases of ideologically motivated violence, Muslims received sentences four times as long as those of non-Muslims convicted of similar crimes.[26]

All of this seemed to confirm the worst suspicions of American Muslims. And each time they turned on their televisions, the future looked increasingly grim. "Sadly, the American dream is dead," Trump had said when he announced his candidacy.[27] Trump had another segment of Americans in mind when he made that claim, but Muslims feared that might well be true for them.

Mainstreaming the Fringe

The anti-Muslim sentiment Trump brought to the White House was fostered by a set of Trump advisers who were deeply embedded in a subculture of Islamophobia that had coalesced in the years since 9/11.

Emblematic was Trump's national security adviser, retired Gen. Michael Flynn, who had been considered for the vice presidency. He saw Islam as "a vicious cancer" and a "political ideology that pretends to be a religion."[28] Flynn argued that Muslim extremists were "dead set on taking us over and drinking our blood."[29] He tweeted in early 2016, "Fear of

Muslims is RATIONAL: please forward this to others: the truth fears no questions."[30]

This wasn't the first time that a minority had been demonized in America. Two generations before, much the same was being said about the pope. Anti-Catholic sentiment—particularly against the Irish and Italians—flourished from the late 1800s through the election of John F. Kennedy. Racism had always had a home in America. A 1941 Dr. Seuss cartoon criticizing the denial of safe haven to Jews during the Holocaust depicted a woman reading *Adolph the Wolf* to two children on her lap: "and the wolf chewed up the children and spit out their bones ... but those were Foreign Children and it really didn't matter."[31] On her sweater were the words "America First."[32]

Jews, Russians, Chinese and Japanese had all been the target of Anglo-Saxon wrath. The assassination of President William McKinley in 1901 by the U.S.-born anarchist son of Polish immigrants sparked a backlash against Poles and ultimately led to the Immigration Act of 1903, which banned anarchists, the first time the U.S. blocked immigration based on political beliefs. But ultimately each new wave of immigrants had been absorbed into the American mosaic. As Senate Majority Leader Mitch McConnell put it at the height of the campaign, "All of us came here from somewhere else."[33]

Nation of Freedom

Two hundred and fifty years before, as Thomas Jefferson shaped the notions of religious freedom that would ultimately be enshrined in the Constitution, he made a series of notes to himself while reading John Locke's 1689 essay about religious freedom in Britain, *A Letter Concerning Toleration*:

> [He] said "neither Pagan nor Mahamedan nor Jew ought to be excluded from the civil rights of the Commonwealth because of his religion."[34]

Locke's defense of "Mahamedans" would ultimately surface again in Jefferson's draft of Virginia's freedom of religion legislation. The bill was aimed first and foremost at ensuring Christian sects other than the dominant Anglicans would be allowed to practice their beliefs, but Jefferson celebrated the fact that the amendments proposed by his colleagues had not limited future interpretation:

> [T]he insertion [of "Jesus Christ"] was rejected by a great majority, in proof that they meant to comprehend, within the mantle of its protection, the Jews and the Gentile, the Christian and Mahometan, the Hindoo, and Infidel of every denomination.[35]

George Washington, too, argued that "the bosom of America" was "open to receive ... the oppressed and the persecuted of all Nations and Religions."[36] It was a sentiment also loudly proclaimed by Thomas Paine in his famous 1776 pamphlet *Common Sense*:

> O! ye that love mankind! Ye that dare oppose not only tyranny but the tyrant, stand forth! Every spot of the Old World is overrun with oppression. Freedom hath been hunted round the globe. Asia and Africa have long expelled her. Europe regards her like a stranger and England hath given her warning to depart. O! receive the fugitive and prepare in time an asylum for mankind.

Jefferson had other lesser-known allies in the fight to provide full rights for Muslims and other religions. Among them was James Iredell of North Carolina, who provided what might be the seminal argument in the debate against a religious test for political office:

> [I]t is to be objected that the people of America may, perhaps, choose representatives who have no religion at all, and that pagans and Mahometans may be admitted into offices. But how is it possible to exclude any set of men, without taking away that principle of religious freedom which we ourselves so warmly contend for?[37]

Theirs was a politically courageous position, according to Denise Spellberg, author of *Thomas Jefferson's Qur'an*:

> At the end of the eighteenth century, it was still theologically and politically dangerous to suggest that Islam retained some merit even for Muslims.[38]

It's worth noting that at one point in his life Jefferson tried to learn Arabic. He and John Adams both owned Qur'ans; Jefferson's was the very copy on which Democratic Congressman Keith Ellison of Minnesota took the oath of office, something considered anathema to pre-Revolutionary tradition:

> It was long held that no oath could be administered but upon the New Testament, except to a Jew, who was allowed to swear upon the Old. According to this notion, none but Jews and Christians could take an oath; heathens were altogether excluded.[39]

Jefferson and his colleagues didn't actually *know* any Muslims; they were considering "the imagined Muslim" as a litmus test for the outer boundaries of religious freedom, but that didn't change the fact that over the course of just a few years, thanks to them, Muslims transitioned from being seen as the spawn of the Devil to potential citizens of the new nation. As scholar Spellberg put it,

> the Federalists charted new territory in their extension of American egalitarianism to the practitioners of Islam.[40]

Yes, Jefferson, the "founding father of Muslim rights in America" was also the father of its first war against Muslims. But while the targets of America's first military adventure abroad may have been practitioners of Islam, it was their piracy, not their religion, that drove America to war. Jefferson's 1797 treaty ending the conflict with the Barbary pirates stated that the U.S. had "no character of enmity against the Laws, Religion and Tranquility of Mussulmen."[41]

Two centuries later, that was an assurance many around the world—and in Muslim communities in America—had reason to doubt.

PART TWO

(MIS) PERCEPTIONS—SEPARATING FACT FROM FICTION

6 NOT ALL ISLAMISTS WANT YOUR HEAD

one more person ask me if i knew the hijackers . . .
one more person assume they know me, or that i represent a people.
or that a people represent an evil. or that evil is as simple as a
flag and words on a page.

SUHEIR HAMMAD
First Writing Since, November 7, 2001

Tiny pieces of U.S. Marines hung from the trees. The four-story building had been reduced to a pile of broken concrete. By the time rescuers dug them out, 241 U.S. servicemen were dead and scores more wounded.

The 23 October 1983 suicide bombing of the U.S. Marine Corps barracks in Beirut was part of a convulsion of anti-American violence that marked the birth of modern 'Islamist' terrorism—the bombings of U.S. embassies in Lebanon and Kuwait; the hijacking of a TWA flight packed with Americans; and the kidnappings of U.S. citizens from the streets of Beirut, some of them my friends.

The group that claimed responsibility for the atrocities called itself 'Islamic Jihad'. Those of us reporting on its activities came under fire for giving Islam a bad name. It was up to us, Muslim critics in America said, to make clear they did not represent Islam. But, of course, they *did* represent Islam—or at least the militant subset of Shi'a Islam championed by the group we now know as Hezbollah, of which Islamic Jihad was the operational wing. The nom de guerre gave Hezbollah deniability, but it gave Islam a black eye.

Fast-forward three and a half decades and 'mainstream' Muslims were still on the defensive, still asking that journalists and politicians make clear the bad guys didn't *really* represent the religion, still struggling to figure out how to battle this virus in their midst. Only now, the worst nightmare of America's three million Muslims had come true: a media-savvy group that made al Qaeda look tame was cutting off heads in the name of Islam, U.S.-born Muslims were carrying out acts of violence on American soil, and there was now a president in the White House who won the job, in part, by inflaming anti-Muslim sentiment to win votes, egged on by a cabal of Islamophobes scattered through his campaign apparatus.

> In next 24 hours, I dare Arab & Persian world 'leaders' to step up to the plate and declare their Islamic ideology sick and must B healed.[1]

That was a tweet sent by Donald Trump's military adviser, Lt. Gen. Michael Flynn, after a horrific massacre in which eighty-three people were killed and almost 500 injured in the French coastal city of Nice at the height of the campaign. The same day, Newt Gingrich told Fox News that the United States must immediately act to prevent similar attacks: "We should frankly test every person here who is of a Muslim background, and if they believe in sharia, they should be deported."[2]

Think about that: the national security "expert" advising the presumptive GOP presidential nominee wanted the world's Muslim leaders to "declare their Islamic ideology sick." Not denounce *terrorism* but denounce *their own religion*. And the former speaker of the U.S. House of Representatives wanted to deport every American Muslim who *believed in the texts upon which her/his religion was based.*

It would later be confirmed that the mass murderer in Nice, an emotionally unstable Tunisian-born Muslim, was inspired by the blood-soaked ideology of the Islamic State. Thus, French president François Hollande's comment that his nation was under the "threat of Islamist terrorism" was understandable. But the problem with that term, as Flynn and Gingrich so readily demonstrated, was it was a short step from there to conflating the tiny minority of extremists with the rest of the world's 1.6 billion Muslims.

Definitions

Despite the insinuation of many simplistic sound bites, "Islamic," "Islamist" and "sharia" were not actually dirty words. Something was

"Islamic" if it had to do with Islam. An "Islamist" was someone who believed Islam was both a religion and a political movement that strived for the incorporation of Islamic teachings in national governance. That did not automatically equate to militancy. Plenty of American allies across the Muslim fit that description.[3]

Voices of Islamists who denounced violence had credibility among fellow Muslims. In them lay the potential to undermine the message of the radicals in ways American anti-extremist Twitter feeds never would. "Islam is a religion. It suffers from the same denominational, sectarian and doctrinal disputes as most other religions. Whereas Islamism is the desire to impose any version of Islam over society," according to Majid Nawaz, an adviser to the British government who was a former member of the Islamist Hizb utTahrir movement. "And where *jihad* traditionally means holy struggle, *Jihadism* is the use of force to spread Islamism. Most Muslims, as you know, are not Islamists."[4] That was particularly true of Muslims in the U.S. One poll of American Muslims found that, like their Christian countrymen, the majority *did not* believe their religion should influence U.S. law.[5]

Meanwhile, sharia, which translates as "the Path," was not a license to cut off heads, as some Muslim critics seemed to imply. It was a term used for the individual and societal mores derived from the texts upon which Islam is based—the Qur'an, the core holy book, and the Hadith, accounts of the Prophet Muhammad's life and teachings. To ask Muslims to disavow them, as Flynn had done, was like asking a Christian to renounce the Bible.

"The Qur'an contains the rules by which the Muslim world is governed (or should govern itself) and forms the basis for relations between man and God, between individuals, whether Muslim or non-Muslim, as well as between man and things which are part of creation," according to M. Cherif Bassiouni of DePaul Law School. "The *Sharia* contains the rules by which a Muslim society is organized and governed, and it provides the means to resolve conflicts among individuals and between the individual and the state."[6]

In other words, there was a world of difference between a Muslim following the teachings of the Qur'an and the Hadith in her/his everyday life and that person insisting those teachings should be the primary law of the land. In fact, only a handful of Muslim-majority countries—such as Saudi Arabia—were governed primarily by sharia law. More commonly, Islamic law took precedence only in family courts or more generally served as a moral compass for civil law, as Judeo-Christian values did in the U.S.[7] A global poll by the Pew Research Center found majority support for the strict application of sharia in just four Muslim-majority countries. Despite the increased influence of Islamic law under Turkey's autocratic Islamist president, the poll found that just 13 percent of Turks supported using sharia as the basis for the law of the land.[8]

Candidate Trump made much of the refusal of President Obama and Hillary Clinton to use "radical" (or "militant") and "Islam" (or "Muslim") in the same sentence. "There's no magic to the phrase 'radical Islam.'" It's a political talking point. It's not a strategy," President Obama said dismissively the morning after the Orlando massacre. "Not once has an adviser of mine said, 'Man, if we use that phrase, we're going to turn this whole thing around.'" But the reality was that refusing to link the two words was an agonizing bit of verbal gymnastics. Supporters of ISIS, al Qaeda and the like *were* Islamists and they *were* radicals. Even many American Muslims—including Islamists—use those terms to differentiate themselves from the violent extremist minority. "To truly understand the world Islamist extremist movement, one must realize it is not just a social phenomenon but is a full-fledged ideological war of words and weapons alike," according to an online primer on "Islamic Radicalism" by the Islamic Supreme Council of America.[9]

Unfortunately, as Clinton and Obama seemed to understand, in America's hyper-inflamed political landscape, the distinction between an "Islamist extremist," an "Islamist" and a 'Muslim,' quickly became lost in the fog of ill-informed of cable news sound bites.

Tim Curry, a counterterrorism official at DHS, summed it up perfectly: "At the end of the day, you can say 'Islamist terrorist' and all that 95 percent of America hears is 'Muslim,' so if that's not your intent, then you should change the language, because what you think you're doing by being clear is actually muddying things."

"Islamism is a political and theoretical philosophy that commands its adherents to wage violent jihad to murder or forcibly convert all infidels," Ted Cruz told CNN's Anderson Cooper in March 2016. "And by 'infidels,' they mean every one of the rest of us. Islamism is our enemy."[10] Cruz would be hard-pressed to find many experts on Islam who would agree. However, such thinking helped justify the patrols of Muslim neighborhoods that Cruz had called for earlier in the GOP primary and that Gingrich and Trump continued to support.

Accuracy Not Appeasement

"Words matter." That was the opening sentence of a 2008 DHS memo written with input from American Muslims. "[E]xperts counseled caution in using terms such as, 'jihadist', 'Islamic terrorist', 'Islamist' and 'holy warrior.'" The purpose of the document, titled "Terminology to Define the Terrorists," was both to avoid offending Muslims and to ensure U.S. government spokespeople did not glamorize the militants.[11] It was produced long before a tiny handful of Muslims in America joined the jihad, before Europe was infiltrated by lethal ISIS networks, and before opportunistic politicians tapped a xenophobic vein in the American body politic. By the 2016 presidential campaign, terminology had become a political tool. Not since the immediate aftermath of 9/11 had the phrase "Islamic terrorism"—and its many variants—been so much a part of the national narrative, or fear of terrorism been so great.

Hillary Clinton's denunciation of "radical jihadists who use Islam to recruit and radicalize others in order to pursue their evil agenda"[12] was portrayed by Trump and others as Muslim appeasement since it did not acknowledge a broad "Muslim" threat. Experts argued that the distinctions drawn by Clinton were necessary both to differentiate the extremists from the majority of Muslims and to differentiate the many threats. Scores of militant groups with wildly different agendas, all claiming to serve Islam, had been spawned since the first attacks on Americans in the early 1980s. Yet from the campaign trail to Capitol Hill, politicians were discussing the ever-growing threat with all the sophistication of a middle school social studies class. "If we lump together the Paris bombings [claimed by ISIS] and the Peshawar school attack [by the Pakistani Taliban], we get seduced by the commonalities and ignore the reality that they are carried out by very different groups for very different reasons," a Saudi diplomat at the UN told me. "The challenge [the West has] with concepts is the same as with language."

But in the U.S. "language has become a political football," according to one official who worked on domestic counterterrorism issues for more than a decade. "We are dealing with an ideology, but instead of trying to communicate and understand its complexity we reduce it all to a sound bite." And it wasn't just on the campaign trail or cable TV. "When I came to State, I was shocked that people still used 'jihadist' and 'Islamist,'" said a State Department official who worried about how policy resonated abroad. "But some things just stick."

There was little in the way of official guidance for U.S. government officials. Aside from a general directive not to refer to the "Islamic State," there wasn't even an agreement on use of the various transliterations of that movement's earlier names: ISIS, ISIL or the pejorative Da'esh (usually incorrectly pronounced by American officials as "Dash," as if the U.S. was fighting a detergent). American officials were all over the linguistic map. The important thing, when it came to advising politicians and government officials who appeared in the media, was "not telling them what to say, it's making sure they understand why they are using a specific term," Tim Curry, the DHS official who authored the U.S. government's terminology document, told me not long after Trump was sworn in.

This issue wasn't just academic. Nor was it about political correctness—though President Obama had been accused of exactly that because he wouldn't use the terms "Islam" or "Islamist" when referring to radicals or militants. It was about winning allies in the war against extremism at home and abroad. Visit any Muslim majority country and it won't be long before someone says dismissively, "You Americans think we are all terrorists." And yet U.S. administrations since 9/11 wanted them to join America's grand coalition against terror.

Among Muslims fed up with being conflated with terrorists, the nerve endings had become raw. Even the term "moderate Muslim" was anathema to some Muslims; they believed it implied "good Muslim" versus one who had been co-opted by the radicals. "From this skewed viewpoint, moderate Muslims are those who adopt no distinctive dress, who consume alcohol and practice their religion 'as we do ours,'" wrote Tariq Ramadan, a professor of contemporary Islam at Oxford who had been labeled an extremist and banned from the U.S. by the Bush administration and embraced as a Muslim reformer by Obama, even as he was denounced as a kafir (unbeliever), *murtad* (apostate) and imposter by extremists among his co-religionists.

Connect the words "Islam" or "Muslim" with almost anything and you were likely to get pushback. At a dinner I attended in Islamabad, Puruesh Chaudhary, a young, British-educated Pakistani head of a nongovernmental organization (NGO), strongly objected when a colleague from a local Islamic university said he was starting a center to study Islamophobia, a term to describe those who are anti-Muslim. "Why would you use the term 'Islamophobia'?" she asked. "It links Islam with a phobia."

Beyond the inaccuracy of equating all Muslims with violence was the fact it was equally misleading to lump together all extremists. Reporting on a rally by an anti-American political alliance, Pakistan's *Dawn* newspaper described it as a "lashing together [of] reactionary and millenarian forces" that included "jihadists, sectarian warriors, orthodox mullahs [and] Islamic revivalists."[13]

You didn't hear those subtleties on the campaign trail. As Aberto Fernandez, a former U.S. State Department Coordinator for Strategic Counterterrorism Communication, wrote, "the unhelpful and superficial rhetoric that exists today, including from high-level political figures," is a "significant obstacle to developing coherent policy to face a very real threat."[14]

Words matter.

Which brought us right back to the challenge I faced in Beirut back in the 1980s: What do we call the enemy? How do we talk about them without offending the very people we need as allies in the fight? It was more complicated in the second decade of the twenty-first century than any time in modern history. Scores of militant groups with wildly different agendas had been spawned since Hezbollah set off that first suicide bomb. There was no simple answer to the conundrum of Islam and language. The extremists *were* carrying out violence in the name of Islam; they *did* represent some subset of the religion. To ignore that *would*, as the denizens of right-wing talk radio constantly reminded us, take political correctness to an unacceptable extreme and undermine America's security. But a campaign narrative that transformed Islam into a derogatory epithet was equally dangerous.

"USG officials should continually emphasize a simple and straightforward truth: Muslims have been, and will continue to be part of the fabric of our country," that 2008 DHS language guidance memo advised. "Muslims are not 'outsiders' looking in but are an integral part of America."

Amid the "perfect storm" of ISIS-inspired attacks and the Islamophobic rhetoric unleashed by the campaign, that message was sounding very hollow.

7 THE MYTH OF THE MUSLIM MONOLITH

The devil can cite Scripture for his purpose.

WILLIAM SHAKESPEARE
The Merchant of Venice

The magnificent palace of Alhambra, rose colored in the Spanish dusk, rests on a rocky spur above the town of Granada in southern Spain. Wandering beneath the arched ceilings, with their ornate inlaid tiles, and through tranquil courtyards dotted with shimmering pools, I soaked in the splendor of what was once the Muslim Caliphate of Córdoba, also known as Al-Andalus.

As I had learned in history books, the palace was the final home of the final Muslim ruler of a 700-year kingdom that came to be known as the "ornament of the world," an intellectual, artistic and spiritual crossroads where "Muslims, Jews, and Christians created a culture of tolerance."[1] But I had spent almost four decades living and working in Muslim-majority countries from Morocco to Indonesia, so I knew that Alhambra was also something more: a vivid reminder of the divisions that had splintered Islam since the dawn of the religion.

I sat for a moment on a stone bench in one of the palace's many anterooms. On the other side of the world, Donald Trump was preparing to take the oath of office. I contemplated the divisive campaign and the central theme that had underscored all the rhetoric: the idea that there was a monolithic thing called "Islam" that "hates us."

I could imagine the last occupant of this palace, his dynasty destroyed by internecine conflict among Muslims, laughing at such a notion through his tears.

Blood and Power

Muslim unity lasted less than thirty years after the death of the Prophet Muhammad. Three of Muhammad's four immediate successors were assassinated by competing Muslim factions.

An Islamic *Game of Thrones* was underway even as the Prophet lay on his deathbed. As in most dynastic rivalries, at the heart of the divisions in those early years of Islam were blood, jealousy and power. With the death of the Prophet in 632, those closest to him—his wives, daughters and his advisers (known as the Senior Companions)—quickly locked horns over the issue of succession. Though Muhammad had left no will, his cousin and son-in-law Ali, husband of Muhammad's daughter Fatima, believed he had been designated as heir. That was based, in part, on a series of comments the Prophet had made over the course of his lifetime, the most famous of which was, "I am the City of Knowledge and Ali is its gateway."[2]

Then there was the fact that Ali was the only one among the potential male *khalifah* ("successors" or caliphs) who was of Muhammad's bloodline (selecting one of the women was not considered an option). Some, such as the future Caliph Umar, feared that Ali would turn the caliphate into a hereditary dynasty.[3] A'isha, Muhammad's youngest and favorite wife, is said to have had a lifelong hatred of Ali, who once reportedly tried to convince the Prophet to divorce her. There was danger for her and her father if Ali inherited Muhammad's spiritual and political mantle. She and another wife, Umar's daughter Hafsa, are said to have prevented Ali from seeing Muhammad on his deathbed to discuss the succession.[4] After much intrigue, A'isha's father and the Prophet's closest Companion, Abu Bakr, was eventually selected as the first of what would come to be known as the Rightly Guided Caliphs, those caliphs drawn from among the Companions.

In the process, several factions among the early Muslims were deeply alienated, including the so-called al-Ansar (The Helpers) of Medina, who had protected the Prophet in his years in exile from Mecca, and the Umayyad clan, which would later rule the caliphate. As scholar Wilferd Madelung noted, "the situation of the caliph was at first highly precarious."[5] Umar was dispatched to Medina, where he bullied the residents into pledging support for Abu Bakr, reportedly even threatening to set fire to the home of the Prophet's daughter Fatima if another of the Prophet's former Companions, who supported Ali, refused to come out.[6] Ali, who was backed by the Ansars, would eventually be compelled—some scholars say forced—to fall into line and pledge support to Abu Bakr, but only after the death of his wife Fatima.[7]

It would take a quarter of a century before Ali would be selected as fourth and last of the Rightly Guided Caliphs. By that point, Islam had descended into all-out civil war and both of Abu Bakr's successors as caliph—Umar and Uthman, father of yet another of Muhammad's wives— had been assassinated. Ali would suffer the same fate five years later at the hands of Muslim Kharijite rebels, but not before A'isha, by then known as Mother of the Faithful, led an army against him in the infamous Battle of the Camel, where the Prophet's wife was wounded and defeated.[8]

Think about that. The Prophet's wife wounded in battle against her brother-in-law, the Prophet's confidant. So much for the Muslim monolith.

Two decades after the assassination of Ali, his son Hussein and a small band of followers were massacred at Karbala, in modern-day Iraq, by an army of the new Umayyad caliphate, founded after Ali's death.[9] In an act that would become an eternal source of anguish for Shi'ites through the ages, Hussein's head was cut off and mounted on a lance. With Ali's death, the bitter rivalry between the Companions and their supporters was torn asunder, creating the seminal division between the two main branches of Islam, the Sunni, who trace their loyalty to Abu Bakr and the other early caliphs, and the Shi'a, the followers of Ali.

Islam descended even deeper into violent conflict. Within a century, the ruling Umayyad dynasty was overthrown by the rival Abbasids, descendants of Muhammad's uncle Abbas, and the Umayyad Caliph Marwan II and his family were murdered. His only surviving heir, a young prince named Abd al-Rahman, whose mother had been a Berber slave, fled west through the Levant, along the North Africa coast, and eventually crossed the narrow Strait of Gibraltar to establish a rival caliphate in "Moorish" Spain.

Thus, even at the height of Muslim political power, when the Islamic empire stretched from India to the Atlantic Ocean, covering a greater land mass than the Roman Empire ever achieved, there were two caliphs, two caliphates and an ever-evolving array of Muslim factions, all laying claim to power and religious truth.

Ironically, it was fellow Muslims, as much as the Spanish Catholics, who were responsible for the collapse of the Caliphate of Córdoba, 700 years after it was founded by al-Rahman. Facing battlefield losses to Catholic monarch Alfonso VI of Castile in the early eleventh century, Mutamid of

Seville, the Muslim ruler of the day, asked for military help from Muslim Berber tribesmen, the Almoravids, who had consolidated control across the strait in North Africa. It would prove to be a fatal miscalculation. As historian Maria Rosa Menocal recorded, "These fanatics considered the Andalusian Muslims intolerably weak" and after defeating Alphonso VI, the "would-be protectors … stayed on as the new tyrants of al-Andalus."[10]

The Almoravids and their successors, the Almohads, had much in common with extremists of the twenty-first century's Islamic State.[11] Their "brand of anti-secular and religiously-intolerant Islam was at irreconcilable odds with" Andalusia's tradition of acceptance.[12] Sufis and other Muslims whom the Almohads considered apostates were persecuted and the works of the legendary Muslim theologian al-Ghazali, known for his "humane" approach to Islam, were burned. The Andalusian Muslims rebelled. Anti-Almohad riots broke out and many Jews and Christians, who had thrived in al-Andalus' Muslim society, fled.

The extremism of the Almohads played into the hands of rival Christian states. Pope Innocent was already uniting European Catholics against Jews, Muslims and Christian heretics. Now the Almohads' campaign of persecution gave Christian armies to the north an excuse to rally to the cause of the Spanish Catholics. In 1212, beneath crosses and papal banners, the Catholic armies inflicted the first of a series of defeats upon the Almohads, marking the beginning of the end.

The swords of the Catholics would ultimately destroy the Spanish caliphate, but it was the divisions among Muslims that had weakened the caliphate from within and laid the groundwork for its demise. When the last of al-Andalus' Muslim rulers, Muhammad XI, known as Boabdil, handed over Alhambra's keys to Catholic monarchs Isabella and Ferdinand on January 2, 1492, the same year Columbus "discovered" the New World, it marked the end of seven centuries of Muslim rule in Spain.

As he left Granada in defeat, the grief-stricken Boabdil is said to have sighed deeply. That moment would enter history as "the Moor's last sigh."[13]

Schisms

Internecine conflict within Islam was certainly not consigned to the fifteenth century. Modern-day Muslims are equally divided by a host of doctrinal, regional, ethnic and political fault lines.

As Islamic scholar Omid Safi put it,

> Salafis, Sufis, modernists, reformers, Wahabis: whichever Muslim group, by whatever name one calls them, and in all their conceivable permutations, portray themselves as bearers of the mantle of the Prophet.... In short, they all claim to speak in Muhammad's name, quoting, misquoting, and contesting the legacy of the Prophet.[14]

There are at least ten major sects and close to 50 splinter groups within Shi'a Islam alone. Iran is dominated by the so-called Twelvers, who believe the twelfth inheritor in the line of Shi'a imams, known as the Hidden Imam, went into occultation (a mystic form of disappearance) at the age of five in the ninth century and will one day return as the Messiah, accompanied by Jesus Christ (Isa).[15] In his absence, the grand ayatollah rules on his behalf. The belief is not just a footnote in the religion. Former Iranian president Mahmoud Ahmadinejad had a block of hotels rooms in Tehran permanently reserved for the return and once accused the United States of planning to arrest the Hidden Imam.[16]

Each of the other Shi'a sects has its own mythology and its own *bab,* or door, to the ultimate Truth. The Ismailis, best known for the charitable works of their leader, the Aga Khan, believe the Mahdi will return to strip away the religions founded by Adam, Noah, Abraham, Moses, Jesus and Muhammad to reveal the one hidden "Religion of Truth";[17] the Ahmadiyya and the Kaysanites each believe their particular founder was the Mahdi;[18] and so it goes.

Among the most esoteric—and furthest from the Muslim mainstream—are the Alawis and the Druzes. The Alawites, a syncretic schism of Twelver Shi'ism, are based mainly in Syria and include President Bashar al-Assad among their followers. They draw their inspiration from a mystic who was a contemporary of the Hidden Imam and worship a "divine triad" that involves three emanations of Allah, an echo of the Christian Holy Trinity.[19] They have also absorbed various Christian practices such as consecrating wine as part of their mass, celebrating several Christian saints' days and drawing teachings from the Gnostics, Aristotle and others.[20]

Particularly anathema to orthodox Islam is the fact that reincarnation is a central element of the teachings of the Alawites, sometimes known as Nusayris. They believe in reincarnation and subscribe to the Gnostic idea that humans were stars or divine lights that were cast to earth as punishment:

When a Nusayri dies his soul moves to another human body, plant, insect or inanimate object until the final stage, when they return to be stars as they were in the beginning.[21]

Another group that believes in reincarnation are the Druze, an eleventh-century offshoot of Ismaili Shi'ism. Most Druze no longer consider themselves Muslim. Their esoteric practices, which include belief in reincarnation, center on seeking the hidden meaning in sacred texts like the Qur'an and the Bible.[22] In the spiritual worldview of the Druze, you cannot convert to Druzism. The only people initiated into the religion are those whose previous incarnations are said to have signed an ancient "Pact of Time" charter and were among the original group of followers massacred in Egypt.[23] All that puts them far outside the Islamic religious mainstream, as one hardline Sunni cleric told his followers in an online post:

> They are worse *kaafirs* [infidels] than many other extremist groups. They believe that this universe has no creator and they deny the resurrection and the duties and prohibitions of Islam.... [T]hey deny the perfect attributes of Allah and they deny the Day of Resurrection with its reckoning and recompense of Paradise and Hell.[24]

In 1959, in an ecumenical move driven by Egyptian president Gamal Abdel Nasser's effort to broaden his political appeal, the Islamic scholars at Al Azhar University in Cairo classified the Druze as Muslims and issued a broader acceptance of Shi'a Islam.[25] But in 2012, with the Muslim Brotherhood in power in Egypt and Salafi views taking hold at Al Azhar, the Grand Mufti issued a fatwa reversing the earlier ruling and declaring not just the Druze but all Shi'a to be heretics, reinforcing Sunni-Shia antipathy as the seminal divide in Islam.[26]

The fatwa followed rising Saudi concerns about Iranian "encroachment" in Egypt after the overthrow of President Hosni Mubarak. According to documents released by Wikileaks, the head of Saudi intelligence sent a secret cable to Egyptian authorities warning that "the Shia sect has found a vast space to expand after the January 25 revolution."[27] The effort at what the Saudi foreign minister described in a secret memo as "resisting the attempts for Shia encroachment in Egypt," was carefully coordinated with Al Azhar. In September 2011, that institution's new head, Grand Sheikh Ahmed al-Tayyeb, issued a fatwa condemning "the attempts to propagate Shia beliefs in Sunni countries, especially Egypt, and next to the minaret of Al-Azhar, the bastion of the people of Sunna."[28]

The Sunni/Shi'a Divide

The impact of such Saudi-fueled Sunni-Shi'a antipathy was felt across the Muslim world. It was evident when I met Mufti Naeem, a Sunni Deobandi cleric, at Pakistan's Jamia Binoria madrassa. Naeem was on the front lines of the Sunni-Shi'a confrontation. Steel doors protected the entrance to the sprawling religious school. As we spoke, we sat sprawled on pillows on the pristine white carpet of his office, which contained no furniture other than a desk. There were no windows. Television screens on the wall Naeem faced weren't tuned to any of Pakistan's plethora of 24-hour news channels, as in many offices. Rather, they showed the feed from security cameras facing the madrassa's gate, outside the front entrance to his office, and on the other side of the office's rear exit.

Security was a fixture of Naeem's life, which was constantly under threat. He was a target of Pakistani Shi'ite militias, just as they appeared to be a target of the more militant of his followers. Western intelligence sources told me that, while Naeem was considered "one of the good ones" who did not target Americans, he was in a constant state of conflict with the Shi'a and some militant Sunni groups. The madrassa was bombed in 2004, killing eight and injuring more than forty. Naeem's son-in-law was assassinated in 2014. Others associated with the madrassa had also been killed or survived attacks. Some incidents were traced back to factions of the Pakistani Taliban, to which the madrassa had ever-shifting political ties; others to Shi'ite militants.

Naeem was coy when I asked him about the Shi'a in our interview, but in 2015 his organization issued a fatwa (religious ruling) declaring that Ismaili Shi'a were infidels. Not long after, a bus attack by Sunni extremists killed at least 45 Shi'a.[29] A hardline Shi'a website, meanwhile, made clear how that organization viewed Naeem:

This particular Saudi-Funded Mullah, his school of thought and his institutions have gone not only against the innate values of Islam but as well were against the creation of an Islamic nation.[30]

Sufis

Another fault line in Islam is between conservatives in both the Sunni and Shi'a camps, and the Sufis, who practice a mystic strain of the religion. There are Sunni and Shi'a Sufis, but they are anathema to hardliners in both branches of the religion. Sufi practice focuses on unity with God through meditation, and they preach an inclusive message characterized by a rich tradition of poetry, such as this from ibn 'Arabi, a thirteenth-century Andalusian philosopher and saint:

> Wonder,
> A garden among the flames!
> My heart can take on
> Any form:
> A meadow for gazelles,
> A cloister for monks,
> For the idols, sacred ground,
> Ka'ba for the circling pilgrim,
> the tables for the Torah,
> the scrolls of the Qur'an.
> My creed is love;
> Wherever its caravan turns along the way,
> That is my belief,
> My faith.[31]

"The whole quest of Sufism is the search for the hidden secret, the desire to know. But the secret can only be known to us through signs," Pir Vilayat Inayat Khan, head of a branch of a major Sufi order, told me when we met in 2000, a few years before his death.[32]

With his snow-white hair and beard and white tunic, Pir Vilayat looked every inch the Eastern master come down from the mountaintop. Yet woven through his esoteric talk of the "Divine Presence," the levels of consciousness, and the interchangeability of the terms "God" and the "Universe," were modern analogies that belied his appearance. "The universe as a being is trying to reveal its software through its hardware, and we're not listening," the Paris-based teacher told me over tea. Interviewing Pir (a religious title meaning Master) Vilayat was both enervating and exhausting; his insights poured forth in an almost non-stop stream of consciousness peppered with illustrations drawn from the works of the great composers, other religions and even physicist David Bohm.

"What we're doing in our [religious] practice for one thing is learning to extend our self-image into the cosmic vastness, so we are not a discreet entity but somehow, we incorporate the totality," Pir Vilayat explained. "The Hindus, the Buddhists all know that things are not the way they look. So what? Any physicist will tell us that." The goal of Sufi contemplation was to see beyond the physical forms that surround us. To the Sufis, he said, we are God, or as Pir Vilayat preferred, "the Universe."

"The Universe can only know itself through those fragments of itself that are us, just as the tree knows itself through the branches of the tree," he said, adding with a laugh, "God knows Himself through our knowledge of God."

"Then, at a certain point, you reach beyond the idea of form," Pir Vilayat went on. "This breakthrough of awakening [comes] when a human being has reached that point where God no more discloses Him/Herself through those devices, but the Divine Mind is knowable directly."

Such a philosophy was the reason some Sunni Muslim conservatives considered Sufis to be apostates, even if most Sufis considered themselves Sunnis. Sufism was outlawed in Saudi Arabia, where Sufis faced prison sentences—and worse—for practicing their religion. They were victimized by Sunni and Shi'a extremists alike and were a favorite target of the Islamic State and its offshoots. From Syria to Egypt to West Africa, ISIS-inspired militants had blown up Sufi mosques and tombs of Sufi saints and slaughtered any Sufis unfortunate enough to fall into their hands. When two Sufis were beheaded in the Sinai in 2017, a videotape released by ISIS showed one of its militants reading what he said was a ruling from the ISIS-run sharia court that sentenced them to death for "apostasy, sorcery, claiming the ability to tell the future, and leading people to polytheism."[33]

Interpreting the Qur'an

The first story involving Islam that I ever covered was the 1977 takeover of the Washington, DC, office of the Jewish charity B'nai B'rith, a mosque, and a district government building by a group of men who called themselves Hanafi Muslims. I was a twenty-one-year-old reporter for Associate Press Radio, about to graduate college. I knew—*sort of*—what a Muslim was. But what the heck was a Hanafi? It turned out the hostage takers weren't too sure either.

It would later emerge that the gunmen—who held more than 100 men and women for three days, killed a radio reporter and wounded the future mayor of Washington—were part of a splinter group of the Nation of Islam, a political and religious movement founded by W. D. Fard in 1931 in Chicago and made famous by Elijah Muhammad and Malcolm X as a black nationalist take on Islam. Its decidedly unorthodox anti-Jewish teachings included the notion that whites were devils.[34] The leader of the B'nai B'rith siege had been a top official of the Nation of Islam until the organization splintered after the death of Elijah Muhammad in 1975. Soon after, gunmen from a rival faction broke into his home and killed seven members of his family, including his nine-day-old grandson. Now he wanted the man responsible, who had been convicted and was in prison, to be turned over to him for some street justice.

The Nation of Islam defector had named his splinter group the Hanafi Movement. Forty years later, in a story marking the anniversary of the siege, *The Washington Post* was still referring to the hostage takers as members of "the Hanafi sect of Islam."[35] In fact, the siege had more to do with black nationalist politics than religion, but it gave me an early glimpse of a reality that would be woven into my reporting for the next four decades: no one person, group or sect speaks for Islam. Nothing better illustrated that than the competition between the *real* Hanafis and their rivals.

Hanafis are the followers of one of the eight main schools of legal doctrine that govern Islam. Muslims believe that the Qur'an is the unaltered word of God, passed down to Muhammad through the Angel Gabriel. "This is the Book in which there is no doubt, a guidance for the reverent … which We … sent down unto thee," according to one of the opening passages of the Qur'an (2:2-4).[36] But what any given injunction actually *means* has been the subject of debate since the dawn of Islam.

To understand why, it's important to know a bit about the history of the Qur'an, which can be translated as "The Work." In the year 610, while meditating in a cave he frequented, Muhammad is said to have heard a voice of the Angel Gabriel who appeared before him and commanded,

Recite in the name of thy Lord who created,
created man, out of a blood clot.
Recite! Thy Lord is most noble,

Who taught by the Pen,
taught man that which he knew not. (96:1–5)

These "revelations" would continue periodically for the next twenty-three years. At the foundation of the transmissions was a sentence that would become the first words of the Call to Prayer that echoes from the minarets five times a day: *La illah il Allah*, there is no god but Allah. The word "Allah" is Arabic for "God," so at face value, the statement seems self-evident, there is no god but God. But in those days, the people of Muhammad's tribe, the Qureshi, worshipped a pantheon of gods. One of them, Allah, was credited with creating man. But he was considered no better or worse than the others. With *la illah il Allah*, Muhammad was being told to forget all those others claiming to be gods; they were just desert jinn. Allah was the only *God* with a capital G. As the Qur'an says elsewhere, "Your God is one God, there is no god but He" (2:163).

In the beginning, Muhammad did not know what to think of what he was hearing. Was it his imagination? Was it an evil spirit trying to confuse him? Was it a false god trying to mislead him? His wife, Khadijah, convinced him it was the Word of the true God. She is therefore considered the first Muslim.

According to the Qur'an, Muhammad was illiterate. "those who follow the messenger, the unlettered Prophet" (7:157). A tradition emerged among some Muslims that it was thus a miracle that he later wrote down some of these Revelations. Scholars are more skeptical, arguing that Muhammad likely recited some passages to his scribes, who transcribed them, while others were committed to memory by the Companions and early Followers. Thus, the Qur'an was not handed down in a single cohesive document. It was only after the Prophet died that Abu Bakr—after much hesitation—ordered the various disparate sections be compiled into a set of codices. Muhammad's scribe, Zayd ibn Thabit, was given the task:

> Thereupon, I traced the *Qur'an*, collecting it from palm branches, flat stones, and the breasts of the people [who had memorized it].[37]

The fact that some passages had been memorized by multiple individuals inevitably led to disagreements over wording and even whether certain memories should be included.[38]

The archive, which was a far better description than "book" since it was initially unbound and the Revelations had not been received in chronological order, was passed down by Abu Bakr to the next caliph, Umar, and on his death to his daughter Hafsa, one of the wives of the Prophet, who some scholars believe was involved in its codification.[39] Before long, at least twenty-eight sometimes conflicting versions of the collection existed as scribes made copies for distribution across the rapidly expanding caliphate.

The next caliph, Uthman, ordered a new codification and re-evaluation of the wording of the Qur'an's "still-fluid pre-canonical text."[40] Once it was complete, previous versions, including Hafsa's archive, were destroyed. And yet, by the time the scribes produced copies of this new version, countless mistakes of grammar and spelling had been made. The challenge this created in parsing meaning was compounded by the undeveloped nature of the Arabic of the day, which lacked vowel marks and dots, potentially transforming phrases like "he killed" (*qatala*) into "he kissed" (*qabala*).[41] As scholar Estelle Whelan observed, "It is clear that even in the Muslim tradition the fact was acknowledged that readings of the Qur'an continually diverged from a supposed original."[42]

Therefore, it shouldn't be surprising that from the beginning Muslims have interpreted many passages of the Qur'an in conflicting ways, not unlike Christians and the Bible. As the centuries passed, an entire class of Qur'anic scholars and jurists emerged. They looked to the "words, deeds rulings, and comportment" of the Prophet and the Companions, what Muslims call the Sunna (Tradition), to help them apply the Qur'an to the real-world issues of their day (the Sunnis take their name from the early moniker "The People of the Sunna").[43]

This corpus, known as Hadith, remains the backbone of Islamic jurisprudence or sharia, the set of principles and legal precedent that guides the life of every Muslim and that so enervated the Islamophobes. However, the Hadith is yet another example of the divisions—or, at very least, different interpretations of aspects of the faith—within Islam. The Sunnis, Shi'a and several smaller sects each have their own set of Hadith. They don't even agree on the proper way to carry out daily prayers.

The Hadith are based on oral history passed down from the time of the Prophet. Unlike the Qur'an they were not necessarily written down. It wasn't until about a century after the death of the Prophet that scholars began compiling Hadith. To judge whether a particular story (*isnad*) was authentic (*sahih*), good (*hasan*), weak (*da'if*) or fabricated (*mawdu*), scholars sought to trace it directly to its source through an unbroken chain of transmitters (*ittisal assanad*). If that could not be achieved, the report was rejected. But human beings—with their subjectivity, prejudices, and preconceived notions—were involved, so of course it wasn't as simple as that. "What one camp considers an authentic and compelling teaching of the Prophet, another considers a forgery," according to Islamic scholar Jonathan Brown of Georgetown University.[44]

It went beyond merely confirming or rejecting a particular Hadith. Literalists argued that the reports passed down from the Companions must be taken at face value, while other emerging schools of Hadith saw them as allegorical. There were eschatological disagreements, such as whether man controlled his own destiny or fate was preordained by God, and less lofty debates, such as whether a woman could lead men in prayers.

These various streams would eventually emerge as what are today four Sunni schools of Islamic thought, two Shi'a schools, and two followed by the Ibadi and Zahiri traditions, small branches of Islam closely aligned with the Sunnis. Each has its own broad geographical and doctrinal zone of influence, often shaped in response to the philosophies of the others. For example, "Sunnis stressed the centrality of literal readings to counter the attractive esoteric interpretations offered by their Shiite competitors," while some Shi'a scholars believed that behind the words of the Qur'an lay hidden, esoteric meanings.[45]

Likewise, each of the competing schools in all traditions has its own emphases and philosophies. Hanbalis, for example, are largely literalists, while the Mu'tazila school believes in the pursuit of reason and rational thought. Meanwhile, a subset of purists, known as the Qur'anists, reject anything but the literal words of the Qur'an.[46] They point to passages like this one:

> And We sent down to unto thee the Book as a clarification of all things, and as a guidance and a mercy and glad tidings for those who submit. (16:89)

In the worldview of this minority, the Word of God is all that counts. "Sadly, the majority of Muslim scholars claim that the Qur'an contains only the headlines of the religion and that we need the hadith and sunna to derive the details!" lamented one literalist website. "*Hadith* and *Sunna* are Satanic innovations."[47] Qur'anists use the following passage from the Qur'an as further evidence that there is no room for Hadith interpretation: "We have neglected nothing in the Book" (6:38). This seemingly straightforward statement is an example of how easily passages can be taken out of context or misinterpreted. Here is the full version of Surah 6, verse 38:

> There is no creature that crawls upon the earth, nor bird that flies upon its wings, but that they are communities like yourselves—We have neglected nothing in the Book—and they shall be gathered unto their Lord in the end.

Thus, the message seems to be closer to the Biblical reference to God creating "Living things small and great" (Psalm 104:24–26) than a claim that the Qur'an answers all questions that could ever be asked.

This was why Islam has long been plagued by dueling fatwas, contradictory religious rulings by clerics of various schools on everything from whether women should drive cars to whether Muslims are obligated to murder Americans.

Salafis and Wahhabis

The distinction between a Salafi, or Salafiyyah, and a Wahhabi is probably one of the most confusing in Islam, even for Muslims. As already noted, some early scholars advocated a literalist method of interpreting the words and actions of the *al-salaf al-salih*, the pious predecessors. Among the most influential champions of this approach was Ibn Taymiyyah, a thirteenth-century theologian and political figure based in Damascus. From his teachings evolved what came to be known as Salafism, a strain of Sunni Islam that looked to the early followers of Muhammad for direction.

Yasir Qadhi, an influential U.S. cleric, identified five common beliefs of all Salafis:

1) They consider themselves alone as correctly espousing the teachings and beliefs of the *salaf al-ṣāliḥ*.
2) They categorically reject any possibility of metaphoric or symbolic interpretation of the *tawḥīd al-asmā' wa'l-ṣifāt* [declaring God one in His names and attributes].
3) They absolutely affirm God's exclusive right to be worshipped (*tawḥīd alulūhiyyah*) and refute anything that may compromise

this directly, or lead to its being compromised. Hence, syncretic practices of certain Sufis (e.g., extreme saint veneration, intercession of the dead etc.) are condemned.

4) They oppose all reprehensible innovations (*bid'a*) and dissociate from those who ascribe to them (*ahl al-bid'ah*). There is especially staunch opposition to Shī'ism, particularly because of the Shī'ite doctrine of dissociating from most of the Companions.

5) They respect and take recourse to the legal and theological opinions of Shaykh al-Islam Ibn Taymiyya. It is important to note, however, that Ibn Taymiyya cannot, and is not, considered a progenitor for the modern Salafi movement, as they view themselves as having no one single founder after the Prophet Muḥammad (*ṣallallāhu 'alayhi wa sallam*).[48]

Today, the majority of Sunni Muslims in Saudi Arabia and the Gulf ascribe to those core Salafi beliefs. But if you ask a Gulf Arab if he or she is a Salafi, the likely response will be, "I am a Muslim," because, after all, part of that core belief system is that "They consider themselves alone as correctly espousing the teachings and beliefs" of Islam.[49]

Qadhi was widely known as a Salafi. When I asked if that was accurate, he replied, "No, I no longer consider myself one. I have left labels and I guess if anything I'm just a generic Sunni. But I'm not anti-Salafi or anti-Sufi or anything. It's pretty complicated, I guess."

Complicated indeed. There are at least seven major subgroups, and a host of splinter groups, among the Salafis, ranging from mainstream Saudi clerics who are "pacifist and loyal to their ruler," to the radical jihadi Salafists, such as al Qaeda and ISIS, committed to the establishment of a "pure" Islamic state and permanent war against all other authority, including Muslims they considered apostates, such as the House of Saud. Other issues that divide them include which *mahdab* or school of Hadith interpretation to follow, adherence to the classic Sunni doctrine of "obeying the legitimate ruler" and the legitimacy of political dissent, and whether specific physical actions –women being veiled, style of prayer or application of the more dramatic aspects of sharia law—are intrinsic to the faith.

Among those splinters of Salafism was the strain most closely associated with Saudi Arabia, the theology known in the West as Wahhabism. If many Salafis did not identify with that term, those called "Wahhabis" were often overtly offended by it.

"This Wahhabism—please define it for us. We're not familiar with it. We don't know about it," Saudi Crown Prince Mohammed bin Salman responded somewhat disingenuously when an American interviewer referred to "Wahhabist ideology." "No one can define Wahhabism. There is no Wahhabism. We don't believe we have Wahhabism. We believe we have, in Saudi Arabia, Sunni and Shiite," he continued. "When people speak of Wahhabism, they don't know exactly what they are talking about."[50]

Notwithstanding bin Salman's protestations, history shows that the Wahabi movement emerged in central Arabia under the leadership of a conservative eighteenth-century Hanbali cleric named Muhammad Ibn Abd al-Wahab, who joined forces with Muhammad ibn Saud to unite the desert tribes. The best way to describe Wahhabis is that they are a subset of Salafism as interpreted by al-Wahhab, who championed a return to the pure faith of the *al-salaf al-salih*, the pious predecessors, who included the Companions (*Sahabh*), the Followers (*Tabi'un*) and Followers of the Followers (*Tabi' al-Tabi'in*). His whose austere interpretation of Islam was rejected by many Sunni clerics of the day, including his father and brother. His power-sharing deal with Muhammad ibn Saud meant his theology, which rejected all who disagreed as apostates and idolaters, spread with ibn Saud's conquests. The mythology around their first meeting describes an instant kinship:
His was a literal interpretation of the Qur'an and the Hadith.

Muhammad ibn Sa'ud greeted Muhammad ibn 'Abd al-Wahhab and said, "This oasis is yours, do not fear your enemies. By the name of God, if all Najd was summoned to throw you out, we will never agree to expel you." Muhammad ibn 'Abd al-Wahhab replied, "You are the settlement's chief and wise man. I want you to grant me an oath that you will perform jihad (holy war) against the unbelievers. In return you will be *imam*, leader of the Muslim community and I will be leader in religious matters."[51]

Ibn Wahab's military alliance with the House of Saud would lead to the defeat of Arabia's other tribes and the creation of the first Saudi state in 1744. A direct line could also be traced from the worldview of al-Wahab to al Qaeda and the Islamic State today.

Wahhabis are generally considered Salafis, but not all Salafis are Wahhabis. Far from it. Counterintuitively, there is even a small subset of Sufi Salafis, who believe the Companions embodied patience and acceptance, key spiritual qualities to which Sufis strive, and blend mystical practice with emulation of a group of dedicated followers of the Prophet, the Ahlus Suffah, who renounced family and possessions and focused on spiritual practice.[52]

As Qadhi puts it,

> The existence of so much disagreement among the various strands of Salafis highlights the very real problem of describing as "salafi" any of the above issues as one collective whole: none of these individual groups is representative of Salafism in its entirety.

Salafis and Terror

Experts who have immersed themselves in the issue of Islam and terror have developed an entire lexicon to define the relationship between Salafism and violent extremism. During the Afghan jihad, French scholar Giles Kepel coined the term "Salafi-*Jihadists*" and "*Jihadist*-Salafism" to describe the "hybrid Islamist ideology" that evolved among foreign recruits to the anti-Soviet jihad.[53] His French colleague Olivier Roy took a different, though equally nuanced tack. "The source of radicalization is not Salafism," Roy wrote in his book *Jihad and Death*. "There is a common matrix, but not a causal relationship."[54] Another way to think about it, said Georgetown's Mohamed-Ali Adraoui, was, "You can get to *Jihadism* without having passed through a Salafist mosque."[55]

This was why the slash-and-burn approach of the Salafists of ISIS was denounced by many other Salafis, and the hardline ideology of the Saudi-funded Wahhabi clerics was anathema to so many other Muslims. Dr. Farid Ahmed Piracha was the deputy *Ameer*, or chief, of Pakistan's largest Islamist movement, the Jamaat-e-Islami (JI), founded in 1941 by Muslim philosopher Abul Ala Maududi with financial support from the Saudis as the vanguard of a global Islamic revolution.[56] JI was a key conduit for CIA funding to the anti-Soviet jihadis during the Afghan war,[57] but more recently had taken an overtly anti-American stance.

"After defeating Russia in Afghanistan, America declared war on Muslims," Piracha told me when we met in his office at JI's Lahore headquarters, known as Mansoora, a sprawling complex of schools, hospitals and social services facilities. "First there was the red danger for world [the color of the Soviet Union] and now there is green danger for world [the color of Islam]."

The JI's political orientation was matched by its religious orientation, at the conservative end of the spectrum. Although the organization itself had never been accused of engaging in violence, JI splinters evolved into various militant groups, including the Pakistani Taliban. Despite that, Piracha had nothing but contempt for ISIS, which he referred to using the derogatory name Daesh.

"Daesh is a trap for Muslims. Their ideology is quite against the teaching of Islam." He took a sip of tea and leaned closer to me. "They are the *khawarij*," he said, grimacing with distaste. He was referring to a group the Prophet Muhammad is said to have prophesized would rise before the return of the Mahdi and the End of Days. "The Prophet, Peace Be Upon Him, said they would recite the Holy Qur'an but they would create terrorism, so they are not representatives of Islam, they are against Islam. This is Daesh."

Navigating Contradictions

As if Islam didn't have enough historic variation, satellite television and the Internet was complicating things even further. Where once Sunni Muslims looked primarily to the scholars of Al Azhar and the Council of Senior Scholars in Saudi Arabia, and Shi'a turned to the ayatollahs of Iran and Iraq, now they switched on their television or computer. In the Middle East alone, dozens of rival religious channels crowded the dial. Meanwhile, the Internet contained an even greater array of sometimes obscure individuals and organizations offering their own rulings, guidance and advice.

Google the term "fatwa" or the phrase "Islamic rulings" and the results will include thousands of websites—from mainstream sites such as FatwaIslam.com, IslamReligion.com and IslamiCity.com to obscure blogs, podcasts and question-and-answer sites—claiming to provide authentic guidance on Islam.

This shifting media environment means that "[r]eligious authority does not have to be embodied in a scholar or ideologue," according Gary Bunt, author of several books on "cyber Islam." Along with traditional voices "are those without traditional Islamic science backgrounds, who use the Internet to present their own personal perspectives."[58] This means that while the "role of the traditional imam has not been negated, ... now authorities are increasingly emerging online, individually or as part of wider organizations." As a result, some Muslims are "shopping around" for religious opinions that bolster their preconceived notions. There is no shortage of opinion from which to choose:

> There may be different answers to similar questions, depending on which sites the surfer visits. While the status and profiles of some scholars have increased, questions arise as to whether greater clarity has been achieved for those seeking advice within this knowledge economy.[59]

Wrestling with the cacophony of voices and inherent ambiguities of his religion, American Muslim convert and iconoclast Muhammad Michael Knight, whom *The New York Times* called "court jester to the Islamic world,"[60] tailored his own solution:

> In my attempt at surrender to the origins, which aren't even the origins beyond doubt, I still have to decide things for myself, namely, which pieces are useful. It sounds like a slacker move, but this is how I navigate the immense textual sea of Hadith.[61]

The bottom line was that how Muslims interpreted the Qur'an and the Hadith—and led their lives—depended in part on which school of legal interpretation they were inclined to follow, what mosque they attended, their country of origin, whom they followed on Facebook and a host of other influences.

As Jonathan Brown put it, "The statement 'the *Shariah* said ...' is thus automatically misleading, as there is almost always more than one answer to any legal question."[62]

Much the same could be said of 2016 political campaign statements that started with the assumption "Islam is ..." or "Muslims are ..."

8 HOW THE WEST CREATED RADICAL ISLAM

I form the light, and create darkness: I make peace, and create evil.

ISAIAH 45
King James Bible

President Barack Obama was "the founder of ISIS."

That wild accusation made by Donald Trump at an August 2016 campaign rally caused his supporters to nod knowingly and Democrats to roll their eyes. "In many respects, you know, they honor President Obama," Trump said, referring to members of the so-called Islamic State. "He's the founder of ISIS. He's the founder of ISIS. He's the founder. He founded ISIS."[1]

There was a grain of truth buried deep in that wild accusation. The West had been creating the circumstances that bred "Islamic" terrorism since the final days of the Ottoman Empire.

The *Ikhwan*, spiritual forefathers of modern extremists, were borne of British perfidy. The Iranian revolution was the fallout of a United States-engineered coup carried out in the 1950s. Hezbollah and al Qaeda were Ronald Reagan's stepchildren. Shi'ite militancy was further inflamed when Iraq's Shi'a were led to the slaughter by George H. W. Bush. His son, George W. Bush, unleashed a sectarian bloodbath and released the power of Iran with his invasion of Iraq. And ISIS was the product of a combination of regional instability created by Bush II and neglect by the Barack Obama administration.

That wasn't a narrative you would often hear in the U.S. media. A significant portion of Americans believed that there was something inherent in the Muslim religion that led its followers to become terrorists. It had nothing to do with *us*.

Make no mistake. There had been violent extremists in Islam since those first years after Muhammad's death, just as history was replete with Catholic fanatics, Jewish zealots, Hindu thugs and even murderous Buddhist ultranationalists. But there was no escaping the fact that the West, particularly America, had created the circumstances that helped fuel the cause of violent Muslim extremists through a combination of cynical self-interest, a thirst for oil and geopolitical naivety.

Terror on Camelback

Manipulation, exploitation and betrayal characterized the twentieth century's first official encounter between the Arabs and the West, as it would for their encounters into the next century. The swords of Islam helped the Allied Powers win World War I, but commitments made in return quickly became promises broken. In the process, Britain served as midwife to modern terrorism, cynically encouraging the rise of an army of Muslim extremists who would serve as an inspiration for generations to come. That cadre of zealots made possible the formation of Saudi Arabia, which in turn gave birth to al Qaeda and the worldview that would feed the zealotry of the Islamic State.

At the outbreak of World War I, much of the Middle East was part of the Ottoman Empire, ruled by the Turks and allied with the Axis Powers. Great Britain called on the Arabs to rise up against the Turks, declaring that "the Islamic Khalifate is a right to the Koresh tribe of the Great Prophet of Islam," referring to Muhammad's Qureshi tribe.[2] This was a message to the sharif of Mecca, Hussein ibn Ali al-Hashemi, that Britain would recognize him as the new caliph if it won the war. He controlled the holy cities of Mecca and Medina and the Arab heartland, and his Hashemite family were believed to be direct descendants of the Prophet Muhammad. In its 1914 proclamation "to the natives of Arabia, Palestine, Syria and Mesopotamia," the British government stated that

[o]ne of [the government's] fundamental traditions is to be a friend of Islam and Muslims [sic] and to defend the Islamic Khalifate even if it was a Khalifate of conquest and necessity.... There is no nation amongst Muslims who is now capable of upholding the Islamic Khalifate except the Arab nation and no country is more fitted for its seat than the Arab countries.[3]

Lest there be any confusion, the British government followed up with a letter to Hussein:

> If the Amir … and Arabs in general assist Great Britain in this conflict that has been forced upon us by Turkey, Great Britain will promise not to intervene in any manner whatsoever whether in things religious or otherwise … It may be that an Arab of true race will assume the Khalifate at Mecca or Medina, and so good may come by the help of God out of all the evil that is now occurring.[4]

In reality, the creation of a new "Khalifate" was the last thing British policymakers wanted. The real goal was to break up the Ottoman Empire and prevent any cohesive body from taking its place. It was all about oil. The British had their eyes on the oil fields of Iraq, then the region's richest, and they didn't want any future Arab/Muslim kingdom messing with their booty—or their empire, as this 1917 dispatch made clear:

> It is … essential that the country to whom Mohammedans look should not be Afghanistan. We should therefore create a state more convenient for ourselves, to whom the attention of Islam should be turned. We have an opportunity in Arabia.[5]

There was also concern that a caliphate could rally anti-colonial movements against British rule in India and Egypt.

Thanks to Hollywood and actor Peter O'Toole, "Lawrence of Arabia" is known to the world as a dashing figure on camelback who was a champion of the Arabs. In real life, T. E. Lawrence was a British agent embedded with the forces of Hussein's son Faisal to coordinate the Hashemite insurgency against the Turks in support of British interests. This 1916 intelligence memo he wrote to his superiors is a reminder that Lawrence wasn't racing around the desert with his Hashemite "brothers" purely for adventure:

> The Arabs are even less stable than the Turks. If properly handled they would remain in a state of political mosaic, a tissue of small jealous principalities incapable of cohesion.[6]

In a cabinet report he filed after the war, Lawrence was even more frank about Britain's motives in befriending the Hashemite leader:

The Sherif [Hussein] was ultimately chosen because of the rift he would create in Islam.[7]

In one of history's great betrayals, the British secretly abandoned Hussein even before the war's end, signing the Sykes-Picot Agreement, which carved up the region between the British, French and Russians. They also began cozying up to Hussein's desert rival, Abdul Aziz ibn Saud, the future founder of Saudi Arabia. The British and ibn Saud both resented Hussein's claim to be "King of the Arabs" and that the *ulema* (clerics) of Mecca had named him to serve as leader of Islam until a new caliphate was formed.[8] Then there was the oil. Hussein had designs on the entirety of the Middle East. Ibn Saud was satisfied ruling the Arabian peninsula, so the British ultimately allowed ibn Saud's forces to crush the armies of Hussein, the man who had fought at their side against the Turks, even though ibn Saud had never raised a sword in support of Britain.

Ibn Saud's weapon in his confrontation with Hussein was the Ikhwan (Brethren), Bedouin Islamic puritans who had revived with renewed vigor Wahhabism, the austere eighteenth-century strain of Islam founded by al-Wahab. Ibn Saud's alliance with the *Ikhwan* predated World War I. The Ikhwan had fought at his side when he and sixty of his relatives launched a military campaign to recapture control of the Arabian Peninsula and restore the Saudi kingdom lost when the Ottomans sacked their capital, Riyadh, in 1818.

Ibn Saud was "aware that religious fanaticism could serve his ambition, and he deliberately fostered it," wrote John Bagot Glubb, known as Glubb Pasha, the British commander of the Arab Legion. "This fanatical brotherhood encouraged his followers to fight and to massacre their Arab rivals, and it helped him to bring many nomadic tribesmen under more immediate control."[9]

While the Ikhwan succeeded in seizing the heart of the Arabian Peninsula, known as the Nejd, on behalf of ibn Saud, Sharif Hussein retained the Hejaz, the Red Sea coastal region, which contained the holy cities of Mecca and Medina. A month after Hussein's declaration that he was the new caliph, ibn Saud set the Ikhwan loose on the Hashemite-controlled city of Ta'if, near Mecca and Medina. A massacre ensued and Hussein called on the British for help. His appeal fell on deaf ears. It was in Britain's interest to see the new caliphate collapse. A few weeks later, Hussein abdicated and fled to Cyprus under British protection. The holy cities quickly fell to the Ikhwan and their patron, ibn Saud.[10]

An indication of the Ikhwan's zealotry and hated of what they considered idolatry was the wave of destruction they unleashed upon entering Mecca and Medina, razing the Mawlid al-Nabi, the shrine that marked the Prophet's birthplace; Bayt Khadija, the house of the Prophet's wife; and Bayt Abu Bakr, the home of the first caliph. As Glubb Pasha wrote, "They religiously clipped their mustaches but massacred their fellow Muslims."[11] *Not following religion*

Winston Churchill may have considered the Wahhabis "austere, intolerant, well-armed and bloodthirsty," as he told the House of Commons in July 1921,[12] but the British had what they wanted, a pliant ally ruling the heart of Arabia who would not threaten their control of Iraq. Ibn Saud's holy warriors would, for the time being, secure the badlands along the frontier between Iraq and the Nejd region of what eventually became Saudi Arabia, safeguarding Britain's oil interests;[13] anti-Western zealots unknowingly serving the interests of the West.

Thus, as Oxford scholar Faisal Devji has observed, "At its birth, Saudi Arabia looked very much like … the vision [of London policymakers who plotted to neuter the caliphate], the center of Islam protected by the Royal Navy and placed firmly in the camp of Christian powers."[14]

However, neither ibn Saud's alliance with the Ikhwan or London's control of the forces of Islamic extremism lasted long. The future Saudi monarch would prove too liberal for their tastes as he sought to consolidate his rule by forging relations with the region's myriad political and religious communities, including Christians. As scholar David Commins relates:

> they faulted ibn Saud for not upholding the sharp separation of belief and infidelity. They noted that two of his sons traveled to idolatrous lands (Faysal to England, Saud to Egypt) and that idolatrous Iraqi and Transjordanian nomads were permitted to pasture their animals in the abode of Islam. They also blamed him for his lenience toward Shiites and the introduction of modern inventions (car, telephone and telegraph).[15]

The rebellious Ikhwan launched a reign of terror across the Arab heartland and "hacked and slashed their way through entire villages that stood in their path, slitting the throats of every male survivor, to ensure that all traces of Western modernity were wiped out."[16] Eventually, ibn Saud brought his zealots to heal:

His Wahhabi army, the Ikhwan, … represented a powerful tool, but one that proved so difficult to control that the ruler ultimately had to destroy it.[17]

A small portion of the Ikhwan were allowed to remain in the service of ibn Saud, who made himself king. This "White Army" (Ikhwan al-Mujahideen) would eventually evolve into the Saudi National Guard, providing a check on the more conventional army that was being formed and safeguarding internal security. Their influence can still be felt today.

The Ikhwan's objection to allowing infidels to pasture their animals in the "abode of Islam" would be echoed a half-century later by their spiritual heir, Osama bin Laden, who laid out his opposition to the presence of U.S. troops in Saudi Arabia in his 1996 fatwa, "Declaration of War against the Americans Occupying the Land of the Two Holy Places."[18] Their intolerance of Christians and all non-Wahhabi Muslims would be reborn in the Islamic State's "grey zone" philosophy, which amounted to, "you're with our puritanical interpretation of Islam or you are an infidel sentenced to die."

Children of the Ikhwan

We didn't know it at the time, but 1979 was the year modern violent extremist Islam was born.

It was the year Shi'ite clerics in Iran overthrew the Shah and established the world's first Islamic theocracy/Islamic state. It was the year Soviet tanks rolled into Afghanistan to crush a rebellion by Muslim tribesmen against a puppet government installed by Moscow. It was the year former Pakistani prime minister Zulfiqar Ali Bhutto was hanged, ushering in the Islamization of that country. And it was the year a group calling themselves the Ikhwan took over the Grand Mosque in Mecca. The Ikhwan were the modern expression of the "fierce hatreds" of their predecessors, which had never disappeared. "The unwavering intolerance, the embrace of an extreme and pitilessly violent form of Islam as a kind of cleansing fire—these would find acceptance into the late 20th century and beyond," author Joby Warrick wrote in *Black Flags: The Rise of ISIS*.[19]

Some of that hatred lay smoldering in the Ikhwan settlement of Sajjir in the Western Najd desert. There, in the 1930s, a boy was born to

Muhammad ibn Sayf al-Otaibi, one of the leaders of the original Ikhwan revolt against ibn Saud. He would name the child Juhayman, which meant Angry Face.[20] Juhayman ibn Muhammad ibn Sayf al-Otaibi would shake the foundations of Saudi Arabia and usher in an era of extremism and terror.

On November 20, 1979, this child of ibn Saud's holy warriors did the unthinkable: he and at least 300 followers stormed the Grand Mosque in Mecca, the holiest sanctum of Islam and took hostage thousands of worshippers. They called themselves the Ikhwan and claimed the prophesized Mahdi, or Messiah, was with them.[21] The date they chose for their assault was the first day of the fifteenth century of the Islamic calendar. Their goal was to fulfil prophecy and anoint the Mahdi beside the black stone of the Kaaba. The group included militants from several Arab countries, and reportedly, two African-American Muslim converts.[22]

It would take the Saudi government two weeks to dislodge the invaders, and then only with the help of Pakistani and French commandos after their own troops failed to gain control of the network of tunnels beneath the sanctuary. Violence inside the mosque was *haram* (forbidden). Infidels—who are banned from even visiting Mecca—killing Muslims in the holiest of holy sites in Islam was the ultimate sacrilege, so before the operation, the French submitted to ritual conversion. No figures were ever released, but it is believed more than 1,000, including many worshippers, died in the fighting.[23] In an historic irony, the assault was complicated by the fact that the Grand Mosque was under renovation by a company called BinLaden Construction, owned by the father of Juhayman's spiritual heir, Osama bin Laden.

Juhayman's Ikhwan was a linear extension of the Ikhwan zealots his father helped lead in revolt against ibn Saud. It was a violent splinter of a larger organization called al-Jama'a al-Salafiyya al-Muhtasiba (the Salafi Group that Commands Right and Forbids Wrong). They represented a "rejectionist" Islam that had a disdain for politics and the institutions of the state, focused myopically on ritual and the Qur'an, opposed the use of reason in religious rulings, rejected the various schools of Hadith interpretation, and argued that even the ultraconservative Wahhabis needed to be purified of innovations (*bid'a*) and misperceptions.

"Juhayman's *Ikhwan* (Brethren) were among the first manifestations of a particular type of Saudi Islamism that outlived Juhayman and has played an important yet subtle role in the shaping of the country's political landscape until today," according to scholars Thomas Hegghammer and Stéphane Lacroix, who wrote a detailed study of him.[24]

That reshaping of Saudi society began as soon as the Grand Mosque was retaken. Even as Juhayman and sixty-two of his followers were beheaded, the House of Saud unleashed the forces of conservatism in the kingdom. Wahhabi clerics were empowered, Western innovations like photos of women in the newspaper were banned, and the *mutawwa'in*, the so-called religious police, were empowered. "The solution to the religious upheaval was simple—more religion," Robert Lacey observed in his study of Saudi Arabia.[25] Just as ibn Saud exploited religious fanaticism to serve his own purposes, so too, his modern descendants.

And what was good for Saudi Arabia, the clerics apparently believed, was good for the world. With the House of Saud's shift back to ultraconservatism in response to the Grand Mosque siege, the global Wahhabi project was born. Fueled by the oil boom of the early 1980s, Saudi Arabia began pouring hundreds of millions of dollars into mosques and madrassas around the world, sending its Salafi missionaries to proselytize abroad and paying for countless tens of thousands of young Muslims to travel to Saudi Arabia to learn the "real" version of Islam. The goal was to become Islam's undisputed leader.

The seeds of zealotry planted by ibn Saud's Ikhwan in the harsh deserts of the Nejd would soon bear fruit around the world.

The Islamic Revolution

The House of Saud's panic in the face of the Grand Mosque siege built on its fear of what was happening across the Gulf. Salafi Islam taught that Shi'a were apostates, and the 1979 Islamic revolution in Iran meant the apostates were now empowered.

Three weeks before the takeover of the Grand Mosque, Iranian students, supported by the Revolutionary Guards, seized the U.S. embassy in Tehran. It was the culmination of a revolution led by the most respected figure in Shi'a Islam, Grand Ayatollah Ruhollah Khomeini, who overthrew the hated Shah of Iran and established the world's first Islamic Republic. When the ailing Shah fled the country, the U.S. gave him sanctuary. The students took over the embassy to force the Carter administration to hand him over for trial.

The embassy takeover, and the failed American mission to rescue the hostages, sent a clear message to would-be Muslim extremists around the world: terror could bring the Great Satan to his knees. And it sent an equally clear message to the Saudis: the age of Sunni dominance was coming to an end.

Western meddling had helped prepare the ground for Khomeini's Islamic revolution. A quarter of a century before, America and Britain mounted a coup that overthrew Iran's democratically elected government, headed by Mohammad Mossadeqh, perceived in the West as a communist-inspired leftist, set the stage for the Shah's brutal dictatorship and froze in time Iran's natural political evolution. Without Western interference, the circumstances that led to Khomeini's revolution may have been avoided. Declassified CIA documents published 60 years after the coup frankly stated America's role:

> The military coup that overthrew Mossadeq [sic] and his National Front cabinet was carried out under CIA direction as an act of U.S. foreign policy, conceived and approved at the highest levels of government.[26]

Codenamed TPAJAX, the coup was engineered in response to a vote by Mossadeqh's left-leaning parliament to nationalize the assets of a British oil company after it refused to allow its books to be audited. Vast amounts of money were involved, but in addition, this was the Cold War. The West believed it couldn't afford to allow Iran to fall into the Soviet sphere of influence. Following a series of meetings between U.S. and British intelligence, according to a declassified CIA cable, "The Director, on April 4, 1953, approved a budget of $1,000,000 which could be used by the Tehran station in any way that would bring about the fall of Mossadegh."[27]

Four months later, Iran's brief experiment in democracy was dead. The CIA's secret history of the coup reported that for the American and British intelligence operatives,

> It was a day that should never have ended. For it carried with it such a sense of excitement, of satisfaction and of jubilation that it is doubtful whether any other can come up to it.[28]

To bolster the Shah's regime, the CIA then helped set up and train SAVAK, the brutal secret police. In a 1976 report, Amnesty International described a common method of interrogation:

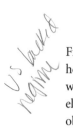

First, he is beaten by several torturers at once, with sticks and clubs. If he doesn't confess, he is hanged upside down and beaten; if this doesn't work, he is raped; and if he still shows signs of resistance, he is given electric shock which turns him into a howling dog; and if he is still obstinate, his nails and sometimes all his teeth are pulled out, and in certain exceptional cases, a hot iron rod is put into one side of the face to force its way to the other side, burning the entire mouth and the tongue.[29]

The Shah's corrupt and oppressive reign—openly supported by the U.S.—crushed all opposition, secular and religious alike, radicalizing the powerful clergy and producing a generation of Iranians who were bitter and angry.

At a 1977 New Year's Eve celebration in Tehran, President Jimmy Carter toasted the Shah with champagne, declaring that thanks to his "great leadership" Iran was "an island of stability in one of the more troubled areas of the world."[30] Barely two years later, angry Iranians stormed the U.S. embassy and began a hostage drama that would last 444 days, bring down Carter's presidency and usher in the era of anti-American terror.

On January 21, 1981, I stood on the tarmac of Algiers International Airport in the chill evening air and watched as the door of the Boeing 727 opened. The plane was one of two carrying the embassy hostages that had taken off from Tehran at the very moment Ronald Reagan concluded his Inaugural Address at the U.S. Capitol. A story took hold in the decades since that Reagan was responsible for the release. In fact, the Iranians had approached the Carter administration the previous September with a proposal to trade the hostages for the release of more than $11 billion in Iranian assets Carter had frozen after the embassy takeover. They wanted to do the deal with Carter so they didn't have to start all over with a new administration.

As our cameras recorded the historic moment, the first of the freed American diplomats stepped onto the stairs, looking dazed and suspicious. Sadly, it would not be the last time I would cover a story involving American hostages. Far from it.

Islamic Jihad Is Born

Ronald Reagan wasn't the architect of the Iran hostage deal, but he *would* play the lead role in the mistakes that ushered in the next phase of Iranian-backed anti-American terror. Nineteen months after the Iran hostages were released, I stood, stunned, in front of the U.S. Marine Corps barracks in Beirut, which had been levelled by a truck bomb. As I recounted in my 2003 book, *Seeds of Hate*:

> The parking lot had become a morgue. Unrecognizable pieces of what had once been United States marines lay on stretchers lined up on the rubble-strewn tarmac. There was no time for the niceties of body bags or blankets. Those would come later. The living took priority now; God only knew how many were still buried under there.
>
> Scores of marines, some in the red gym shorts they slept in, others wearing camouflage pants and T-shirts, scrambled over the smoking wreckage, prying at the broken concrete with shovels, picks, and their bare hands, desperately trying to reach the buddies they could hear pleading for help below. Italian peacekeepers, Lebanese troops, and teenagers clad in the white aprons of the local rescue squads, toiled beside them. As the survivors were dug out, stretcher-bearers rushed them to hastily set up first aid stations or waiting ambulances.
>
> The roof of the four-story Battalion Landing Team (BLT) headquarters now stood at eye level. The phenomenal force of the blast had literally lifted the building from its foundation, sheared off concrete columns 15 feet around, blown out the lower walls, and caused the structure to collapse onto itself.[31]

The American military, along with troops from the United Kingdom, France and Italy, had arrived in Beirut in the summer of 1982 to coordinate the evacuation of units of the Palestinian Liberation Organization (PLO), cornered in Beirut, which was under Israeli siege. The mission complete, the multinational forces withdrew. But when hundreds of Palestinian and Shi'ite civilians were massacred by Israeli-backed Christian militias, the U.S. was blamed. "This shameful crime of genocide is an international responsibility, and first it is an American responsibility," PLO leader Yasser Arafat told me when we showed him the footage of the massacre at his office in Damascus hours after reporters gained access to the scene.

Washington panicked. The Marines and the European forces were rushed back to Beirut. But this time they came without a clearly defined mission. Over the coming months, the White House would variously claim American forces were there as observers, neutral peacekeepers or to support the "legitimate government of Lebanon." In Reagan's eyes, good guys wore white hats and bad guys wore black. What he didn't understand was that in Lebanon, there were only shades of grey. There was no "legitimate" government of Lebanon. It was a minority Christian regime that talked about unity even as it took measures to further undermine and isolate the Sunni and Shi'ite Muslim communities.

When war broke out between largely Christian government forces on one side and Shi'ite and Druze militias on the other, the White House sided with the Christians, even as American diplomats and Marine officers on the ground pleaded to stay neutral. Reagan's White House won the argument. Before long, one-ton shells from the battleship *U.S.S. New Jersey* were hurdling over the city, pounding Druze and Shi'ite positions. "Is it more brave to shoot bombs from the sea?" asked Akram, a member of the Shi'ite militia Amal, as we sat drinking sweet tea in a building facing the Marine positions while shells passed overhead. "We do not have jet planes. We have many trucks, so we use them. What is the difference between dropping a bomb on a building from the sky and driving it from the street?"

America's brief encounter with Lebanon lasted less than two years. But it was long enough to show the world that a handful of men and women with a few hundred pounds of explosives and a willingness to give their lives could defeat a superpower. It was in Lebanon that America told Muslim civilians it would protect them, then watched them die. It was in Lebanon that supposedly neutral U.S. forces fired in anger on Muslim forces for the first time since World War II. It was amid the crusader fortresses of Lebanon that American "peacekeepers" sided with the Christians and their Israeli allies against Muslim militiamen, reopening a thousand-year-old wound. And it was in Lebanon that Khomeini and the newly empowered Shi'a would exploit the anger produced by America's ill-conceived policies to launch a campaign of terror.

Ronald Reagan defeated communism. But the seeds of hate he planted in Beirut spawned a new confrontation that was, in many ways, even more frightening and unpredictable than his worst Cold War nightmares.[32]

On Afghanistan's Plains

In February 1983, President Ronald Reagan welcomed seven guests in the Oval Office. They were a mix of villagers who had suffered under the Soviets and Afghan warlords then locked in a guerrilla war against the Soviets. The CIA, in partnership with Pakistan's Inter-Services Intelligence (ISI) and the Saudis, eager to bolster their credentials as the vanguard of Islam, had been secretly arming these rebel fighters since 1979. In the process, they unwittingly helped create the first generation of extremists who would go on to wage jihad against the West.

"If this aggression should succeed, it will have dangerous impact on the safety of free men everywhere," Reagan had declared a few months earlier, on the third anniversary of the Russian invasion.[33] Reagan was prescient in ways he could not imagine. The Soviets *were* ultimately defeated by the U.S.-backed mujahideen rebels, but the fallout would plunge America into an endless war without borders.

An entire mythology was created around the Afghan guerrillas. "They are our brothers, these freedom fighters, and we owe them our help," Reagan told guests at a fundraising dinner in 1985, acknowledging Afghan resistance leaders in the audience.[34] But the reality was that the resistance included both moderate anti-Islamists and hardliners who would become some of America's most persistent enemies.

Over the course of the next decade, the U.S. would pour hundreds of millions of dollars into Afghanistan to support the anti-Soviet jihad. American policy was heavily influenced by Pakistan's ISI, which was dominated by conservative Islamists; so Islamist-oriented that, according to journalist Steve Coll, they would later seek funding from Osama bin Laden to overthrow both Pakistani prime minister Benazir Bhutto, who openly campaigned against the Islamization of Pakistan, and the moderate Afghan government that took office after the Soviet withdrawal, "the perceived twin enemies of Islam they saw holding power in Kabul and Islamabad."[35] Bhutto was assassinated several years later. A letter she wrote before her death implicated Pakistani intelligence.[36]

The CIA's reliance on the ISI meant the U.S. would ultimately favor Gulbuddin Hekmatyar, an Islamist hardliner heavily funded by Osama bin Laden and largely responsible for the brutal civil war after the Soviet defeat, which paved the way for the rise of the Taliban. The U.S. would also, at least indirectly, get in bed with bin Laden himself. During the anti-Soviet jihad, bin Laden ran the Maktab al-Khadamat (Services Office), also known as MAK, in Peshawar, Pakistan, a kind of Welcome Wagon for would-be jihadis, offering guests houses and orientation.[37] When each recruit arrived, bin Laden's team gathered as much information as possible so their families could be contacted if they were "martyred." The resulting database would become the foundation for al Qaeda (one translation of al Qaeda is "The Base," which some have argued is a reference to the MAK database). Bin Laden openly raised money in the U.S. through his al-Kifah (Struggle) charity, based at a Brooklyn mosque. His mentor, Abdullah Azzam, who later became al Qaeda's chief ideologue, mounted a fifty-city fundraising and recruitment tour of the U.S. during which he invited audiences to "send cheques to the various bank accounts he had opened in Western countries."[38]

As many as 35,000 foreign volunteers flocked to Afghanistan to fight in the jihad.[39] They came from around the world. In the process, the U.S. not only trained the first generation of anti-American jihadis but also created the infrastructure that would nourish generations of jihadis to come as "[n]ew *madrassas* (Islamic schools) sprouted, funded and supported by Saudi Arabia and the U.S. Central Intelligence Agency, where students were encouraged to join the Afghan resistance."[40]

Indonesia's Jemaah Islamiyah (JI) offers a case study of the impact of the Afghan war on global terrorism. JI, which was effectively al Qaeda's Southeast Asian franchise, carried out a campaign of attacks in Indonesia beginning in the late 1990s that claimed hundreds of lives. The entire JI leadership fought in the Afghan war in the late 1980s and early 1990s before the organization was founded. On their arrival in Pakistan, they all funneled through bin Laden's Services Office. From there, they went to Camp Saddah, on the Afghanistan border, run by an Afghan named Abdul Rasul Sayyaf, said to have had the closest ties with Saudi Arabia of any mujahideen commander.[41] The money that made it possible for the Indonesians to travel to Pakistan came from a variety of Saudi-funded agencies, including the Muslim World League, Rabitat al-Alam al-Islami, often referred to as "the Rabitah."[42]

One of the top figures in JI, known as Hambali, rose to become a top aide to bin Laden before returning to Southeast Asia to help set up JI. Another of the founders was a key recruiter in Indonesia for the Afghan jihad. As the International Crisis Group observed in a study of Jemaah Islamiyah,

The jihad in Afghanistan had a huge influence in shaping their worldview, reinforcing their commitment to jihad, and providing them with lethal skills. Their experience there was also critical in terms of forging bonds among themselves and building an international network that included members of al-Qaeda.[43]

As bin Laden himself told one reporter, speaking of his early jihadi recruitment operations on the Pakistan-Afghan border, "The weapons were supplied by the Americans, the money by the Saudis."[44]

against USSR and Hussein in Iraq

Enter al Qaeda

From the perspective of the U.S. and its Gulf allies, the 1990–1 Gulf war was a huge victory. Saddam Hussein's Iraqi army was driven out of Kuwait, his designs on the Saudi oil fields were thwarted and his hopes of becoming the dominant force in the Middle East were crushed. Yet, Operation Desert Storm also led to the birth of al Qaeda and it further stirred Shi'ite antipathy for America.

Iraq's invasion of Kuwait, which sparked the war, had deeply shaken the neighboring Saudis, so much so that the official Saudi media was banned from making any mention of the crisis for the first three days while the government struggled to respond. The administration of George H. W. Bush immediately offered to send troops and air cover. Bin Laden, who had returned from Afghanistan as a hero, went to the Saudi defense minister and pleaded to be allowed to activate his jihadi network to defend the kingdom, rather than invite in the Americans. The offer was rejected, but the House of Saud agreed to a compromise: as soon as Saddam was defeated, officials told bin Laden, the Americans would leave. The royals ultimately went back on their word and after the war Saudi Arabia became the primary American base in the Middle East. Bin Laden was enraged. He began to actively speak out against the king. The only thing that protected him was the fact that he was a scion of one of the most influential non-royal families. The royals advised the elder bin Laden to get his son out of the country, or else. In 1991, Osama bin Laden left for Sudan.

Al Qaeda was the product of that confrontation. To bin Laden, the presence of American troops in Saudi Arabia was *haram* (forbidden) and the House of Saud had made itself the enemy of Islam for breaking its promise to remove the infidels. "The king told lies to the *ulema* [clerics]," bin Laden charged in his 1996 *Declaration of War Against the Americans Occupying the Land of the Two Holy Places*. "The king said that, 'The issue is simple, the American and the alliance forces will leave the area in a few months.' Today, it is seven years since their arrival and the regime is not able to move them out of the country.... To push the enemy—the greatest *kufr* [infidel]—out of the country is a prime duty."[45]

"Our country has become an American colony," he told British journalist Robert Fisk of *The Independent* that same year.[46]

This was no "fanatic" with "millennial visions of the Apocalypse,"[47] as some so-called terrorist experts described him in years to come. Bin Laden was a devout Muslim motivated by religious conviction and the pragmatism to recognize that, as he once told his followers, "the presence of the world's largest oil reserve makes the land of the two Holy Places an important economical power in the Islamic world."[48]

Two years after bin Laden fled to Sudan, militants with ties to him killed six and wounded hundreds in the first attack on the World Trade Center in New York. Soon after, bin Laden issued a fatwa declaring jihad against American troops in Somalia, and he was tied to a truck bombing at a U.S. military base in Saudi Arabia that killed five Americans and two others. Al Qaeda was hitting its stride.

Even as the U.S. was lighting the fires of the Sunni anti-American jihad of al Qaeda, it was simultaneously creating new hatred of the U.S. among the Shi'a. As the U.S. prepared its military assault to dislodge Iraqi troops from Kuwait, President George H. W. Bush had called on "the Iraqi people to take matters into their own hands and force Saddam Hussein, the dictator, to step aside." Bush issued the call in two separate speeches on the same day.[49] Two weeks later, after the 100-hour U.S.-led blitzkrieg that devastated the Iraqi army, the Kurds in the north and the Shi'a in the south rose up against the dictator. And then America abandoned them. Under the terms of the ceasefire that ended the war, the U.S. prohibited fixed-wing Iraqi aircraft from flying over southern Iraq and Kurdistan. "You fly, you die," was how Gen. Norman Schwarzkopf, the U.S. commander, summed up the deal. But helicopters were permitted, ostensibly to ferry Iraqi officials, as well as units of Saddam's elite Republican Guard. That would seal the fate of the Shi'a and the Kurds. "Saddam almost immediately began using the helicopters as gunships to put down the uprisings," Bush and his national security adviser, Brent Scowcroft, recalled in their book.[50] Saddam decimated the rebels and their supporters, killing as many as 60,000 Shi'a in the south and some 20,000 Kurds in the north. American jets patrolling the regions held their fire as the slaughter was carried out and, instead of providing stockpiles of captured Iraqi weapons to the insurgents, the U.S. destroyed them or shipped them to the Afghan mujahideen.

American officials would later claim that they had Iran uppermost in their minds when they gave Gen. Schwarzkopf the order not to pursue Iraqi troops into Iraq or come to the aid of the Shi'a and Kurds who, at Bush's urging, had rebelled against the regime. "Our practical intention was to leave Baghdad enough power to survive as a threat to an Iran that remained bitterly hostile toward the United States," then-Secretary of State Colin Powell wrote in his autobiography.[51] And then there was regional reaction. Occupying Iraq, Bush and Scowcroft wrote, "could instantly shatter our coalition, turning the whole Arab world against us, and make a broken tyrant into a latter-day Arab hero."[52]

Twenty years later, James F. Jeffrey, the U.S. ambassador to Iraq, apologized to the Shi'a for America's failure to support them. "The apology of the U.S. has come too late, and does not change what happened," the spokesman for Ayatollah Bashir al-Najafi, a top Shi'ite leader, told *The New York Times*. "The apology is not going to bring back to the widows their husbands, and bereaved mothers their sons and brothers that they lost in the massacre following the uprising."[53]

Creating "the New Middle East"

George H. W. Bush feared that pursuing Iraqi troops beyond the Kuwaiti border would risk that the U.S. would be perceived by the Arab world as an occupier. His son, George W. Bush set out not only to occupy Iraq but also to redraw the borders of the Arab world and create "the new Middle East."[54]

There are shelves of books analyzing the American invasion of Iraq and parsing the justifications, miscalculations and implications for the Iraqis. Suffice to say, hundreds of thousands of Iraqis died and the country was reduced to a near failed state. Beyond the terrible toll suffered by the Iraqi people, the war created the circumstances that produced ISIS and unleashed Iran.

In 1980, more than two decades before George W. Bush rained "shock and awe" on Bagdad, I squatted in the desert somewhere near the Iranian city of Khorramshahr trying to keep the blowing sand out of my eyes and fully absorb what I was seeing. There were bodies of Iranian Pasardan troops and poorly trained Basiji conscripts as far as we could see; a carpet of corpses that disappeared into the haze. The metal of destroyed tanks and armored personnel carriers had melted in the heat of the explosions and puddled in the sand. Iran and Iraq were locked in what would become the longest conflict of the twentieth century. More than a million soldiers would die.[55]

Saddam Hussein had declared himself leader of the Arab world, and his propagandists portrayed the war as a modern-day Qadissiya, the seventh-century victory of Arab armies over the Persians. He sensed weakness in the chaos of post-revolution Iran and was angry that Ayatollah Khomeini had called on Iraq's Shi'ite majority to rise up in their own Islamic revolution against Saddam's minority Sunni, secular, regime.

On September 24, 1980, the war began. My first indication that morning was the sound of air raid sirens at dawn. I ran out onto the balcony of my room near the top of Baghdad's Mansour Melia hotel, tape recorder in hand to describe the scene for a radio report, and immediately dropped to the floor as an Iranian jet came straight at me, close enough that I could see the pilot, then lifted up and over the hotel, one of the highest buildings in the city, which the Iranians were using as a navigation beacon for their bombing runs.

For the U.S., Saudi Arabia and the other Gulf states, the Iran-Iraq War was a geopolitical godsend. Saddam had increasingly been bullying the other Arab autocrats. Khomeini's revolution threatened to stir Shi'ite rebellions across the Gulf. The war meant that these two regional powers held each other in check, easing the pressure on other governments in the region. The U.S. remained neutral in the conflict, but when it appeared Saddam might be defeated in 1982, the Reagan administration secretly provided intelligence and arms,[56] which kept the two sides in a stand-off even after the war officially ended.

George W. Bush destroyed all that when he invaded Iraq. He failed to see what his father had known: by overthrowing Saddam Hussein's secular, Sunni regime, Iran was unleashed. Iraqi Shi'ite militias that Iran had trained and armed for many years took to the streets. Iraqi Shi'ite politicians the Iranians had nourished came to power. By ignoring the experts, and his own father, George W. Bush upset the Middle East balance of power and opened the way for the "Shi'a crescent" to become a reality.

Iraq was the birthplace of Shi'a Islam. With four million Shi'a in Saudi Arabia and a Shi'ite majority in Sunni-ruled Bahrain, the Shi'a were regarded as a fifth column by Gulf regimes. If Iraq's Shi'ite majority came to power, it could shift the balance of power in the Middle East. The Saudis and other Sunni leaders of the Gulf were enraged by George W. Bush's decision to topple Saddam Hussein. King Abdullah reminded the Americans that in the Middle East, history is never far from the present. In an angry 2007 meeting, the eighty-two-year-old Saudi monarch berated a top adviser to Secretary of State Condoleezza Rice: "You have allowed the Persians, the Safavids, to take over Iraq," he said, referring to the Shi'a dynasty that invaded Baghdad in the seventeenth century, destroying Sunni mosques and killing thousands.[57]

Saudi Arabia's Western-educated foreign minister, Saud al-Faisal, put it in terms more likely to resonate with the Americans. "Iran is being handed … Iraq on a golden platter," he said during 2005 visit to the U.S.[58] If the Sunni-Shi'a sectarian violence continued, "Iraq is finished forever. It will be dismembered, it will cause so many conflicts in the region that it will bring the whole region into turmoil."[59]

That was precisely the milieu from which ISIS would rise.

Empty Promises

In June of 2009, U.S. president Barack Obama stood on the dais at Cairo University and proclaimed "a new beginning between the United States and Muslims around the world."[60] It was a verbal shot heard 'round the Muslim world. Wherever I went in Cairo that week, conversation turned to the speech. This was potentially a watershed moment after the long years of George W. Bush, who had invaded Afghanistan and Iraq and referred to his battle against terrorism as a "crusade," which many Arabs and Muslims heard as a continuation of the Christian Crusades against Islam that began in the eleventh century.

"Without any exaggeration, Obama's address will go down in history as one of the most important documents conveying the desires of the West, led by the United States, for a different dealing with Islam and the Muslims after centuries of aggression and hatred," gushed Egypt's semi-official *Al-Ahram* newspaper.[61] Others were more cautiously optimistic. Lebanon's *Al-Anwar* newspaper said Obama offered "a realistic call—even though it seemed a romantic one,"[62] and the pan-Arab daily *Al-Hayat* heard "clear messages that carried reassurances and challenges."[63] However, some, like Adel Bari Atwan, editor of the Palestinian-owned *Al-Quds al-Arabi*, were not ready to push aside the past:

President Obama wants to open a new page with the Islamic world, which is both possible and welcomed as long as it is accompanied by a clear apology for America's crimes against the Muslims and its ongoing wars against them and by a full compensation for all the material and human losses that these wars entailed.[64]

For the most part, the average Arab and non-Arab Muslim welcomed this new tone. My students at the American University in Cairo were ecstatic. My cynical journalist and activist friends were intrigued.

This "new beginning," Obama told Arabs and Muslims watching on television around the world, was "one based on mutual interest and mutual respect, and one based upon the truth that America and Islam ... share common principles ... of justice and progress; tolerance and the dignity of all human beings." Obama sketched out a shared "challenge" which required that "we act boldly in the years ahead," adding, "Words alone cannot meet the needs of our people."

But as Obama ended his term in office eight years later, many Arabs and Muslims felt words were *all* Obama ever delivered. In their eyes, he had failed the challenge miserably on every level. In Cairo, Obama declared, "we reject the same thing that people of all faiths reject: the killing of innocent men, women, and children," yet he dramatically ramped up the CIA drone campaign in Pakistan, Afghanistan, Somalia, Libya and Yemen, killing at least 7,000 alleged militants and upward of 1,000 of civilians, including dozens of children.[65]

"When innocents in Bosnia and Darfur are slaughtered, that is a stain on our collective conscience," Obama said in Cairo. But when Bashar al-Assad unleashed chemical attacks on his own people, an action the American president had declared to be a red line the Syrian president must not cross, America struck back with words not weapons. Close to a half million Syrians would die on Obama's watch. "Barack Obama feared that protecting Syrian civilians could anger Iran and cause it to walk away from nuclear talks. From his point of view, the prices paid by Syrians, Syria's neighbors, and American allies in the region and beyond were worth the grand prize," according to Frederick Hof, Obama's special envoy on Syria. "Such was the mindset that considered Syrian lives expendable for a higher cause."[66]

In Cairo, Obama quoted Thomas Jefferson: "[M]ilitary power alone is not going to solve the problems in Afghanistan and Pakistan.... I hope that our wisdom will grow with our power and teach us that the less we use our power the greater it will be." But Obama dramatically escalated the number of U.S. troops in Afghanistan, from 30,000 when he gave that Cairo speech to a peak of 100,000, declaring it "a war we have to win." In the end, he drew those troops down to 10,000 but only because he finally acknowledged the conflict was unwinnable. Afghanistan, he would explain, "was riven with all kinds of ethnic and tribal divisions before we got there. It's still there."[67]

In Cairo, Obama announced, "I have ordered the prison at Guantanamo Bay closed by early next year." When he left office in January 2017, Gitmo was still open and forty-one Muslim prisoners still languished there, most without ever receiving a trial.

In Cairo, Obama declared that "The situation for the Palestinian people is intolerable. And America will not turn our backs on the legitimate Palestinian aspiration for dignity, opportunity, and a state of their own … Too many tears have been shed. Too much blood has been shed." But during Obama's presidency, the number of Israeli settlers on the West Bank increased by a third to 400,000; more than 2,200 Palestinians died and 17,000 more were wounded in Israel's 2014 war in Gaza, the highest toll since the 1967 war; and Israel was given the largest military aid package in history.

In Cairo, Obama declared his commitment "to governments that reflect the will of the people" and his "unyielding belief that all people yearn for certain things: the ability to speak your mind and have a say in how you are governed; … the freedom to live as you choose." And he promised, "we will support them everywhere."

> [N]o matter where it takes hold, government of the people and by the people sets a single standard for all who would hold power: You must maintain your power through consent, not coercion; you must respect the rights of minorities, and participate with a spirit of tolerance and compromise; you must place the interests of your people and the legitimate workings of the political process above your party.

But many Arabs and Muslims believe he failed with what they saw as his administration's ambivalent handling of the 2011 Arab Spring uprisings that overthrew Egyptian autocrat Hosni Mubarak and two other dictators, as well as its response to the coup that later ousted Egypt's first democratically elected government. By the time Obama left office a new Egyptian tyrant was in place, supported by U.S. financial and military

Obama continually saying one thing and doing the opposite

aid, and thousands of democracy activists, journalists and bloggers were in jail—or dead.

On the day Obama metaphorically handed the White House keys to Donald Trump, the forces of autocracy were once more firmly in control across the Middle East. The only exceptions were Tunisia, which was moving toward democracy, and Syria, Yemen and Libya, which had been reduced to failed states.

"Barack Obama, we love you!" an audience member had interjected at one point in the Cairo speech. That exhilaration ultimately proved elusive, the promises empty. The dominant sentiment as the Obama presidency came to an end was summed up by a headline on the website of one of the most influential news organizations in the Middle East: "Why Arabs hate Obama."[68]

Today's Solution, Tomorrow's Problem

In the corridors of power in Washington and the capitals of Europe, there were reams of policy documents that justified each of the West's actions over the course of a century: supporting the Ikhwan to prevent the rise of a new caliphate that would threaten British interests in the region; overthrowing Mossadeqh to protect Western businesses and stop Iran from falling into the Soviet sphere of influence; basing troops in Saudi Arabia to defend the vital oil fields that supplied the West; supporting the Christian-dominated Lebanese regime on the principle that it was the elected government of the land; funding and equipping the Afghan jihad to checkmate the Soviets; abandoning the Iraqi Shi'a to avoid becoming bogged down in a civil war or causing the Arab world to turn against the U.S; invading Iraq to prevent the spread of weapons of mass destruction that the CIA claimed Saddam had stockpiled; launching a military "surge" in Afghanistan in yet another doomed effort to defeat the Taliban; withdrawing from Iraq and refusing overt engagement in the Syrian civil war for fear of jeopardizing the Iran nuclear deal and repeating the mistakes of the past.

There was plenty of room for honest debate about the pros and cons of decisions made at each juncture. But that did not change the fact that every one of those actions enraged old enemies or created new ones, throwing ever more fuel on the fires of terror.

9 THE ISLAMIC STATES OF AMERICA

Bear patiently that which they say and take leave of them in a beautiful manner. Leave to Me the deniers living in luxury, and be gentle with them for a while.

QUR'AN (73:10–11)

"Let them call you racists. Let them call you xenophobes. Let them call you nativists," Steve Bannon told members of France's far right National Front. "Wear it as a badge of honor."[1] Bannon certainly displayed it that way. So, too, the cadre of Islamophobes who found their way from the extreme fringes of the political right to the center of power during the presidential campaign.

"Everything has changed," Sebastian Gorka, Trump's senior adviser on terrorism, said a few hours after Trump's dystopian Inaugural speech. "When he used those three words today—radical Islamic terrorism—he put the marker down for the whole national security establishment."[2]

Donald Trump's White House staff list read like a *Who's Who* of the anti-Islam lobby, beginning with Bannon. Years before his alliance with Trump, Bannon proposed a documentary tracking a "fifth column" made up of "Islamic front groups" seeking to transform the United States into the "Islamic States of America."[3]

That theory resonated with the views of National Security Adviser Michael Flynn, who had called Islam "a cancer."[4] Other anti-Islam campaigners in the president's orbit included Frank Gaffney, a national security adviser on the Trump transition team who ran a bevy of anti-Muslim websites; Muslim immigration ban author Stephen Miller, an acolyte of David Horowitz, whom the Southern Poverty Law Center called "the Godfather of the modern anti-Muslim movement";[5] Attorney

General Jeff Sessions, who considered Islam "a toxic ideology";[6] Kellyanne Conway, who had conducted flawed surveys commissioned by Gaffney that claimed more than a quarter of American Muslims want to "punish unbelievers";[7] and Gorka, a British-born immigrant who two top Obama administration counterterrorism officials called the "Islamophobic huckster in the White House."[8]

Other informal advisers who had Trump's ear included Eric Prince, founder of the controversial Blackwater private army and brother of Trump Education Secretary Betsy DeVos, who reportedly viewed himself "as a Christian crusader tasked with eliminating Muslims and the Islamic faith from the globe";[9] Roger Stone, who had claimed the Clinton State Department "was permeated at the highest levels by Saudi intelligence and others who are not loyal Americans";[10] and author and provocateur Ann Coulter, who had made a career Islam-bashing since her comment after 9/11 that "we should invade their countries, kill their leaders and convert them to Christianity."[11]

These anti-Muslim activists and an array of Islamophobic websites, *Breitbart* the most prominent among them, were bound to the president through a web of funding that led back to conservative financier Robert Mercer and his daughter Rebekah, according to an investigation by the Bridge Initiative at Georgetown University.[12] Mercer also reportedly gave $2 million to a secretive non-profit called Secure America Now, which placed a series of ads on Facebook and Google targeting swing voters in the presidential election. The ads included a pseudo-travel promo that showed an America taken over by Syrian refugees, with the iconic Hollywood sign replaced by one reading Allah Akbar [sic] and the Statue of Liberty wearing a burka and holding a star and crescent, the symbol of Islam.[13]

There were two other notable figures with access to the president. They brought to American politics a visceral hatred of Muslims forged in the sectarian wars of their native Lebanon.

I first encountered Walid Phares in the early 1980s when he was a propagandist for a right-wing Christian militia known as the Phalangists. The private army had been at war with the PLO and Lebanon's Muslim militias for more than a decade. We first met when Phares facilitated an interview for me with Phalangist leader Bechir Gemayel. A year later, Gemayel was elected president of Lebanon. He was assassinated soon after. Within 48 hours, Phalangist militiamen were engaged in a frenzy of rape, murder and dismemberment that left at least 800 Palestinian and

Shi'ite civilians dead in the Beirut refugee camps of Sabra and Satilla. The Phalangists "now have just one thing left to do, and that is revenge; and it will be terrible," the Israeli chief of staff told the cabinet as Israeli troops, who were laying siege to Beirut, allowed the Phalangists into the camps. "I know what the meaning of revenge is for them, what kind of slaughter," Deputy Prime Minister David Levy responded.[14]

Phares "was a prominent ideologue indoctrinating people who went out and murdered people and he has never accounted for that," Yossi Alpher, the former director of Israel's Jaffee Center for Strategic Studies, told the *Jerusalem Post*.[15] Three decades later, after emigrating and becoming a U.S. citizen, Phares emerged as Trump's Middle East adviser, bringing to American politics his militant take on Islam.

Brigitte Gabriel's anti-Muslim fervor was also a product of her Lebanese upbringing. The head of ACT! for America, arguably the largest anti-Islam organization in the U.S., Gabriel styled herself as "a survivor of Islamic terror."

For her, it seemed, there was no such thing as a "good" Muslim. In a 2007 speech at the military's Joint Forces Staff College, she warned:

[A] practicing Muslim who believes the word of the Koran to be the word of Allah, who abides by Islam, who goes to mosque and prays every Friday, who prays five times a day — this practicing Muslim, who believes in the teachings of the Koran, cannot be a loyal citizen to the United States of America.[16]

Gabriel was born in a narrow strip of land along the Israeli border controlled by the South Lebanon Army (SLA), another right-wing Lebanese Christian militia loosely allied with the Phalangists. According to Lebanese columnist Michael Young, Gabriel's birth name was Nour Saman;[17] before she became Brigitte Gabriel, she was also reportedly known as Hanan Qawaji, Brigitte Qawaji and Brigitte Qawaji Tudor.[18] She frequently regaled American audiences with grisly tales of Muslim butchery of Christians. At age ten, she told a 2006 "Intelligence Summit" in Washington, DC, her home was destroyed "burying me under the rubble and leaving me to drink my blood to survive."

The SLA's enclave was established by Israel as a buffer zone between its forces and the Palestine Liberation Organization (PLO), which occupied South Lebanon at the time. Gabriel writes of being under siege from

"Islamic militias" as a child in the mid-1970s when "Muslim rockets exploded in my bedroom."

> I lived for seven years in pitch darkness, freezing cold, drinking stale water and eating grass to live. At the age of 13 I dressed in my burial clothes going to bed at night, waiting to be slaughtered.[19]

It was, she wrote, part of "a religious war, declared by the Muslims against the Christians." That characterization raised eyebrows among those familiar with the Lebanon conflict. The confrontation in South Lebanon in the 1970s and early 1980s pitted the PLO against the Israelis, with Christians in the buffer strip sandwiched in between. The PLO was a decidedly secular organization that included Christians like Popular Front for the Liberation of Palestine (PFLP) chief George Habash in key positions of power. The rise of the Shi'ite jihadis of Hezbollah would not come until after the 1982 Israeli invasion. Up until then, the Shi'a were vassals of the Palestinians. So, while South Lebanon was certainly a war zone likely to traumatize any child, there were no ISIS-style "Islamic militias." Columnist Michael Young called it all part of "her con act."[20]

Yet indisputable was the fact that tens of thousands of Palestinian refugees arrived in Lebanon in 1970, upsetting the country's delicate communal balance and plunging it into civil war, forever shaping how the future Brigitte Gabriel would view refugees. It was that worldview, and the anti-Muslim rhetoric she absorbed as an anchor on the SLA's propaganda station, founded by American evangelical missionaries, that she brought with her to the U.S. in 1989.[21] "My past is America's future," was her frequent refrain.[22]

"Our enemy is not an organization of people living overseas plotting to attack," Gabriel wrote in *Because They Hate: A Survivor of Islamic Terror Warns America.* "Our enemies are the neighbors next door, the doctors practicing in our hospitals, and the workers who share our lunch break."

In a fundraising letter a month after Trump was elected, Gabriel boasted, "Two of our board of advisors Dr. Walid Phares and General Michael Flynn were, and will continue to be President-elect Donald Trump's National Security Advisors. In addition to this, the next CIA Director Rep. Mike Pompeo has been a steadfast ally of ours since the day he was elected to Congress."[23]

The fringe was now the center.

The Anti-Brotherhood Campaign

The idea that operatives of the Islamist Muslim Brotherhood had infiltrated former president Barack Obama's administration was a favorite of the Islamophobes.[24] The accusation was repeatedly featured by *Breitbart News* when it was headed by Bannon[25] and for years had bounced around the anti-Muslim echo chamber from alt-right bloggers like Gaffney[26] to more mainstream conservative commentators such as Jeffrey Lord[27] and talk show host Glenn Beck.[28]

The alleged Muslim Brotherhood infiltrators included Hillary Clinton's top aide, Huma Abedin, a handful of Muslims serving in various government agencies, and conservative activists Grover Norquist and Suhail Khan. "It's not just Huma," Roger Stone said. "It's her mother and her father who are, who are hardcore Islamic ideologues, her brothers."[29] Stone even accused Khizr Khan, the Gold Star father who upset Trump with his speech at the Democratic National Convention, of being "a Muslim Brotherhood agent."[30]

The allegation that Abedin and five other individuals associated with Obama administration were Brotherhood operatives could be traced back to a piece of disinformation published in the Egyptian magazine *Rose al-Yusuf* six months before the military coup that ousted that country's democratically elected Muslim Brotherhood government headed by Mohamed Morsi.[31] The story appeared to have been planted by loyalists to ousted autocrat Hosni Mubarak and was likely designed to embarrass the Obama administration, which the anti-democratic forces blamed for supporting Morsi's elected government.

"Do these six individuals mark a turning point for Obama's administration from a position of opposition to Islamic organizations and groups to being the largest and most important supporter of the Muslim Brotherhood in the world?" asked the unsourced article, which included a photo gallery of the U.S. government staffers.[32]

America's anti-Muslim lobby seized on the story, which had been published in Cairo with no evidence to back it up. Their interests coincided with those of the Mubarak loyalists. The Holy Grail of the American anti-Muslim lobby was the designation of the Muslim Brotherhood as a "Foreign Terrorist Organization" (FTO) by the U.S. government. No issue better encapsulated the Islamophobe's visceral hatred of Islam or what happened when the complexities of Middle East geopolitics were lost in a flurry of anti-Muslim campaign rhetoric.

Just weeks after taking office, the Trump administration began discussing an executive order to officially classify the Muslim Brotherhood as a terrorist group, while like-minded members of Congress pushed legislation with the same objective. There were huge implications for foreign policy and domestic civil rights.

"It will absolutely fuel the line in the Middle East that we are inherently anti-Muslim," argued Ryan Crocker, who served as U.S. ambassador in four Arab countries, as well as Pakistan and Afghanistan. "Because while Trump and his nearest and dearest may not have any clue of how the Brothers are organized and how much autonomy each country's organization has, this will just send a broad-brush message: all you need to be is Muslim to be blacklisted."

Domestically, the proposed designation of the Muslim Brotherhood as a terrorist group was "a cluster bomb that's going to cause damage everywhere," said James Zogby, president of the Arab American Institute. The Muslim Brotherhood was the granddaddy of most Muslim political movements around the world—both peaceful and violent. Many politically active Muslims who immigrated to the U.S. and helped found Muslim civic associations were either members of the Brotherhood or had friends who were. So, as with the Kevin Bacon parlor game, look hard enough at almost any Muslim organization in the U.S. and you were likely to find six degrees of separation—or less—from the Brotherhood. And if the Brotherhood was on the terrorist list, that opened the door to aggressive investigation of any organization perceived to be linked to the group.

"The designation would make any associate of the Muslim Brotherhood a criminal and would justify designating them as a supporter of terrorism, which would then make any of their associates a criminal and justify the designation of them," former FBI agent Michael German told me.

That was precisely the scenario sketched by another former FBI agent, John Guandolo, whose anti-Muslim views became the cornerstone of a business, called Understanding the Threat, training law enforcement professionals about Islam.[33] "I came to understand and see how deeply they were embedded in our national apparatus, portraying themselves as nice, helpful [and] wanting to be patriotic. But," he told a conservative blog, "in fact, we could identify all the leaders of the Islamic organizations as members of the Muslim Brotherhood—and [identify] all of the key Islamic organizations in the United States as part of their network."[34]

Representative Keith Ellison (D-MN), one of two Muslims in Congress, knew about the power of the Islamophobes who now had influence in the White House. A network of anti-Muslim websites linked to several of these figures regularly accused Ellison, without evidence, of being a "Muslim Brotherhood shill"[35] or operative,[36] a campaign that took on new vigor when he announced his candidacy to chair the Democratic National Committee.[37] "You sound paranoid when you say there is a well-financed, organized movement to promote anti-Muslim hate," Ellison told me in the fall of 2016 as he rushed to the House floor for a vote. "But the fact is, it's true and well documented."

For the Muslim Brotherhood to be added to the FTO list, there were three requirements. It had to be determined that the group 1) was "a foreign organization"; 2) "engages in terrorist activities ... or retains the capability and intent to engage in terrorist activity or terrorism"; and 3) "threatens the security of United States nationals or the national security of the United States."

"This is an issue that, just knowing their history, is a no-brainer," said Rep. Mario Diaz-Balart, R-Fl, Sen. Ted Cruz's co-sponsor on the Congressional bill. Critics said the comment betrayed Diaz-Balart's own ignorance. The Brotherhood's history included winning Egypt's first democratic election, being recognized as the elected government of Egypt by the Obama White House, then being ousted in a military coup.

"The Brotherhood's stated goal is to wage violent jihad against its enemies," said Cruz. That wasn't true either, most experts said. The Brotherhood was a hugely complex organization. There were what most Americans would consider "good" guys and "bad" guys within the organization's ranks. Before joining al Qaeda, bin Laden's second-in-command, Egyptian Ayman al-Zawahiri, led a breakaway Brotherhood faction that carried out brutal acts of terror. Likewise, the Palestinian group Hamas, already on the U.S. government's terrorism list, was an offshoot of the Egyptian Muslim Brotherhood. More recently, the military coup that ousted Egypt's first freely elected president and the subsequent massacres and mass jailing of Brotherhood members radicalized some elements within the group, who turned to violence.

However, many experts agreed with Gehad el-Haddad, a former spokesman for the then-Egyptian president, Mohamed Morsi, who rejected the idea that the Brotherhood should be held responsible for such offshoots. "This is wildly misleading," he wrote from solitary confinement in Egypt's Tora Prison where he was being held by the Sisi regime. "In the cases where people did leave the Muslim Brotherhood to embrace violence, they did so specifically because they found no path in our philosophy, vision of society or movement for such extremism."[38]

"This bill would impose tough sanctions on a hateful group that has spread violence and spawned extremist movements throughout the Middle East," Diaz-Balart said as he introduced his legislation. "Designating the Muslim Brotherhood as a terrorist organization is an important step in defeating violent extremists." That was a deeply flawed, simplistic assessment. Depending on how you looked at it, the Muslim Brotherhood was "a terrorist organization or a firewall against violent extremism," wrote Marc Lynch of George Washington University.[39] Founded in Egypt in 1928, the group was the forerunner of Islamist political movements around the world. But to portray it as a monolithic organization with a central leadership and single goal was simply wrong.

"There is a common DNA, there's a common core of ideas and beliefs," Lorenzo Vidino, director of the Program on Extremism at George Washington University, told me. "But you have such different groups, such different entities. If the Brotherhood in Yemen has current links to terrorism and has been involved in violence, the Brotherhood in Tunisia is a completely different beast, which has behaved in a completely different way."

"The MB universe is a 'broad church'—the Libyan MB is not like the Jordanian MB, the Egyptians are not like the Tunisians, and so on," H. A. Hellyer, author of *Revolution Undone: Egypt's Road Beyond Revolt*, told me. "It is important not to assume too much of a connectivity between the different MB inspired groupings."

Ryan Crocker said that when he was U.S. ambassador to Iraq, the Muslim Brotherhood was America's main ally among the country's Sunnis. Without them, "we wouldn't have had anyone to talk to." If the Brotherhood was put on the terrorism list, American diplomats from Tunisia to Kuwait would find themselves barred from speaking to members of parliament and key political opposition groups. That, Crocker predicted, would cripple American diplomacy and produce even more extremism. "What I would see coming out of this, if we are crazy enough to list them, is that the option of working with Sunni Muslim groups opposed to radical extremists like Islamic State is taken off the table, since even the moderates were likely have ties to the Brotherhood. That would leave the U.S. with no alternative but to back authoritarian regimes to take on the terrorists," he told me. "I think it will get really bad, particularly in places like Jordan. It's certainly going to help some of the younger Brothers make the case for moving to violence."

Bizarrely, in laying out the case for declaring the Brotherhood a terrorist group, the Cruz/Diaz-Balart bill justified the listing by noting that Egypt, Syria and Russia had all done the same. But in each of those three countries, the declaration of the Brotherhood as a terrorist group led to violent crackdowns by the government that fed a cycle of terrorism. As noted by Paul Pillar, former CIA national intelligence officer for the Middle East, "closing peaceful channels for the expression of political Islam moves more people into the violent channels."[40]

The British government opted not to declare the Brotherhood a terrorist group after a House of Commons report concluded there was "no indication" the group sought to create an Islamic state in Britain and "has not been linked to terrorist-related activity in and against the UK."[41] American backers of the listing would likewise be hard-pressed to identify terrorist activity by the Brotherhood "in and against" the U.S., as law required. In fact, some radical jihadists had identified the Muslim Brotherhood as an enemy rather than a potential ally. Al Qaeda leader Ayman al-Zawahiri, himself once a member of the Egyptian Muslim Brotherhood, likened the group to a "poultry farm" and its members to "chickens."[42] The leader of the al Qaeda-linked Jabhat al-Nusra in Syria said he hoped that one day, "the [Syrian] Muslim Brotherhood will realize that their plan of action is wrong.... They should take up their arms and wage *Jihad* for the sake of Allah."[43]

The decision by the United Arab Emirates (UAE) and several other Gulf countries to declare the Brotherhood a terrorist organization, lumping it together with the Islamic State, had more to do with the potential threat political threat it posed to those feudal regimes than any perceived terrorism threat. Referring to Saudi Prince Mohammed bin Salman's warning that both groups sought to create an "Islamic empire," exiled Saudi journalist Jamal Khashoggi noted, "He treats IS and the Brotherhood as the same thing—the only difference being that IS tried to create the caliphate immediately by violence while the Brotherhood wants to create the caliphate slowly, through democracy."[44] The irony was, as *The Economist* observed, "Brothers are often less puritanical in Islamic practices than [S]alafists [among Gulf leaders] but, because they permit rebellion against impious leaders, they are regarded as more subversive."[45]

In the U.S., the listing of the Muslim Brotherhood risked dramatic implications for the civil liberties of American Muslims. "The conspiracy theory has been that essentially every Muslim organization in the United States is a front for the Muslim Brotherhood and we're all part of a plot to undermine the United States from within," explained Corey Saylor of CAIR, the group most often accused of being a Brotherhood front by the anti-Muslim lobby, a charge it vehemently denied. Former FBI agent Michael German said the experience of other groups charged with terrorism ties during the Bush administration showed that U.S. organizations accused of being associated with the Muslim Brotherhood could find themselves in a Kafkaesque nightmare. "Much of the evidence in the administrative file used to justify the designation [of terrorist groups] is classified.... So the entity is in a position of trying to argue against facts they don't even know and accusations they haven't even heard," said German, a fellow at New York University's Brennan Center for Justice. Numerous groups accused of links to terror had their assets seized, even though they were never convicted of a crime.

Among the potential targets was the Muslim Students' Association (MSA), which has branches on campuses across the U.S. and describes itself as "a non-profit organization that strives to facilitate networking, educating, and empowering the students of today to be citizens of tomorrow's community."[46] Anti-Muslim campaigner David Horowitz has been quoted as saying that the MSA's campus branches are "arms of the Muslim Brotherhood, which is the fountainhead of the terrorist jihad against the West."[47] The charges against the MSA were emblematic of the situation that could be faced by other American Muslim groups. A handful of individuals who were members of the MSA when they attended university have been convicted of terrorism, accused of terrorism-related crimes or deported. These include 9/11 mastermind Khaled Sheikh Muhammad and al Qaeda propagandist and recruiter Anwar al-Awlaki, a U.S. citizen who was president of the MSA chapter at Colorado State University and was assassinated in a U.S. drone strike. But the majority of Muslim college students in the U.S. were also members of the MSA. Yale president Richard D. Levin said the MSA "has been an important source of support for Yale students during a period when Muslims and Islam itself have too often been the target of thoughtless stereotyping, misplaced fear and bigotry."[48] Levin made the comments after news broke in 2012 that the New York City Police Department was monitoring MSA chapters on campuses across the Northeast.

America had not had an official litmus test for political ideas since the "red baiting" of the McCarthy era of the 1950s, and many Muslims worried that "red baiting" was about to be replaced by "green baiting," a reference to the color associated with Islam.

"Not only does this put at risk of prosecution all such nonviolent associations, but it also risks potentially any independent scholars or journalists who provide them even with the assistance of defending or propagating their views," warned Yale law professor Andrew March.[49] In other words, they could end up accused of "un-American activities" much like the diplomats, academics, journalists and Hollywood figures who found themselves on the blacklist of a certain junior senator from Wisconsin 60 years ago.

The Anti-Sharia Campaign

The effort to declare the Brotherhood a terrorist group was closely associated with the campaign to prevent sharia law from being adopted in the U.S. This was the issue with which Brigitte Gabriel was most closely associated. She launched the Stop Sharia Now campaign shortly after founding her organization. "We, at ACT for America, are committed to protecting women and children from *Sharia* Law," the group's website declared. "We must ensure that every woman and child enjoy the protection afforded by the U.S. Constitution."

Most experts said there was nothing to protect against. Surveys showed that only 10 percent of American Muslims wanted their religion to be "the main source" of U.S. law and 55 percent said Islam should not even be "a source" of American law. Contrary to the rhetoric of the anti-Muslim lobby, strong religious identity among American Muslims actually correlated with strong identity as Americans.[50]

Ruling on an anti-sharia amendment to the Oklahoma constitution, passed by 70 percent of the state's voters, a federal judge found the measure both unconstitutional and ridiculous, saying that proponents had failed to "identify any actual problem the challenged amendment seeks to solve."[51]

Despite all that, between 2010 and early 2018, Gabriel and her allies managed to convince legislators in forty-eight states to introduce more than 200 anti-sharia bills, with fourteen states enacting such legislation,[52] on the grounds sharia threatened "infringements on due process, freedom of religion, speech, or press, equal protection, and any right of privacy or marriage as specifically defined by the constitution of the state."[53]

The movement was bolstered by scare tactics, such as a *Breitbart* article titled "Islamic Tribunal Confirmed in Texas," which the *Houston Chronicle* named "2015 Texas Hoax of the Year."[54] The reality was that voluntary arbitration panels where Christians, Jews or Muslims could work out family and business disputes in the context of their own religious beliefs were common. There was no issue of "foreign" laws superseding those of the U.S. The Texas Islamic Tribunal's website explicitly stated: "These proceedings must be conducted in accordance with the law of the land; local, state and federal within the United States."[55]

The template language used in many of the anti-sharia bills was written by Robert Spencer and David Yerushalmi. Spencer had reportedly called the Prophet Muhammad a "con man. Someone who is knowing [sic] that what he is saying is false, but is fooling his followers," adding that, "From a historical stand point, it is not even clear that Muhammad existed."[56] Yerushalmi believed "[t]he Mythical 'moderate' Muslim … who embraces traditional Islam but wants a peaceful coexistence with the West, is effectively non-existent."[57]

The real goal of the campaign was not the passage of anti-sharia laws per se; rather, it was to generate debate about the role of Muslims in American society. As Yerushalmi told *The New York Times*,

> If this thing passed in every state without any friction, it would have not served its purpose. The purpose was heuristic—to get people asking this question, "What is *Shariah*?"[58]

The movement had long received support in the halls of power. Former House Speaker Newt Gingrich said he believed "*Sharia* is a mortal threat to the survival of freedom in the United States and in the world as we know it." Former Minnesota Representative Michele Bachmann insisted that sharia "must be resisted across the United States," and Herman Cain, who ran for the GOP presidential nomination in 2012, condemned the "attempt to gradually ease *Sharia* law and the Muslim faith into our government."[59]

But those were yesterday's politicians. Now Gabriel, Yerushalmi and the other anti-*Sharia* crusaders had even more powerful new allies in the White House. "If you boil this down to its operational essence," Sebastian Gorka said in 2012, referring to Muslims, "this is about anybody in that camp who wishes to undermine the U.S. Constitution, whether by killing 3,000 civilians in 102 minutes on a beautiful Tuesday morning in New York or by instigating *Sharia*-compliant mortgages in twenty-six states in this great nation. Both of those things are a form of attack."[60]

Idaho's Heart of Darkness

A yogurt company might seem a strange terrorist Trojan Horse, but it was precisely such a looming threat that brought Gabriel to the tiny town of Twin Falls, Idaho, in the summer of 2016. She was there to prevent the Muslim takeover of America. Nestled on the shores of the Snake River, Twin Falls had become ground zero for the champions of the proposed Muslim immigration ban. It was also a case study in the modus operandi of the Islamophobic extreme right.

"Radical Islam has declared war on America," Gabriel told a cheering crowd that packed the high school auditorium. The Three Percenters, which the Anti-Discrimination League described as an anti-government extremist movement, provided security, according to local reporters, and the John Birch Society was a co-sponsor.[61]

Since the 1980s, Twin Falls had welcomed about 300 refugees a year from an assortment of countries to work in its agricultural industry. Two months before Gabriel arrived in Twin Falls, police arrested two Eritrean boys, aged ten and fourteen, and a seven-year-old Somali boy, for sexually assaulting a five-year-old white girl in a laundry room and videotaping it. Minors were involved, so police records were sealed. Rumors began circulating. Social media lit up. Hard-right websites piled on. Amid all the campaign talk about the threat of Syrian refugees, the story morphed: three Syrian refugees had raped and urinated on a little girl at knifepoint and the police did nothing. At a town meeting, anti-refugee activists shouted down the board. "ISIS is here," one man declared, "the Muslim Brotherhood is here."

"There was no gang rape, there was no Syrian involvement, there were no Syrian refugees involved, there was no knife used, there was no inactivity by the police," Twin Falls County Prosecutor Grant Loebs told a newspaper in nearby Washington state. "I'm looking at the Drudge Report headline: "Syrian Refugees Rape Little Girl at Knifepoint in Idaho"—all false."[62]

It didn't matter. The story ricocheted through the alt-right media echo chamber—*Creeping Shariah*, *Jihad Watch* and *World Net Daily* all went with variations on the story. *Breitbart* launched a series of articles.

Anti-Islam campaigner Pam Geller arrived in town and wrote, "The Muslim migrants have devastated Twin Falls."[63] Another *Breitbart* writer claimed the "gang rape" frightened "local activists, particularly when it became clear that ISIS was using the Syrian refugee crisis ... to bring terrorists into the West."[64] A third piece "revealed" that four years before, tuberculosis cases had increased by 500 percent due to the refugees.[65] Readers had to do the math to realize that was a total of two new cases.

"Idaho Yogurt Maker Caught Importing Migrant Rapists," announced a tweet from *InfoWars*, run by right-wing provocateur Alex Jones.[66] The tweet linked to a story blaming Chobani founder Hamdi Ulukaya for a TB outbreak and the town's alleged crime wave. Ulukaya, a Kurdish-born Turk, had been praised by the state of Idaho for making a $100 million investment and employing 2,000 workers to create what the governor called "the Magic Valley Miracle" that attracted investments by other food manufacturers. However, he drew the wrath of anti-immigration activists for employing hundreds of refugees and urging other American companies to do the same.

When Ulukaya sued for defamation, Jones's defense of his team's reporting offered a telling window on the anti-Muslim echo chamber. "The point is, they did their research, and it depends on how you look at it, but *a lot of it* is accurate," he explained on his webcast. Twin Falls mayor Shawn Bariger, who received death threats for defending the town's refugees, told me, "It's too easy to go out and find misinformation or no information at all and frame it in the context of your personal beliefs and fail to even listen to rational facts."

Brigitte Gabriel, who had fled war-torn Lebanon three decades before, wasn't buying that. She knew all about the danger posed by refugees. As her Twin Falls speech ended and the music surged on a dramatic video of military tanks juxtaposed with the U.S. Capitol, a voiceover told the people of Idaho, "There comes a time when we have to make sure that the enemy does not conquer us from within."[67]

Tacos with a Terrorist

The men and women who *were* actually fighting on the front lines of the war on terror understood the landscape of extremism was far more nuanced than the good and bad dichotomy presented by the anti-Islam movement.

Tim Curry was a top counterterrorism official in the Department of Homeland Security. His intersections with terror came long before he started his career. Curry's grad school dorm-mate was a terrorist. So were many of his Irish drinking buddies. And one of his college Lacrosse teammates at Boston College died saving others in the World Trade Center.

Boston Irish to his core, Curry went to graduate school in Belfast and became friends with former members of the Irish Republican Army (IRA) who were convicted terrorists. "They wouldn't ascribe that term to themselves, but they were in jail for terrorist offenses and they killed people. They moved past that," he told me over dinner one evening.

The guy across the hall in his Belfast dorm took a different trajectory. He became a suicide bomber. Curry had moved to Northern Ireland six days after 9/11 to work on a dissertation examining the role of religion in the formation of terrorist groups in Ireland and Lebanon. When he wasn't out with his Irish pals, Curry frequently hung out with Kafeel Ahmed, his Indian Muslim dorm neighbor. "We shared a common room, shared a bathroom, shared a kitchen. We became close and we became good friends," Curry recalled as we finished our meal. "I taught him to cook tacos. He knew about my brother and I knew about his. We just had a good time." Coming home many evenings after doing research at the library, Curry peppered Ahmed with questions about Islam. Ahmed's answers were straightforward, never doctrinaire or polemical.

Curry took a sip of Irish whiskey and continued. "He worked at a kebab shop, so I'd go there late at night. It was in the Loyalist area. They were paying protection money to Loyalists, and many of the people there were Loyalist paramilitaries. My Catholic friends were like, 'I'm not going to that kebab shop. You go.'"

After graduating, he and his dorm-mate went their separate ways. Curry joined DHS, and Ahmed went home to Bangalore where, Curry learned later, he was drawn into the sectarian rift between Muslims and Hindu nationalists and began reading Chechen Islamist literature. From there he went back to the United Kingdom, where he became involved with Hizb ut-Tahrir (Party of Liberation), an Islamist group dedicated to the re-creation of the caliphate.

"It got to the point where he felt that he needed to do something," Curry recounted. "Tried to blow up nightclubs in London. Bombs didn't work." The next day, Ahmed and an accomplice targeted Glasgow airport. "They knew the clock was ticking on them," Curry continued. "Drives the car full of explosives. It doesn't ignite. He self-immolates. He is attacking other people, involving other people [in the flames]. He has burns over 70 percent of his body. He's alive for about seventy-one days, then he passes away."

Curry heard about the attack while writing congressional testimony on counterterrorism for Homeland Security director Michael Chertoff. At the office the next morning he started reviewing the initial intelligence from Glasgow, and the more he read, the more it sounded like his old dorm-mate. Then he saw the picture and knew. "I walked into my boss's office and I said, 'You know this attack in Glasgow?' He's like, 'Yeah, it's crazy.' I'm like, 'That's my friend.' He's like, 'What do you mean he's my friend?' I'm like, 'I knew him.' He's like, 'How well do you know him?' I'm like, 'I lived across the hall from him, I saw him every day.'"

Curry finished his whisky and shook his head at the irony. "At the end of his life, I epitomized what he hated the most, and if he had the chance at that time, he would have liked nothing more than for me to have been one of those victims because of who I was and what I did. Three years prior, we were friends and colleagues and had a mutual understanding and could talk about life, could talk about Islam and could talk about 9/11."

Beyond the irony, Curry found an important lesson in the tragedy of his former friend: terrorism was not preordained. It involved roads not taken. He took that pragmatic view even though terrorism claimed the life of one of his American friends. His lacrosse teammate at Boston College was Welles Crowther, a stock trader who saved many lives before the second tower of the World Trade Center collapsed on him. He was the "man in the red bandanna" featured in a documentary on the tragedy. "Their lives had been saved by the man in the red bandanna," President Obama said during the dedication of the National September 11 Museum.[68]

Curry, who carried a red scarf in memory of Crowther, knew that terrorism was about more than good and evil. It involved human nature. He was fascinated by the process that produced a terrorist. How did Shirwa Ahmed go from being a student at the University of Minnesota to becoming the first American suicide bomber, one of three Somali-American kids from Minneapolis who blew themselves up in Somalia for the militant group al Shabab? How did a white Southern Baptist kid who was president of his high school class in Daphne, Alabama, become one of al Qaeda's most prolific recruiters, make it to the FBI's Most Wanted list with a $5 million bounty on his head, only to be assassinated by al Qaeda when he tried to jump ship to a Somali militant group?

Curry found it comforting that the answers to those questions weren't straightforward. "Doing the work that I do, it reassures me that there is a process of radicalization. Some people are just born bad dudes; there are serial killers and psychopaths or whatever. There is another group that are radicalized to violence, manipulated."

People were not born terrorists, they became terrorists. It had nothing to do with their DNA.

PART THREE

POLICIES—SEEING BLACK AND WHITE IN A SEA OF GRAY

10 BROTHERHOOD OF THE ORB

*A nation/tribe will be coming forth from the Farsi direction,
saying: "You Arabs! You have been too zealous! If you don't give
them their due rights, nobody will have alliance with you . . ."*

AL BARZEENJI
Signs of the Judgment Day

April 2017

It was a scene that launched a thousand memes.

Fourteen centuries after the death of the Prophet Muhammad and 500 miles from Mecca, Donald Trump stood with the man who was the closest thing to the caliph of the modern era, King Salman of Saudi Arabia, and President Abdul Fatah al-Sisi, the brutal dictator of Egypt, their hands resting on a glowing orb.[1]

The Twittersphere lit up with comparisons to movie scenes from the *Lord of the Rings* to the *Wizard of Oz.*

oh my god this is how space jam started.[2]

Attention, Marvel heroes, we found the last Infinity Stone![3]

The power of Riyadh is at your command, Sauron, Lord of the Earth[4]

There comes a time in every deal when you'll be required to siphon energy from an orb . . .[5]

Trump's participation in a traditional Saudi *ardah* sword dance, and a photo of adviser Steve Bannon looking dazed amid a sea of Saudi men in robes, provided even more fodder for late-night comedians and Twitter trolls:

That moment you realize you're surrounded by people that you've claimed for years want to kill you[6]

Even more head-spinning than the images were the words. Trump, who had called the Saudis "the world's biggest funders of terrorism,"[7] and said the country was responsible for 9/11,[8] was now praising the Saudi king for his "strong demonstration of leadership" in "combatting radicalization."[9] And the Saudis returned the favor. The president, who had campaigned on the idea that "Islam hates us," was now being hailed by the king's son, the future crown prince, as "a true friend of the Muslims."[10]

The sense of dissonance became even more pronounced when contemplating the ostensible purpose of the summit: "to meet history's great test—to conquer extremism and vanquish the forces of terrorism."[11]

"This is not a battle between different faiths, different sects or different civilizations," proclaimed Donald Trump, whose entire campaign was based on just such imagined fault lines. "This is a battle between Good and Evil."[12]

But the overriding focus of the summit was not a battle against al Qaeda or the Islamic State, which had carried out scores of terror attacks across the Middle East, Asia, Europe and the United States. In this Saudi-authored drama, the role of Evil Incarnate was played by Iran. Consciously or not, Trump had stepped directly into the rift between Saudi Arabia and Iran, a rivalry as old as Islam itself. The two Middle East powers were locked in a politically and religiously polarizing Cold War that had already cost tens of thousands of lives across the Middle East and fueled sectarian violence around the world.

The Saudis, thanks to an accident of geography that gave them both oil and the holy city of Mecca, were the most influential force in Sunni Islam. The Islamic Republic of Iran was home to both the world's largest Shi'a population and to the grand ayatollah, the Shi'a equivalent of the pope. Their confrontation was the modern manifestation of the succession crisis at the dawn of Islam that had resulted in the Sunni-Shi'a split. It was about geopolitics as much as religion. The Saudis wanted to dominate and impose their will on the Middle East. Iran had a different plan. Years before, King Abdullah II of Jordan, a Sunni Muslim, had warned of the creation of a "Shi'a crescent" that would stretch from Iran, across Bahrain, Iraq and Syria to Lebanon, where Iran's proxy militia-cum-political party, Hezbollah, operated a state-within-a-state.[13] Now that threat had become a reality. With Iranian troops operating in Iraq and Syria, Hezbollah had an unbroken supply line that stretched straight back to Tehran. The Saudis were not happy and set out to marshal the American president to their cause.

In a blur of glittering chandeliers, glowing orbs and billions of dollars in trade deals, Saudi Arabia deftly transformed itself into America's soulmate and Iran secured its place as Public Enemy #1. In the process, the two fundamentally different issues were conflated as American foreign policy became an extension of Saudi regional policy.

One Man's Terrorist

The numbers told the real story. About 140 Americans had died in terrorist attacks by ISIS, al Qaeda and related Sunni Muslim groups over the previous two years (outside the wars in Afghanistan and Iraq).[14] During that same period, Iran and its Shi'ite proxies had not killed a single American. The last incident in which Iranian proxies were tied to a terrorist act that claimed American lives was the 1996 bombing of the Khobar Towers barracks in Saudi Arabia, carried out by Hezbollah al-Hejaz (Saudi Hezbollah), which killed nineteen U.S. Air Force personnel and injured 372.[15]

"Iran's state sponsorship of terrorism worldwide remained undiminished," the State Department said in its 2016 *Country Reports on Terrorism*. Yet that study could not name a single Iranian-backed attack on American interests,[16] and terrorism databases recorded only one attack by Hezbollah outside the Middle East in decades. A top expert told Congress that while Iran's main proxy, Hezbollah, "remains bitterly anti-Israel and anti-American," it "has even less interest in a direct clash with the United States" than with Israel.[17] But like everything in the Middle East, Iran's role was complex. Though it had been holding a top al Qaeda operative under house arrest for years, Iran also allowed Sunni militants free transit across its borders en route to Afghanistan and Pakistan.

Complicating this picture was the fact that the U.S. and Iran had fought on the same side in the war against ISIS. When an Iraqi assault on Islamic State forces occupying the Iraqi city of Tikrit bogged down in the spring of 2015, the U.S. launched airstrikes and provided aerial reconnaissance to support a ground offensive by Iraqi troops, Iranian-backed Shi'ite militias and elements of the Iranian Revolution Guard, including its commander. A spokesman for U.S. Central Command insisted, "We do not coordinate our operations in any way with Iran,"[18] but the fact was that the U.S. and Iran were working in tandem with the Iraqi government to defeat ISIS. The long game for each country was to increase its influence with the Iraqi government, but they shared an immediate goal, to crush the extremist group threatening them both and their mutual ally, the government of Iraq.

Based on two years of interviews in Iran, scholars Ariane Tabatabai of Harvard and Dina Esfandiary of King's College in London concluded:

> Iran's strategy against ISIS is similar to that pursued by the United States. Tehran wants to eliminate ISIS in Iraq and push it back in Syria, while ensuring that both countries preserve their territorial integrity; destroy ISIS' capacity to launch terrorist attacks outside of its territories; undermine its appeal to local and foreign fighters; and stop it from spilling into neighboring Afghanistan.[19]

There was a precedent for U.S.-Iranian cooperation: The Afghan war. Iran was battling the Taliban alongside the Northern Alliance and India long before the U.S. intervened in 2001. After the U.S. invasion, it worked with the Americans on the ground and committed substantial aid for reconstruction.[20]

"The Iran of 2017 is not the Iran of 1981," a group of retired intelligence officers wrote to the White House at the end of 2017.[21] In the 1980s, Iran *was* synonymous with anti-American terror. It effectively invented modern suicide bombing in Lebanon, beginning with the 1983 destruction of the U.S. embassy, followed in short order by the bombings of the U.S. Marine Corps barracks in Beirut, the U.S. embassy in Kuwait, and the Beirut embassy "Annex," which replaced the destroyed embassy. Two years later, Shi'ite militiamen hijacked a TWA flight, killing a U.S. Navy diver and holding thirty-nine passengers for seventeen days. Meanwhile, two dozen other Americans, some of them my friends, were kidnapped, along with more than forty Europeans, and held for up to seven years.

I covered that wave of terror, which claimed more than 300 lives, including those of 260 Americans. It was carried out by the operational arm of Hezbollah using the nom de guerre Islamic Jihad. But there was no doubt who was pulling the strings. Hezbollah had its roots in a coalition of Lebanese Shi'a clerics who had grown disillusioned with what they considered the failure of the main Shi'a militia, Amal, to adequately confront America troops in Beirut.

The Iranians weren't shy about their role in confronting the U.S. At the height of this wave of anti-American terror, I met with the man U.S. intelligence said was pulling Hezbollah's strings, Ali Akhbar Mohtashmipur, a cleric who was Iran's ambassador to Syria. One intelligence source called his office "the center for terrorism in the Levant." As I recounted in my 2003 book *Seeds of Hate*:

Greeting me, Mohtashami reached out with the mangled remains of his left hand. Only the thumb was intact. The two index fingers ended at the second joint. The other fingers were gone. The right hand was a rubber fake. The detailed work, complete with fingernails and skin creases at the joints, looked so realistic that I was at first deceived.

The disfigurement had been caused by a booby-trapped *Qur'an* sent to the ambassador several months after the Marine bombing. The gift had blown up in Mohtashami's face when he had opened it. He had spent six months in a German hospital recovering from his wounds. This man of the cloth was a man with enemies . . .

The ambassador was reported to be one of the most vehemently anti-American members of Iran's leadership. He blamed the CIA for the bomb that had almost killed him and regularly left the room at diplomatic gatherings if an American entered. Mohtashami said that this was the first time he had spoken to an American journalist . . .

"We think that as long as America as a superpower looks to Israel in a special way and prefers it to all other countries, and until the U.S. can be nonaligned in the Middle East, there will be difficulties." The Farsi words came out in short, sharp phrases that sounded almost like a chant.

There was a globe and small Iranian flag on the ambassador's desk at the opposite end of the room. A larger, freestanding flag of the Islamic Republic stood behind it, flanking the obligatory portrait of Khomeini in a gilt-edged frame. A silhouette of Jerusalem's al-Aqsa Mosque hung on another wall.

When I said I had been told that he was a key figure behind the attacks against Americans and that the Council for Lebanon met in the room in which we sat, Mohtashami's face split in a wide grin.

He was silent for a few moments, then shifted in his seat, cleared his throat and replied enigmatically. "Let me tell you clearly that I have 20 years of struggle in Iran and Iraq against the American intervention in our countries. A person like me is not afraid if it is said about him this or that." There was amusement, not anger, on his face.

"This is one of the American faults that America thinks every accident, every activity in every place should be attributed to Iran."

When we spoke at the end of May 1985, seven Americans were being held captive by Islamic Jihad. One of them was a friend, Associated Press Middle East correspondent Terry Anderson. Based in Beirut, Anderson and his staff had written extensively on the Israeli occupation of South Lebanon. I pointed out to Mohtashami the irony that a reporter whose work had benefited the Shi'ites was being held captive by them.

"Yes, it is too bad about your friend," Khomeini's man in Damascus said as he walked me to the door. "He is innocent. They are all innocent as individuals. It is a very unfortunate situation. They are suffering for the policy of your government, just as others will suffer until that policy changes."

Two weeks later, TWA flight 847 was hijacked to Beirut.[22]

A quarter of a century later, anti-American terrorism by Iran and its agents had largely been confined to history. Iranian nukes were a *potential* threat, but the Islamic State, al Qaeda and their offshoots were a very *real-time* threat.

Was Iran culpable for regional instability in the spring of 2017? Absolutely. Iranian-backed Shi'ite militias in Iraq had fueled the sectarian strife that caused the country to collapse in the wake of the American invasion. But so, too, Saudi and Gulf backing for Sunni militias. Iranian Revolutionary Guards and Hezbollah fighting in support of the Assad regime in Syria had made possible the carnage that had taken at least a half-million lives and created more than 10 million Syrian refugees since 2011, but so, too, Saudi/Gulf-backed Sunni militias fighting Assad, including al Qaeda offshoots and the Islamic State. Iranian-backed Houthi tribesmen rebelled against the Yemen government in 2014, but upward of 200 airstrikes a day by the Saudi-led coalition, which included Saudi Arabia's Gulf allies, Jordan and Sudan, using American-made weapons and with operational support from the U.S. and the United Kingdom, had "indiscriminately killed and wounded thousands of civilians in violation of the laws of war," according to Human Rights Watch.[23] As Trump was feted in Riyadh, a few hundred miles away almost 20 million Yemenis were being threatened by what the UN called "the world's largest hunger crisis"[24] and thousands more were dying in the worst cholera outbreak in modern history, all the result of the Saudi-led war.

Like most things in the Middle East, the issue of Saudi Arabia's relationship to terror was complicated. Fifteen of the nineteen 9/11 hijackers were Saudis; Saudi Arabia provided the bulk of both foreign suicide bombers in Iraq and foreign volunteers serving the Islamic State; and financial support for a range of violent extremist groups had been traced back to Saudi Arabia, Qatar, Kuwait and the UAE. As then-Secretary of State Hillary Clinton said in a 2014 e-mail released by Wikileaks: "We need to use our diplomatic and more traditional intelligence assets to bring pressure on the governments of Qatar and Saudi Arabia, which are providing clandestine financial and logistic support to ISIL and other radical Sunni groups in the region."[25]

Elements within the Saudi government *had* cooperated with the U.S. on counterterrorism efforts since 9/11. After all, the House of Saud was bin Laden's ultimate target. Crown Prince Mohammed bin Nayef, who had survived several assassination attempts by the extremists, was considered by some in the CIA to be one of the world's preeminent counter-terrorists. But there were many centers of power in the kingdom. "Donors in Saudi Arabia constitute the most significant source of funding to Sunni terrorist groups worldwide," Clinton said a 2008 e-mail that was also part of the Wikileaks trove. "More needs to be done since Saudi Arabia remains a critical financial support base for al-Qaida, the Taliban, LeT [Lashkar-e-Taiba] and other terrorist groups."[26] Saudi leaders had been talking for years about cutting out the "malignant cancer" of terrorism,[27] and it was still metastasizing.

Ryan Crocker knew the complicated nexus of terror and Middle East politics better than anyone. He was the number two diplomat in the U.S. embassy in Beirut when it was leveled by a suicide bomber in 1983. He went on to become U.S. ambassador to four Arab countries, including Syria and Iraq, as well as Pakistan and Afghanistan. George W. Bush called Crocker "America's Lawrence of Arabia" and awarded him the Presidential Medal of Freedom. Crocker had worked with the Saudis and Pakistanis to support the anti-Soviet jihadis in Afghanistan. Then in Baghdad years later, he was involved in developing the strategy to fight what would become the Islamic State. He reopened the U.S. embassy in Afghanistan after the U.S. invasion in 2001 and was brought back from retirement by Barack Obama to return to Afghanistan at the height of the U.S. surge.

Crocker and I first met in Beirut in the brief period between Iran's Islamic revolution and the embassy bombing, in which he lost dozens of friends and colleagues. That bombing meant Crocker had more reason than most to hate Iran, yet he was troubled by the Riyadh summit's focus on the Tehran regime. "Clearly fighting terror is important, but you've gotta remember, terror isn't a country, it's not a policy. It's a tactic," he told me, frustration in his voice. "The Islamic Republic of Iran kind of invented the large-scale suicide bomb attacks, but then they got out of the business. So [suicide bombing] has transferred from being an exclusively Shia instrument to now being a Sunni Arab instrument."

Crocker paused, gathering his thoughts. "Islamic State is not the disease itself, it's the symptom of the disease. So yeah, that's the conversation I wish the president had had. It is important that we do it."

Bankrolling Terror

Saudi Arabia's historic complicity in terror—whether official or through the web of wealthy private donors—was well documented by Western intelligence. One example: During interrogation, convicted al Qaeda courier Zacarias Moussaoui directly implicated top Saudi officials as providing support for al Qaeda. In testimony for a lawsuit brought against Saudi Arabia by the families of 9/11 victims, Moussaoui claimed he brought messages from Osama bin Laden to Saudi officials including King Salman, then a prince. He also claimed that in the late 1990s, he was tasked by bin Laden with setting up a computer database of al Qaeda donors, which included the names of key members of the royal family, including the former intelligence chief and a former ambassador to the U.S. "Sheikh Osama wanted to keep a record who give money; who is to be listened to or who contributed to the *jihad*," the deposition records him saying in imperfect English.[28]

"I am convinced that there was a direct line between at least some of the terrorists who carried out the September 11th attacks and the government of Saudi Arabia," former Senator Bob Graham, who headed the 9/11 inquiry, wrote in an affidavit for the lawsuit. In his own affidavit, another member of the commission, former Senator Bob Kerry, wrote that it was "fundamentally inaccurate and misleading" to argue that the 9/11 Commission exonerated the Saudi government.

And then there was the supposed funding crackdown. Just one week before Trump arrived in Saudi Arabia, the U.S. Treasury Department added Pakistani cleric Ali Muhammad Abu Turab to its list of Specially Designated Global Terrorists "for facilitat[ing] the movement of tens of thousands of dollars from the Gulf to Pakistan" for use by militant groups implicated in anti-Shi'a terror campaigns. That was the good news for U.S. anti-terrorism officials. The bad news was that Turab was reportedly in Saudi Arabia raising money the very day the U.S. added him to the terrorist list, even as U.S. and Saudi officials were putting the finishing touches on their grand anti-terror summit.

While Saudi royals traded compliments with Trump on camera, off-camera they were pursuing what Bruce Riedel of Brookings called "the most aggressively sectarian and anti-Iran policy in modern Saudi history" with the "Wahhabi clerical establishment [as] an enthusiastic partner."[29] That involved ongoing cynical efforts to ramp up anti-Shi'a violence in proxy wars across the region. Along with increasing the presence of Salafi clerics in the morass of Yemen,[30] Saudi funds had been pouring into militant madrasas in Pakistan's Baluchistan province to stir unrest on Iran's southeastern border and threaten its Indian-built port at Chabahar, a few dozen miles from the Pakistani border.[31] More than 2,000 Shi'a had been killed in sectarian attacks there over the previous twenty years. "Saudi Arabia funds pan-Sunnism, while Iran funds Pan-Shia-ism in Pakistan. In order to counter pan-Shia-ism, a "systematic" killing of Shia is ongoing," wrote Pakistani journalist Sajid Hussain.[32]

The visceral antipathy for Muslim minorities among some Saudi Wahhabi purists was illustrated by the response of Saudi TV host Abdullellah al-Dosari to the death of 300 Shi'ite Iranian pilgrims in a stampede during the 2015 Hajj in Mecca: "Praise be to Allah, who relieved Islam and the Muslims from their evil. We pray that Allah will usher them into Hell for all eternities."[33]

11 THE WAHHABI PROJECT

A man who is convinced of the truth of his religion is indeed never tolerant.

ALBERT EINSTEIN

Despite what it wanted the world to believe, the interests of the House of Saud were not necessarily the interests of the world's Muslims. Since the early 1980s the Saudi government had been developing a network of Wahhabi-inspired mosques and madrassas around the world that was a breeding ground for extremism and was fundamentally reshaping the very nature of Islam itself. "The Saudis have exported more extreme ideology than any other place on Earth over the course of the last 30 years," Hillary Clinton told the Jewish United Fund at a 2013 dinner.[1]

In these schools and houses of worship, Saudi-trained clerics set the tone and al-Wahhab's key tracts, *Kitab al-Tawhid* (*The Book of Monotheism*) and *al-Usul al-Thalatha* (*The Three Fundamental Principles*), were closely studied. Estimates of how much the Saudis invested in this global Wahhabi project varied wildly, from $80 billion to $200 billion.[2] Western intelligence identified a range of Saudi charities as the main conduits for this funding, including the Muslim World League, the International Islamic Relief Organization, the al-Haramain Foundation, the World Assembly of Muslim Youth, and the Medical Emergency Relief Charity.[3]

The United States had long been among the targets of Wahhabi proselytizing. A 2006 Freedom House report accused the Saudi government of systematically distributing in U.S. mosques publications filled with a "totalitarian ideology of hatred that can incite to violence."[4] Farah Pandith, appointed America's first special representative to Muslim communities by President Obama, traveled to more than eighty countries. She warned of the role played by Saudi Arabia in fueling extremism:

In each place I visited, the Wahhabi influence was an insidious presence, changing the local sense of identity; displacing historic, culturally vibrant forms of Islamic practice; and pulling along individuals who were either paid to follow their rules or who became on their own custodians of the Wahhabi world view. Funding all this was Saudi money, which paid for things like the textbooks, mosques, TV stations and the training of Imams.[5]

Just weeks before the Riyadh summit, the Bangladesh government announced it had approved a plan for Saudi Arabia to spend $1 billion to build a new mosque in each of Bangladesh's 560 towns, adding to the 50,000 privately funded mosques that had sprung up in that country since 2009, operating alongside a network of privately funded, religiously conservative *Qawami* madrassas, with 1.4 million students. The move prompted a backlash from Sufis and Shi'a, who had been targeted for violence by Wahhabi-trained Bangladeshi Muslims.[6]

Saudization

"The evil empire." That's what many Pakistani Muslims called Saudi Arabia. They bemoaned the "Saudization" of their country. At least half of all Pakistani Muslims belong to the Barlevi Sufi school of Islam, but Saudi money had poured into the expansion of mosques and madrassas run by the conservative Deobandi and Ahl al-Hadith schools, more closely aligned with Saudi Wahhabism.

Estimates of the total number of madrassas in Pakistan varied. One set of figures released by the government at the end of 2014 reported that some 3.5 million students were being educated in about 35,000 registered madrassas, up from less than 3,000 in 1988, but thousands of others operated illegally. "Saudi money is being invested in madrassas that equip people with a particular mindset that does not jell with what we are trying to do," a former Pakistani ambassador who headed a government-funded think tank told me.

Noted Islamic scholar Tariq Ramadan has written that the Pakistani "madrassas, which were associated with conservatism, ossification and stagnation of Islam earlier, are now seen as hotbeds of militancy in the name of Islam." Pervez Hoodbhoy, chairman of the NGO Quaid-i-Azam in Islamabad, observed that "Pakistani schools—and not just madrassas—are churning out fiery zealots, fueled with a passion for jihad and martyrdom,"[7] providing what the UN called a rich pool of suicide bombers for extremist groups across the border in Afghanistan.[8]

A 2008 cable released by Wikileaks, purportedly written by U.S. embassy employees after a visit to the southern Punjab, reported a "growing extremist threat" in the state as a result of "exponential" growth in hardline mosques and madrassas over the previous two years:

> Government and non-governmental sources claimed that financial support estimated at nearly 100 million USD annually was making its way to Deobandi and Ahl-e-Hadith clerics in the region from "missionary" and "Islamic charitable" organizations in Saudi Arabia and the United Arab Emirates ostensibly with the direct support of those governments.[9]

In late 2017, Pakistan's military chief decried the fact that some 2.5 million students were enrolled in madrassas run by the Saudi-aligned Deobandi school. "So what will they become: will they become *Maulvis* [clerics] or they will become terrorists?" General Qamar Javed Bajwa asked, answering his own question by adding that there could never be enough mosques to employ all those students as clerics.[10]

Pakistan's civilian authorities were cracking down on what they called "the terrorist financing system," but the challenges were large, not least because the military's Inter-Services Intelligence (ISI) had supported the growth of militant groups to achieve its own ends in Afghanistan and Kashmir. Another complication in stemming the flow of money to the extremists from Saudi Arabia and other Gulf countries was the fact that Saudi Arabia also provided hundreds of millions of dollars in government-to-government support. When sanctions were slapped on Pakistan after its 1998 nuclear test, Saudi Arabia provided a bailout. And its influence extended deep into the Pakistani government. Pakistani prime minister Nawaz Sharif, one of the guests at the Riyadh summit, had spent his political exile in Saudi Arabia after he was ousted in a military coup. Meanwhile, remittances from Pakistani workers in Saudi Arabia brought $20 billion a year into the Pakistani economy. "That money is vital to the country," one politician told me, "but it gives the Saudis tremendous leverage over us. And there is also the problem that many of our workers spend years in Saudi Arabia and in they come back with the Wahhabi mentality."

One other weapon the Saudis held over the Pakistanis—and all countries with a sizable Muslim population—was the quota for the annual Hajj pilgrimage. One of the pillars of Islam is that all Muslims with the means must take part in the Hajj pilgrimage at least once in their lives. As Ali Shihabi, executive director of the Arabia Foundation in the U.S., put it, "Whoever controls Mecca and Medina has tremendous soft power."[11] In 2018, the Saudis increased Pakistan's Hajj allotment by 5,000. That was the same year Pakistan agreed to send troops to defend Saudi Arabia's border with Yemen against Iranian-backed rebels, a step the Islamabad government had been trying to avoid for more than a year.

It was also the same year the Saudis froze Hajj visas for more than 600,000 Palestinians as Riyadh stepped up pressure on Palestinian leaders to bend to Saudi foreign policy on the future of Palestine.[12]

Southeast Asia

The impact of Wahhabi proselytizing could be seen in the dramatic increase in the number of Muslim women covering their heads in countries from Indonesia to Nigeria and increased support for harsh Islamic practices such as corporal punishment in places like Pakistan, Egypt and Malaysia.[13] A British study of the influence of Saudi funding in the United Kingdom reported,

> The most profound impact has been in other parts of the Islamic world, where funding from Gulf States has been used to promote a more extreme interpretation of Islam, often overriding local practices and traditions that are more moderate.[14]

Indonesia, the world's most populous Muslim country, had long been known as "the smiling face of Islam."[15] The country embodied a tolerant, syncretic approach to Islam. I vividly recall a business meeting with an Indonesian media executive when I lived in Jakarta in the 1990s. He suggested we meet at midday in the coffee shop of the Hilton Hotel. It was Ramadan, the month during which Muslims fast from dawn to dusk, so I thought the suggestion was odd. I happened to arrive first. When he joined me, he asked if I had ordered lunch. I had not and, fearful I would imply he was a bad Muslim, hesitantly asked whether he was planning to eat. He confirmed he was fasting and told me to go ahead and order.

I didn't, but in my decades living in the Arab world, where most countries ban food or beverages in public places during the fasting hours, I had never had a similar conversation.

In those years, plenty of Indonesian women wore the jilbab head covering, but on my trips back in the following decades I was stunned at how pervasive it had become. The jilbab was now a symbol of Muslim identity, and an intolerant, Saudi-style conservatism had taken root. It was a symptom of the tens of millions of dollars in money from Saudi Arabia and its Gulf allies, Kuwait, Qatar, Bahrain and the United Arab Emirates,[16] that funded a string of some 150 mosques and 100 madrassas teaching Saudi Arabia's Wahhabi *madab* (doctrine), threatening to undermine Indonesia's inclusive *Pancasila* (Five Principles) ideology, which was based on religious tolerance.

"While the 1979 Iranian revolution showed Indonesians how women could play a more active role, the adoption of *Salafi* precepts by (male) leaders of *Darul Islam,* and later *Jemaah Islamiyah,* focused on absolute obedience to male authority and a stricter dress code, with more women wearing headscarves and in some cases, face veils," according to a report on female radicalization by Indonesia's Institute for Policy Analysis of Conflict.[17]

It is important to put this in context: institutions funded by the Saudis and Salafis elsewhere in the Gulf were a tiny portion of the hundreds of thousands of mosques and more than ten thousand madrassas and *pesantren* (Islamic boarding schools) in Indonesia. But they had an outsized influence on the religion and culture.

Just two months before the Riyadh summit, King Salman had made a nine-day visit to Indonesia, accompanied by an entourage of some 1,500 relatives, retainers and businessmen, and 500 tons of luggage, including four Mercedes limousines and two gold-plated escalators. It was part of a month-long Asian trade mission, but for Saudi Arabia, money and religion went hand in hand. Morocco could attest to that. When it needed Saudi financial support for its war in the Western Sahara, the money came with strings attached: allow in Wahhabi clerics or forget about funding. The Moroccans accepted, and the presence of the extremist preachers ultimately fueled domestic extremism.[18]

During Salman's Jakarta visit, the Saudis announced $1 billion in social aid, including a long-term partnership between seven Indonesian public universities and the Islamic Development Bank to upgrade campuses, "improve" curriculum and train faculty. The first university to undergo upgrades was in Aceh, the only Indonesia province governed by sharia law.

"The efflorescence of Salafism in Indonesia cannot be isolated from Saudi Arabia's immensely ambitious global campaign for the Wahhabization of the Muslim *umma*," according to Indonesia scholar Robert Hefner of Boston University.[19]

The Saudi Alums

"University of Terror: The Jihadi school on Australia's doorstep funded by Donald Trump's friend Saudi Arabia." That was the headline on Australia's largest news website, run by Rupert Murdoch's News Corp, a month after the Riyadh summit.[20]

While the terror tag may have been wildly sensational, the Institute for the Study of Islam and Arabic (LIPIA), a university offering degrees in Islamic studies, was the cornerstone of Saudi proselytizing in Indonesia. Indonesian students were provided free tuition. Graduates were offered scholarships to continue their studies in Saudi Arabia. Only Arabic was spoken on campus. Music, television and loud laughter were banned. Men and women were segregated. It was an approach to Islam a world apart from what Indonesians had practiced for generations.

An entire generation of "Saudi alumni," as they were referred to in Indonesia, had moved into positions of power in politics and religion, from the cabinet to the mosque. Most espoused moderation, but not all. These "alumni" include Jafar Umar Thalib, the founder of Lashkar Jihad, a militant group that waged Holy War against Christians in Indonesia in the 1990s, supported by fatwas issued by Salafi clerics in the Middle East.[21] An extensive study of the organization by Indonesian researcher Noorhaidi Hasan concluded,

> the very existence of *Lashkar Jihad* cannot be dissociated from Saudi Arabia's immensely ambitious global campaign for the Wahhabization of the Muslim *umma*.[22]

Thalib was a case study in the international connections that fueled the spread of Saudi religious doctrine and, too often, extremist violence. An Indonesian Arab of Hadrami Yemeni descent, he grew up immersed in Salafism at home and at a *pesantren* (religious boarding school) in Surabaya. He then attended LIPIA but dropped out after clashing with a professor, whom he accused of failing to provide enough references to the Qur'an and Hadith. However, the head of LIPIA at the time intervened and sent Thalib to Pakistan to study at the Maududi Islamic Institute inside the Mansoora headquarters complex of Jemaat-e-Islami, where I had met the JI deputy *Ameer*. From there, Thalib moved on to the training camps of Saudi-backed militants in Pakistan, and then fought in the Afghan jihad as part of a unit supported by private sources in Saudi Arabia and Yemen. That experience laid the groundwork for much of what was to come:[23]

[D]uring the war he directly witnessed how Wahhabi doctrines were implemented by Afghan *mujāhids* and voluntary *jihad* fighters associated with the Wahhabi-supported factions.[24]

After the war, Thalib taught at a Salafi *pesantren* in Indonesia, then traveled to Yemen to study under a Wahhabi cleric who had been accused of involvement in the 1979 takeover of the Grand Mosque in Mecca. When Thalib returned to Indonesia, he was considered one of the country's leading Salafi teachers, which enabled him to mobilize 7,000 jihadis in a war against Christians in the Moluccan Islands of Indonesia. That holy war was strengthened and legitimized by fatwas from prominent religious authorities in Saudi Arabia and Yemen calling on Indonesian Muslims "to arise and conduct *jihad* in the name of God and overthrow Christians who occupy Muslim territory."[25]

There was also a strong Saudi connection to a *pesantren* in the Central Java city of Solo tied to Indonesia's most notorious militant group. The school was founded by Abu Bakar Bashir and Abdullah Sungkar. Bashir is considered the spiritual father, and Sungkar, the founder of Jemaah Islamiyah (JI), which carried out a campaign of attacks in the 2000s that claimed more than 300 lives. Effectively the Southeast Asian branch of al Qaeda, it reportedly received Saudi funding in its early days.[26] Bashir publicly pledged loyalty to the founder of ISIS, Abu Bakr al-Baghdadi. He was eventually arrested and sentenced to fifteen years in prison for running a terrorist training camp.

According to the International Crisis Group, the school was part of "a small circle of *pesantrens*" that JI depended on to propagate *jihadist* teachings. Of the more than 14,000 such schools in Indonesia, only a tiny number are committed to *jihadist* principles, but there is a kind of JI "Ivy League" to which JI members send their own children.[27]

JI's operational chief, known as Hambali, was another product of this network of schools. He went on to become a key aide to Osama bin Laden in Afghanistan before returning to Indonesia to plan the wave of terror by JI, which reported received funding from Saudi charities. Hambali was ultimately captured and send to the U.S. detention center in Guantanamo Bay.

The intolerance bred through Gulf-funded mosques and educational institutions in Indonesia was having a profound effect on culture, society and governance. By 2017, one in four Indonesian high school and college students favored the establishment of an Islamic caliphate in their country, up from just 10 percent in 2009.[28] "Indonesia is facing red-alert status in ideology," said Nusron Wahid of Indonesia's forty-million-member Nahdlatul Ulama (NU), the largest Muslim organization in the world. "I always believed one who can control universities will control the public. If the idea of a caliphate has its own space in the universities, it will grow bigger in the next few years."

"Wahhabist money going into Indonesia," said the former head of one of Australia's intelligence agencies, "is a far more dangerous trend, I think, than some of the things that have received more publicity, like some of the extremist groups such as *al-Qaeda*."[29]

No one knew that better than Jakarta governor Basuki Tjahaja Purnama, popularly known as "Ahok." A Chinese Christian and technocrat, Ahok was the first non-Muslim elected to his post. He was widely popular for his stand against Indonesia's endemic corruption and for advocating reforms such as free education and healthcare. But weeks after the Riyadh summit, he would lose a run-off election to a conservative Muslim and ultimately be sentenced to two years in prison for blasphemy. The Islamic Defenders Front (FPI), the head of which was another "Saudi alumni," had posted online an edited video of a speech by Ahok in which they claimed he had mocked a passage in the Qur'an. In his comments to fisherman on an island group off the Jakarta coast, Ahok had claimed his opponents were misusing the passage, widely debated among Islamic scholars, to forbid Muslims from voting for a non-Muslim.

Indonesia's "pious democracy" was under threat; the tolerance for which Indonesian Islam had long been known was wearing thin. One Indonesian Muslim friend complained to me that peer pressure meant that he even had to change his prayer practice and adopt the Saudi style. "From our point of view, if the Saudis want to be Wahhabi in Saudi Arabia, that's their business; but if they want to export this worldwide, it's highly problematic," C. Holland Taylor, an NU official, told me.

There had been self-proclaimed *al-salaf al-salih* in Indonesia since the 1800s. But it been kept in check. In 1922, one of NU's founders, Muhammad Faqih Maskumambang, published a pamphlet entitled *Menolak Wahhabi* (*Wahhabism Rejected*). The NU was founded in 1926 in response to the *Ikhwan's* destruction of tombs and other holy places in Mecca and Medina. Now, NU acquaintances told me, they were beginning to feel like the boy with his finger in the dike trying to hold back the tide.

And the pressure was mounting. In 2016, the Saudis had begun a project to dramatically grow the number of graduates being produced by LIPIA from 3,500 a year to 10,000. The Saudi ambassador bragged to a reporter that the expansion would better counter the ideology of ISIS. "We need to protect our children and the best way is to teach pure Islam."[30]

"Pure" according to the Saudi-trained clerics teaching the students. On his gold-plated Indonesia visit, King Salman again pressed Indonesia to approve the project. The "Custodian of the Two Holy Mosques" left behind a little gift to sweeten the deal: an increase of 50,000 in the annual Hajj quota, meaning 230,000 Indonesians each year would now be able to take part in the pilgrimage that was an obligation of every Muslim.

Arabization

Malaysia, also on the king's tour, was another example of the contradictions in Saudi Arabia's newfound commitment to stopping ISIS. The Malaysian prime minister had only recently been cleared of corruption charges. His defense? The $681 million found in his bank account was a gift from the Saudi royal family.

"This is just Arabisation. Our culture—it's colonialism, Arab colonialism," Marina Mahathir, the daughter of former prime minister, Mahathir Mohamad, told a local newspaper. The impact, Mahathir said, extended from culture, such as the increased popularity of Arab-style women's kaftans rather than traditional *baju Melayu*, to religious practices themselves. "Islam has a very strong intellectual history, but there's no intellect at all in the way Islam is taught here. We're taught rituals; we're not taught about the great thinkers and differences between them," she said.[31] In fact, officially sanctioned sermons at Friday prayers often warned against the evils of liberalism and pluralism and condemned "deviant" Muslims, including Shi'a, who were outlawed from practicing their version of Islam.

Southeast Asian leaders "are too intimidated by Saudi Arabia's religious credentials and too mesmerized by its wealth for their own good," argued Dennis Ignatius, who served as Malaysia's ambassador to Canada and several South American countries. "Worse still, negligence has often been compounded by complicity with some political leaders exploiting religion for their own purposes."[32]

During the king's visit to Malaysia, the two countries announced plans to establish the King Salman Centre for International Peace, designed to "counter radical ideologies and promote Islam as a religion of peace and moderation." The center was to be a joint venture between the Islamic Science University of Malaysia and the Muslim World League, the Saudi-funded organization that has been a primary conduit for propagating Wahhabism around the world,[33] which raised questions about exactly what kind of Islam the new center would promote. Wahhabism/Salafism was banned in six of Malaysia's eleven states,[34] but the country's Sufi and Shi'a minorities feared the new center would only fuel more religious extremism. "The West cannot have it both ways," a Malaysian Shi'ite activist told a local news website. "In order to eliminate terrorists, you need to stop the ideology that creates terrorism."[35]

Plenty of others in the Sunni mainstream and closer to the center of political power agreed. In late 2017, Mohamad Sabu, who would become Malaysian minister of defense a year after the king's visit, published an article arguing that Malaysia should "keep a safe distance" from "a Wahabi state that seeks to punish and police every behavior" and whose internal politics "are toxic."

"Saudi Arabia is governed by hyper-orthodox Salafi or Wahhabi ideology, where Islam is taken in a literal form," he wrote. "Yet true Islam requires understanding Islam, not merely in its Quranic form, but Quranic spirit."[36]

Arsonists and Firefighters

By the time Trump took office, the Saudis and their Gulf allies *were* stepping up their cooperation with the U.S. to stem the flow of money to some extremist groups because, more than ever before, they were in the firing line. From his earliest days in exile, Osama bin Laden had sought the overthrow of the House of Saud. But al Qaeda strategy focused on destroying "the far enemy"—the U.S.—as a path to toppling the "near enemy," the Saudi regime. The so-called Islamic State did not buy into that roundabout route. It had been carrying out a campaign of bombings and assassinations in Saudi Arabia for the past several years. The dog was biting the hand that fed it. "The Saudis are really spooked, so they are ready to play ball on blocking funds—or at least as far as it is convenient for them," an American security source told me.

William McCants, author of a book on ISIS, summed up America's relationship with the Saudis. They were, he told *The New York Times*, "both the arsonists and the firefighters. They promote a very toxic form of Islam that draws sharp lines between a small number of true believers and everyone else, Muslim and non-Muslim … providing ideological fodder for violent jihadists." Yet at the same time, "they're our partners in counterterrorism."[37]

Muddling the issue of Saudi cooperation/collusion was the fact that much of the funding for violent extremist groups came from private sources in the kingdom, some of them influential members of the Wahhabi clergy. In 2016 testimony on Capitol Hill, Daniel Byman of Brookings explained that "the regime has at times supported, at times deliberately ignored, and at still other times cracked down on these actors. Some of these figures are important for regime legitimacy, and it is difficult for the regime to openly oppose them."[38]

That otherworldly scene with Trump, Salman and Sisi gathered around a globing orb was an example of such cooperation. It was the photo op at the opening of the new Global Center for Combating Extremist Ideology, the mission of which was "to expose, combat and refute extremist ideology."[39]

The Saudis *were* cooperating with the U.S. Behind the scenes, they *were* working with the Treasury Department to block accounts funneling money to ISIS and some other extremist groups. But not *all*. They *were* trading information with the CIA and the FBI on the movements of operatives of ISIS and some other extremist groups. But not *all*. Even as some branches of the Saudi state cooperated, Byman told Congress, others in the kingdom continued their "support for an array of preachers and non-government organizations that contributes to an overall climate of radicalization, making it far harder to counter violent extremism."[40]

12 TEMPEST IN THE GULF

And Cain talked with Abel his brother: and it came to pass, when they were in the field, that Cain rose up against Abel his brother, and slew him.

GENESIS 4:8

May 2017

It had been a hell of a week in the Middle East. It began with Saudi Arabia and its friends imposing the modern equivalent of a feudal siege on tiny Qatar. Next came an assault on the Iranian parliament and a suicide bombing at a Tehran landmark. Then the Turkish parliament voted to send troops to Qatar to defend it from its Arab brothers.[1]

By week's end, as I arrived in Dubai, the tidy "good versus evil" dichotomy of the new U.S.-Saudi alliance against "terror"—and against Iran—was looking pretty tattered. It had been less than a month since the Riyadh summit. Black and white had morphed into shades of grey. The events playing out might have been laughable if they weren't so tragic— and dangerous. The story had all the elements of a bad spy thriller: Arab potentates. A glaring Ayatollah. Hooded *jihadis*. Russian hackers. Turkish troops. American airbases. And lots and lots of fake news.

This was a part of the world, after all, where sometimes the enemy of my enemy was *in fact* my enemy. It was also a place obsessed with conspiracies, real, imagined or a bit of both. Was the Tehran attack a ploy by ISIS trying to recoup some credibility as it was being forced out of its Iraqi and Syrian capitals? Was this the Saudis using terror to fight terror under a false flag? Or the Russians throwing more kindling on the Middle East bonfire? Or the CIA? Or perhaps the Iranians putting on a Potemkin attack to discredit the Saudis and/or generate sympathy for themselves?

There had been a lot going on since the Riyadh anti-terror summit. The *Cliffs Notes* version of events.

In early May, Mohammed bin Salman gave an interview to Saudi television describing Iran as his country's irreconcilable enemy. As the Saudis saw it, while the moderate strains in the Iranian government negotiated a nuclear deal and preached reconciliation, the hardliners in the government pursued an expeditionary and expansionary policy, using overt troop deployments, proxy forces and covert action in Iraq, Syria, Yemen, Bahrain and parts of Saudi Arabia as well. MBS, as he was universally known, said he wanted to take the fight to Iran before Iran brought any more of it to Saudi Arabia. "We know we are a major target for the Iranian regime," he told the interviewer. "Reaching the Muslims' *qibla* [Mecca] is a major aim for the Iranian regime. We will not wait until the battle is in Saudi Arabia, but we will work so the battle is there in Iran and not in Saudi Arabia."[2]

When Trump met with the world's Muslim leaders in Riyadh, Iran was not on the guest list. Among those who *were* invited was the thirty-seven-year-old emir of Qatar, Sheikh Tamim bin Hamad al-Thani, who was praised as a strategic partner, not least because his country hosted more than 10,000 American service personnel and the forward command centers for all the U.S. military operations in the region from Syria to Afghanistan. But Qatar, in part to assert its independence from Saudi Arabia, had long cultivated warm relations with Iran and the international Muslim Brotherhood, which the Saudis saw as direct threats to their monarchy. After all, Qatar and its Al Jazeera satellite channel had championed the Arab Spring revolt that unleashed forces of democracy across the region, sparked a Shi'a uprising in Bahrain and Saudi Arabia's majority Shi'a Eastern province and brought the Muslim Brotherhood to power in Egypt, unnerving the House of Saud next door.

Arabic Fake News

The wheels of Air Force One had barely lifted off the tarmac at Riyadh airport bound for Israel—on arrival, Trump told Israeli officials that he "just got back from the Middle East"[3]—when Qatar's emir was quoted by Qatar's official news agency criticizing his fellow Arab leaders and saying nice things about Iran.

Qatar was being unfairly attacked by "some governments which promote terrorism by adopting a radical version of Islam which doesn't represent its tolerant reality," Sheikh Tamim bin Hamad al Thani reportedly said, adding he would sue "the countries and organizations behind this smear campaign."[4] The story went on to quote him saying, "There is no wisdom in harboring hostility toward Iran," which he allegedly called "an Islamic power," something the Saudis considered close to blasphemy, adding that Trump's Saudi visit was an attempt to distract from the Russia investigation.

As if on cue, an uproar ensued in the rest of the Gulf media. A few hours later, the same Qatari news agency said it was hacked and the quotes were fake news. The FBI and Britain's National Crime Agency eventually traced the breach to freelance Russian hackers, believed to have been hired by parties in the UAE or Saudi Arabia.[5] Investigators said the hackers were unlikely to have accepted the assignment without the blessing of the Putin government; Moscow certainly had plenty to gain from throwing Molotov cocktails into America's plans for a so-called Arab NATO led by Saudi Arabia.

As the investigation was underway, Gulf media descended into a war of words. "Since its inception, Qatar has been an emirate of coups, treachery and playing with fire," declared Saudi Arabia's *Al Eqtisadiya* in one typical broadside. "Bark as you wish, Qatar won't change its principles," Qatar's *Al Raya* newspaper responded.[6]

Saudi Arabia and its allies soon announced a complete diplomatic and economic break with Qatar. Land, sea and air ties were cut. "[T]his decisive decision" was being taken because of "grave violations" such as "adopting various terrorist and sectarian groups" including "the Muslim Brotherhood Group, Daesh (ISIS) and al Qaeda," the Saudis said in their declaration.[7] Qatari citizens had 48 hours to get out of Saudi and the Emirates and vice versa. Most of Qatar's food and supplies were from, or trans-shipped through, Saudi Arabia and the Emirates. That was now rotting on the border. A few days later, the Turkish parliament rammed through approval for its military to deploy troops to Qatar, with which it had a mutual defense treaty. "We will not allow Qatar to be beaten up," a senior Turkish official was quoted saying.[8]

And the incendiary media battle continued. Influential Saudi columnist Abdul Rahman Al-Rashed, adopting one of the American president's favorite characterizations, called Qatar's emir a "nut job."[9] Qatar has "chosen to ride the tiger of terrorism and extremism," said

UAE foreign minister Anwar Mohammed Gargash.[10] His government announced that anyone expressing sympathy for Qatar online faced up to fifteen years in prison.[11] Influential Emiratis even started an anti-Qatar Twitter campaign that included sexually suggestive memes involving Sheikha Mozah bint Nasser al-Missned, the mother of the emir.

The speed with which other Gulf news organizations had begun attacking the Qatari emir was striking. Editors in the Gulf faced jail for criticizing the heads of state of other Gulf countries. They would never have dared do so without the blessing of the palace. Yet they began firing their broadsides against the Qatari emir just twenty minutes after the hacked story appeared—as if the whole thing had been planned in advance. Which it had. "They made it very clear to us how this is to be reported," a journalist at a Saudi-owned television channel told me, referring to the Saudi government.

It was all part of a multi-million-dollar information war between the former Gulf allies that involved dueling tranches of leaked e-mails, shouting matches between the rival foreign ministers and, ultimately, a battle for influence that filled the coffers of lobbyists, think tanks and PR firms, and was visible in pro-Qatar billboards and newspaper ads and anti-Qatar websites and infomercials that appeared in Washington, New York and London.

Mixed Signals

Gulf unity was the cornerstone of the new United States-backed alliance. When he was in Riyadh, Trump had what seemed to have a positive meeting with the emir of Qatar. "Qatar, which hosts the U.S. Central Command, is a crucial strategic partner," the president told the summit.[12] However, immediately after the siege was announced, he seemed to take credit with what Marwan Bishara, an analyst for Qatar-based Al Jazeera, called a "hate tweet": "During my recent trip to the Middle East I stated that there can no longer be funding of Radical Ideology. Leaders pointed to Qatar—look!"[13]

The State Department and the Pentagon were horrified. The U.S. ambassador to Qatar tweeted her praise for Qatar's "strong efforts" to stem the flow of money to extremists;[14] Secretary of State Rex Tillerson called for negotiations between the feuding Arab cousins;[15] and the U.S. Central Command, which operates America's huge military base there, said it was "grateful" to Qatar.[16] Trump then doubled down. "So good to see the Saudi Arabia visit with the King and 50 countries already paying off. They said they would take a hard line on funding.... Perhaps this will be the beginning of the end to the horror of terrorism!"[17]

Hours after Tillerson called for an easing of the blockade, Trump made clear he wanted nothing of the kind. "The nation of Qatar, unfortunately, has historically been a funder of terrorism at a very high level, and in the wake of that conference, nations came together and spoke to me about confronting Qatar over its behavior," he told a Rose Garden news conference. "I decided, along with Secretary of State Rex Tillerson, our great generals and military people, the time had come to call on Qatar to end its funding—they have to end that funding, and its extremist ideology in terms of funding."[18]

Within a few days, in a striking bit of policy whiplash, the president was on the phone with the Qatari emir and the Saudi king offering to get everyone together at the White House to make nice because Gulf unity was "critical to defeating terrorism and promoting regional stability."[19]

But the threads that tied together decades of U.S. Middle East policy were already beginning to unravel.

The Emirate That Roared

Qatar and Saudi Arabia had a long history of animosity. On the surface, they were Gulf allies. But under Sheikh Tamim's father, Hamad bin Khalifa al-Thani, Qatari foreign policy had diverged from that of the Saudis, most recently in the case of the Arab Spring, when they each backed different sides. They had been also at loggerheads over crises from South Asia to West Africa as Qatar pursued an interventionist foreign policy designed by the emir's father, who ousted his own father in a bloodless coup in 1995, to allow his tiny country to punch outside its weight class and stand up to the Saudis by pursuing a set of diplomatic objects that included "converting financial strength into political influence, helping to bring down hostile regimes, gaining economic benefits and promoting its Islamist agenda."[20]

Money was at the basis of some of these disputes, as in the West African country of Mali, where the European Parliament reported Qatar had been funding the government's war against rebels in order "to take control of the hydrocarbon resources of an emergent state of Azawad on the Malian territory."[21] The policy differences were highlighted every day on the airwaves of Al Jazeera, the Qatar-based satellite channel that regularly criticized Saudi Arabia. Further angering the Saudis and their Emirati allies was the fact that Qatar also had a working relationship with Iran, with which it shared vast natural gas fields. Their differences also extended to Syria, where they had supported different rebel groups. Qatar had recently enraged the Saudis and Emiratis by paying hundreds of millions of dollars to Shi'ite militants in Iraq to secure the release of a group of kidnapped Qataris and another $200 million to Sunni militants in Syria to allow humanitarian aid to reach civilians.[22]

Saudi accusations that Qatar supported terrorism were just slightly problematic. "While entities from across the Gulf and Iran have been guilty of advancing extremism, those in Saudi Arabia are undoubtedly at the top of the list," according to a report issued by Britain's Henry Jackson Society a few weeks after the siege began.[23] Yet, despite the decades of backbiting, Saudi and Qatar also cooperated, most recently in Yemen, where Qatari troops were fighting alongside the Saudis in Yemen until they were ejected from the coalition after the siege was imposed.

For the U.S., relations with Saudi Arabia and Qatar involved "a balancing act," a diplomat with deep experience in the region told me. "Both are deeply flawed. People in both countries have been implicated in supporting terror, both regimes are guilty of flagrant human rights violations, both are close to bad guys we don't like, but they are also important pillars of U.S. policy in the region."

When Iran's parliament was stormed at roughly the same time the siege of Qatar was imposed, Iran blamed the Saudis and their Arab allies. "Terror-sponsoring despots threaten to bring the fight to our homeland. Proxies attack what their masters despise most: the seat of democracy," Iranian foreign minister Javad Zarif tweeted.[24] But then the conspiracy theories appeared in the region's media. Inevitably, one involved the Middle East's favorite bogeyman, America. Some articles pointed out that the CIA had just appointed as head of Iran operations an agent known as the Dark Prince, who led the search for bin Laden and directed the drone program that killed thousands of people—good and bad.[25] Perhaps this was the inaugural operation of his new assignment? Or Tehran might want the Muslim world to think that.

It would later emerge that ISIS really did manage to stage the attack in Tehran, posting video of the slaughter in progress. The attack was a morale booster for ISIS as it was losing its hold on Mosul and Raqqa, its two greatest conquests, carried out with the goal of provoking an all-out war between Sunnis and Shiites—an apocalyptic objective far dearer to it than confrontation with the West.

13 BETWEEN IRAN AND A HARD PLACE

Never interrupt your enemy when he is making a mistake.

Napoléon Bonaparte

As the wheels came off Donald Trump's grand Muslim anti-terror coalition there was a quiet sigh of relief in Pakistan.[1]

The Riyadh summit "has widened the sectarian divide in the Muslim world," reported *Dawn*, Pakistan's leading newspaper. "The Saudi-led Islamic Military Alliance against terrorism may have some counter-militancy aims, but it is also increasingly clear that it has been conceived by the kingdom as an anti-Iran alliance," the paper said in an editorial entitled "Dangerous Alliance."[2]

America's bare-chested, muscle-flexing entry into the Middle East's seminal religious and geographic divide had left Pakistan—a Sunni-majority country with a sizable Shiite population—in a no-win situation. After all, while Saudi Arabia provided billions in aid to Muslim Pakistan, Iran was right next door.

The optics and timing of the Saudi summit were particularly challenging for Pakistan. Less than two weeks earlier the head of Iran's armed forces had threatened military strikes on Pakistan after ten Iranian soldiers were killed by Pakistan-based Sunni militants. "Iran's eastern border regions with Pakistan have become a safe haven for training and equipping terrorists recruited by Saudi Arabia and supported by the United States," the Iran News Agency quoted Chief of Army Staff Maj. Gen. Mohammad Hossein Bagheri as saying. "We will not tolerate this situation in the joint borders. If continued, we will hit the terrorists' safe havens anywhere they are."[3]

Making matters worse, Pakistan had recently agreed to allow its former top general to command the military wing of the new Saudi-led alliance. The fact that this was now an overtly anti-Iranian military force was a real problem for Islamabad policymakers. "We have to walk a very fine line between Saudi Arabia and Iran," a senior government official told me. "It can be quite dangerous." It was dangerous for everyone else, as well, since Pakistan happened to have nuclear weapons. Iran might not be willing to strike directly at Saudi Arabia, but Pakistan would be a tempting place to send a message via its proxies if Islamabad didn't play its cards right. After all, Iran and Saudi Arabia were already fighting proxy wars in Syria and Yemen. What was one more?

Even if Iran's military kept its weapons sheathed, there were plenty of other ways Tehran could cause headaches for Pakistan by cutting trade; killing plans to supply electricity, desperately needed in a country suffering twelve-to-fourteen-hour-a-day power cuts; and, most crucially, stirring up trouble in the restive province of Baluchistan, on the shared border, as well as via Pakistani Shi'ite militant groups that could be found in every corner of the country.

Adding humiliation to diplomatic discomfort, Pakistani prime minister Nawaz Sharif—who reportedly practiced his speech while flying to Riyadh—was not allowed to address the Saudi-American summit, presumably because the Saudis knew he would make a case for his country's difficult geopolitical position. The snub angered many Pakistanis.

"Trump's speech itself further added salt to the wounds," wrote columnist Kunware Khuldune Shahid in *The Diplomat*. "Not only did the U.S. president identify India as a victim of terror, he failed to acknowledge Pakistan as one."[4] Trump also refused a private meeting with Sharif, rubbing in the salt. That's probably because the Americans wanted Pakistan, widely accused of cynically supporting militants, to do more to crack down on terrorist groups operating inside the country. Ironically, the militant organizations Washington was most concerned about were Sunni groups often spawned in the extremist Saudi-funded madrassas that littered Pakistan, not Shi'ite militias supported by Iran. But why let complicated facts ruin a good versus evil policy?

The diplomatic bloodletting among erstwhile Gulf brethren gave hope to some observers in Pakistan that the so-called Muslim NATO, haughtily announced by the Saudis without much consultation with its erstwhile allies, might amount to little more than a Trump photo op. "One summit meeting does not create an organization," Ambassador Ali Sarwar Naqvi of the Institute for International Strategic Studies in Islamabad told me as we sat in his office near Parliament. "This was already nebulous. This was all very much in the air, nothing concrete. I don't think this alliance has much of a future."

With the Arabs once more lashing out at one another in what had become a family feud on steroids, that appeared to be a pretty good bet. A Foreign Ministry spokesman told me there were no plans to follow in the footsteps of Saudi vassals like Yemen and the Maldives and cut ties with Qatar.

"The overriding imperative is that Islamabad keeps a healthy distance between itself and the conflicts raging across the Arab world," the *Express Tribune* said in an editorial the morning after the break. "This is not our fight."[5] That was easier said than done. The newspaper reported that at a private meeting in Riyadh shortly after the siege began, King Salman demanded Sharif take sides: "Are you with us or with Qatar?"[6]

The Good, the Bad, the Taliban

Donald Trump's first tweet of 2018 wasn't about Russia, the wall or "Crooked Hillary." It was about Pakistan.

> The United States has foolishly given Pakistan more than 33 billion dollars in aid over the last 15 years, and they have given us nothing but lies & deceit. They give safe haven to the terrorists we hunt in Afghanistan, with little help. No more![7]

As with the Middle East, the reality of what was going on in Pakistan was a little too complicated to fit in a 280-character tweet. Pakistan had long played both ends against the middle, training and equipping a variety of extremist groups to do its bidding in Kashmir and Afghanistan, allowing some of those groups to maintain bases inside Pakistan and providing cover to some extremists sought by the United States—such as Osama bin Laden—while also reigning in militant groups operating against the interests of the Pakistani state.

A Pakistani journalist friend provided a snapshot of the complicated dynamics of the Pakistani military's relationship with the militants. In 2007, the year former prime minister Benazir Bhutto was assassinated and 5,000 people were killed in suicide attacks, my friend was assigned to do a story on how devout Muslims in the military ranks were handling the task of killing militants fighting in the name of Islam. In the militant-held Swat Valley, he encountered the commander of a unit who was drowning his sorrows in Scotch. Days before, this lieutenant colonel had taken a handful of his most loyal troops to attack a militant camp. As they assembled on a ridge overlooking the militants, his troops hold him they would not follow him into battle. "This is not a just war," they told him. "We cannot fight them." A few years later, my friend met another Army officer who told him he was also in Swat at that time. Over beer one night, he tearfully recounted the story of another battle in Swat. On a cold winter night, he led a group of 100 of his best soldiers into battle against the militants. Six died. The officer still felt responsible. "They died for me, not a cause or the government," he told my friend, who summed up for me the lesson. "One story is, people left because they were not prepared to kill other Muslims; the other story is that people died," my friend told me. "Neither fought for the government. Neither gave their lives for the Army or for the idea of Pakistan."

When seven Taliban militants strapped with explosives stormed into a school for the children of Pakistani Army personnel in the border city of Peshawar in 2014, it marked the beginning of a shift in mindset on the part of that country's military and civilian leadership. There could no longer be any distinction between "good and bad Taliban," Pakistani prime minister Nawaz Sharif insisted, referring to the government's controversial policy of supporting militant groups in Afghanistan and Kashmir but battling their offshoots operating on Pakistani soil. "Terrorism and the fight against extremism is our fight. To defeat it we must unite to defeat terrorists and root out their hideouts ... All parliamentary and political leaders will decide a national consensus to defeat terrorism."[8]

The truth of the matter lay somewhere between Trump's outrage and Sharif's feigned policy reversal. "The jihadis have, since 1989, been an instrument of Pakistani policy for regional influence," according to Hussain Haqqani, former Pakistani ambassador to the U.S.[9] Sharif himself admitted as much. In an interview after he was forced from office in a corruption scandal, he lamented the fact that the country had "two or three parallel governments," at least one of which, the military, was supporting select militant groups. "Militant organizations are active. Call them non-state actors, should we allow them to cross the border and kill 150 people in Mumbai? Explain it to me."[10]

Despite that cynical sleight of hand, there was no escaping the fact that the 2014 attack on the Army school in Peshawar had jolted the Pakistani body politic, civilian and military alike. Militants had massacred more than 130 students, most of them children of Pakistani military officers, along with about twenty adult teachers and staff. The *Tehrik-i-Taliban* (TTP)—the Pakistani branch of the *Taliban*—claimed responsibility for the attack, which was carried out by three Arabs, two Afghans and a Chechen. "We have killed all the children in the auditorium. What do we do now?" the attackers were recorded saying in the chilling transcript of a phone call to their handler "Skip," released by the Pakistani military. His response: "Wait for the army people, kill them before blowing yourself."[11]

The Peshawar Army school massacre appeared to be payback for a devastating assault on militant strongholds in the tribal areas along the Afghan border that the government had launched six months earlier after a militant attack on the Karachi airport. Some 30,000 troops had poured into Waziristan in Operation Zarb-e-Azb (Cutting Strike), a bid to reclaim the region from the TTP and other militant groups, driving them back across the border into Afghanistan. The government ultimately claimed to have killed more than 3,500 militants, shut down 7,500 bombing-making factories and seized huge quantities of "modern weapons ... which they had stolen from American troops."[12]

"Due to [*Zarb-e-Azb*], the nation regained peace that was snatched by terrorists and anti-state elements," Prime Minister Nawaz Sharif somewhat optimistically told Pakistanis on the second anniversary of the massive operation.[13] However, in the process, the Army created almost a million internal refugees and killed an unknown number of civilians, radicalizing a new crop of extremist recruits. "If our women and children die as martyrs, your children will not escape," Umar Mansoor, the handler behind the school attack, said addressing the Pakistani military in a video posted online. "We will fight against you in such a style that you attack us, and we will take revenge on innocents."[14]

TTP leader Maulana Fazlullah conveyed a similar message: "Our men attacked the school and killed children of Army personnel—not civilians. They asked about their identity before killing them. These people will always be our target and we will kill them in the streets, markets, everywhere." Fazlullah was the man accused of ordering the attempted murder of schoolgirl activist Malala Yousafzai, who was shot in the head but survived. In the spring of 2018, the U.S. would put a $5 million bounty on Fazlullah's head, the same day American drones killed his son and other key TTP leaders. That spring, Malala, now a Nobel Peace Prize winner, made her first visit back to Pakistan since she was shot. The Urdu press, a mirror of the rising tide of anti-American sentiment inflamed by Trump's rhetoric about Pakistan, pilloried her as a patsy of the West.

City on Edge

Waziristan wasn't the only part of Pakistan the military set out to purge of militants, a fact that further muddied the Trump administration's narrative about Pakistani collusion with militants. The Army Rangers were in the midst of a years-long campaign to restore law and order in the commercial port of Karachi, where kidnappings, targeted killings and bombings had become the norm. The city was controlled by the Muttahida Quami Movement (MQM), a political party-cum-crime organization at odds with the rest of the country's establishment and which the military had repeatedly accused of being supported by India's intelligence services. Until the Army arrived in force, armed MQM militants controlled whole sections of the city, which was also riddled with operatives of al Qaeda, ISIS and countless other militant groups. Karachi's mayor, an MQM official, would eventually be jailed on thirty-nine terrorism-related charges and run for re-election from prison.

It was in Karachi that *Wall Street Journal* reporter Daniel Pearl had been kidnapped by British-Pakistani militant Omar Saeed Sheikh and ultimately beheaded by alleged 9/11 mastermind Khalid Sheikh Mohammed. I was reminded of that every time I entered my Karachi hotel, which was located directly across the street from the restaurant where Pearl was last seen.

In 2015, on one of my periodic visits to Karachi, the city was particularly on edge. "We live in a kingdom of fear, fortified by religious extremism and intolerance," columnist Ghazi Salahiddin wrote in *The News on Sunday* the day I arrived.[15] Such hyperbole reinforced the stereotypes about Pakistan. But sometimes, stereotypes contain more than a grain of truth. Karachi was Pakistan's business and media capital. It was also one of the most violent cities in the world. One indication: the crime log in the *Express Tribune* newspaper was subtitled "Grenade Attacks and Encounters." Those were the kinds of "encounters" you didn't want to have.

One day when I checked, it included the ambush of a convoy carrying the city's chief of counterterrorism; the attempted assassination of another government official; nine other targeted killings; a grenade attack on a bus stop; a shoot-out that killed four armed militants; and a man who had been burned alive by an angry crowd after he shot a policeman.

Some of the violence involved crime gangs; some battles between political factions or religious sects. A wave of targeted assassinations in Karachi in the spring of 2015 had shaken Pakistan's intelligentsia. Killings included a university professor, the owner of a bookshop that hosted frequent free speech events, and the marketing manager of one of the largest media groups. An American medical school administrator was also shot and wounded.

Among the educated elite, discussions inevitably included speculation about who was behind the killings. As columnist Saroop Ijaz wrote in the *Express Tribune*, "Public and private conversations in Pakistan have been reduced to obituaries." Conspiracy theories abounded; the more Machiavellian, the better. They could make your head spin. A dominant line of speculation involved the rebellious province of Baluchistan, where the military had used brutal tactics to put down an insurgency.

China was building a major port there, which threatened the efficacy of rival ports in Iran, India and the Arabian Gulf, and gave the Chinese Navy a base less than 200 miles from the strategic Straits of Hormuz. That was of serious concern to U.S. military strategists. Each of those governments was alleged to be stirring the Baluchistan pot.

Islamist militants. Sectarian rivalries. A "foreign hand." Unnamed "dark forces." Circles within circles. Shadows within shadows. All this added to the complex geopolitical matrix that Trump had reduced to that New Year's tweet.

And this was just one Pakistani city.

Blasphemy

Another sign of the growing power of the extremists—and the threat they posed to the Pakistani government—was the 2011 assassination of Punjab governor Salmaan Taseer. When he called for the blasphemy laws to be reformed, the extremists accused him of blasphemy just for suggesting that. The killing—by his own bodyguard—took place at an Islamabad cafe.

In the spring of 2016, on a visit to Islamabad, I went out to dinner with an acquaintance. When I returned, the street in front of my hotel was barricaded with metal cargo crates stacked three levels high. Heavily armed riot police were taking up positions behind the barricades and overlooking the street beyond the crates.

I had seen something similar a few years before, when the government announced it had executed Taseer's assassin after he lost an appeal. The court's ruling was an indication of the way religious extremism was shaping Pakistani society. The High Court confirmed that Muslims had the right to kill blasphemers, referring to a Hadith that quoted the Prophet Muhammad saying, "Kill the person who abuses a Prophet and whip by stripes the one who abuses my companions." However, the court said the real issue was that Islam did not allow such an act "without any proof and merely on perceptions. This act of appellant cannot be termed as Islamic and moral."[16] The Supreme Court upheld that ruling, saying the assassin, Mumtaz Qadri, had violated a passage in the Qur'an by acting on "hearsay without getting his information ascertained, verified."[17] Two months later, Qadri was hanged in a secret location. The news galvanized ultraconservative religion groups who seized the highway connecting Islamabad with the military capital, Rawalpindi.

Now, it was happening again. This time the issue was a change to the oath of office taken by government officials. The new version would contain fewer references to the Prophet Muhammad. The protesters claimed the change was blasphemous. After a three-week stand-off, accompanied by demonstrations in Lahore and Karachi, the government capitulated. The law minister responsible for the bill resigned and taped a video in which he groveled to the protestors, swearing, "I love *Hazrat* (Presence) Muhammad, Peace Be Upon Him, from the depth of my heart. My family and I are prepared to lay down our lives for the honor and sanctity of Prophet Muhammad." In another sign of the power of the fundamentalists, the government asked them to promise that they would not issue a fatwa ordering the death of the law minister.

China

Little of this seemed to have been factored into the Trump administration's decision to slash military aid to Pakistan by $1.1 billion in the weeks after his tweet, which left many Pakistanis baffled. Just a year before, he told

Pakistani prime minister Nawaz Sharif, "You are a terrific guy. You are doing amazing work which is visible in every way," adding that he would "would love to come to a fantastic country, fantastic place of fantastic people," according to a read-out released by Sharif's office.[18]

"We do not have any alliance," Pakistan foreign minister Khawaja Muhammad Asif told the *Wall Street Journal* after the January 2018 tweet. "This is not how allies behave." He accused America of turning Pakistan into a "whipping boy" and described the U.S. as a "friend who always betrays."[19]

Amid Trump's mixed signals, more and more Pakistanis were looking north. That was a message I heard repeatedly in Islamabad's corridors of power. The $62 billion China-Pakistan Economic Corridor, designed to become an express lane to China from the Chinese-built port in Baluchistan, was already having a visible impact on Pakistan, right down to hotels adding congee and dumplings to their breakfast buffets to cater to the Chinese businesspeople filling their rooms.

"They've come in, in a massive way. The [Pakistani] state is reorienting with the Chinese," *Dawn* columnist Cyril Almeida told me. "You have the political, the foreign policy, the military, the bureaucracy, the sort of infrastructure building things, they're all going that way." The chairman of the Karachi Stock Exchange, Munir Kamal, saw China as more important to Pakistan than the U.S. in the long run. "We are converting the Chinese political and military relationship to an economic relationship," he said as we sat on the terrace of the colonial-era Sindh Club.

"We see China as a good friend because China never tried to influence Pakistan," added Ali Sarwar Naqvi, former Pakistani ambassador to the UN. "They never tried to export communism to Pakistan. They respected our system, our way of life and never interfered. In this, people find the U.S.—and now Donald Trump—at fault."

Existential Threat

If the White House's misreading of Pakistan's complex internal politics wasn't doing enough damage, the simplification of South Asian religion-based regional rivalries threatened to further complicate U.S. efforts to extricate itself from Afghanistan. In a speech outlining his strategy toward the war, Trump called on India "to help us more with Afghanistan, especially in the area of economic assistance and development."[20]

Those words struck directly at Pakistan's rawest nerve, the threat posed by India. Pakistan was created in 1947 when the British partitioned India; the Northwest became a Muslim-majority country and the rest a Hindu-dominated nation. Pakistani intelligence had fostered the rise of Afghan and Kashmiri militant groups to avoid being encircled by its rival. Trump wasn't far off. Pakistan was "housing the very terrorists that we are fighting."[21] But it was also true that Pakistan feared an Afghanistan aligned with India, with which the Kabul government was already close. Until Pakistan was convinced it would not be trapped in a Hindu pincer move, Islamabad was unlikely to give up support for the militants.

To Pakistan, the dispute with the U.S. over whether it was doing enough to fight terror was a strategic issue. The confrontation between South Asia's largest Muslim-majority country and its Hindu-dominated rival was existential.

14 RETURN OF THE OTTOMANS

From the ashes, a fire shall be woken, A light from the shadows shall spring.

J. R. R. TOLKIEN
The Fellowship of the Ring

February 2018

The Qatar Airways Boeing 777-300 taxied to a halt in front of the gleaning terminal at Doha International Airport. The nonstop flight from LAX had taken almost sixteen hours. Getting from my home in Eastern Washington state to Los Angeles via Seattle had tacked on another six hours. I was ready for a hot shower and a comfortable bed.

Normally when I went to Qatar, I took Emirates Airlines, the flag carrier of the United Arab Emirates. It flew non-stop from Seattle to Dubai, cutting six hours off the flight. Not this time. The continuing siege made that impossible.

America's allies were still at each other's throats and the damage was spreading. A new fault line had opened in the Middle East, pitting Saudi Arabia, Egypt and its Gulf partners against Qatar and America's NATO ally Turkey. Meanwhile, Qatar was being driven deeper into the embrace of Iran. As a Lebanese newspaper put it, "The gates of the Gulf are opening wide for a 'cluster' conflict."[1]

Most troubling for U.S. policymakers who understood the region was the fact that the fissures encouraged by recent U.S. statements opened the way for Turkey to step into the breach in a new activist role that threatened to further upend American strategy.

Turkey's increasingly autocratic Islamist president, Recep Erdoğan, aspired to return to the glory days of the Ottoman Empire, when his country dominated the Middle East. Turkey had largely been exiled from the Arab world since the end of World War I. The Syrian conflict, where Turkey joined the battle against ISIS, and a 2014 alliance with Qatar allowed Erdoğan to put boots on Arab sand for the first time in almost a century. Turkey and Qatar had similar policies toward Iran and the Muslim Brotherhood. The Saudi-Qatar rift gave Erdoğan the opportunity to project his influence into the heart of the Arab nation and play the role of savior of an Arab state. A few dozen Turkish troops were dispatched to the tiny emirate, where Turkey already maintained a small military base with several hundred soldiers.

The idea that Qatar would need Turkish troops to prevent a Saudi/Emirati invasion seemed unthinkable, but regional experts speculated that Riyadh had designs on Qatar's $320 billion sovereign wealth fund to help refill the dwindling Saudi coffers.[2] Qatari officials later insisted that an invasion was only averted through the threatened intervention of the Turks. American officials would later tell me that pressure from the State Department and the Pentagon was at least as important as Turkey's troop deployment in preventing the conflict.

The House of Saud eyed Erdoğan's growing ambition with concern. A year after Erdoğan's exercise in muscle flexing, Crown Prince Mohammed bin Salman accused Turkey of trying to "reinstate the Islamic Caliphate,"[3] said Iran was seeking to "export revolution"[4] and warned an "evil triad" had been formed by the "Ottomans, Iran and the terrorist organizations."[5] Most U.S. news organizations reported that MBS criticized "the Turks," missing not only the actual reference to "the Ottomans" but also the historic significance of the comment. This was about leadership of the Islamic world, which the Saudis saw as their birthright.

History made them hyper-sensitive to Erdoğan's aspirations: They knew that it was only the British defeat of the Ottoman Empire and the discovery of oil that had allowed them to transform their geographic control of the holy cities into political control of Islam. Before that, as Oxford scholar Faisal Devji has noted, "Muslim kings rarely visited Mecca and Medina. Instead, those cities served as places of exile for their enemies."[6] "In the eyes of the Saudi crown prince, Turkey and its president, Recep Tayyip Erdoğan, are exploiting all the crises to serve their interests and are thus practically pulling the rug of the Islamic leadership away from Saudi Arabia," said London-based *Rai al-Youm* in an article about MBS's comments.[7]

Erdoğan was also exploiting the Syrian crisis to crush Turkey's ancient enemy the Kurds. Memories are long in the Middle East. History informs modern decision-making. Kurdistan was divided between Turkey, Syria, Iraq and Iran when the Western powers carved up the Middle East. The Kurds had been fighting for an independent state ever since. Turkish troops were now advancing across Kurdistan, ostensibly with the mission of defeating ISIS, but driving back Kurdish forces in the process, even as Erdoğan reminisced about the glories of the Turkish-controlled Ottoman Empire. "The Republic of Turkey, just like our previous states that are a continuation of one another, is also a continuation of the Ottomans," Erdoğan said in remarks at a ceremony marking the centenary of the death of Ottoman Sultan Abdulhamid II, who died four years before the collapse of the Ottoman Empire.[8]

The Turkish offensive against the Kurds meant Erdoğan's government was turning its weapons on the very Kurdish militias the U.S. was increasingly relying on in the war against ISIS. And Turkey's influence was rising even as the White House grew ever more reliant on the Saudis.

"The Turkey of Erdoğan ... smartly pulled a number of other files away from the Saudi Crown Prince," *Rai al-Youm* reported, using the Arab term for political relationships or policies. "This has practically flipped over the leadership equation in the Islamic world and the balance is now tipping in favor of the Ottoman state or Ottomans, as per the term used by the controversial young prince."[9]

Jerusalem

Further complicating inter-Arab/Muslim relations and strengthening Turkey's leadership claim was Trump's controversial decision to recognize Jerusalem as Israel's capital, which followed news that MBS and Trump son-in-law and adviser Jared Kushner had worked out a deal to impose what Hamas leader Isma'il Haniyah sarcastically labeled "the deal of the century" to end the Israel-Palestine conflict.[10] The former upended fifty years of U.S. policy, while the latter called for an autonomous Palestinian entity that did not have sovereignty or Jerusalem as its capital. Palestinians in exile would not have a right of return and few of the existing Israeli settlements would be removed.[11]

The so-called "Arab street"—the Arab public—was horrified by the news. The response from Arab governments underlined the hypocrisy of those undemocratic regimes that had long paid little more than lip service to the Palestinians. Most issued carefully scripted, though in some cases sclerotic, statements. "The official Egyptian reaction to the decision of President Donald Trump on acknowledging Jerusalem as the capital of Israel and launching the measures of moving the U.S. embassy from Tel Aviv to the occupied city was a faint one," Lebanon's *Al Akhbar* newspaper reported.[12]

Even that "faint" criticism was duplicitous. *The New York Times* obtained recordings of phone calls from a top Egyptian intelligence officer to influential Egyptian talk show hosts telling them to subtly make comments on the air arguing that it was time to bow to the inevitable and recognize Jerusalem as Israeli's capital. "How is Jerusalem different from Ramallah, really?" Capt. Ashraf al-Kholi was heard telling one of the TV hosts, arguing that the Palestinians should accept the West Bank town as their capital.[13]

President Abdel Fattah el-Sisi was furious that the ruse had been exposed and fired the general in charge of intelligence. The reality was that the incident was just the latest example of the disconnect between public statements and secret policy when it came to Israel. In recent years, Arab regimes, including the Saudis, had been secretly meeting with Israeli intelligence agents and policymakers to coordinate their response to ISIS and lay the groundwork for the secret deal.

That created another opening for Turkey. "Those who believe that they are the owners of Jerusalem today will not find a tree to hide behind tomorrow," Erdoğan defiantly asserted after Trump's Jerusalem announcement.[14] The same day, a newspaper considered a mouthpiece of his Justice & Development Party published an article arguing for the formation of a Muslim army to confront Israel. "The military power of the members of the Organization of Islamic Cooperation is wide and strong enough to envelop Israel," the paper, *Yeni Safak*, said, noting the importance of Pakistan's nuclear weapons.[15]

Bear in the Room

Vladimir Putin was the biggest beneficiary of this chaos in American Middle East policy. In the final years of the Obama administration, Russia had aggressively projected itself into the void created by the absence of American leadership. It strengthened ties with Iran and stepped up its military involvement in defending the regime of Bashar al-Assad in Syria, which had been its last toehold in the Arab world.

A survey of Arab youth conducted weeks after Trump's inauguration found that Russia was now considered the Arab world's top ally, with the percentage of youth who believed America held that honor dropping precipitously from 2016.[16] Now Russia was finding even more space in the new cracks being formed by the U.S. administration's actions. No government had been more opposed to Moscow's involvement in the region than Saudi Arabia. But less than one year after Donald Trump first set foot in the region, Mohammed bin Salman told reporters in Egypt, "Russia enjoys strong relations with Egypt and Saudi Arabia, and what it is gaining from its Arab relations is much greater than [what it is gaining] from its relationship with Iran."[17]

Meanwhile, Saudi Arabia signed $65 billion in bilateral trade deals with China and began harmonizing its development plan with China's Belt and Road initiative; Egypt agreed to a Suez Canal Cooperation Zone with China; and Chinese capital was funding an $11 billion Sino-Oman Industrial City.[18]

By the spring of 2018, in the eyes of the Arab public only Israel posed a greater threat than the U.S. Their view of Russia and China was far more favorable.[19]

Much the same was happening in South Asia. In the summer of 2018, intelligence chiefs from Russia, China and Iran met in Pakistan to strategize over Afghanistan and the broader region. The "Great Game"— the historic rivalry between Russia and the West over Central Asia— had been turned on its head. "Pakistan's army is frantically mending its historically weak ties with the Russian army and making progress through defense diplomacy at a dizzying pace by making a pivot to Russia instead of its traditionally close military ties with the US," Britain's Royal United Services Institute (RUSI) reported.[20] A few months after the spy chiefs' meeting, U.S. Secretary of State Mike Pompeo made a brief three-hour visit to Islamabad before jetting off to New Delhi. The following day, the Chinese foreign minister arrived in town and stayed for three days. The contrast was not lost on the Pakistanis.

The Russian bear was on the prowl. China was on the march. The Ottoman Empire was attempting to rise from the dead. The chimera of a monolithic Muslim enemy continued to fade. So did American influence.

PART FOUR

PROSPECTS—ISLAM BEYOND TRUMP

15 THE PRINCE

Everyone sees what you appear to be, few experience what you really are.

NICCOLÒ MACHIAVELLI
The Prince

April 2018

"Saudi Officials Apologise after Images of Scantily Clad Women Appear at Wrestling Event," read the headline in London's *Independent* newspaper.[1] Those were three phrases I never expected to see in the same sentence. The times they were a-changin', at least on the surface.

"We will end extremism very soon," Mohammed bin Salman vowed a few months after the Riyadh summit. He was now crown prince. In a soft coup, he had succeeded in convincing his father to purge Crown Prince Nayef, who American officials respected for his commitment to counterterrorism. Bin Salman promised to restore "moderate, open" Islam and eliminate extremist ideas "immediately."

> We will not spend the next 30 years of our lives dealing with destructive ideas. We will destroy them today ... returning to what we were before—a country of moderate Islam that is open to all religions and to the world.[2]

Cinemas, outlawed since the 1980s, were reopened. Music concerts were permitted. Women would soon be allowed to drive. And yes, WWE wrestling arrived in Saudi Arabia, albeit with a TV ad for women wrestlers that was supposed to have been blocked. It was all designed to bolster the crown prince's support among young, educated Saudis who chafed at the restrictions imposed by the Wahhabi clerics who had been so vital to the credibility of the royal family in generations past. And score even more points in the White House.

MBS introduced measures to make it more difficult for private individuals and foundations to funnel money to extremists, moved to detain dozens of hardline clerics, disbanded the religious police and ordered clerics to include positive comments about other religions in their sermons and fatwas. He also explained away the global Wahhabi project as Saudi Arabia's contribution to the Cold War. "We worked with whomever we could use to get rid of communism," he told an interviewer. "This is what America wanted us to do."[3]

Beyond steps to rein in religious extremism, MBS also announced that the country would embark on a modernization campaign, including a $500 billion city of the future powered by alternative energy and outfitted with drones and driverless cars, and where women would jog in sports bras. The project marked a "civilizational leap for humanity" and was closely tied to a major campaign to boost foreign investment in the kingdom.

The dramatic announcement had generated headlines around the world, not least in the United States. "Saudi Arabia's Arab Spring, at Last," gushed *The New York Times*. "If this virus of an antipluralistic, misogynistic Islam that came out of Saudi Arabia in 1979 can be reversed by Saudi Arabia, it would drive moderation across the Muslim world," wrote columnist Thomas Friedman. "The Saudi clerics have completely acquiesced."[4] Tell that to the Saudi Sports Authority, which apologized for those scantily clad women wrestlers in the face of outrage from the clerics and vowed "to eliminate anything that goes against the community's values."

Regional rivals dismissed MBS's grand plan as a hypocritical power play to bolster his American alliance and generate desperately needed foreign investment in the kingdom, further driving a wedge into the political and religious fissures splintering the region. MBS's rival for Muslim leadership, Turkish President Recep Erdoğan, was among the most scathing. 'You say 'moderate Islam', but you do not allow women to drive. Is there any restriction in Islam banning women from driving? There is no such thing."[5] To Erdoğan, the whole idea of "moderate Islam" was a Western plot: "What they really want to do is weaken Islam."

Luxury Prison

The Saudi crown prince's attempt to put a new face on his kingdom was immediately undermined by his round-up of 200 top Saudi businessmen, government officials, generals and princes, including members of a rival wing of the royal family. The Ritz Carlton in Riyadh was transformed into a luxury prison. The arrests were widely perceived as both a power grab by MBS and a financial shakedown. Among those jailed was Al-Waleed bin Talal, said to be the richest man in the world with a fortune estimated at almost $19 billion.

The "guests" at the Ritz Carlton were kept largely incommunicado, but tales of abuse and brutal torture would emerge. *The New York Times* reported that least one detainee, a major general, was apparently tortured to death. His neck had been twisted and his body was marked by burns. The officer had been an aide to an MBS rival, who was both the commander of the Saudi National Guard—formed from the remnants of the Ikhwan almost a century before—and son of King Abdullah, the Saudi ruler who preceded MBS's father, Salman, on the throne. Even after they were released, many of the detainees were forced to wear ankle bracelets to monitor their movements. Billions of dollars were reportedly signed over to the king by the detained businessmen as the price of freedom.[6]

The businessmen weren't MBS's only target. The day before the roundup, the crown prince summoned to Saudi Arabia Lebanese prime minister Rafiq Hariri, a Saudi ally who bin Salman had decided was not being tough enough on Hezbollah, Iran's Lebanese surrogate. Expecting a late-night outing to the desert, Hariri turned up at the palace in jeans and T-shirt only to find himself separated from his bodyguards, stripped of his cell phones, manhandled by Saudi guards and locked away in the palace.

Kept incommunicado, Hariri was handed a script and forced to go on television the next day to announce he was stepping down as prime minister, blaming threats from Iran for his decision. He spent the next month under house arrest in his Riyadh villa. Few in Lebanon or elsewhere believed the ruse. Eventually, after much international pressure, Hariri was allowed to return to Beirut where he abruptly withdrew his resignation, handing bin Salman his first public defeat and leaving Hezbollah and Iran more influential than ever in Lebanon. "The competition for power and influence in today's Middle East has changed significantly," Brian Katulis, a senior fellow at the Center for American Progress in Washington, told *The New York Times*, "and the Saudis are playing catch-up, with very mixed results."[7]

Mohammed bin Salman claimed the round-up of the businessmen was part of an anti-corruption and austerity drive tied to his reform campaign. However, news that the "reformist" prince had recently spent $1.3 billion to buy a 440-foot yacht, a 50,000-square-foot palace near Versailles and a da Vinci portrait of Christ made that sound a bit disingenuous. So did his response to a question about the extravagance. "As far as my private expenses, I'm a rich person and not a poor person. I'm not Gandhi or [Nelson] Mandela," he said in an interview with CBS's *60 Minutes*.[8]

Further complicating PR efforts around the reform campaign was the fact that Saudi Arabia was in the midst of a two-year "execution spree." More than 300 people—many of them Shi'a—would die by the executioner's sword before the end of 2017. As Amnesty International observed:

> The Saudi authorities have been using the death penalty as a tool to crush dissent and rein in minorities with callous disregard for human life.[9]

Activists, journalists and bloggers languished in the country's prisons, and the country sat at the bottom of Freedom House's global rankings, alongside North Korea, Equatorial Guinea and Turkmenistan.

> The regime relies on extensive surveillance, the criminalization of dissent, appeals to sectarianism, and public spending supported by oil revenues to maintain power.[10]

Such criticism was not well received by the thin-skinned young crown price and his acolytes. Barely three months after MBS ended a three-week, seven-city PR tour of the U.S., during which he met with media moguls and business titans, projecting an image of modernity and openness, the Canadian foreign minister sent a tweet criticizing the jailing of two prominent Saudi women's rights activists. Bin Salman responded by ordering the Canadian ambassador expelled from the kingdom, a freeze on Saudi investment in Canada, the suspension of flights to Canada by the national carrier and the immediate return of all Saudi students studying in Canada.

"Canada needs to fix its big mistake," insisted Saudi Foreign Minister Adel al-Jubeir,[11] as the Saudi media launched a bizarre propaganda campaign claiming that Canada is the world's worst oppressor of women and that 75 percent of detainees in Canadian prisons die before standing trial.[12]

That same week, a series of stories broke that made the Saudi defense of its human rights record seem somewhat disingenuous. Saudi fighter jets in Yemen rocketed a school bus en route to a summer camp, killing dozens of children;[13] the Associated Press revealed that the Saudi-led coalition in Yemen was working with Al Qaeda;[14] and Saudi authorities beheaded a Burmese convicted of murder, then crucified the body.[15]

Cultural Dance

MBS's ulterior motives—and lifestyle—aside, there was a huge constituency in Saudi Arabia for the kinds of reforms he proposed. Saudis were not all Wahhabi zealots funneling money to extremists. Far from it. The Kingdom suffered from a severe case of national schizophrenia. Liberal Saudis engaged in a constant cultural dance.

Muna Abu Sulayman was one of the highest-profile, most powerful and internationally minded women in Saudi Arabia. Over lunch in a Jeddah Lebanese restaurant a few years before the Saudi leadership change, we talked about the forces shaping Saudi society. A young couple sat nearby. Midway through our meal, another woman joined them. "Did you notice what just happened?" Muna asked me, subtly nodding toward the table. She obviously knew the group. The Saudi elite is relatively small. "Her brother arrived unexpectedly a few minutes ago. She is having lunch alone with a guy, which she is not allowed to do. That guy is her best friend's brother, so she ran out to call her friend to rush to the restaurant and make it look like the plan all along was for the three of them to have lunch, so she wasn't alone with the man."

On another occasion, I sat chatting with another female Saudi acquaintance at a Starbucks in the center of a popular shopping mall. At the edge of the seating area was a glass elevator. I watched with fascination as twenty-something Saudi men went up and down in the elevator holding slips of paper up to the glass. My companion noticed what I was watching. "They've written their mobile phone numbers on the paper, so the girls can call them," she explained. The same thing often happened in cars, particularly out in the desert on Thursday nights, the end of the Saudi workweek. Men would cruise up to cars containing women and their drivers and hold up their phone numbers. Sometimes, they would roll down the window and toss into the other car a cell phone preprogrammed with their own number.

"Mobile phones have changed everything," my acquaintance told me. "When I was young, we couldn't talk to boys. Now, with video on the cell phones, who knows what's going on. I don't know how I'm going to handle it when my girls reach that age."

The cultural dance was also a geographical dance. Both of those conversations took place in the Red Sea port of Jeddah. If I had sat alone with either woman in the capital Riyadh, in the more conservative Nejd heartland, we would likely have been harassed and possibly arrested by the *mutawwa'in*, the Committee for the Promotion of Virtue and the Prevention of Vice, the so-called religious police.

The contrast between the two cities was stark. When I was invited to a Saudi home in Riyadh, I almost never encountered the women. On the rare occasions I had a brief glance, they were always completely covered, either fully veiled so there was not even a glimpse of skin, or wearing a niqab, the stereotypical "veil" that included a cloth covering the nose and mouth so that only the eyes were visible. At dinner parties in Jeddah, women arrived covered in a flowing black abaya robe, but as soon as the door closed, the robes were handed to an attendant to reveal the latest Paris fashion.

Jeddah had plenty of other cultural contradictions. Effat University was an elite women's college in the city, which I visited periodically to advise on its communication curriculum. Wherever I went on the campus I was accompanied by a non-Saudi Arab female escort who walked twenty feet ahead of me shouting in Arabic, "*Rajul! Rajul!*" ("Man! Man!") to give the women a chance to cover before I came into view. A friend of mine, Egyptian-Canadian journalist Shereen el-Feki, worked with me on the project. She didn't need an escort. Shireen happened to be writing a book about sex in the Arab world and spent much time alone with the girls, who told her all about their piercings. At first Shereen thought they meant ear piercings. But they corrected her. They had piercings in *all sorts* of places, the giggling girls confided to Shereen. My friend was perplexed. "But why?" she asked. They obviously didn't have boyfriends or husbands to see them. "We show them off at the parties," they told her. All-girl parties.

Such contradictions weren't confined to Saudi Arabia. They could be found in all the Gulf states, where Salafism held sway. At Qatar University, where I also visited frequently, the campus was divided into separate sections for men and women. Qatari men were banned from the women's side, but foreign professors were allowed. The first time I visited, I walked into a lounge and I felt like I had accidently entered the ladies' room. Some of the girls had the hoods of their abayas down. Others who wore the niqab, which covered the lower half of their face, or the full burka face veil, had also removed those, so their faces were on full view. I backed out of the room, embarrassed. But I quickly learned there was no real issue with my seeing them "uncovered."

"What is forbidden," a young Qatari woman told me later, "is for a man our age to see us, especially someone who knows us."

The whole issue of the "veil" was one rife with controversy and misunderstanding. There are various references to women "covering" in the Qur'an and the Hadith, such as:

> O you Children of Adam! We have bestowed on you raiment to cover your shame as well as to be an adornment to you. (Qur'an 7:26)

And

> [T]he believing women ... should lower their gaze and guard their modesty; ... they should draw their veils over their bosoms and not display their beauty except to their husbands, [immediate relatives], or the servants whom their right hands possess, or male servants free of physical needs, or small children who have no sense of the shame of sex. (Qur'an 24:31)

I apparently fell into the "male servants free of physical needs" category, or at least I would be free of them if I tried anything. Many Muslims who did not believe women needed to cover their head or face interpreted the admonishments "cover your shame" and "draw veils over their breasts" as an instruction for basic modesty. The passages also had to be read in the context of the time and place. According to the Hadith, the caliph Abu Bakr actually had to make an announcement that "no naked person is allowed to perform the Tawaf [circumambulation] around the Ka'ba."[16]

Two Qatari women who were my students in Egypt told me that it wasn't until they came to Cairo that they learned that women covering was a cultural issue and not a religious requirement. That wasn't how most of the conservative Salafi clergy saw it. The head of the Mecca branch of the Saudi Committee for the Promotion of Virtue and the Prevention of Vice, Sheikh Ahmed al-Ghamdi, found that out the hard way. He was someone with impeccable religious credentials: the regional chief of a force so dogmatic in their Wahhabi beliefs that more than a dozen young girls died in 2002 when the *mutawwa'in* forced them back into a burning school and prevented rescue workers from entering because the girls were not properly attired. But when al-Ghamdi made public statements arguing that certain prohibitions, such as the degree to which a woman must be covered and the separation of the sexes were Arab cultural practices, not religious injunctions, he received an avalanche of threats.

"There is no doubt that this man is bad," said a member of the Supreme Judicial Council. "It is necessary for the state to assign someone to summon and torture him."[17]

16 THE AMERICANIZATION OF ISLAM

I, too, am America.

LANGSTON HUGHES
The Collected Poems of Langston Hughes

Even as U.S. foreign policy was being upended by stereotype, cliché and wishful thinking, Islam back in the United States was in the throes of an American revolution.[1]

If you were a Sunni Muslim in America in the 1970s and 1980s and wanted to study more about your religion, the odds are you ended up with a textbook written in Saudi Arabia. The Saudis called the shots when it came to Islamic orthodoxy. It was also likely that the imam in your local mosque was a Saudi, Egyptian or Pakistani who espoused a Saudi-inspired conservative brand of the religion and brought with him all his cultural and religious baggage.

By the time Donald Trump was elected president, those old-school clerics were yesterday's news for a growing number of American Muslims. If anything, the rise of the so-called Islamic State had only sped up that process. "The light of Islam will shine from the West," Dr. Farouq Khan of the Islamic Center of Long Island told me with pride in his voice. "And the reason is because we have all the constitutional protections. We have the freedom to write, freedom to speak and freedom to interpret." Unlike Muslims in much of the world.

There is no Vatican in Sunni Islam, the largest branch of the religion, but the chief clerics in Saudi Arabia and their counterparts at Egypt's Al Azhar University came awfully close. Or at least they once did. That was also changing. "We're no longer talking about a group of Egyptian,

Pakistani or Iranian sheikhs who are imported here to teach Americans about Islam," Omid Safi, a professor of Islamic Studies at Duke University, told me. "More American Muslims want to have someone who articulates their vision of Islam with an American accent."

A new generation of American Muslim religious leaders were making their voices heard. They were American born or arrived young and grew up in the U.S. Some were white converts, like Hamza Yusuf, co-founder of Zaytuna College, an Islamic university in Berkeley, California, and Suhaib Webb, a former hip-hop DJ from Oklahoma. Others were African Americans, such as Amina Wadud, who in 2005 became the first woman to lead Friday prayers in the U.S. (a woman also gave the call to prayer).

They bridged what many American Muslims see as a huge disconnect in their religion. "The foreign Imams make the mosques irrelevant for the majority of people who might otherwise go. They're speaking a foreign language literally and figuratively," argued Jihad Turk, the second-generation Palestinian-American president of Bayan Claremont, which offers graduate degrees to future imams. One vivid example of that foreign worldview: a Virginia imam who told his congregants to circumcise their daughters so they did not become "hypersexually active," adding that "in societies where circumcision of girls is completely prohibited, hypersexuality takes over the entire society and a woman is not satisfied with one person or two or three."[2]

This, said Turk, was exactly why "we need to have a cadre of American-Muslim religious leaders that were born and raised here, who get it, who can speak to the diversity first of all, in our own community."

Khaled Abou Fadl of University of California, Los Angeles (UCLA), one of the most renowned scholars of Islamic law in the U.S., said that—counterintuitively—American convert imams resonated even with immigrant Muslims: "The white guy that is all-American converts to Islam and then tells them Islam is wonderful, so it affirms to the immigrant that Islam is not all these horrible things that the public stereotypically believes in."

Dogma

Worldview, not just accent, was the key issue. Many of the old guard— and there were still plenty of them around—wore what some in their erstwhile flock saw as cultural and religious blinders. "A reinterpreted

Islam is no Islam at all," Jaafar Idris, a U.S.-based Saudi cleric, preached in 2005. "When we insist on keeping Islam in its pristine purity, and when we invite people in the West to accept it as such, we are in fact doing them a great service."[3] "Hogwash," responded Omid Safi. "This notion that Islam somehow dropped from Heaven in a hermetically sealed envelope and our job is to simply preserve it can only come from somebody who doesn't understand the way that history works and the way that religious traditions work." That dogmatic adherence to a particular school of Islam was fading in the U.S. One major survey of U.S. mosques found that only about one-fifth reported following a literalist approach, 10 percent reported observing a specific madhab, or school of Hadith interpretation, and just 1 percent identified as Salafi.[4] The vast majority just considered themselves Muslims.

Even the conservatives among this new generation of American-Muslim preachers agreed that Islam could and should adapt to its time and place. "American Muslims by and large do need to understand that the environment they're living in is not third-century Byzantium, nor is it twenty-first-century Saudi Arabia," said Yasir Qadhi, an influential American imam who had more than one million followers on social media. "If you wish Islam to flourish in this land, you have to find and create local clergy, you have to bring about a new generation of scholars who are fully Western and fully in sync with the tradition of Islam."

These new American imams are not (necessarily) anti-Saudi. Many owe their expertise to Saudi Arabia, Egypt and Pakistan, or, in the case of Shi'ite Muslims, Iran. Qadhi was an example. After doing his bachelor's degree at the University of Houston and his PhD at Yale, he spent years in the holy city of Medina, where he earned graduate degrees in Arabic and Islamic theology. But these American imams were taking what they learned in those years in the seat of Islamic orthodoxy and putting their own spin on it. Qadhi said this wasn't about "fixing" Islam to placate the anti-Muslim crowd; nor was it an overnight spiritual revolution. It was a cultural *evolution*. "This is going to be an ongoing struggle, I believe, for at least another generation," he told me.

It was not only those who grew up in the U.S. who were leading the evolution of the religion. Many recent arrivals also embraced the movement. "A Muslim American has to understand his religion in American context not in Arabian context, not in Sudanese context, not in Egyptian context," explained Mohamed Magid, an influential Sudan-born cleric who came to the U.S. in 1987 after studying in Saudi Arabia and now ran a network of mosques and community centers in the Washington, DC, suburbs. "They must also understand American history [and] celebrate American freedom."

Manifestations of this new, "American" Islam could be seen in the removal of the walls that divide men and women in the mosque, though women imams, like female Catholic priests, were still *haram* (forbidden); in the provision of social services and interfaith community engagement; and in heightened levels of political and social activism—whether on the front lines in Ferguson, at the Dakota pipeline protests or in get-out-the-vote drives. It came down to this, said lawyer Cherrefe Kadri, one of the first women in the U.S. elected to head a U.S. Muslim community: "What should Islamic centers be doing? Are we just some place to go and pray and grow a beard and five times a day open a door? Or are we more than that?"

PrIslam

Jihad Saafir was a young African-American imam in south LA running a social welfare organization and prison ministry. When we spoke, he was working to reconcile his formal religious education with the realities of the streets and life behind bars. "There's not one Islam. The thing that they imported is the thing that they imported, but it always changes forms," he said with a gentle smile. "The structure of the mosque is different in America." As American-Muslim leaders, he continued, "it's important for us to engage the Western mind set as well as the more Eastern mind set." That wasn't always easy. "It can be a culture shock."

Saafir embodied two realities of Islam in America. The first reality was that the fastest rate of conversion to Islam was among African Americans and Hispanics.[5] The second reality was that many of those conversions were taking place in prison.[6] Estimates of the number of Muslims in American prisons ranged as high as 350,000, an astounding 10 percent of the U.S. Muslim population.[7] Some of that involved what the New York police department dubbed "PrIslam," temporary conversion for self-protection: you join a gang or you become a Muslim. Statistics like those generated sensational headlines: "Ripe for Radicalization: Federal Prisons 'Breeding Ground' for Terrorists."[8] There *were* cases of prisoners becoming radicalized behind bars, including a foiled 2005 California terror plot with roots in Folsom prison, but studies of *actual* radicalization in U.S. prisons, as opposed to the *potential* for radicalization, did not bear out the hype.[9]

Yahya Malik knew all about the perception of prison as a breeding ground for radicalism. Malik was a retired information technology (IT) professional who volunteered as a prison imam in the Seattle area. We met for lunch a few days before I accompanied him on a visit to meet some of the men who make up America's Muslim prison population.

"I always make sure I've got two people sitting in our sessions," he told me of his prison visits. "I have a chaplain and then someone else. The chaplain was telling me last week, "That teaching, you should be doing it on your own." I said, 'No, I want you to be there.' I don't want anybody to come out tomorrow and say, 'What he was saying was extremist.'"

Malik emigrated from Pakistan where he was raised in a conservative Islamic school of thought. Now, like so many American Muslims, he refused to be labeled. "Honestly, I'm lost," he said, when I asked how he identified himself. "I have close Shi'a friends, I have close Sufi friends, my parents were Hanafi. Where do I fit it? I fit in with Islam." Malik had facilitated many prison conversions. I asked him what reasons the men gave for turning to Islam. "My experience is they became Muslim because, number one, they read something which stuck their mind, and number two they might have somebody within the [prison] unit who was a Muslim trying to tell them what's right and what's wrong. Number three could be whatever I was saying appealed to them; that 'this is how you need to live your life.'"

For some African-American prisoners, he said, there was also a desire to reconnect with their heritage. "I hear, 'Our forefathers were Muslims. Then the masters took away our faith, they took our language and [as a result] here I am, in prison.'"

When I accompanied him to the county jail, about forty men filed quietly into a multipurpose room, where chairs had been arranged in a semicircle and mats laid on the floor for prayers. The majority were African American, with about a dozen Hispanics and a handful of white prisoners. The jail was adjacent to the courthouse, and most were awaiting sentencing or appeals hearings. The oldest in the room was probably in his late thirties. He wore a skullcap signifying his faith. He told me he had spent much of his life in prison. "Islam gave me a path beyond all this," he said, gesturing to the locked door and bulletproof guard station across the hall. I watched with surprise when a pale, gangly white prisoner with a wispy Salafi-style beard walked to the front of the room and began reciting the Qur'an in fluent Arabic, then gave the sermon, applying the lessons of the Hadith to the lives of the men in the room. Jamal, the Muslim name he took when he converted in prison, was twenty years into a thirty-four-year sentence. He had taught himself Arabic in his prison cell and committed the entire Qur'an to memory.

When it was time to pray, about half of the men gathered on the mats. The others, who were not Muslim, had just come to listen. When I asked one later why he was there, he smiled and said it was better than sitting in his cell. "And it's kind of interesting."

Malik had asked me to say a few words about the different approaches to Islam that I had encountered in my years of reporting. The response belied my stereotypes about those who end up in prison. Even the non-Muslims were attentive and asked interesting questions. One had been reading about Islam in Indonesia and wanted to know the impact the growing Islamist movement was having on the country's politics. Several of the prisoners were Iraq war veterans. One had converted after returning from his tour of duty: "I was amazed that the guys we were fighting would stop shooting at the call to prayer." After he returned to the States, a Saudi acquaintance introduced him to Islam. Like many converts to any religion who have been lost, he dived in head first. He went to Saudi Arabia for several years, and even did a three-month walking pilgrimage between the holy cities of Medina and Mecca. Now he was back in jail for domestic abuse. "Iraq?" I asked. He nodded sadly, "I have flashbacks."

"Blackamerican" Islam

Even as immigrant Muslims were reinventing the religion in America, so, too, black American Muslims were in the midst of a reformation. I first encountered Islam in the African-American community in the mid-1970s when I was a college journalism student and accompanied two black reporter friends to a huge rally by Nation of Islam leader Elijah Muhammad on the South Side of Chicago. They were skeptical when I asked if I could go with them. "You *do* know he preaches that white people are devils, don't you?' one of them asked, with an expression that said I was crazy. A lot of people at the rally looked at me the same way, but nothing untoward happened, though my friends did have to tell a few people, "He's with us."

The Nation taught that its founder, Wallace D. Fard, was an incarnation of God, and that Elijah Poole, who had taken the name Muhammad, was God's Messenger, just as his namesake Muhammad had been.

"Black Muslims, Elijah Muhammad taught, were the first people of the earth, whose beautiful way of life was upset when a mad, evil scientist named Yacub genetically engineered a race of white devils," according to historian Edward E. Curtis IV.[10] Four decades later, the majority of Muslims in the black community had moved into the mainstream of the religion.

About 60 percent of native-born American Muslims identified as African American or black, as did about 20 percent of all Muslims in the U.S.[11] Those facts were often lost in the debates over Muslims, which tended to focus on immigrants. The shift from the black nationalism of the Nation of Islam to mainstream Sunni Islam was epitomized by the journey of Malcolm X, whose autobiography had "influenced the religious lives of not only converts but also born-and-raised Muslims of transnational backgrounds."[12]

African Americans were quietly striving to put their own stamp on Islam in America, moving beyond "immigrant Islam" into an era in which African Americans would "emerge as self-authenticating subjects rather than dependent objects of and in" what scholar Sherman Jackson labeled the "Blackamerican" Sunni tradition.[13]

Beyond "textual stone"

An "Americanized" Islam did not necessarily mean a "liberal" Islam, though the reality was that most of this new generation of preachers were moving away from what Islamic scholar Vali Nasr described as Saudi Arabia's "very legalistic ... very austere" and "very black-and-white" approach to the religion.[14] Yet drill below the broad agreement over the need for cultural adaptation and you quickly came up against the question of what constitutes reform and what amounts to heresy.

"Mainstream traditionalists, by and large, are not going to be willing to explicitly discard commandments that have been agreed upon historically, commandments that are essentially etched in what we would call textual stone," explained Yasir Qadhi, who counted himself among the traditionalists. He drew red lines around issues like premarital sex, women leading prayers and homosexual acts, although, regarding the latter, he added, "we've essentially permitted and humanized the feelings and we have forbidden the actions on them." Others, like Omid Safi, rejected such an approach. He represented the self-styled "progressive" wing of American Islam and quoted Bishop Desmond Tutu's line that "I will not worship a homophobic God," calling it "powerful" and "truth-telling."

Somewhere in the middle was Mohamed Magid, whom anti-Muslim campaigners called "Obama's Sharia czar" for his role as a White House adviser,[15] whom ISIS threatened to kill and who *Breitbart* claimed "has deep ties to radicalism."[16] Magid chuckled proudly as he recalled telling Muslim parents that they needed to give their teenagers space "as long as the girl doesn't get pregnant," which led to horrified reactions. "I say, 'You need to deal with the situation with an American context,'" Magid explained as we sat in his Islamic center near Dulles airport. "Religion is not about you [the] parents, feeling good. The social manifestation of Islam has to be completely American."

Like so many who trained under the Saudis, Magid said he initially adopted their ultraconservative Salafi, or Wahhabi, ideology. "I don't call myself Salafi anymore, I call myself orthodox." He smiled. "Even the Salafis in America evolve."

Not all American imams rode motorcycles and played in punk rock bands like Saad Tasleem, who had his own clothing line and was an instructor at AlMaghrib Institute, which billed itself as a place that doesn't "turn learning Islam into a snoozefest." Nor did most advocate mixing drugs and religion, like hip-hop Muslim Michael Muhammad Knight, author of *Tripping with Allah: Islam, Drugs and Writing*. Many imams—from places like Egypt, Pakistan and Malaysia—still hewed to an approach more in keeping with the societies from which they emigrated or where they had studied. At the most conservative (not a synonym for "extremist") end of the spectrum, bodies like the Assembly of Muslim Jurists in America were fighting a rearguard action for an approach to Islam that would find support in a fundamentalist Pakistani madrassa. Emblematic was the organization's publication "Recommendations of the Conference on Contemporary Dawah Issues in the West," which included this ruling on the *fiqh*, or understanding, of the fundamentals of Islam:

> Music that excites the desires and leads one to immoral acts is, by agreement, unacceptable. As for other types of music, there is a difference of opinion. The majority are of the opinion that they are all forbidden and that is the strongest view from a *fiqh* perspective. The least that could be said is that it is from the doubtful matters and it is safest to avoid it.[17]

But the greybeards of the old guard were, increasingly, losing their grip. So, too, were reactionaries among immigrant Muslims who periodically generated headlines such as, "Parents Burned and Beat Their Teen Daughter after She Said No to 'Arranged' Marriage, Police Say."[18] With a generation of American Muslims—children of the immigrants of the 1980s and 1990s—raised on social media and hip-hop, reformers argued that to be relevant, the cultural accoutrements of the religion, though not the core values, had to adapt, not unlike Catholic priests in the 1960s who advocated such heresies as guitar masses.

Religious Authority

At the heart of this evolution of American Islam was the question of religious authority. As noted earlier, sharia, a dirty word to the Islamophobes, refers to the corpus of Islamic teachings, which includes both the Qur'an, the holy book said to be the word of God, and the Hadith, the voluminous compilation of the teachings and accounts of the Prophet's life, and opinions from religious scholars through the centuries on the meaning and application of those words and deeds. At least in the modern era, Saudi Arabia and Egypt for the Sunnis, and Iran for the Shia, had traditionally seen it has *their* responsibility to determine the proper application of Islamic laws. American Muslims believe the day is coming soon when that religious authority will reside in the U.S. "I *do* think that the scholars who are rooted in the realities and the complexities of America have increasingly more religious authority," said Sohaib Sultan, the imam at Princeton University. "Knowing people's customs and traditions is very important when making any sort of religious ruling."

"Islamic authority has moved around the world," added Magid. "It was in Mecca, then it went to Medina. Then it went to Damascus, then it went to Baghdad. Then it went to Spain, then it went to Turkey. Now it's in America."

A significant wave of immigration between 1990 and 2010 meant that the Muslim population in the U.S. roughly doubled to an estimated 3.45 million by 2017.[19] As a result, the number of American mosques in the first decade of this century grew to more than 2,000.[20] Gulf money—particularly Saudi money—had played a major role in the expansion of Islam in America. But that was all changing.

"Saudi money is nowhere near as available as it was," according to Khaled Abou Fadl of UCLA. "I've seen a very clear rolling back on the availability of funds, and a great reluctance to bankroll blindly various organizations in the way that used to be in the 1980s and 1990s especially." The catalyst was 9/11. Various Saudi-funded charities, such as the al-Haramain Foundation, were accused of ties to al Qaeda; a Saudi-backed Islamic training center in suburban Virginia was raided by the FBI and some of its clergy, who carried Saudi diplomatic passports, were expelled. The declassified "missing" twenty-eight pages from the 9/11 Commission report alleged—without providing evidence—that at least one Los Angeles mosque was laundering terrorist funds. All this, coupled with the drop in oil prices, which led to belt-tightening at home, meant the Saudis and the Gulf emirates had significantly reduced their largesse. Even before Crown Prince Mohammed bin Salman announced his "moderate Islam" campaign, Abou Fadl, who had close ties with members of the royal family, told me that another reason behind the House of Saud's increased parsimoniousness towards overseas religious projects was that "they wish they could rid themselves of the Wahhabism all together, but they know that it's impossible domestically." Would-be American imams could still study for free in Saudi Arabia but, Abou Fadl said, "they're not going to have the type of easy power that comes from having the means of controlling the flow of money" like in the old days.

The Arab Spring intensified the turn away from the traditional centers of Islamic teaching as leading religious figures in places like Egypt became apologists for authoritarian regimes that crushed the revolution. "On a moral level, you have a big problem. The figures you were previously looking to for religious knowledge are now supporting political decisions that you think are very obviously terrible," explained Jonathan Brown of Georgetown University, author of *Misquoting Muhammad*. "One of the biggest changes in Islam, at least at an intellectual level, since 2013 has been that Muslim scholars in America have really been more and more on their own, which I think is good; they're forced to think about things on their own."

To Indonesian-born Imam Shamsi Ali, who stood with President George W. Bush on Ground Zero in the aftermath of 9/11 but ultimately ran afoul of the Muslim traditionalists for his dedication to interfaith dialogue, that was very good news. "People around the world look to America as the superpower and I think American Muslims can play an important role to balance the Saudis' rigid interpretation of Islam."

The growth of homegrown centers of Islamic learning meant that tomorrow's imams might not even need to leave the borders of the U.S. These included institutions such as Zaytuna and Bayan Claremont in California, AlMaghrib and Bayyinah in Texas, and Chicago's American Islamic College. Back in the traditional centers of learning abroad, there was a—sometimes grudging—acknowledgment that the baton was gradually being passed, even in Shi'a Islam, where the Iranian ayatollahs play a role much more akin to that of the Catholic clergy in dictating orthodoxy. "I speak to scholars there and they say it's up to you to come up with solutions to these things," reported Hadi Qazwini, a Shi'ite Muslim PhD student at the University of Southern California who spent years studying at the Shi'a Islamic Seminary of Qum. "There is recognition, I think slowly but surely, that Muslims in the United States also have a developing authority to find solutions for the various challenges that they're facing."

Mohamed Magid summed up the change. "People don't like the word 'American Islam,' but this *is* Islam in America. It's unique, it is very integrated, it's holistic, it's diverse and it should be always tolerant and tolerated."

17 VOICES OF REASON

The opening of a true consciousness to what is actually occurring would be purgatory.

SAUL BELLOW
More Die of Heartbreak

Back at the Riyadh summit, Donald Trump had declared, "Young Muslim boys and girls should be able to grow up free from fear, safe from violence and innocent of hatred." Around the world, millions of Muslims were working to achieve exactly that.

From Lagos to Lahore, Muslims were thinking outside Twitter's 280-character box and far beyond the Trump presidency. In countries that had long suffered from Wahhabi proselytization, they weren't waiting to see if MBS was serious, whether he could truly rein in the ultraconservative *ulema*, or even if he would survive. They were taking steps, large and small, to tame the extremist beast; waging a battle for the soul of their religion.

Cartoon Jihad

"How do we prevent the five-year-old in Pakistan from becoming a radical?" House Speaker Paul Ryan once asked.[1] Imran Azhar had a ready answer: "You make him a hero. And you redefine what it is to be a hero." Azhar was part of a small group of Pakistani artists, activists and entrepreneurs trying to do that through cartoons.[2]

In Pakistan, "intolerance and extremism ... is so deep as to be ... a part of the national genetic code," the *Express-Tribune* wrote in a 2016 editorial about the assassination of an anti-extremist blogger.[3] Religious intolerance. Ethnic intolerance. Socio-economic intolerance. It was a narrative that painted a bloody path across newspapers and television screens on a daily basis. More than 50,000 Pakistanis had been killed in the previous decade.[4]

"What is this sickness?" Gauher Affab asked rhetorically when we met in a Lahore cafe. He was the co-creator of a series of comic books designed to provide a counternarrative for young people in rural areas. "It is essentially injustice and helplessness. The moment a person is born in a third world country, they realize their life is worthless; that the social contract here does not exist." That left them prey to whomever portended to be their protector. Those would-be heroes too often became the soldiers of jihad.

"This kind of ideology that they're tackling is very widespread," said Dr. Faisa Musthaq, chair of the Department of Social Sciences at Karachi's Institute of Business Administration (IBA), referring to Gauher and the other cartoon creators. "If you look at any public school textbook, even some of those textbooks which are taught in private schools, they're carrying these very extremist messages without any counternarrative at all." That reality was underlined in a 2014 United Nations Development Programme (UNDP) study that reported, "No young Pakistani man or woman, school going or not, socio-economically deprived or affluent, can escape exposure to this: the narratives are public, they are loud, and they are bold."[5]

The producers waging this cartoon counter-jihad were trying to present alternative ideas in ways that captured the imagination of Pakistan's youth. The vehicles ranged from comic books to apps to full-fledged animated television series. Topics covered the spectrum of Pakistan's societal problems, including violence, corruption, pollution, health, discrimination, sexual harassment and child trafficking. The storylines were serious, but the bad guys were buffoons, the main characters were endearing, and, as with Wile E. Coyote and the Road Runner, no one ever died. The idea was to open young minds before they were co-opted by the extremists. "These kids are not born to hate. We need to catch them early," said Azhar.

Burka Avenger was the poster child for the movement. Its animated star was Jiya, a schoolteacher who transformed into her alter ego, Burka Avenger, "whenever evil is afoot." She practiced an imaginary martial art that involved throwing pens and books at her enemies, a symbolic swipe at the Taliban's opposition to education. Her name and costume were an ironic twist on the head-to-foot burka robes worn by some religiously conservative Muslim women. The idea was to reclaim the symbol from the extremists and to empower women.

That theme of empowerment, education, equality and social justice was woven through the various cartoon projects. Gauher Affab said such innovative approaches were vital. "We're going to have to shake the foundation, get them thinking and then provide the alternative." Affab knew first-hand the dangers of extremist ideology. He was radicalized at age twelve. Only a fluke stopped him from joining the jihad in Kashmir. His Islamic studies teacher had fought as a mujahideen in the Afghan war against the Soviets and "he didn't teach Islam, he just stood in class giving jihadi lectures." The young Affab was fascinated. "Why can't I just take this little shortcut?" he recalled asking himself. "Why do I need to study, get a job and do all these things that are difficult? Why should I do that when I can just jump right to the end, give up my life in some sort of glorious battle and get eternal salvation? It was the epitome of everything I wanted."

As was often the case, the *mujahid* (fighter) never overtly tried to recruit Affab, "but he inspired me toward violence." After a year, the young boy told his teacher he wanted to join the jihad. Arrangements were made for him to board a bus to Kashmir where he would become part of a militant group. But fate intervened. His grandmother fell ill on the day of his departure. "My parents just randomly showed up. I was in the car before I knew what happened."

In that pre-cell phone age, he had no way to reach the teacher. Affab spent the summer reading the Qur'an and the Hadith. He emerged with a new perspective on Islam. "None of it gave me any radical inclination; violence was not in it at all." He had dodged the bullet, literally. Twenty years later, he was trying to help other young Pakistanis do the same. *The Guardian Pasban*, one of the comic series produced by Affab's CFxComcs, took on jihadist recruitment of young people. "Sometimes you forget you even had a choice. But you do. It's just not always easy to know the right ones," read the text of one edition.

Another comic series produced by Affab's team featured Pakistani military heroes in order to recapture the martial narrative from the extremists. "We are using those martial myths, rather than using something fluffy like Care Bears, in order to redefine words like 'jihad' and 'mujahid' [fighter]," he said. "'Jihad' means being a protector, not an aggressor. And my hope is that if we can get the kids to read this before the jihadi walks in, he's on unstable enough ground that [the young person] can make a decision and reject that person."

That effort to instill critical thinking was at the heart of the animated TV short series *Quaid Say Baatein* (Talking to the Guide), in which the heroine, Zainab, confronted moral and ethical challenges with the help of Pakistan's founder, Muhammad Al Jinnah, known to Pakistanis as *Quaid-e-Azam* (Great Leader), who comes to her in dreams. "The Guide is never didactic; he never tells Zainab, 'This is what you have to do, this is the solution,'" creator Daniyal Noorani explained. "He always ends a dream by saying, 'You have to decide for yourself by taking the first step.'"

Critical thinking, Noorani said, was essential to combating extremism, "whether it is the way you see it emerging in the United States through Trump or whether it's in Pakistan with religious extremists, it stems from the person's willingness to say, 'You make the decisions for me, I'm not going to analyze or question what you say.'" A musician, Noorani, first came upon the idea of animated messages for Pakistani children when he was working at a biotech company in Boston. Feeling helpless about the rising violence in his homeland, he wrote a song asking, "Hey, what's going on over there? ... Why is there injustice? Where is the God in this?" A friend did a simple animation that he posted online. It went viral. That inspired him.

Noorani eventually came up with the idea of *Quaid Say Baatein*, which was aired by Pakistan's largest broadcaster and distributed to classrooms. By adopting Jinnah as Zeinab's muse and drawing on the Pakistani founder's actual teachings, *Quaid Say Baatein* was able to gain credibility beyond Pakistani liberal circles. One episode about the privileges of the corrupt elite was posted on the Facebook page of the youth wing of the largest Islamist political party and received more than 4.5 million views. I was surprised that a conservative Islamist organization, accused of links to radical splinter groups, would endorse such a project. But Dr. Farid Piracha, deputy secretary general of Jaamat-e-Islamiya, told me that *Quaid Say Baatain's* message "is clear, ethical, and according to basic teaching of Islam,"

The projects were having an effect. *Burka Avenger* was the most-watched children's television show in Pakistan. *Quaid Say Baatein* was the highest-rated animated series in the months it aired. Meanwhile, a PDF version of Affab's comics, made available through a Pakistani messaging app, resulted in more than 500,000 downloads.

Before distributing his comic books at schools in rural Punjab, Affab and his team surveyed 250 students age twelve to eighteen. Sixty-six percent of them "believed that if you had a religious opinion about something, you had the right to take violent action to enforce it." "*The right*," he told me, emphasizing the words. "They're *already* radicalized; they just haven't been recruited yet." But after they read the comic books, Affab reported, the worldview among half the students began to shift. "It wasn't that they said, 'Our preacher is bad,' or 'We're going to become pacifists,' they just took a critical thinking approach." That, to Affab, was the key.

Dr. Feriha Peracha was working on an even bigger challenge: changing the minds of young men who *had* been recruited. A neurosurgeon, Peracha ran a camp for young jihadis captured by the Pakistani military. Her pitch: "You don't have to go to heaven; you can carve out your own life here on earth." With a team of psychologists and social workers, she worked to integrate the former fighters back into civilian life. Many had joined the militants for a steady paycheck, not religious glory. Training them to put down their guns and earn a living was the main focus. "It's not just hearts and minds," Peracha told me. "It's creating change that can last. It's lifestyle." The challenges were huge. Some boys rejoined the militants. Peracha blamed the Saudis for much of the extremism. "This whole Wahhabism just festers. It builds sympathies for the extremists."

But there were success stories as well. Many graduated from the camps and went to work as tailors or motorcycle repairmen. A few became teachers or engineers, and one even applied for a Fulbright fellowship to the U.S. Others helped the army capture their own brothers or uncles to save them from a life of violence. Peracha was convinced education was the key to defeating extremism. "A mother doesn't send all her children to the madrassa," she told me. "Just the ones that drop out of school." She also believed that those women had an important role in the strategy to defeat extremism. When her team was having particular issues with a young former jihadi, "we sometimes warn him that we're going to tell his mother, and they shape right up!"

The reintegration camp sat in the middle of an area once controlled by the militants. "I get threats, but I also think the students will protect me," Peracha told me, with a nervous smile. "My husband doesn't stop me, but I know he doesn't sleep until I'm home again."

When I next saw cartoonist Affab, I asked him Paul Ryan's question about what the U.S. could do to prevent a five-year-old from becoming radicalized. Stop the drone strikes that were radicalizing even more Pakistanis and give money to projects like his that worked to prevent radicalization, he said dryly. But beyond that, he argued, Americans simply couldn't do much. "You have to go behind enemy lines and talk to them and get their trust; you have to empathize with their problems. And that's impossible for a Westerner to do."

Islam Nusantara

Three thousand miles away, Indonesians were also working to recapture the narrative from the extremists—and the Saudis.

The Middle East is on fire; the Middle East is shaking; it is terrifying to look at what is happening in those societies, Indonesian President Joko Widodo told 40,000 of his countrymen at Jakarta's main mosque in June 2015. "*Alhamdulillah* (thank God), our Islamic archipelago, our Islam, is full of manners, full of etiquette and tolerance. It is Islam Nusantara."[6]

With that, the battle was joined.

The Indonesian archipelago (*nusantara*) has had more Muslims than the entire Arab world. It is also home to the Nahdlatul Ulama (NU). With some forty million members, NU is one of the largest Muslim organizations in the world. The NU conceived the Islam Nusantara campaign around the argument that Indonesians had as much right as the Arabs to determine how to interpret their religion.

The idea of Indonesian Islam as embodying the Qur'anic call for *al-wasatiyyah* (a justly balanced) approach to the religion, distinguished from the austere and polarizing teachings of Wahhabi Islam, was nothing new. It was the arrival of Wahhabism in the archipelago that had led to the founding of the NU decades before. Indonesian Islam had always respected—and in some ways absorbed—local traditions and mystical practices, which Wahhabis rejected as "deviant."

What *was* new was the decision to use Islam Nusantara as a brand under which to aggressively take on the extremists.

Islam, said proponents of Islam Nusantara and the closely related *Islam Berkemajuan* (Progressive Islam) of the thirty-million-member Muhammadiyah organization, should be a living religion receptive to the modern world, not trapped in a medieval past. "We [should] not understand the issues in the time of the Prophet or the apostles only … but also the Islam" of Indonesia's various historic kingdoms "up to Islam in the era of President Jokowi," the head of the NU's student association wrote in 2016.[7] Such an approach was anathema to strict Wahhabis. Many

Indonesian Muslims in turn rejected Wahhabi *hudud* practices such as amputation as a punishment for theft.

The stark difference between Indonesian Islam and that of the Saudis was embodied in the Festival of the Wali Sangha (Nine Saints), a celebration that honored the role of the Islamic teachers credited with bringing Islam to Indonesia in the fifteenth and sixteenth centuries. The Sufi notion of saints was blasphemous to the Wahhabis.

The Indonesian effort to take leadership in challenging the extremists was evident in the Indonesian Ulema Council's invitation to clerics from Afghanistan and Pakistan to join them for a gathering at which the seventy participants issued a joint fatwa against violence carried out in the name of Islam—and were in turn denounced by the Taliban for helping the "invading infidels in Afghanistan" attain "their malicious objective."[8]

The concept of Islam Nusantara was developed by NU leader Abdurrahman Wahid, known as Gus Dur, a highly respected Islamic scholar, who was Indonesia's president from 1999 to 2001. "It's based on a worldview which emerges, as Gus Dur would say, 'from the depths of human experience,' not from specific teachings; but, rather, a spiritual apprehension of reality, which is incompatible with extremist Islam," C. Holland Taylor explained to me. Taylor was a student of Gus Dur and international spokesman for the NU.

Indonesia's challenge to the Muslim world was embedded in a video publicizing the campaign. Over images of Islamic State jihadis slaughtering a group of prisoners, Gus Dur read a Javanese poem:

Many who memorize the Qur'an and Hadith love to condemn others as infidels while ignoring their own infidelity to God, their hearts and minds still mired in filth.

It was an argument that resonated with hundreds of millions of Muslims around the world.

18 ISLAM UNTRUMPED

[H]appily the Government of the United States … gives to bigotry no sanction, to persecution no assistance.

GEORGE WASHINGTON

If Donald Trump had set out to mobilize the American Muslim community, he could not have done a better job. As the 2018 bi-elections approached, Muslims across the country were organizing rallies, coordinating voter registration drives and running for office, from local city councils to Capitol Hill.

One of those was Abdul El-Sayed, a thirty-three-year-old doctor who was a contender for the Democratic nomination for Michigan governor. "Reminds me of someone I used to work for," a former Obama speechwriter tweeted when El-Sayed entered the race.[1] El-Sayed's candidacy inevitably provoked the anti-Islam lobby, with Patrick Colbeck, a candidate for the GOP gubernatorial nomination, accusing him of ties to the Muslim Brotherhood and trotting out the conspiracy theory about the jihad infiltrating the U.S. government. Senator Ted Cruz and Sean Hannity of Fox News endorsed Colbeck, but a GOP spokesperson said, "We categorically condemn any sort of hate speech, regardless of the source."[2]

El-Sayed dismissed the controversy about his religion. "Michiganders don't care how you pray, but what you pray for," El-Sayed told a radio interviewer. "I pray for my family, my state, my country and for Michigan football. I know a lot of Michiganders pray for the same things."[3] El-Sayed would eventually lose the Democratic primary, but polls showed that had more to do with his close association with the Bernie Sanders wing of the party than his religion.

Like El-Sayed, many of the Muslims who sought nomination in the 2018 primaries were also viciously trolled. So, too, were those with names that some believed sounded Muslim. "He wants to behead you all," said one post on the campaign Facebook page of Kia Hamadachy, the son of Iranian immigrants who sought the Democratic nomination for Congress in Republican Irvine, California, and was not a practicing Muslim.[4] "Nice try but your first love is Satan (AKA Allah) and your second love is to a litter box your 'people' come from. You are as American as Chinese checkers," said a comment on the Facebook page of Deedra Abboud, a U.S.-born former Southern Baptist and long-time Phoenix lawyer who sought the Democratic nomination for U.S. Senate.[5] Abboud said it was just such rhetoric that inspired her to run for office. "Unfortunately ... this is actually what we hear on the street; this is what we hear in the media even," she told the *Arizona Republic*. "That's what we really have to talk about."[6]

Most Muslim politicians—and would-be politicians—just shook off such attacks as inevitable and focused on the energy of Arabs and Muslims who felt a new empowerment in the face of the Trump administration. "There is a fire lit under them. They see their rights being stripped away, day in and day out," said Abdullah Hammoud, a Michigan state legislator.[7]

In Washington, Bannon and Flynn were gone, but they had been replaced by an ever-expanding circle of officials with a history of anti-Muslim statements, including CIA director Mike Pompeo, who eventually replaced Rex Tillerson as secretary of state, and John Bolton, Flynn's replacement as national security adviser. Meanwhile, it was hard to escape the steady drumbeat of anti-Muslim and anti-immigrant outrage that continued in some sections of the media, such as the complaint by Laura Ingraham of Fox News that "massive demographic changes" involving immigrants meant "the America that we know and love doesn't exist anymore."[8]

The biggest shock to American Muslims was the Supreme Court's ruling upholding the president's so-called Muslim ban. Also troubling was the administration's decision to block plans to add a "Middle Eastern/ North African" category to the U.S. Census, a move that would have more clearly identified the country's estimated 3.7 million Arabs—who often choose "White" on the existing census forms. Meanwhile, the Trump administration announced that the Census would for the first time ask respondents whether they were U.S. citizens. That was likely to reduce the count of non-citizens, already fearful of deportation. Changes in who is counted and how they are categorized had implications for federal funding, the drawing of congressional districts, votes in the Electoral College and civil rights laws.

But there were victories, too. A Hispanic blogger and political appointee at the Department of Health and Human Services was forced to resign after tweeting anti-Muslim conspiracy theories with the hashtag #BanIslam and #DeportLSarsour, referring to Arab-American activist Linda Sarsour;[9] the administration's nominee for the top UN migration post was rejected by the international body in part because of his history of anti-Muslim comments;[10] and the revival of Roseanne Barr's situation comedy was canceled after the actor posted racist comments about former Obama adviser Valerie Jarrett that included the false charge that she was a member of the Muslim Brotherhood.[11]

Hashtags like #CanYouHearUsNow and #AmericanMuslimFaces served as rallying points for activism on Twitter and other social media platforms, Muslim Americans ramped up their donations to political causes,[12] and they pushed back at reporting that gave seven times more coverage to acts of violence by Muslims than non-Muslims.[13] Hashtags such as #CallingAllMuslims and #MyMuslimVote circulated widely in the days before the midterms, as Muslim volunteers mounted a get-out-the-vote campaign via mosques and phone banks.

Muslim women especially were moved to action by the Trump presidency. Faiza N. Ali, a young New York Democratic activist tweeted this on Muslim Women's Day in the spring of 2018:

Q: What's the status of Muslim women?
A: Fierce.[14]

As journalist Shaheen Pasha observed, Muslim women bore a special burden in Trump's America: they were both Muslim *and* women,[15] so the Women's March on Washington, the day after Trump's inauguration, had special meaning for Muslim women. An Arab-American woman, Linda Sarsour, was one of the organizers of the massive event and #muslimwomensday and #muslimgirlarmy became social media rallying cries in the campaign to confront violence against women and discrimination against Muslim women.

It was, after all, women who were most readily identifiable as Muslims. The hijab, worn regularly by 40 percent of American Muslim women, was catnip for Islamophobes.[16] Hate crimes commonly involved the hijab, whether harassment or actual to attempts to pull it off. Two-thirds of women who wore the headscarf or other forms of hijab reported discrimination.[17] The twisted mindset that caused the reaction was evident in a bizarre report from the U.S. Air Force Research Center that claimed the hijab contributed to "passive terrorism."[18] Tell that to the massive crowds at the women's march on Washington—Muslim and non-Muslim—who adopted the iconic Shepard Fairey poster of a defiant Muslim woman wearing an American flag hijab.

The much-maligned hijab was even emerging as a fashion statement. Boutique designers and industry leaders like Oscar de la Renta developed clothing lines that married modesty and style for fashion-forward American Muslim women and non-Muslim women inspired by their struggle. The Islamophobes—and ill-informed would-be experts—were right: the "veil" *was* a symbol, but in Donald Trump's America it was embraced as a symbol not of Muslim oppression, backwardness or extremism, but one celebrating the nation's religious, ethnic and racial diversity. From podcasts to Haute Hijabi fashion sites, from health clinics in South LA to a woman-centered LGBT mosque in Chicago, Muslim women were tackling—and wrestling into submission—stereotypes that once defined them.

Thanks to Donald Trump, American Muslims had entered an era of contradictions. Never had they been more under attack, but never had they been so accepted and outspokenly proud to be American. Journalist Amani Al-Khatahtbeh summed up the new spirit in her *Letter to My Future Muslim Daughter*:

Yes, *habibti*, a presidential candidate for the free United States of America did offer a ban on Muslim immigration as an actual part of his policy platform. Yes, he stood at a podium and talked about shooting Muslims with bullets dipped in pigs' blood, and his numbers did rise in the polls every time he said something bad about us. I know, it's hard to believe millions of Americans supported him, but, yes, it happened, dear.

… I will remind you … of the legacy of Muslim women in speaking truth to power: the beautiful tradition you will inherit of not just resisting adversity in whatever form it may take, but also in defying it. . . .

And … even though Muslim women became the targets of anti-Muslim bigotry, they also became the symbols of the strength and resiliency of American Muslims in the fabric of our nation.[19]

Trump's rhetoric was having an unintended effect: more Americans now felt positively toward Muslims and Islam than ever before.[20] That helped many American Muslims cling to their faith in America, even as they tried to forget that 20 percent of Americans were ready to deny them the right to vote and 56 percent still believed American Muslims did not want to fit in.[21]

Gallows humor also played a healthy role. Suleiman Din, a Muslim-American journalist, posted this on Facebook: "Was walking to work today, laughing at a joke from a friend, and some lady yelled at me, 'Jesus loves you!' … Not to make light of her intent, but I wonder how freaked out people would be if I randomly yelled 'Allahu Akbar' at them?"

Fighting Radicalism

The arrest of a group of American Muslims at a New Mexico compound where they were allegedly training children for a wave of school shootings underlined the challenge still facing American Muslims in preventing "home-grown" terrorism. The group was led by the son of a New York imam who had been a character witness for the so-called "blind sheikh," Omar Abdel Rahman, who was convicted in the 1993 bombing of the World Trade Center.[22]

As political activists celebrated their 2018 victories and prepared for the 2020 presidential election, Muslim clerics and community leaders across the country ramped up their efforts to prevent radicalization. Whether in informal dialogues with youth groups or confidential chats with young people who were alienated by their treatment in America and enticed by the extremists, many American imams worked hard to "walk the walk" and not just "talk the talk" about Islam being a religion of peace.

"I have encountered some of young that are really, really angry towards Donald Trump's political rhetoric. There is truly a big responsibility on us to bring them back on track and provide the genuine Islamic stand on issues," said Shamsi Ali, an Indonesian-born imam in New York. "We try to let them know, we can disagree on policy but doing something bad in the name of disagreement is certainly not American."

Muhammad Magid personally counseled dozens of would-be ISIS recruits who were actively engaged in online conversations with extremists. "I can tell you that the number one issue is not ideology, number one is psychology. It's just like in cult recruitment and in gang recruitment," Magid told me when we met at his Islamic center near Dulles airport. He explained that

one of the most powerful recruitment tools [used by extremist recruiters] is presenting a picture of a young person or a child killed in Syria, in Gaza, overseas, and say, "Are you going to do something about this?" This child's soul is calling you, you're in the comfort of your home in America and there's the urgency this cannot wait. They create this kind of sense of purpose at the same time disconnect [the recruit] socially.

Islam itself was the tool used by Magid and others who tried to prevent radicalization. He told me of his conversation with one would-be recruit who was determined to join the Islamic State in Syria. "'You want Paradise?' I asked him. He said, 'yes.'" Magid quoted the Prophet Muhammad saying that the route to Paradise involved spreading peace, praying and feeding the hungry. "I said, 'Do you believe the Prophet or [ISIS leader Abu Bakr al-] Baghdadi?' He said, 'I believe the Prophet.' I said, 'Then if you want shortcut to Paradise, you don't have to go to Syria, you can do these three things here.' One of the things radical extremism does, it makes you suspend your critical thinking because it's a cult and a cult is emotional-driven, it's not intellectual-driven mission and therefore that's the intervention we do," he explained.

Daisy Khan, the co-founder of the so-called Ground Zero Mosque, the mosque and interfaith community center in New York City that had been blocked by anti-Muslim activists, published *WISE UP!*, a book that combined tips for helping Muslim children cope with racist bullying and a how-to guide for early intervention with those being seduced by extremist ideologies. "By providing in-depth Islamic knowledge to these potential recruits, we can challenge their way of thinking and bring them back to the straight path," wrote former militant Mubin Shaikh, one of the book's contributors.

WISE UP! Was just one of many initiatives to address the twin challenges of Islamophobia and terrorist recruitment. A fundamental piece of many of these formal and informal initiatives was to encourage adults in the community to listen. "I think oftentimes young people just feel like they have no other alternative, and that's what leads them down these dark paths," Yale imam Sohaib Sultan told me. "I think as Muslim-American leaders and as religious leaders, part of our responsibility is showing young people alternative paths of engagement, alternative paths of bringing some sense to their world, rather than dismissing their grievances."

The shift in mindset from the defensiveness and denial that previously permeated the American Muslim community during the 2016 presidential campaign to one of engagement after the shock of the election wore off was seen in the introduction to the *Safe Spaces* early intervention toolkit published by the Muslim Public Affairs Council (MPAC). MPAC directly took on those in the Muslim community who pretended radicalization was the sole product of FBI stings. Yes, it was true that just under half of all terrorism convictions involved potential entrapment by informants, the publication's authors said. However, "This means that slightly more than half of the plots studied did not involve an informant." In other words, half of all alleged terrorist plots were likely to be *real*. As a result, MPAC said, American Muslims needed "to strengthen our communities in ways that protect its most vulnerable members from being tempted into making harmful decisions—whether that temptation comes from paid informants or actual violent criminals."[23]

"Our critics will say, you're admitting that the Muslim community has a problem. We're saying, no, the Muslim community is part of the solution," MPAC president Salam al-Marathi told me when we met in his LA office, unmarked to avoid the attention of anti-Muslim extremists. "We have to align ourselves with realities and with needs."

Terrorism by American Muslims had become a reality and there was a pressing need to address that. "Nobody wants to see their son go join ISIS or bomb a school," he said. Nor did the community want to see one of its own go to jail. However, that was part of the new reality. "We're looking at the situation as a public health matter, not a criminal justice matter," al-Marathi said. "But when it becomes a criminal justice matter, then the authorities will be informed and then they have to deal with the situation after that."

For a growing cadre of leaders in American law enforcement, such early interventions by Muslim communities were an increasingly important weapon in the counterterrorism arsenal. These local cops and federal agents brought a pragmatic, rather than political, approach to their job. Their files were full of examples of American Muslims who might not have been radicalized if someone had intervened while they were moving down the path to extremism. What, for example, would have happened if a North Carolina mosque hadn't tossed out Dana Patrick Boyd for spouting radical ideas? Would he still have set up his own prayer group, radicalized his own sons and been sentenced to eighteen years in prison for "participating in terrorist activities abroad and committing acts of murder, kidnapping, or maiming persons abroad"?[24]

They also knew learning to trust America's Muslim communities was critical. If law enforcement had taken seriously a Boston imam's concerns about the Tsarnaev brothers instead of cross-examining him about his own views, would three people have died and several hundred others been injured or maimed in the Boston Marathon bombings?[25]

While the Islamophobes constructed walls, these law enforcement professionals built bridges and substituted cooperation for the confrontation too common in the past. "There's no doubt we have to hunt and pursue those that are trying to do horrible things to innocent people," Michael Downing, head of counterterrorism for the Los Angeles Police Department, said when I spoke with him a few months before he retired. "But on the other side of the equation, those people that are on the fence, that haven't yet mobilized to violence, that are being recruited into this dysfunctional ideology, there's an opportunity, as we did with the gangs, to build intervention models where we talk about character development and job placement and perhaps mental illness issues, where we get the mental health experts involved, social services involved."

"You cannot arrest your way out of this problem," Downing continued. "It's got to be a balanced approach between arresting the very bad, prosecuting and putting in prison, but on the other side building communities so that they are hostile to this type of recruitment and financing and pre-operational planning."

When Will Johnson became chief of the Arlington, Texas, police department, he attended Friday prayers at every mosque in the city. His goal was to ease suspicions in the Muslim community, which he saw as a natural outgrowth of the often-aggressive law enforcement tactics after 9/11. "If you're a first-generation immigrant, you're going to look at the police department, your municipal police department, through the eyes of whatever policing looked like in your country of origin," he told me. By becoming a presence in the community, attending fairs and holiday celebrations, police departments like Arlington built a level of trust. As a result, local police departments and the FBI were increasingly involved in early interventions to reorient young Muslims by working with the community to bring to bear mental health counseling, job training and other forms of social services.

It also meant such departments were in a better position to detect actual terrorist plots before they reached fruition. "Our experience is we've seen those results," said Johnson, who was chair of the Civil Rights Committee for the International Association Chiefs of Police. "We've seen the ability for our mosques to call us and identify individuals that are engaged in criminal activity," leading to arrests.

In Portland, where there had been so many issues between the FBI and the Muslim community in the decade after 9/11, Jessica Anderson, head of one of the counterterrorism teams at the local FBI office, told me they were experimenting with intervention—rather than arrest—as an option even in some of the most troubling cases:

> We have instances of this, where subjects who are talking about killing people, killing non-believers, putting heads on spikes, kidnapping non-believers, all sorts of stuff, but we see them stabilize, we see them get jobs. There's a stability to their life that increases, and then we can start to decrease our attention to the point where we're like, "You know what? I'm comfortable closing this."

This evolving and multidimensional approach to counterterrorism, which involved the participation of the American Muslim community, was critical to the future. With the collapse of the Islamic State in Syria and Iraq, new threats arose. About 300 American jihadis fought in Syria. How many of these would try to come home? Most of the handful who did had been arrested, but a few slipped in undetected.[26] Would the loss of Syria as a release valve mean more American extremists would try to carry out their jihadi aspirations at home? How would American law enforcement face the challenge?

Deradicalization

One controversial strategy for handling returning jihadis involved deradicalization therapy. Experts said the U.S. was fifteen to twenty years behind Europe and Muslim-majority countries such as Saudi Arabia and Indonesia in developing such programs to reintegrate those who had joined the jihad.

"I believe that people can correct these errors and can reform and reintegrate," German expert Daniel Koehler told a Minneapolis court.

Without deradicalization programs, "They go into prison, they radicalize others, they become more radicalized. Some of those folks may get out sooner than these folks and carry out lone wolf terrorist acts."[27]

In a groundbreaking move in 2016, a federal judge in Minneapolis ordered deradicalization therapy for one member of a group of Somali youth convicted of trying to join ISIS. As Donald Trump marked the first anniversary of his election, twenty-one-year-old Abdullahi Yusuf, walked out of the federal courthouse in Minneapolis a free man. Yusuf, who had cooperated with authorities from early in the investigation and convinced the judge of his regret, was the first American who had completed a program of deradicalization. His life would be under a microscope as counterterrorism experts and the courts evaluated the Minneapolis experiment to determine the future of others convicted of terrorism in the years to come.

There would certainly be more. The ideology behind ISIS was alive and well. Online recruitment continued unabated, despite the Islamic State's losses on the ground. The U.S. coalition had systematically targeted the leadership of the IS's sophisticated media operation, but its vast trove of sophisticated videos lived on across the Web, endlessly spread in chat rooms, on Facebook and through encrypted messaging apps like Telegram and WhatsApp. Evidence of that was the 90 videos and 3,800 photos of ISIS-related propaganda found on the cell phones of an extremist who carried out a truck attack in New York City in November 2017.[28]

Even as ISIS worked to rebuild its media operations, splinter groups emerging in its wake were posting their own videos and online propaganda, raising new virtual flags of extremism and spreading messages that fueled sectarian violence from Southeast Asia to West Africa.[29]

The Way Forward

By 2050, Islam will supplant Judaism as the second-most populous religion in the U.S. By 2070, it will pass Christianity as the most populous religion on earth. A "clash of civilizations" on such a scale is unthinkable. As extremists on the right hurled insults at America's Muslims and extremists on the Muslim fringe continued to kill in the name of Islam, rational minds in policy circles, law enforcement and at the grass roots worked to craft strategies for the long game. But the most important work was being done by those who will be in charge long after the Trump era is consigned to history.

On a gray, drizzly Sunday, I sat in a crowd of proud parents on the football field at Ithaca College for the 2018 graduation ceremony. Four years before, when we received news our son had been awarded a small minority scholarship, we had joked that it was a sign of Ithaca's lack of diversity that the school would consider a half-Asian student a minority while other universities were being accused of turning away Asians because they had so many.

Now I watched as the new president, Shirley M. Collado, was introduced as the first Dominican-American leader of an American university. Moments later, a leading transgender activist and a ninety-three-year-old African-American civil rights leader were recognized with honorary doctorates. It was all a clear riposte to the reactionary rhetoric beyond the campus gates.

But it was when the senior class president stepped to the podium that my jaw dropped. Her graduation cap sat atop a brown hijab.

"Good morning, *As-salamu-Alaikum, Al-sama, Jawali.* These are greetings from my cultures and religion. I am a first-generation, Gambian, Muslim American," Fatoumata B. Jallow proudly told the thousands gathered on the field. "*Ramadan Mubarak* to all my fellow fasting Muslim brothers and sisters, as I am fasting too," she said, referring to the Muslim month of fasting, which happened to fall in May that year.

I thought of that Kenyan-American man on the Emirates flight two years before who had asked permission to pray on the floor in front of my seat. At the time, I had wondered if he and other Muslims would be afraid to openly practice their religion after the election. So much had happened since. Hateful rhetoric; policies based on stereotype and cliché; rule by executive order and tweet. Now I had my answer. It was embodied in the young woman on the stage. A graduating class that was more than 70 percent white and had come of age during the Trump presidency had elected a Muslim immigrant to lead them.

Donald Trump's rhetoric *had* produced very real fallout for American Muslims: the rate of immigration by Muslim refugees was down 91 percent from the early days of the GOP primary,[30] and anti-Muslim hate speech had become a fixture of American life. Yet efforts to turn the politics of fear into the law of the land had been consistently confronted by the power of decency and common sense. The Muslim ban was repeatedly challenged in the courts; the plot to undermine

American Muslim organizations by adding the Muslim Brotherhood to the terrorism list languished in committee on Capitol Hill; and threats to shutter mosques remained nothing more than unconstitutional campaign bombast.

Donald Trump would inevitably bring more turmoil for American Muslims and angst for their co-religionists around the world. But the fact that Fatoumata B. Jallow stood almost defiantly on the stage thanking her professors, her family and Allah for her success—as her classmates cheered and many parents around me surreptitiously wiped away tears at the moving scene—left me reassured.

By electing her, Ithaca's class of 2018 reminded us the values that truly *did* make America great *were* alive and safely in the hands of the next generation.

POSTSCRIPT

On January 3, 2019, Ilhan Omar strode onto the floor of the U.S. House of Representatives proudly wearing a maroon and burnt orange hijab. A Somali immigrant who had spent four long years in a Kenyan refugee camp as a child, Omar was one of two Muslim-American women elected to Congress in the 2018 midterm elections.

Back in 2016, American Muslims had faced a "perfect storm" that combined Islamophobic election-year rhetoric and the first instances of domestic terrorism by American Muslims. Now it was Donald Trump who faced a very different kind of political storm that saw Omar and Rashida Tlaib, a second-generation Palestinian American, elected to Congress as part of a "pink wave" of women who won their party's nomination for Congress in 2018.

"I will uplift you in so many ways," Tlaib told supporters in her victory speech. "Not only through service but fighting back, against every single oppressive, racist structure that needs to be dismantled, because you deserve better than what we have today in our country."[1]

The numbers told the story. More than 160 American Muslims ran for office in the 2018 midterms, from governor of Michigan down to local boards of education. Most striking, of the eighty-one candidates for Congress, statewide office and state legislatures, more than 80 percent were first- or second-generation immigrants and all but two of the rest were African Americans.[2] For most, the decision to run was a direct response to the election of Donald Trump. "Most of us who ran took our stance to oppose fear and hatred," Gregory Jones, a candidate for Congress from Alaska, told me.

Predictably, Muslim candidates faced sometimes vicious pushback from the Right. "Let's hope she doesn't have a spiritual crisis and decide to blow herself up to grantee [sic] her entry into heaven," said the first hate comment posted on the Facebook site of Deedra Abboud, a white convert to Islam who wears a hijab, four days after she declared her candidacy in April 2017.[3] It would only get worse from there. More than half of the candidates said they were threatened—physically, verbally or online—and some were forced to call in the police.[4]

Others were targeted in the ecosystem of Islamophobic trolls and blogs. "Jihadi Cult Member Files to Run for Congress," was the headline on the website of the anti-Muslim extremist Clarion Project, reporting on the Congressional candidacies of Gregory Jones in Alaska and Tahira Amatul-Wadud in Massachusetts.[5] Frontpagemag.com called 2018 "The Terror-Reinforcing Primary."[6] Anti-Muslim provocateur Laura Loomer targeted Omar and Tlaib in person at their rallies and through her Twitter account, which was eventually shut down for violating the company's rules against "hateful comment" for a tweet attacking Omar after her election:[7]

> Isn't it ironic how the twitter moment used to celebrate "women, LGBTQ, and minorities" is a picture of Ilhan Omar? Ilhan is pro Sharia Ilhan is pro-FGM Under Sharia, homosexuals are oppressed & killed. Women are abused & forced to wear the hijab. Ilhan is anti Jewish.[8]

At least 10 percent of the Muslims running for office said they even heard disparaging remarks about Islam from competing candidates. But in a sign of how the winds of public opinion were shifting, of the eighty-three candidates in the 2018 midterms identified as "anti-Muslim" by the activist group Muslim Advocates, only nineteen were elected. And of those, leading anti-Muslim voices such as Representative Steven King of Iowa, Peter King of New York, Duncan Hunter of California and Senator Ted Cruz of Texas all saw significant drops in their level of support.[9]

Saudi Trolls

Ironically, the Saudis and their allies were among those trolling the newly elected Muslims members of Congress. A month after the election, the English-language website of the Saudi-owned Al Arabiya television channel accused the pair, along with American Muslim activist Linda Sarsour, of being part of "an alliance with Political Islamist movements … to infiltrate" the U.S. government.[10]

It was a desperate play on the part of Saudi Crown Prince Mohammed bin Salman—MBS—to shore up his alliance with Donald Trump as the

Saudi leader's support crumbed elsewhere in Washington and around the world as a result of the fallout from the murder of Saudi journalist and dissident Jamal Khashoggi at the Saudi consulate in Istanbul. Saudi Arabia's multimillion-dollar effort designed to present MBS to the American people as a liberal reformer was undone in the few hours it took to slaughter and dismember a single writer.

"A mad prince who murders a journalist, kidnaps a prime minister and starves millions of children should never be celebrated at state dinners, but instead belongs in a prison cell," wrote *New York Times* columnist Nicholas Kristof. "In the end, Saudi Arabia played Kushner, Trump and his other American acolytes for suckers."[11]

As part of their campaign against the newly elected Muslim members of Congress, the Saudis recycled the old right-wing claim of a Muslim Brotherhood plot to subvert the U.S. system from inside. Omar, the Al Arabiya article claimed, was "the spiritual daughter of Obama" and the goal of these "Muslim sisters" was "to topple Trump."

But their real concern was that the pair would lead a move in Congress to shift U.S. Middle East policy away from the cozy relationship between Trump and the authoritarian regimes in Saudi Arabia, Egypt and their allies established at that glitzy summit in Riyadh, and back to the Obama-era policy that factored human rights into the equation.

Omar "will be hostile to the Gulf and a supporter of the political Islam represented in the Brotherhood in the Middle East," Faisal al-Shammeri, a cultural adviser at the Saudi Arabian Cultural Mission to the United States, reportedly tweeted.[12] Omar, Tlaib and the other recent Muslim immigrants who ran for office in the U.S. also muddied the message of the authoritarians that their citizens were not ready for democracy.

"People would not have access to power in their countries, but they *would* if they leave," Egypt-born Abdul El-Sayed, who ran for governor in Michigan, told a reporter. [T]his destroys the argument by [Egyptian President Abdel Fatel el-] Sisi or bin Salman."[13]

Another player the Saudis claimed was part of this imagined conspiracy was Turkish President Recip Tayyib Erdoğan, MBS' rival for leadership of the world's Muslims. Erdogan had masterfully undermined MBS by manipulating the leak of details of the Khashoggi murder.

But the Saudis were swimming against the tide. Even before Omar and Tlaib took office, the lame-duck, Republican-controlled Congress voted to end U.S. support for the Saudi-led coalition in Yemen. It was a major rebuke to Donald Trump; it left his Saudi-centric Middle East policy in tatters, much to the delight of China and Russia, which had fewer concerns about the slaughter of a mere journalist—or tens of thousands of Yemenis.

Meanwhile, despite the president's continued rhetoric about the threat of Islamist-inspired terrorism, and his spurious claim that "unknown Middle Easterners" were "mixed in" with a caravan of South American asylum seekers, not a single act of terrorism was carried out by a Muslim on U.S. soil in 2018, while right-wing extremists were responsible for a wave of terror attacks, from the murder of eleven people at a Pittsburgh synagogue and the slaughter of seventeen students and teachers at a Florida school, to a wave of mail bombs sent to leading Democratic figures and CNN, [14] part of an explosion of religious and ethnically focused hate crimes since the primaries began in 2015.[15]

The Way Forward

As news organizations published their 2018 year-in-review articles, two iconic images stood out. One epitomized the tattered remnants of American influence in the Middle East. It showed a grinning MBS and Russian President Vladimir Putin giving each other a high five. The other showed the new Congressional "Dream Team" of Omar, Tlaib and two other young, progressive women of color, Ayanna Pressley of Boston and New York's Alexandria Ocasio-Cortez.

There was one more image that summed up the new reality. It was a tweet from Ilhan Omar directed at a conservative pastor who complained that "[t]he floor of Congress is now going to look like an Islamic republic,"[16] but the tweet, which included a smiley face laughing so hard it was crying, could just as well have been aimed at Donald Trump:

> Well sir, the floor of Congress is going to look like America . . .
>   And you're gonna have to just deal

Lawrence Pintak
Seattle, Washington
January 2018

NOTES

Introduction

1 Theodore Schleifer, "Donald Trump: 'I Think Islam Hates Us,'" (2016), https://www.cnn.com/2016/03/09/politics/donald-trump-islam-hates-us/.

2 Samuel P. Huntington, *The Clash of Civilizations and the Remaking of World Order* (New York: Simon & Schuster, 1996).

3 David Sherfinski, "Donald Trump: We Will 'Eradicate' 'Radical Islamic Terrorism' 'from the Face of the Earth,'" *washingtontimes. com* (2017), http://www.washingtontimes.com/news/2017/jan/20/ donald-trump-we-will-eradicate-radical-islamic-ter/.

4 Ryan Devereaux, "An Interview with Michael T. Flynn, the Ex-Pentagon Spy Who Supports Donald Trump," *The Intercept* (2016), https:// theintercept.com/2016/07/13/an-interview-with-lt-gen-michael-flynn/.

5 Gabrielle Seunagal, "No Islam in America," Twitter, https://twitter.com/ ClassySnobbb/status/796224917905833984?lang=en].

6 Jimmy Carter, "Relations with Islamic Nations Statement by the President," (The American Presidency Project, 1980).

7 Lawrence Pintak, *Reflections in a Bloodshot Lens: America, Islam and the War of Ideas* (London; Ann Arbor, MI: Pluto, 2006).

8 Ibid., p. 15.

9 Nina Shapiro, "CEO Makes Fiery Emails about Muslims Part of the Workday," *Seattle Times*, April 29, 2016.

10 Portions of this chapter were previously published as Lawrence Pintak, "The Muslims Are Coming! The Muslims Are Coming!," *ForeignPolicy.com* (2016), https://bit.ly/1WN6XDS.

11 Thomas S. Kidd, *American Christians and Islam: Evangelical Culture and Muslims from the Colonial Period to the Age of Terrorism* (Princeton, NJ: Princeton University Press, 2009).

12 Kambiz GhaneaBassiri, *A History of Islam in America: From the New World to the New World Order* (New York: Cambridge University Press, 2010).

13 Sylviane A. Diouf, *Servants of Allah: African Muslims Enslaved in the Americas*, 15th anniversary edn. (New York: New York University Press, 2013), 71, Kindle edition.

14   Ibid.

15   Denise A. Spellberg, *Thomas Jefferson's Qur'an: Islam and the Founders*, 1st edn. (New York: Alfred A. Knopf, 2013), 7.

16   Michael A. Gomez, "Muslims in Early America," *Journal of Southern History* 60, no. 4 (1994), 671.

17   Dan Merica, "Trump: Frederick Douglass 'Is Being Recognized More and More'," *CNN.com* (2017), https://cnn.it/2vK8Yum.

18   Spellberg.

19   Gomez.

20   Diouf, 96–97.

21   Kidd.

22   Timothy J. Johnson, *Franciscans and Preaching: Every Miracle from the Beginning of the World Came About through Words*, The Medieval Franciscans (Leiden; Boston: Brill, 2012). Quoted in, p. 336.

23   Malcolm Lambert, *Crusade and Jihad* (London: Profile Books Ltd., 2016).

24   William Muir, *The Life of Mahomet and History of Islam, to the Era of the Hegira*, 4 vols. (n.p., 1858).

25   Voltaire et al., *Mahomet, the Imposter* (London: C. Bathurst etc., 1777).

26   Spellberg, 33.

27   Ibid., 9.

28   Daniel L. Dreisbach and Mark David Hall, *Faith and the Founders of the American Republic* (New York: Oxford University Press, 2014), 92.

29   Robert J. Allison, *The Crescent Obscured: The United States and the Muslim World, 1776–1815* (New York: Oxford University Press, 1995), 40.

30   "Barbary Wars, 1801–1805 and 1815–1816," *Milestones: 1801–1829*, https://history.state.gov/milestones/1801–1829/barbary-wars.

31   "Francis Scott Key," *Strangers to Us All: Lawyers and Poetry* (2001), http://myweb.wvnet.edu/~jelkins/lp-2001/key.html.

32   "Vaccination for Smallpox? The Paper War during Boston's Smallpox Epidemic of 1721," *National Humanities Center Resource Toolbox*, http://nationalhumanitiescenter.org/pds/becomingamer/ideas/text5/smallpoxvaccination.pdf.

33   Jonathan Edwards and Jonathan Edwards, *Apocalyptic Writings*, The Works of Jonathan Edwards, vol. 5 (New Haven: Yale University Press, 1977).

34   Timothy Marr, *The Cultural Roots of American Islamicism* (Cambridge; New York: Cambridge University Press, 2006), 92.

35   Jann Bellamy, "NY Federal Court Hands Triple Loss to Anti-Vaccination Ideology," *Science-Based Medicine* (2014), https://sciencebasedmedicine.org/ny-federal-court-hands-triple-loss-to-anti-vaccination-ideology/.

36 Soumya Chatterjee and Haritha John, "Video of Kerala Islamic Leader
    Calling Vaccination 'Work of Devil' Surfaces, Group Denies," (2015),
    http://www.thenewsminute.com/article/video-kerala-islamic-leader-
    calling-vaccination-work-devil-surfaces-group-denies-35347.

37 "Pat Robertson Praises 'Mideast Beast' on 'the 700 Club'," *endureinstrength.
    org*, http://www.endureinstrength.org/pages.asp?pageid=119412.

38 CNN, "Transcript of Republican Debate in Miami, Full Text" (Atlanta:
    CNN.com, 2016).

Chapter 1

1   Ron Elving, "What Trump Really Meant When He Said Obama Has
    'Something Else in Mind'," *NPR* (2016), https://n.pr/2HwvlJm.

2   Jesse Byrnes, "Trump on Obama and Islam: 'There's Something Going
    On'," *thehill.com* (2016), http://thehill.com/blogs/blog-briefing-room/
    news/283246-trump-on-obama-and-islam-theres-something-going-on.

3   Maggie Haberman, "Donald Trump Calls for Surveillance of "Certain
    Mosques" and a Syrian Refugee Database," *Newyorktimes.com* (2015),
    https://www.nytimes.com/2015/11/22/us/politics/donald-trump-syrian-
    muslims-surveillance.html.

4   Donald J. Trump, "Presidential Announcement Speech," *time.com* (2015),
    http://time.com/3923128/donald-trump-announcement-speech/.

5   CNN.

6   Joe Scarborough, "Trump: 'Something Going on' with Islam and
    Violence" (2015), http://www.msnbc.com/morning-joe/watch/
    trump--something-going-on-with-islam-and-violence-576200259724.

7   Max Ehrenfreund, "The Four Cryptic Words Donald Trump Can't Stop
    Saying," *Washingtonpost.com* (2016), https://www.washingtonpost.com/
    news/wonk/wp/2016/06/13/the-four-cryptic-words-donald-trump-cant-
    stop-saying/?utm_term=.cf5bf1efa4b3.

8   Mark Wilstein, "Bobby Jindal on Muslim Americans: 'That's Not
    Immigration', It's 'Invasion'," *Mediaite* (2015), https://www.mediaite.com/
    online/bobby-jindal-on-muslim-americans-thats-not-immigration-
    its-invasion/.

9   Omar Suleiman, "Exploring the Faith and Identity Crisis of American
    Muslim Youth" (Yaqeen Institute for Islamic Research, 2017).

10 Jenna Johnson, "Donald Trump Says He 'Absolutely' Wants a Database of
    Syrian Refugees," *Washington Post* (2015), https://www.washingtonpost.
    com/news/post-politics/wp/2015/11/21/donald-trump-says-he-absolutely-
    wants-a-database-of-syrian-refugees/?utm_term=.fe5393caa3eb.

11 " 'This Week' Transcript: Donald Trump and Ben Carson," *This Week* (2015), http://abcnews.go.com/Politics/week-transcript-donald-trump-ben-carson/story?id=35336008.

12 "Rubio: Senate Dems Will Back Bill to Pause Refugee Program," *The Kelly File* (2015), http://video.foxnews.com/v/4622536839001/?playlist_id=2694949842001#sp=show-clips.

13 "Trump Calls for 'Total and Complete Shutdown of Muslims Entering the United States'," *Washington Post* (2015), https://www.washingtonpost.com/news/post-politics/wp/2015/12/07/donald-trump-calls-for-total-and-complete-shutdown-of-muslims-entering-the-united-states/?utm_term=.5faf050567b5.

14 Donald J. Trump, "Extraordinary Influx," *Twitter* (2015), https://bit.ly/2FhOfO8.

15 Nick Kim Sexton, "GOP Hopeful Carly Fiorina under Fire for 'Praising Muslims'," *MSNBC.com* (2015), https://nbcnews.to/2vLnyle.

16 "Je Suis Charlie," *Real Time with Bill Maher* (2015), http://www.real-time-with-bill-maher-blog.com/index/2015/1/10/je-suis-charlie-january-9-2015.

17 Dylan Stableford, "Marco Rubio Bought a Gun to Be 'Last Line of Defense between ISIS and My Family'," *Yahoo!* (2016), https://www.yahoo.com/news/rubio-bought-gun-isis-174728777.html.

18 November 1, 2015–October 31, 2016. Author's e-mail exchange with mediaQuant COO Mary Harris, April 3–4, 2018.

19 Mary Harris, "A Media Post-Mortem on the 2016 Presidential Election" (Portland, OR: mediaQuant, 2016).

20 Jonathan Mahler, "CNN Had a Problem. Donald Trump Solved It," *New York Times Magazine* (2017), https://www.nytimes.com/2017/04/04/magazine/cnn-had-a-problem-donald-trump-solved-it.html.

21 Barbara Sprunt and Ally Mutnick, "On the Clock: Trump Gets Most Time in GOP Debate," *It's All Politics* (2015), https://www.npr.org/sections/itsallpolitics/2015/09/16/440827414/on-the-clock-who-spoke-the-longest.

22 Alicia Parlapiano, "A Final Count of Candidate Speaking Time," *New York Times* (2015), https://www.nytimes.com/live/republican-debate-election-2016-cleveland/a-final-count-of-candidate-speaking-time/.

23 "Anderson Cooper Interviewed Trump, and It Was a Disgrace," *Slate.com* (2016), http://www.slate.com/blogs/the_slatest/2016/03/09/anderson_cooper_s_interview_with_donald_trump_was_a_disgrace.html.

24 Mahler.

25 Nick Visser, "CBS Chief Les Moonves Says Trump's 'Damn Good' for Business," *Huffington Post Media* (2016), https://www.huffingtonpost.com/entry/les-moonves-donald-trump_us_56d52ce8e4b03260bf780275.

26 The Editorial Board, "Mr. Trump's Applause Lies," *New York Times* (2015), https://www.nytimes.com/2015/11/24/opinion/mr-trumps-applause-lies.html.

27 "Truth and Lies in the Age of Trump," *New York Times* (2016), https://www. nytimes.com/2016/12/10/opinion/truth-and-lies-in-the-age-of-trump. html.

28 Edward W. Said, *Covering Islam: How the Media and the Experts Determine How We See the Rest of the World* (New York: Vintage Books, 1997), xxii; italics in original.

29 Mariam Duranni, "A Portrait of Islamophobia?" *Religion Dispatches* (2015), http://religiondispatches.org/a-portrait-of-islamophobia/.

30 Lawrence Pintak and Syed Javid Nazir, "Inside the (Muslim) Journalist's Mind," *New York Times*, February 12, 2011.

31 Lawrence Pintak, *Reflections in a Bloodshot Lens: America, Islam and the War of Ideas* (London; Ann Arbor, MI: Pluto, 2006), 30.

32 "US TV Primetime News Prefer Stereotypes: Muslims Framed Mostly as Criminals" (London: Media Tenor, 2013).

33 Owais Arshad, Varun Setlur and Usaid Siddiqui, "Are Muslims Collectively Responsible?" (416Labs, 2015).

34 Youssef Chouhoud and Dalia Mogahed, "American Muslim Poll 2018" (Dearborn, MI: ISPU, 2018).

35 Meighan Stone, "Snake and Stranger: Media Coverage of Muslims and Refugee Policy," (Cambridge, MA: Joan Shorenstein Center on Media, Politics, and Public Policy; Kennedy School; Harvard University, 2017).

36 Chouhoud and Mogahed.

37 Suleiman.

38 Hend Amry, "So True," *Twitter* (2016), https://twitter.com/LibyaLiberty/ status/719551173766864897.

39 Shaya Tafeye Mohajer, "Q&A: Hannah Allam on Covering Muslim Life in America for BuzzFeed," *Columbia Journalism Review* (2017), https://www. cjr.org/q_and_a/qa-hannah-allam-on-covering-muslim-life-in-america-for-buzzfeed.php.

40 "2017 Survey of U.S. Muslims" (Washington, DC: Pew Research Center, 2017).

41 Brian J. Bowe and Taj W. Makki, "Muslim Neighbors or an Islamic Threat? A Constructionist Framing Analysis of Newspaper Coverage of Mosque Controversies," *Media, Culture & Society* 38, no. 4 (2015).

42 "Donald Trump Orlando Tweet" (2016), https://twitter.com/ realDonaldTrump/status/742096033207844864.

43 "Trump Tweet: Right on Radical Islam" (2017), https://twitter.com/ realdonaldtrump/status/742034549232766976?lang=en.

44 "A Joint Muslim Statement on the Carnage in Orlando," http:// orlandostatement.com/.

45 "Do American Muslims Need to Speak Out against Radical Islam?," *Foxnews.com* (2016), http://www.foxnews.com/transcript/2016/12/27/

amb-oren-israel-was-hurt-by-this-appalling-resolution-do-american-muslims-need.html.

46   Rupert Murdoch, "Maybe Most Moslems," *Twitter* (2015), https://twitter.com/rupertmurdoch/status/553734788881076225?lang=en.

47   "Cair Video Calls out Fox News' Faux 'Condemn Islamic Extremism' Challenge to Muslim Leaders." News release, November 13, 2014.

48   Ibid.

49   Max Fisher, "It's Not Just Fox News: Islamophobia on Cable News Is Out of Control," *Vox.com* (2015), https://www.vox.com/2014/10/8/6918485/the-overt-islamophobia-on-american-tv-news-is-out-of-control.

50   "Kill the Imams of Kufr in the West," *Dabiq*, no. 14, 1437 Rajab (2016), https://clarionproject.org/docs/Dabiq-Issue-14.pdf.

51   Khizr Khan, "Khizr Khan's DNC 2016 Speech," *The Independent*, https://www.independent.co.uk/news/world/americas/dnc-2016-khizr-khan-donald-trump-read-full-transcript-father-muslim-soldier-a7161616.html.

52   Steve Turnham, "Donald Trump to Father of Fallen Soldier: 'I've Made a Lot of Sacrifices,'" *ABC News* (2016), http://abcnews.go.com/Politics/donald-trump-father-fallen-soldier-ive-made-lot/story?id=41015051.

53   Scott Detrow, "GOP Criticism Mounts as Trump Continues Attacks on Khan Family," *NPR* (2016), https://www.npr.org/2016/08/01/488213964/gop-criticism-mounts-as-trump-continues-attacks-on-khan-family.

54   ps://thehill.com/blogs/ballot-box/presidential-races/289938-graham-trump-going-to-a-place-where-weve-never-gone.

55   Christina Gregg, "Why Us Veterans Voted 2-to-1 for Donald Trump," *AOL.com* (2016), https://www.aol.com/article/news/2016/11/11/why-veterans-voted-donald-trump-swing-states/21603486/.

56   Jesse Byrnes, "Nikki Haley Denounces Trump's Muslim Ban Idea," *The Hill* (2015), http://thehill.com/blogs/ballot-box/presidential-races/262589-nikki-haley-denounces-trumps-muslim-ban-idea.

57   S. A. Miller, "Speaker Paul Ryan Blasts Trump's Muslim Ban: 'This Is Not Conservatism,'" *Washingtontimes.com* (2015), http://www.washingtontimes.com/news/2015/dec/8/paul-ryan-blasts-trump-muslim-ban-not-conservatism/.

58   Leigh Ann Caldwell and Andrew Rafferty, "GOP Leaders Denounce Trump's Plan as Anti-American," *NBC News* (2016), https://www.nbcnews.com/politics/2016-election/paul-ryan-denounces-donald-trumps-anti-muslim-plan-n476201.

59   Lisa Mascaro, "Speaker Paul Ryan Defends Trump's Immigrant and Refugee Ban, as Congress Grumbles about Being Left Out," *LATimes.com* (2017), http://www.latimes.com/politics/washington/la-na-trailguide-updates-speaker-paul-ryan-stands-behind-trump-s-1485881647-htmlstory.html.

Chapter 2

1   Portions of this chapter were first published as Lawrence Pintak, "Portland Is the Most Livable City in America—Except If You're Muslim," *ForeignPolicy.com* (2016), https://bit.ly/1VFldfK.

2   Office of the Inspector General, "A Review of the FBI's Handling of the Brandon Mayfield Case" (Washington, DC: Department of Justice, 2006).

3   Michael Price, "Community Outreach or Intelligence Gathering?" (Brennan Center for Justice at New York University School of Law, 2015).

4   Ibid.

5   "Portland Passes Resolution for Welcoming Muslims," *KGW.com* (2016), https://bit.ly/2JuliRq.

6   "A Resolution to Declare Support for the Muslim Community and Reaffirm Beaverton as a Welcoming City" (Beaverton, OR: City Council, 2017).

7   Dalia Mogahed and Youssef Chouhoud, "American Muslim Poll" (Dearborn, MI: ISPU, 2017).

8   Judge John B. Owens, "United States of America v. Mohamed Osman Mahomud," ed. Ninth Circuit United States Court of Appeals (San Francisco, 2016).

9   Judge John V. Acosta, "Arrest Warrant," ed. United States District Court for the District of Oregon (Vancouver, WA, 2010).

10 Owens.

11 Ibid.

12 Ibid.

13 Kumar Rao, Carey Shenkman and Sarrah Buageila, "Equal Treatment? Measuring the Legal and Media Responses to Ideologically Motivated Violence in the United States," ed. Dalia Mogahed (Washington, DC; Dearborn, MI: Institute for Social Policy and Understanding, 2018).

14 Glenn Greenwald and Murtaza Hussain, "Meet the Muslim-American Leaders the FBI and NSA Have Been Spying On," *The Intercept* (2014), https://theintercept.com/2014/07/09/under-surveillance/.

15 Spencer Ackerman, "FBI Fired Sebastian Gorka for Anti-Muslim Diatribes," *Daily Beast* (2017), https://www.thedailybeast.com/fbi-fired-sebastian-gorka-for-anti-muslim-diatribes.

16 Greenwald and Hussain.

17 Owens.

18 Ibid.

19 Shawn Scott Hare, "Affidavit in Support." United States of America v. Erick Jamal Hendricks, United States District Court for the Northern District of Ohio. (Cleveland: 2016).

20 "United States of America v. Justin Nojan Sullivan a/K/a 'the Mujahid'. Bill of Indictment," ed. Asheville Division United States District Court for the Western District of North Carolina (Asheville, NC, 2016).

21 Rao, Shenkman and Buageila.

22 Yasmeen Abutaleb and Kristina Cooke, "A Teen's Turn to Radicalism and the U.S. Safety Net That Failed to Stop It," *Reuters Investigates* (2016), https://www.reuters.com/investigates/special-report/usa-extremists-teen/.

23 Matt Apuzzo, "Only Hard Choices for Parents Whose Children Flirt with Terror," *New York Times* (2016), https://www.nytimes.com/2016/04/10/us/parents-face-limited-options-to-keep-children-from-terrorism.html.

24 Alex Nowrasteh, "Terrorism and Immigration: A Risk Analysis," in *Policy Analysis* (Washington, DC: Cato Institute, 2016).

25 Kristine Phillips, "In the Latest JFK Files: The FBI's Ugly Analysis on Martin Luther King Jr., Filled with Falsehoods," *Washington Post*, November 12, 2017, https://wapo.st/2qgJijY.

26 Adam Nossiter, "Too Radical for France, a Muslim Clergyman Faces Deportation," *New York Times* (2018), https://nyti.ms/2qay13W.

27 Bob Graham et al., "Part Four: Finding, Discussion and Narrative Regarding Certain Sensitive National Security Matters; Report of the U.S. Senate Select Committee on Intelligence and U.S. House Permanent Select Committee on Intelligence" (Washington, DC: U.S. Congress, 2002), 435.

28 Rowan Scarborough, "Saudi Government Funded Extremism in U.S. Mosques and Charities: Report," *Washington Times* (2016), https://www.washingtontimes.com/news/2016/jul/19/911-report-details-saudi-arabia-funding-of-muslim-/.

29 Graham et al., 417.

30 Ibid., 435.

31 James Zogby, "Saudis Reject Bin Laden and Terrorism" (2003), http://www.aaiusa.org/w081103.

32 Graham et al., 418.

33 Dan Christensen, "Saudi Arabia Cites FBI's Meese Commission in Asking Judge to Toss 9/11 Victims' Lawsuit," *Florida Bulldog* (2017), http://www.floridabulldog.org/2017/08/saudi-arabia-cites-fbis-meese-commission-in-asking-judge-to-toss-911-victims-lawsuit/.

34 Ibid.

35 Ibid.

Chapter 3

1 Portions of this chapter were first published as Lawrence Pintak, "The Rise of the American Taliban," *ForeignPolicy.com* (2016), https://bit.ly/2FqfCFz.

2 Tahir Khan, "Remarks by Pakistani Cleric Spark Controversy, Stir Up Pak-Afghan Tension," *Express Tribune* (2013), https://bit.ly/2qZUIZI.

3 "From the MEMRI Archives: Reports on Pakistani School, Radical Mosque That Played a Role in CA Jihadi Tashfeen Malik's Radicalization," *MEMRI* (2016), https://bit.ly/2HSKN1z.

Chapter 4

1 Portions of this chapter were first published as Lawrence Pintak, "Black and White and Trump All Over," *ForeignPolicy.com* (2016), https://bit.ly/2r6we12.

2 Shahzad Raza, "A Religious Edict against Pakistan's Information Minister Is a Worrying Sign," *Friday Times* (2015), http://www.thefridaytimes.com/tft/fatwa-fears/.

3 Zachary Laub, "International Sanctions on Iran" (New York: Council on Foreign Relations, 2015).

4 Charlotte Alter, "Transcript: Read the Full Text of the Fourth Republican Debate in Milwaukee," *Time.com* (2015), http://time.com/4107636/transcript-read-the-full-text-of-the-fourth-republican-debate-in-milwaukee/.

5 Nicole Gaouette and Barbara Starr, "Trump Is Calling for 30,000 Troops. Would That Defeat Isis?" *CNN.com* (2016), https://www.cnn.com/2016/03/11/politics/donald-trump-30000-troops-isis/.

6 "Transcript: Donald Trump's Full Immigration Speech, Annotated," *Los Angeles Times* (2016), https://lat.ms/2bEhguL.

7 Pamela Engel, "Donald Trump: 'I Would Bomb the S--- out of' Isis," *Businessinsider.com* (2015), http://www.businessinsider.com/donald-trump-bomb-isis-2015-11.

8 "Donald Trump Calls Pakistan Most Dangerous Country," *Reuters* (2015), https://bit.ly/2Jtg1cR.

9 "Donald Trump Says May Seek India's Help on 'Unstable' Pakistan Nukes," *Press Trust of India* (2016), https://bit.ly/2Jttstf.

Chapter 5

1 Portions of this chapter were first published as Lawrence Pintak, "For Muslim Americans, Fear and Shock at a Trump Presidency," *ForeignPolicy.com* (2016), https://bit.ly/2eWMQQG.

2 Donald J. Trump, "Statement on Preventing Muslim Immigration." News release, December 7, 2015, https://www.donaldjtrump.com/press-releases/donald-j.-trump-statement-on-preventing-muslim-immigration.

3 Bill Morlin, "Experts Seeing Spike in Possible Anti-Muslim Hate Crimes" (Atlanta: Southern Poverty Law Center, 2016).

4   Theodore Schleifer, "Donald Trump: 'I Think Islam Hates Us,'" *CNN.com* (2016), http://www.cnn.com/2016/03/09/politics/donald-trump-islam-hates-us/.

5   "Transcript: Donald Trump's Victory Speech," *New York Times* (2017), https://www.nytimes.com/2016/11/10/us/politics/trump-speech-transcript.html.

6   Maha Abdul Gawad, "My First Racist Encounter," Facebook, https://www.facebook.com/shaunking/photos/a.799605230078397.1073741828.7995399 10084929/1194283823943867/?type=3.

7   Seunagal.

8   Shaheen Pasha, "Voices: Donald Trump Is My Son's Bogeyman," *usatoday.com* (2015), http://www.usatoday.com/story/opinion/voices/2015/12/10/voices-donald-trump-my-sons-bogeyman/77088272/.

9   "Complaint for Injunctive and Declaratory Relief," ed. Eastern District of Virginia United States District Court (Richmond, VA, 2017).

10   Rachel Weiner and Justin Jouvenal, "Government Reveals More Than 100,000 Visas Revoked Due to Travel Ban," *washingtonpost.com* (2017), https://www.washingtonpost.com/local/public-safety/government-reveals-over-100000-visas-revoked-due-to-travel-ban/2017/02/03/7d529eec-ea2c-11e6-b82f-687d6e6a3e7c_story.html?hpid=hp_hp-top-table-main_visas-1246pm%3Ahomepage%2Fstory&utm_term=.7277cc050267.

11   Alexander Meleagrou-Hitchens, "As American as Apple Pie: How Anwar Al-Awlaki Became the Face of Western Jihad" (London: ICSR, King's College, 2011), 75.

12   Rebecca Savransky, "Giuliani: Trump Asked Me How to Do a Muslim Ban 'Legally,'" *thehill.com* (2017), http://thehill.com/homenews/administration/316726-giuliani-trump-asked-me-how-to-do-a-muslim-ban-legally.

13   Donald J. Trump, "Call It What You Will," *Twitter* (2017), https://bit.ly/2r4TDPt.

14   "Pouring In," *Twitter* (2015), https://bit.ly/2pJl3ZW.

15   Amy B. Wang, "Trump Lashes Out at 'So-Called Judge' Who Temporarily Blocked Travel Ban," *Washington Post* (2017), https://wapo.st/2vLbXCI.

16   Chris Sommerfeldt, "Texas Pastor Who Calls Islam 'Evil,' Homosexuals 'Filthy' to Give Donald Trump Private Inauguration Sermon," *nydailynews.com* (2017), http://www.nydailynews.com/news/politics/trump-inauguration-sermon-rev-calls-islam-evil-article-1.2951078. That same preacher would lead the prayer at the dedication of the U.S. embassy in Jerusalem.

17   Juliet Eilperin and Sandhya Somashekhar, "Trump Considering Order on Religious Freedom That Critics Warn Could Lead to Discrimination,"

Sltrib.com (2017), http://www.sltrib.com/home/4899090-155/
trump-considering-order-on-religious-freedom.

18 Philip Bump, "Why Did Sean Spicer Suggest That the Quebec Shooting
Validated Trump's Policy Initiatives?" *Washington Post* (2017), https://
wapo.st/2vOCoro.

19 Mahita Gajanan, "President Trump Says Media 'Doesn't Want to
Report' on Terror Attacks," *Time.com* (2017), http://time.com/4661625/
president-trump-media-report-terrorism/.

20 Carl Bildt, "That's Ludicrous" (2017), https://bit.ly/2JvnzvM.

21 Josh Feldman, "CBS' Scott Pelley: 'It Has Been a Busy Day for Presidential
Statements Divorced from Reality'," *Mediaite* (2017), https://bit.
ly/2Hy2FeU.

22 Dean Obeidallah, "The Terror Trial We're Really Ignoring," *dailybeast.com*
(2017), http://www.thedailybeast.com/articles/2017/02/07/mr-president-a-
terrorist-is-on-trial-right-now-but-he-s-christian.html.

23 J. Herbert Altschull, "What Is News," *Mass Comm Review*, no. Dec. (1974).

24 Rao, Shenkman and Buageila.

25 "When Is It 'Terrorism'? How the Media Cover Attacks by
Muslim Perpetrators," *The Hidden Brain* (2017), https://www.npr.
org/2017/06/19/532963059/when-is-it-terrorism-how-the-media-covers-
attacks-by-muslim-perpetrators.

26 Rao, Shenkman and Buageila.

27 Trump, "Presidential Announcement Speech."

28 Oli Smith, "Video Shows Trump's New National Security Advisor Brand
Islam a 'Malignant Cancer'," *Express.com.uk* (2016), http://www.
express.co.uk/news/world/734285/Michael-Flynn-Donald-Trump-
National-Security-Advisor-Islam.

29 Paul McLeary and Dan De Luce, "Trump's Possible VP Believes Isis Could
Conquer the U.S. and Drink Americans' Blood," *Foreignpolicy.com* (2016),
http://foreignpolicy.com/2016/07/12/trumps-possible-vp-believes-isis-
could-conquer-the-u-s-and-drink-americans-blood/.

30 Andrew Kaczynski, "On Twitter, Michael Flynn Interacted with Alt-
Right, Made Controversial Comments on Muslims, Shared Fake News,"
Flynn on Twitter (2016), http://www.cnn.com/2016/11/18/politics/
kfile-flynn-tweets/.

31 Jennie Rothenberg Gritz, "When Dr. Seuss Took on Adolf Hitler,"
theatlantic.com (2013), https://www.theatlantic.com/national/
archive/2013/01/when-dr-seuss-took-on-adolf-hitler/267151/.

32 Kim LaCapria, "Horton Hears a Hitler," *Snopes.com* (2015), http://www.
snopes.com/dr-seuss-adolf-wolf/.

33 Sally Bronston, "McConnell on Trump Judge Comments: 'I Couldn't
Disagree More'," *Meet the Press* (2016), http://www.nbcnews.com/

meet-the-press/mcconnell-trump-judge-comments-i-couldn-t-disagree-more-n586056.

34 Spellberg, 106.

35 Ibid. Quoted in, 118.

36 Ibid., 5.

37 Ibid., 174.

38 Ibid., 40.

39 Ibid. Quoted in, 177

40 Ibid., 168.

41 Thomas Williams, *The American Spirit: The Story of Commodore William Phillip Bainbridge*, Kindle ed. (AuthorHouse, 2010), 204.

Chapter 6

1   Lt. Gen. Michael T. Flynn, "'I Dare'," *Twitter* (2016), https://twitter.com/genflynn/status/753772080471179264?lang=en.

2   "Newt Gingrich: Deport Every Muslim Who Believes in Sharia," *Foxnews.com* (2016), http://video.foxnews.com/v/5036444136001/?#sp=show-clips.

3   Portions of this chapter were first published as Lawrence Pintak, "Not All Islamists Are Out to Kill Us," *ForeignPolicy.com* (2016), https://bit.ly/2HFI9Ja.

4   Maajid Nawaz, "My Open Letter to a Jailed Muslim Brotherhood Leader," *Daily Beast* (2017), https://www.thedailybeast.com/my-open-letter-to-a-jailed-muslim-brotherhood-leader.

5   Mogahed and Chouhoud.

6   M. Cherif Bassiouni, "Islamic Law—the Sharia" (2012), http://www.mei.edu/content/islamic-law-shariah.

7   Toni Johnson and Mohammed Aly Sergie, "Islam: Governing under Sharia," (2014), https://www.cfr.org/backgrounder/islam-governing-under-sharia.

8   Jacob Poushter, "The Divide over Islam and National Laws in the Muslim World" (Washington, DC: Pew Research Center, 2016).

9   "Islamic Radicalism: Its Wahhabi Roots and Current Representation," https://bit.ly/1E1YEKQ.

10 Eugene Scott, "Ted Cruz: Program Patrolling Muslim Neighborhoods Was a Success," *CNN.com* (2016), https://cnn.it/2vRNhJ3.

11 "Terminology to Define the Terrorists: Recommendations from American Muslims" (Washington, DC: Department of Homeland Security, 2008).

12 Sophie Tatum, "France Attack Highlights Differences in Trump, Clinton Terror Responses," *CNN.com* (2016), https://cnn.it/2FjI77O.

13 Cyril Almeida, "Rally in Lahore Sends Alarm Bells Ringing," *Dawn.com* (2011), https://bit.ly/2HPGOTL.

14 Alberto Gonzales, "Countering the Islamic State's Message," *Journal of International Security Affairs* 30 (2016).

Chapter 7

1 Maria Rosa Menocal, *The Ornament of the World: How Muslims, Jews, and Christians Created a Culture of Tolerance in Medieval Spain*, Kindle ed. (Boston: Little, Brown, 2002). Loc. 136.

2 Lesley Hazleton, *After the Prophet: The Epic Story of the Shia-Sunni Split in Islam*, 1st ed. (New York: Doubleday, 2009), 34.

3 Wilferd Madelung, *The Succession to Muhammad: A Study of the Early Caliphate*, Kindle edn. (Cambridge; New York: Cambridge University Press, 1997), Loc. 739.

4 Ibid., Loc. 719.

5 Ibid., Loc. 1529.

6 Ibid.

7 Ibid.

8 Ibid., Loc. 633.

9 His son, Hasan, ruled for about six months before handing power to the founder of the Umayyad dynasty.

10 Menocal., Loc. 631

11 Matthew Carr, *Blood and Faith: The Purging of Muslim Spain*, Kindle ed. (New York: New Press, 2009), Loc. 5.

12 Menocal, Loc. 663.

13 Ibid., Loc. 3440.

14 Jonathan Brown, *Misquoting Muhammad: The Challenge and Choices of Interpreting the Prophet's Legacy*, Kindle ed. (London: Oneworld, 2014), Loc. 147.

15 Mohammad Ali Amir-Moezzi, *The Divine Guide in Early Shi'ism: The Sources of Esotericism in Islam* (Albany: State University of New York Press, 1994). 111–23.

16 Golnaz Esfandiari, "Iranian Ex-President Says U.S. Seeks Arrest of Hidden Imam," *Radio Free Europe/Radio Liberty* (2015), https://www.rferl.org/a/iran-ahmadinejad-hidden-imam-us/27086798.html.

17 Brown, Loc. 3717.

18 "Ahmadiyya Muslim Community," (2018), https://www.alislam.org/library/ahmadiyya-muslim-community/. Cyril Glassé, *The Concise Encyclopædia of Islam* (London: Stacey International, 1989), 252.

19   Gisela Procházka-Eisl and Stephan Procházka, *The Plain of Saints and Prophets: The Nusayri-Alawi Community of Cilicia (Southern Turkey) and Its Sacred Places* (Wiesbaden: Harrassowitz Verlag, 2010).

20   Yaron Friedman, *The NuṣAyrī-ʿalawīS: An Introduction to the Religion, History, and Identity of the Leading Minority in Syria*, Islamic History and Civilization (Leiden; Boston: Brill, 2010).

21   Yvette Talhamy, "The Fatwas and the Nusayri/Alawis of Syria," *Middle Eastern Studies* 46, no. 2 (2010): 176.

22   Samy S. Swayd, *Historical Dictionary of the Druzes*, 2nd ed., Historical Dictionaries of Peoples and Cultures (Lanham, MD: Rowman & Littlefield, 2015), 56.

23   Col. Charles Churchill, *The Druzes and the Maronites* (London: Bernard Quaritch, 1982).

24   Muhammad Saalih al-Munajjid, "A Brief Look at the Beliefs of the Druze," *Islam Question and Answer* (2003), https://islamqa.info/en/26139.

25   Saïd K. Aburish, *Nasser: The Last Arab*, 1st ed. (New York: St. Martin's Press/Thomas Dunne Books, 2004).

26   Amr Ezzat and Islam Barakat, "State's Islam and Forbidden Diversity" (Cairo: Egypt Initiative for Personal Rights, 2016).

27   "Wikileaks: Saudi Arabia and Azhar on the 'Shia Encroachment' in Egypt," *Mada Masr* (2015), https://www.madamasr.com/en/2015/07/09/feature/politics/wikileaks-saudi-arabia-and-azhar-on-the-shia-encroachment-in-egypt/.

28   Ibid.

29   "The Killing of Ismaili Start from Fatwa of Mufti Naeem Madarsa," *Jhang TV* (2015), http://jhangtv.com/the-killing-of-ismaili-started-from-the-fatwa-of-mufti-naeem-madarsas-must-watch/.

30   Super User, "Anti-Pakistan Mufti Naeem Declares Quaid-E-Azam Was an Infidel," (2015), http://www.shiitenews.org/index.php/pakistan/item/15936-anti-pakistan-mufti-naeem-declares-quaid-e-azam-was-an-infidel/15936-anti-pakistan-mufti-naeem-declares-quaid-e-azam-was-an-infidel.

31   Ibn ʿArabi, "Garden among the Flames," Poem, http://www.ibnarabisociety.org/poetry/ibn-arabi-poetry-index.html.

32   Lawrence Pintak, "Translating Spirituality into Real Life," *Beliefnet.net* (2000), https://bit.ly/2vKIoRQ.

33   Reuters, "Islamic State Beheads Two for 'Sorcery' in Egypt's Sinai," (2017), https://www.reuters.com/article/uk-egypt-insurgency/islamic-state-beheads-two-for-sorcery-in-egypts-sinai-idUSKBN16Z2PX.

34   Scholars say this is a distortion of a line in the Qur'an that describes criminals who will be gathered on Judgment Day as "blue-eyed."

35 Aaron C. Davis, "The Day Terrorists Took D.C. Hostage," *Washington Post* (2017), https://www.washingtonpost.com/local/dc-politics/the-day-muslim-terrorists-took-dc-hostage--and-there-was-a-happy-ending/2017/03/10/e7cf4918-0517-11e7-ad5b-d22680e18d10_story.html?utm_term=.5204aa06b519.

36 All Qur'an quotations in the book are from *Seyyed Hossein Nasr, The Study Quran: A New Translation and Commentary*, 1st ed. (New York: HarperOne, 2015).

37 Muhammad Ibn Ishmail Bukhari, *Sahih Al-Bukhari*, ed. Muhammed Muhsin Khan (Alexandria, VA: Saadwai Publications, 1996), 6: 477–8.

38 Estelle Whelan, "Forgotten Witness: Evidence for the Early Codification of the Qur'an," *Journal of the American Oriental Society* 118 (1998).

39 Ruqayya Yasmine Khan, "Did a Woman Edit the Qur'an?: Hafṣa and Her Famed 'Codex'," *Journal of the American Academy of Religion* 82, no. 1 (2014).

40 Angelika Neuwirth, "Two Faces of the Qur'an: Qur'an and Mushar," *Oral Traditions* 25, no. 1 (2010): 142.

41 C. H. M. Versteegh, *Arabic Grammar and Qur'anic Exegesis in Early Islam*, Studies in Semitic Languages and Linguistics (Leiden; New York: E. J. Brill, 1993).

42 Whelan, 3.

43 Brown, Loc. 567.

44 Ibid., Loc. 381.

45 Ibid., Loc. 3651 and 3765.

46 "Quran: All You Need for Salvation," *True Islam* (2010), http://www.quran-islam.org/main_topics/quran/new_information/quran_is_all_we_need_(P1253).html.

47 "Does 20:130 Imply or Authorise 5 Salat?," *True Islam* (2010), http://www.quran-islam.org/main_topics/misinterpreted_verses/manipulation_of_20:130_(P1251).html.

48 Yusuf Qadhi, "On Salafi Islam," (2014), https://muslimmatters.org/2014/04/22/on-salafi-islam-dr-yasir-qadhi/.

49 Ibid.

50 Jeffrey Goldberg, "Saudi Crown Prince: Iran's Supreme Leader 'Makes Hitler Look Good'," *The Atlantic* (2018), https://www.theatlantic.com/international/archive/2018/04/mohammed-bin-salman-iran-israel/557036/.

51 Ahmad Mustafa-Hakima, *History of Eastern Arabia 1750–1800: The Rise and Development of Bahrain, Kuwait and Wahhabi Saudi Arabia*, 2nd ed. London (Probsthain, 1988), 30.

52 Julia Day Howell, "Indonesia's Salafist Sufis," *Modern Asian Studies* 44, no. 5 (2009).

53 Gilles Kepel, *Jihad: The Trail of Political Islam* (Cambridge, MA: Harvard University Press, 2002).

54 Olivier Roy and Cynthia Schoch, *Jihad and Death: The Global Appeal of Islamic State* (New York: Oxford University Press, 2017), 58.

55 Nossiter; italics added.

56 Noorhaidi Hasan, *Laskar Jihad: Islam, Militancy, and the Quest for Identity in Post-New Order Indonesia*, Studies on Southeast Asia (Ithaca, NY: Southeast Asia Program Publications, Southeast Asia Program, Cornell University, 2006).

57 Husain Haqqani, "Islamism and the Pakistani State," in *Current Trends in Islamist Ideology* (Washington, DC: Hudson Institute, 2013).

58 Gary R. Bunt, *Imuslims: Rewiring the House of Islam*, Islamic Civilization and Muslim Networks (Chapel Hill: University of North Carolina Press, 2009), 114–16.

59 Ibid., 118.

60 "Convert Straddles Worlds of Islam and Hip-Hop," *New York Times*, October 29, 2011.

61 Muhammad Michael Knight, *Why I Am a Salafi*, Kindle ed. (Berkeley, CA: Soft Skull Press, 2015), Loc. 127.

62 Brown, Loc. 1232.

Chapter 8

1 Daniel Arkin and Erik Ortiz, "Trump Calls Obama the 'Founder of Isis' over Anti-Terror Strategy," (2016), https://www.nbcnews.com/politics/politics-news/trump-calls-obama-founder-isis-over-anti-terror-strategy-n628096.

2 Elie Kedourie, *In the Anglo-Arab Labyrinth: The Mcmahon-Husayn Correspondence and Its Interpretations, 1914–1939*, Cambridge Studies in the History and Theory of Politics (Cambridge; New York: Cambridge University Press, 1976), 22.

3 "An Official Proclamation from the Government of Great Britain to the Natives of Arabia and Arab Provinces, Public Record Office, 1914 (Pro), Fo141/710/9," cited in *Secret Affairs: Britain's Collusion with Radical Islam*, ed. Mark Curtis (London: Serpent's Tail, 2018), 6.

4 "Government Letter to Sherif of Mecca, November 1914, (Pro), Fo141/710/9," cited in *Secret Affairs: Britain's Collusion with Radical Islam*, ed. Mark Curtis (London: Serpent's Tail, 2018), 7.

5 Mark Curtis, *Secret Affairs: Britain's Collusion with Radical Islam*, Kindle ed. (London: Serpent's Tail, 2018).

6 Ibid., 6.

7 Ibid.

8 T. G. Fraser, Andrew Mango and Robert McNamara, *Making the Modern Middle East*, rev. and updated paperback ed. (London: Gingko Library, 2017), 228.

9 John Bagot Glubb, "Ibn Sa'ūd: King of Saudi Arabia," *Britannica.com*.

10 Sherifa Zuhur, *Saudi Arabia*, Middle East in Focus (Santa Barbara, CA: ABC-CLIO, 2011), 44.

11 John Bagot Glubb, *War in the Desert, an R.A.F. Frontier Campaign*, 1st American ed. (New York: Norton, 1961), 75.

12 Winston Churchill and Winston S. Churchill, *Never Give In! Winston Churchill's Speeches*, Bloomsbury revelations ed. (London: Bloomsbury Academic, 2013), 68.

13 Clive Leatherdale, *Britain and Saudi Arabia, 1925–1939: The Imperial Oasis* (London; Totowa, NJ: F. Cass, 1983), 126.

14 Faisal Devji, "Will Saudi Arabia Cease to Be the Center of Islam?," *New York Times* (2018), https://www.nytimes.com/2018/09/07/opinion/saudi-arabia-islam-mbs.html?rref=collection%2Fsectioncollection%2Fopinion&action=click&contentCollection=opinion&region=rank&module=package&version=highlights&contentPlacement=7&pgtype=sectionfront.

15 David Dean Commins, *The Wahhabi Mission and Saudi Arabia* (London; New York: I. B. Tauris, 2006), 88.

16 Joby Warrick, *Black Flags: The Rise of Isis* (New York: Doubleday, 2015. 1st ed., 28.

17 Richard F. Nyrop, *Saudi Arabia, a Country Study*, 4th ed., Area Handbook Series (Washington, DC: US GPO, 1984).

18 Osama bin Laden, "Declaration of War against the Americans Occupying the Land of the Two Holy Places," *al-Quds al-Arabi*, no. April 15, 2002 (1996), http://www.pbs.org/newshour/terrorism/international/fatwa_1996.html.

19 Warrick, 28–9.

20 Thomas Hegghammer and Stéphane Lacroix, "Rejectionist Islamism in Saudi Arabia: The Story of Juhayman Al-'Utaybi Revisited," *International Journal of Middle East Studies* 39, no. 1 (2007), 103–22. It has been widely reported that Juhayman's grandfather was a leader of the Ikhwan revolt, but Hegghammer interviewed members of Juhayman's group who said that was not accurate.

21 Karen Elliott House, *On Saudi Arabia: Its People, Past, Religion, Fault Lines--and Future*, 1st edn (New York: Alfred A. Knopf, 2012).

22 Yaroslav Trofimov, *The Siege of Mecca: The Forgotten Uprising in Islam's Holiest Shrine and the Birth of Al Qaeda*, 1st edn (New York: Doubleday, 2007), 64.

23   Stephen Rakowski, "How the 1979 Siege of Mecca Haunts the House of Saud," *Worldview* (2017), https://worldview.stratfor.com/article/how-1979-siege-mecca-haunts-house-saud.

24   Hegghammer and Lacroix, 105–6.

25   Robert Lacey, *The Kingdom*, 1st American ed. (New York: Harcourt Brace Jovanovich, 1982), 48.

26   "CIA Confirms Role in 1953 Iran Coup," *National Security Archive Electronic Briefing Book No. 435* (2013), https://nsarchive2.gwu.edu/NSAEBB/NSAEBB435/.

27   James Risen, "The C.I.A. In Iran," *New York Times* (2000), https://archive.nytimes.com/www.nytimes.com/library/world/mideast/041600iran-cia-chapter4.html.

28   James Risen, "The C.I.A. In Iran," *New York Times* (2000), https://archive.nytimes.com/www.nytimes.com/library/world/mideast/041600iran-cia-chapter4.html.

29   "Iran," in *Amnesty International Briefing* (London: Amnesty International, 1976).

30   "Jimmy Carter Toasting with the Shah," YouTube, https://www.youtube.com/watch?v=DqrHQpRHwws.

31   Lawrence Pintak, *Seeds of Hate: How America's Flawed Lebanon Policy Ignited the Jihad* (Sterling, VA: Pluto Press, 2003).

32   Ibid.

33   Ronald Reagan, "Statement on the Third Anniversary of the Soviet Invasion of Afghanistan," ed. The White House (Washington, DC: Ronald Reagan Presidential Library and Museum, 1982).

34   "Remarks at the Annual Dinner of the Conservative Political Action Conference," in *The American Presidency Project* (Santa Barbara: University of California, Santa Barbara, 1985).

35   Steve Coll, *Ghost Wars: The Secret History of the Cia, Afghanistan, and Bin Laden, from the Soviet Invasion to September 10, 2001* (New York: Penguin Books, 2005).

36   "PPP Demands Probe Based on Benazir's Letter," *dawn.com* (2007), https://www.dawn.com/news/282349.

37   John Roth, Douglas Greenburg and Serena Wille, "Monograph on Terrorist Financing: Staff Report to the Commission" (National Commission on Terrorist Attacks upon the United States), 88.

38   Alison Pargeter, *The New Frontiers of Jihad: Radical Islam in Europe* (Philadelphia: University of Pennsylvania Press, 2008), 32.

39   Ahmed Rashid, *Taliban: Militant Islam, Oil and Fundamentalism in Central Asia*, 2nd ed. (New Haven, CT: Yale University Press, 2010), 129.

40 Jayshree Bajoria, "Pakistan's Education System and Links to Extremism" (New York: Council on Foreign Relations, 2009).

41 "Jemaah Islamiyah in South East Asia: Damaged But Still Dangerous" (Jakarta/Brussels: International Crisis Group, 2003).

42 Barnett R. Rubin, *The Fragmentation of Afghanistan: State Formation and Collapse in the International System*, 2nd ed. (New Haven, CT: Yale University Press, 2002), 146.

43 "Jemaah Islamiyah in South East Asia: Damaged But Still Dangerous," 2.

44 Kate Zernike and Michael T. Kaufman, "The Most Wanted Face of Terrorism," *New York Times* (2011), http://www.nytimes.com/2011/05/02/world/02osama-bin-laden-obituary.html?hp=&pagewanted=all.

45 Osama bin Laden, "Declaration of Jihad against the Americans Occupying the Land of the Two Holiest Sites." Combating Terrorism Center at West Point; U.S. Military Academy, West Point, NY, 1996.

46 Robert Fisk, "Why We Reject the West—by the Saudis' Fiercest Arab Critic," *The Independent*, 10 July 1996.

47 Matthew J. Morgan, "The Origins of the New Terrorism," *Parameters* 34, no. 1. 29. 2004.

48 bin Laden, "Declaration of Jihad against the Americans Occupying the Land of the Two Holiest Sites."

49 Reuters, "War in the Gulf: Bush Statement; Excerpts from 2 Statements by Bush on Iraq's Proposal for Ending Conflict," *New York Times* (1991), https://www.nytimes.com/1991/02/16/world/war-gulf-bush-statement-excerpts-2-statements-bush-iraq-s-proposal-for-ending.html.

50 George Bush and Brent Scowcroft, *A World Transformed*, 1st ed. (New York: Knopf: Distributed by Random House, 1998), 490.

51 Colin L. Powell and Joseph E. Persico, *My American Journey*, 1st Ballentine Books rev. ed. (New York: Ballantine Books, 2003), 531.

52 Bush and Scowcroft, 464.

53 Tim Arango, "A Long-Awaited Apology for Shiites, But the Wounds Run Deep," *New York Times* (2011), http://www.nytimes.com/2011/11/09/world/middleeast/iraqi-shiite-anger-at-united-states-remains-strong.html.

54 Jeremy Bransten, "Middle East: Rice Calls for a 'New Middle East'," *Radio Free Europe/Radio Liberty* (2006), https://www.rferl.org/a/1070088.html.

55 Charles Kurzman, "Death Tolls of the Iran-Iraq War" (2013), http://kurzman.unc.edu/death-tolls-of-the-iran-iraq-war/.

56 Seymour Hersh, "U.S. Secretly Gave Aid to Iraq Early in Its War against Iran," *New York Times* (1992), https://www.nytimes.com/1992/01/26/world/us-secretly-gave-aid-to-iraq-early-in-its-war-against-iran.html.

57 Bob Woodward, *The War Within: A Secret White House History, 2006–2008*, 1st Simon & Schuster trade pbk. ed. (New York: Simon & Schuster Paperbacks, 2009).

58 Saud al Faisal, "Saudi Arabia and the International Oil Markets" (Houston: James A. Baker III Institute for Public Policy, Rice University, 2005).

59 "The Fight against Extremism and the Search for Peace" (New York: Council on Foreign Relations, 2005).

60 Barack Obama, "Remarks by the President on a New Beginning," ed. The White House (Cairo: The White House, 2009).

61 "An Exceptional Summit and a Historic Speech," *Al Ahram* (2009), https://mideastwire.com/page/article.php?id=30118.

62 Rafiq Khuri, "An American Speech with an Islamic and Universal Taste," *Al-Anwar* (2009), https://mideastwire.com/page/article.php?id=30119.

63 Ghassan Charbel, "The Confusing Visitor," *Al-Hayat* (2009), https://mideastwire.com/page/article.php?id=30131.

64 Adel Bari Atwan, "Half an Apology Is Not Enough," *Al-Quds al-Arabi* (2005), https://mideastwire.com/page/article.php?id=30107.

65 Official U.S. government figures are consistently lower than those reported by independent organizations. The Bureau of Investigative Journalism maintains a real-time online database at https://thebureauinvestigates.com/projects/drone-war. That site does not include strikes in Libya. Another organization, Long War Journal, maintains its own database that includes Libya at https://www.longwarjournal.org/us-airstrikes-in-the-long-war.

66 Frederick Hof, "Leaving," *Syria Source* (2018), http://www.atlanticcouncil.org/blogs/syriasource/leaving?tmpl=component&print=1.

67 Mark Landler, "The Afghan War and the Evolution of Obama," *New York Times* (2017), https://www.nytimes.com/2017/01/01/world/asia/obama-afghanistan-war.html.

68 Mamdouh AlMuhaini, "Why Arabs Hate Obama," *Al Arabiyah English* (2017), https://english.alarabiya.net/en/views/news/middle-east/2017/01/06/Why-Arabs-hate-Obama-.html.

Chapter 9

1 Adam Nossiter, " 'Let Them Call You Racists': Bannon's Pep Talk to National Front," *New York Times* (2018), https://www.nytimes.com/2018/03/10/world/europe/steve-bannon-france-national-front.html?module=WatchingPortal&region=c-column-middle-span-region&pgType=Homepage&action=click&mediaId=thumb_square&state=standard&contentPlacement=7&version=internal&contentCollection=www.

nytimes.com&contentId=https%3A%2F%2Fwww.nytimes.com%2F2018%
2F03%2F10%2Fworld%2Feurope%2Fsteve-bannon-france-national-front.
html&eventName=Watching-article-click.

2 Greg Jaffe, "For a Trump Adviser, an Odyssey from the Fringes of
Washington to the Center of Power," *Washington Post* (2017), https://
www.washingtonpost.com/world/national-security/for-a-trump-
adviser-an-odyssey-from-the-fringes-of-washington-to-the-center-
of-power/2017/02/20/0a326260-f2cb-11e6-b9c9-e83fce42fb61_story.
html?utm_term=.5477516b0d20.

3 Matea Gold, "Bannon Film Outline Warned U.S. Could Turn into
'Islamic States of America," ibid., https://www.washingtonpost.com/
politics/bannon-film-outline-warned-us-could-turn-into-islamic-states-
of-america/2017/02/03/f73832f4-e8be-11e6-b82f-687d6e6a3e7c_story.
html?utm_term=.dffe65ed5df4.

4 Miriam Khan, "Donald Trump National Security Adviser Mike Flynn
Has Called Islam 'a Cancer," *ABC News* (2016), http://abcnews.go.com/
Politics/donald-trump-national-security-adviser-mike-flynn-called/
story?id=43575658.

5 "The Godfather," *Intelligence Report* (2014), https://www.splcenter.org/
fighting-hate/intelligence-report/2014/godfather.

6 David Cole, "More Dangerous Than Trump," *New York Review
of Books* (2017), http://www.nybooks.com/daily/2017/05/23/
more-dangerous-than-trump-jeff-sessions/.

7 Pema Levy, "Long before Trump, Kellyanne Conway Worked
for Anti-Muslim and Anti-Immigrant Extremists," *Mother
Jones* (2016), https://www.motherjones.com/politics/2016/12/
kellyanne-conway-immigration-islam-bannon-trump/.

8 Steven Simon and Daniel Benjamin, "The Islamophobic Huckster in the
White House," *New York Times* (2017), https://nyti.ms/2lF12C2.

9 Jeremy Scahill, "Blackwater Founder Erik Prince Implicated
in Murder," *The Nation* (2018), https://thenation.com/article/
blackwarer-founder-implicated-murder/.

10 Nick Gass, "Trump Ally: Clinton Aide Could Be 'Terrorist Agent,"
Politico.com (2016), https://www.politico.com/story/2016/06/
roger-stone-huma-abedin-terrorist-agent-224261.

11 "Ann Coulter Explains How to Talk to a Liberal ..." *Foxnews.com* (2004),
http://www.foxnews.com/story/2004/10/05/ann-coulter-explains-how-to-
talk-to-liberal.html.

12 Mobashra Tazamal, "Robert Mercer's Financing of Islamophobia" (2018),
http://bridge.georgetown.edu/robert-mercers-financing-islamophobia/.

13 Robert Macguire, "Exclusive: Robert Mercer Backed a Secretive Group
That Worked with Facebook, Google to Target Anti-Muslim Ads at

Swing Voters," *OpenSecrets,org* (2018), https://www.opensecrets.org/
news/2018/04/exclusive-robert-mercer-backed-a-secretive-group-that-
worked-with-facebook-google-to-target-anti-muslim-ads-at-swing-voters/.

14   A. Eban, *The Beirut Massacre: The Complete Kahan Commission Report*
(Princeton; New York: Karz-Cohl Publishing, 1983), 27–8.

15   Ben Lynfield, "Who Is Walid Phares, Trump's Mideast Adviser?"
Jerusalem Post (216), http://www.jpost.com/Us-Elections/
Who-is-Walid-Phares-Trumps-Mideast-adviser-472741.

16   Chris Rodda, "Maher Season Premiere Includes Islamophobe Who
Said Muslim-Americans Shouldn't Be Allowed to Hold Public Office,"
Huffington Post (2017), https://www.huffingtonpost.com/chris-rodda/
maher-season-premiere-inc_b_168972.html.

17   Michael Young, "The Dark Angel Gabriel," *Now Lebanon* (2011), http://
michaelyoungscolumns.blogspot.com/2011/03/dark-angel-gabriel.html.

18   Bob Smietana, "Covering the Anti-Islam Movement," in *Islam for
Journalists (and Everyone Else)*, ed. Lawrence Pintak and Stephen Franklin
(Columbia, MO: Donald W. Reynolds Journalism Institute, 2017).

19   Brigitte Gabriel, "A Survivor of Islamic Terror Warns America.," *Frontpage
Mag* (2006), http://archive.frontpagemag.com/Printable.aspx?ArtId=5480.

20   Young.

21   Irene Mosalli, "Brigitte Gabriel et sa 'Marche contre la charia," *L'Orient
du Jour* (2017), https://www.lorientlejour.com/article/1057222/brigitte-
gabriel-et-sa-marche-contre-la-charia-.html.

22   Brigitte Gabriel, "Brigitte Gabriel Twin Falls Idaho" (2016), https://www.
youtube.com/watch?v=YFL7LQ7TKiM.

23   "Personal Message from Brigitte" (2016), http://www.actforamerica.org/
bgeoy.

24   Portions of this chapter were first published at Lawrence Pintak, "The
Trump Administration's Islamophobic Holy Grail," *ForeignPolicy.com*
(2017), https://bit.ly/2I0iE98.

25   "Capt. Joseph John: Muslim Brotherhood 'Fifth Column' Has Infiltrated
U.S. Government," *Breitbart News* (2016), http://www.breitbart.com/
big-government/2016/06/30/capt-joseph-john-muslim-brotherhood-fifth-
column-infiltrated-u-s-government/.

26   "The Muslim Brotherhood Infiltrates Obama Administration,"
Frontpage Mag (2013), https://www.frontpagemag.com/fpm/183352/
muslim-brotherhood-infiltrates-obama-frontpagemagcom.

27   Jeffrey Lord, "Hannity, Cleric, Fight over Muslim Brotherhood's
Nazi Link," *American Spectator* (2011), https://spectator.
org/24993_hannity-cleric-fight-over-muslim-brotherhoods-nazi-link/.

28   Glenn Beck, "Obama's Shocking Ties to the Muslim Brotherhood,"
The Blaze (Undated), http://www.glennbeck.com/2012/04/27/

obama%e2%80%99s-shocking-ties-to-the-muslim-brotherhood/?utm_
source=glennbeck&utm_medium=contentcopy_link.

29 Gass.

30 Ben Mathis-Lilley, "Longtime Trump Adviser Claims Khizr Khan
    Is a Terrorist Agent," *Slate* (2016), http://www.slate.
    com/blogs/
    the_slatest/2016/08/01/roger_stone_says_khizr_khan_is_a_muslim_
    brotherhood_saboteur.html.

31 Ahmed Shawky, "A Man and Brothers in the White House," *Rose al-Yusuf*
    (2012), https://bit.ly/2uC6CND.

32 Max Blumenthal, "How an American Right-Wing Conspiracy Traveled
    to Egypt and Has People Thinking Obama Is in Deep with the Muslim
    Brotherhood," *Alternet* (2013), https://www.alternet.org/world/how-
    islamophobic-sleeper-cell-conspiracy-started-american-right-wingers-
    michele-bachmann-has.

33 "Disgraced Ex-FBI Agent John Guandolo Training Law Enforcement This
    Week in San Angelo, Texas," *Hate Watch* (2018), https://www.splcenter.org/
    hatewatch/2018/05/02/disgraced-ex-fbi-agent-john-guandolo-training-
    law-enforcement-week-san-angelo-texas.

34 Chad Groening, "Muslim Brotherhood Embedded in National Security,"
    OneNewsNow.com (2018), https://www.onenewsnow.com/national-
    security/2018/07/19/muslim-brotherhood-embedded-in-national-security.

35 Mark Tapson, "Harry Reid Endorses Muslim Brotherhood Shill Keith
    Ellison for DNC Chairman," *Truth Revolt* (2016), https://www.truthrevolt.
    org/news/harry-reid-endorses-muslim-brotherhood-shill-keith-ellison-
    dnc-chairman.

36 Leo Hohmann, "Keith Ellison Is 'Muslim Brotherhood
    Operative'," *WND* (2016), http://www.wnd.com/2016/12/
    keith-ellison-is-muslim-brotherhood-operative/.

37 Matt Gertz, "Here Come the Anti-Muslim Attacks on Keith Ellison,"
    Media Matters for America (2016), https://www.mediamatters.org/
    blog/2016/11/16/here-come-anti-muslim-attacks-keith-ellison/214496.

38 Gehad El-Haddad, "I Am a Member of the Muslim Brotherhood, Not a
    Terrorist," *New York Times* (2017), https://mobile.nytimes.com/2017/02/22/
    opinion/i-am-a-member-of-the-muslim-brotherhood-not-a-terrorist.html.

39 Marc Lynch, "Is the Muslim Brotherhood a Terrorist Organization or a
    Firewall against Violent Extremism?" *Washington Post* (2016), https://
    www.washingtonpost.com/news/monkey-cage/wp/2016/03/07/is-the-
    muslim-brotherhood-a-terrorist-organization-or-a-firewall-against-
    violent-extremism/?utm_term=.3c743eb24922.

40 Paul R. Pillar, "Ideological Warfare against Nonviolent Political Islam,"
    National Interest (2017), http://nationalinterest.org/blog/paul-pillar/
    ideological-warfare-against-nonviolent-political-islam-19068?page=2.

41 "Muslim Brotherhood Review: Main Findings" (London: House of Commons, 2015).

42 Thomas Joscelyn, "Zawahiri Compares Members of the Muslim Brotherhood to Chickens," *Long War Journal* (2016), https://www. longwarjournal.org/archives/2016/08/zawahiri-compares-members-of-muslim-brotherhood-to-chickens.php?utm_source=feedburner&utm_ medium=email&utm_campaign=Feed%3A+LongWarJournalSiteWide+%2 8The+Long+War+Journal+%28Site-Wide%29%29.

43 "Jabhat Al-Nusra Commander Abu Muhammad Al-Jourlani: The Muslim Brotherhood Should Bear Arms and Wage Jihad," *MEMRI* (2015), https:// www.memri.org/tv/jabhat-al-nusra-commander-abu-muhammad-al-joulani-muslim-brotherhood-should-bear-arms-and-wage.

44 "Saudi Arabia Turns against Political Islam," *The Economist* (2018), https://www.economist.com/special-report/2018/06/23/ saudi-arabia-turns-against-political-islam?frsc=dg%7Ce.

45 Ibid.

46 MSA National, "Who We Are," Muslim Students Association, http:// msanational.org/about-us/who-we-are/.

47 "The Godfather."

48 Al Baker and Kate Taylor, "Bloomberg Defends Police's Monitoring of Muslim Students on Web," *New York Times* (2012), https://www.nytimes. com/2012/02/22/nyregion/bloomberg-defends-polices-monitoring-of-muslim-student-web-sites.html.

49 Andrew March, "Designating the Muslim Brotherhood a 'Terrorist Organization' Puts Academic Researchers at Risk," *Washington Post* (2017), https://www.washingtonpost.com/news/monkey-cage/wp/2017/01/25/ how-the-courts-have-put-middle-east-researchers-at-risk/?utm_term=. b1fbad38b993.

50 Mogahed and Chouhoud.

51 "Awad v. Ziriax et al," in *10–6273*, ed. U.S. Court of Appeals for the Tenth Circuit (Denver, 2012).

52 "Anti-Sharia Law Bills in the United States," Southern Poverty Law Center, https://www.splcenter.org/hatewatch/2018/02/05/ anti-sharia-law-bills-united-states.

53 http://ibh.554.myftpupload.com/issues-2/shariah-law/

54 "The 2015 Texas Hoax of the Year: Rumors about Sharia Courts," *Houston Chronicle* (2015), https://www.chron.com/news/houston-texas/texas/ article/The-2015-Texas-Hoax-of-the-Year-Rumors-about-6716157.php.

55 Islamictribunal.org.

56 Committee on the Judiciary. Subcommittee on the Constitution, Civil Rights and Human Rights, *Written Statement of the Council on*

American-Islamic Relations on Hate Crimes and the Threat of Domestic Extremism, 2017.

57 Mordechai Kedar and David Yerushalmi, "Shari'a and Violence in American Mosques," *Middle East Quarterly* 18, no. 3 (2011).

58 Andrea Elliott, "The Man Behind the Anti-Shariah Movement," *New York Times* (2011), https://www.nytimes.com/2011/07/31/us/31shariah.html.

59 Abed Awad, "The True Story of Sharia in American Courts," *The Nation* (2012), https://www.thenation.com/article/true-story-sharia-american-courts/.

60 Spencer Ackerman, "FBI Fired Sebastian Gorka for Anti-Muslim Diatribes," *Daily Beast* (2017), https://www.thedailybeast.com/fbi-fired-sebastian-gorka-for-anti-muslim-diatribes.

61 Nathan Brown, "Activist Calls for Action in Twin Falls before Muslims 'Take Over,'" *Times-News* (2016), http://www.idahostatesman.com/news/state/idaho/article94057222.html.

62 Betsy K. Russell, "False Story on Social Media Charges Syrian Refugees Raped Idaho Girl," *Spokesman-Review* (2016), http://www.spokesman.com/stories/2016/jun/20/false-story-social-media-charges-syrian-refugees-r/.

63 Pam Geller, "Pamela Geller: How Muslim Migrants Devastate a Community," *Breitbart* (2016), http://www.breitbart.com/immigration/2016/07/26/geller-muslim-migrants-devastate-community/.

64 Lee Stranahan, "Twin Falls Refugee Rape Special Report: Why Are the Refugees Moving In?" ibid., http://www.breitbart.com/big-government/2016/08/10/twin-falls-refugee-rape-special-report-refugees/.

65 Michael Patrick Leahy, "TB Spiked 500 Percent in Twin Falls during 2012, as Chobani Yogurt Opened Plant," ibid., http://www.breitbart.com/big-government/2016/08/26/tb-spiked-500-percent-twin-falls-2012-year-chobani-opened-local-plant/.

66 Alex Jones, "Infowars "Migrant Rapists" Tweet," *InfoWars* (2017), https://twitter.com/PrisonPlanetTV/status/851850584508567552.

67 Gabriel, "Brigitte Gabriel Twin Falls Idaho."

68 Lia Eustachewitz, "Obama Honors 9/11 Hero behind 'the Red Bandanna'" (2014), https://nypost.com/2014/05/16/obama-honors-911-hero-behind-the-red-bandanna/.

Chapter 10

1 In photos of the scene, First Lady Melania Trump can be seen reaching for the orb between her husband and the Saudi king, effectively shouldered out, perhaps a subtle comment on the worldview of the three men illuminated by the eerie light.

2   Obi-Sean Kenobi, "Spacejam," *Twitter* (2017), https://bit.ly/2JxBTUx.

3   Jim Geraghty, "Attention Marvel Heros," ibid., https://bit.ly/2Fk86MG.

4   Daniel Larison, "The Power of Riyadh," ibid., https://bit.ly/2KkjdZs.

5   Jordan Stratton, "Art of the Deal," ibid., https://bit.ly/2FkkkVr.

6   Shahed Amanullah, "That Moment," Twitter, https://twitter.com/shahed/sta
    tus/865920245105651712?lang=en.

7   "Meet the Press Transcript" (2015), https://www.nbcnews.com/
    meet-the-press/meet-press-transcript-august-16-2015-n412636.

8   Pamela Engel, "Fox News Hosts Grill Donald Trump in Tense Interview
    about His George W. Bush Criticism," *Businessinsider.com* (2016),
    http://www.businessinsider.com/donald-trump-fox-news-george-w-
    bush-9-11-iraq-2016-2.

9   "President Trump's Speech to the Arab Islamic American Summit," ed. The
    White House (Washington, DC, May 21, 2017).

10 "Saudi Prince Sees Trump as 'True Friend' to Muslims (Full Text),"
    Bloomberg (2017), https://www.bloomberg.com/news/articles/2017-03-15/
    saudi-prince-sees-trump-as-true-friend-to-muslims-full-text.

11 "President Trump's Speech to the Arab Islamic American Summit."

12 Ibid. "Saudi Prince Sees Trump as 'True Friend' to Muslims (Full Text)."
    [12] "President Trump's Speech to the Arab Islamic American Summit."

13 Robin Wright and Peter Baker, "Iraq, Jordan See Threat to Election from
    Iran," *Washington Post*, December 8, 2004.

14 Dr. Erin Miller and Michael Jensen, "American Deaths in Terrorist Attacks,
    1995–2016" (College Park, MD: The National Consortium for the Study of
    Terrorism and Responses to Terrorism (START), 2017).

15 Bruce Riedel, "Captured: Mastermind behind the 1996 Khobar Towers
    Attack" (2015), https://www.brookings.edu/blog/markaz/2015/08/26/
    captured-mastermind-behind-the-1996-khobar-towers-attack/.

16 "Country Reports on Terrorism 2016," ed. U.S. Department of State
    (Washington, DC, 2016).

17 Daniel L. Byman, "Hezbollah's Growing Threat against U.S. National
    Security Interests in the Middle East," Congressional Testimony, *Testimony
    before the House Committee on Foreign Affairs. Subcommittee on the Middle
    East and North Africa* (2016), https://www.brookings.edu/testimonies/
    hezbollahs-growing-threat-against-u-s-national-security-interests-in-the-
    middle-east/.

18 Loveday Morris, Karen DeYoung DeYoung and Missy Ryan, "U.S. Forces
    Begin Airstrikes in Tikrit, Where Iran-Backed Militias Are in Lead,"
    Washington Post (2015), https://www.washingtonpost.com/world/
    middle_east/us-providing-surveillance-to-iraqi-forces-fighting-islamic-

state-in-tikrit/2015/03/25/1851a070-d236-11e4-8b1e-274d670aa9c9_story. html?utm_term=.2ff369d790a2.

19 Ariane Tabatabai and Dina Esfandiary, "Partnering with Iran to Counter Isis?" *Lawfare Blog* (2016), https://www.lawfareblog.com/partnering-iran-counter-isis.

20 Ibid.

21 Veteran Intelligence Professionals for Sanity, "Intel Vets Tell Trump Iran Is Not Top Terror Sponsor" (2017), http://www.ronpaulinstitute.org/archives/featured-articles/2017/december/26/intel-vets-tell-trump-iran-is-not-top-terror-sponsor/.

22 Pintak, *Seeds of Hate: How America's Flawed Lebanon Policy Ignited the Jihad.*

23 "Yemen: Events of 2016," *World Report 2017* (2017), https://www.hrw.org/world-report/2017/country-chapters/yemen.

24 "A Cry for Help: Millions Facing Famine in Yemen," *Al Jazeera English* (2017), https://www.aljazeera.com/video/news/2017/04/raises-famine-alarm-yemen-170425075042281.html.

25 Ben Norton, "Leaked Hillary Clinton Emails Show U.S. Allies Saudi Arabia and Qatar Supported Isis," *Salon.com* (2016), https://www.salon.com/2016/10/11/leaked-hillary-clinton-emails-show-u-s-allies-saudi-arabia-and-qatar-supported-isis/.

26 Hillary Rodham Clinton, "Terrorist Finance: Action Request for Senior Level Engagement on Terrorism Finance," *The Guardian* (2010), https://www.theguardian.com/world/us-embassy-cables-documents/242073.

27 "Prince Saud Al-Faisal / Speech / the Council on Foreign Relations New York 20/-09-2005." News release, 2005, http://www.mofa.gov.sa/sites/mofaen/Minister/MinisterMedia/OfficialSpeeches/Pages/NewsArticleID39973.aspx.

28 Scott Shane, "Moussaoui Calls Saudi Princes Patrons of Al Qaeda," *New York Times* (2015), https://www.nytimes.com/2015/02/04/us/zacarias-moussaoui-calls-saudi-princes-patrons-of-al-qaeda.html?_r=0&mtrref=undefined&assetType=nyt_now.

29 Bruce Riedel, "Saudi Arabia Uses Aggression Abroad to Calm Clerics at Home" (2018), http://www.crpme.gr/analysis/saudi-arabia/saudi-arabia-uses-aggression-abroad-to-calm-clerics-at-home.

30 "Saudi Invasion of Al-Mahrah: A Salafist 'Princedom' on Oman's Borders?" *Al-Akhbar* (2018).

31 James Dorsey, "The U.S.-Saudi Plot for Iran That Spells Trouble for China's New Silk Road," *South China Morning Post* (2017), http://www.scmp.com/week-asia/geopolitics/article/2095734/us-saudi-plot-iran-spells-trouble-chinas-new-silk-road.

32   Muhammad Akhbar Notezai, "The Rise of Religious Extremism in Balochistan," *The Diplomat* (2017), https://thediplomat.com/2017/01/the-rise-of-religious-extremism-in-balochistan/.

33   "Saudi TV Host Abdullellah Al-Dosari Celebrates Death of Iranian Pilgrims in Hajj Stampede in Mecca," *Clip #5134* (2015), https://www.memri.org/tv/saudi-tv-host-abdulellah-al-dosari-celebrates-death-iranian-pilgrims-hajj-stampede-mecca.

Chapter 11

1   Michael Biesecker, Chad Day and Jeff Horowitz, "Private Clinton Speeches Leaked in Hacking Blamed on Russia," *AP News* (2016), https://apnews.com/1fad9d4a8f004bcd99ead31e8509e437.

2   For some of these estimates, see Tom Wilson, "Foreign Funded Islamist Extremism in the UK" (London: Centre for the Response to Radicalisation and Terrorism, 2017); James Dorsey, "Creating Frankenstein: The Saudi Export of Wahhabism," *Straits-Times* (2016), http://www.straitstimes.com/opinion/creating-frankenstein-the-saudi-export-of-wahhabism; Brahma Chellaney, "How to Shut Down the 'Jihad Factories'," *Toronto Globe and Mail* (2016), https://www.theglobeandmail.com/opinion/how-to-shut-down-the-jihad-factories/article29452621/.

3   Claude Moniquet, "The Involvement of Salafism/Wahabbism in the Support and Supply of Arms to Rebel Groups around the World," (Brussels: Directorate-General for External Policies, Directorate B, European Parliament, 2013), 5.

4   Nina Shea, "Saudi Publications on Hate Ideology Invade American Mosques" (New York Center for Religious Freedom, Freedom House, 2005).

5   Farah Pandith, "The World Needs a Long-Term Strategy for Defeating Extremism," *New York Times* (2015), https://www.nytimes.com/roomfordebate/2015/12/08/is-saudi-arabia-a-unique-generator-of-extremism/the-world-needs-a-long-term-strategy-for-defeating-extremism.

6   "Bangladesh to Build Hundreds of Mosques with Saudi Cash," *The Star* (2017), https://www.thestar.com.my/news/regional/2017/04/26/bangladesh-to-build-hundreds-of-mosques-with-saudi-cash/#tMggoEkgdIUSZHhI.99.

7   Pervez Hoodbhoy, "Can Pakistan Work? A Country in Search of Itself," *Foreign Affairs* (2004).

8   "Suicide Attacks in Afghanistan (2001–2007)" (Kabul: UN Assistance Mission to Afghanistan, 2008).

9   "'Extremist Recruitment on the Rise in Southern Punjab', Bureau of Security and Consular Affairs, Bureau of South and Central

Asian Affairs," *Wikileaks* (2008), https://www.wikileaks.org/plusd/cables/08LAHORE302_a.html.

10   Drazen Jorgic, "Army Chief Says Pakistan Should 'Revisit' Islamic Madrassa Schools," *Reuters* (2017), https://www.reuters.com/article/us-pakistan-religion-army/army-chief-says-pakistan-should-revisit-islamic-madrassa-schools-idUSKBN1E12F6.

11   "Saudi Politics Entangle Hajj Pilgrimage," *Associated Press* (2017), https://www.cbsnews.com/news/hajj-pilgrimage-entangled-in-web-of-saudi-politics/.

12   "Saudi Arabia Bars 600,000 Palestinians from Hajj and Umrah with Passport Ban," *Middle East Eye* (2018), https://www.middleeasteye.net/news/saudi-arabia-bans-issuing-visas-600000-palestinians-visiting-mecca-929133513.

13   "Chapter 1: Beliefs About Sharia," *The World's Muslims: Religion, Politics and Society* (2013), http://www.pewforum.org/2013/04/30/the-worlds-muslims-religion-politics-society-beliefs-about-sharia/.

14   Wilson.

15   Martin van Bruinessen, *Contemporary Developments in Indonesian Islam: Explaining the "Conservative Turn"* (Singapore: Institute of Southeast Asian Studies, 2013).

16   Wahid Din, "Nurturing Salafi Manhaj: A Study of Salafi Pesantren in Contemporary Indonesia" (PhD dissertation, Utrecht University, 2014).

17   Nava Nuraniyah, "Mothers to Bombers: The Evolution of Indonesian Women Extremists" (Jakarta: Institute for Policy Analysis of Conflict, 2017).

18   Ilhem Rachidi, "Morocco Struggles to Tamp Down Radical Islam," *Christian Science Monitor* (2003), https://www.csmonitor.com/2003/1215/p07s01-woaf.html.

19   Robert W. Hefner and Barbara Watson Andaya, *Routledge Handbook of Contemporary Indonesia* (New York: Routledge, 2018), 254.

20   "University of Terror: The Jihadi School on Australia's Doorstep Funded by Donald Trump's Friend Saudi Arabia," *News.com.au*, http://www.news.com.au/world/asia/university-of-terror-the-jihadi-school-on-australias-doorstep-funded-by-donald-trumps-friend-saudi-arabia/news-story/267fcd2904925182cc3092833efff0f2.

21   Noorhaidi Hasan, "Laskar Jihad: Islam, Militancy, and the Quest for Identity in Post-New Order Indonesia," in *Southeast Asia Program Publications* (Ithaca, NY: Cornell University, 2006).

22   Ibid., 45.

23   Ibid., 67.

24   Ibid., 68.

25 Ibid., 118.

26 "Saudi Influence and Islamic Radicalization in Indonesia," *Lausanne Global Analysis* 6, no. 5 (2017).

27 "Jemaah Islamiyah in South East Asia: Damaged But Still Dangerous," 2.

28 Zahara Tiba, "Concept of Islamic Caliphate Grows More Popular among Indonesian Students: Survey," *BenarNews* (2017), https://www.benarnews.org/english/news/indonesian/indonesia-militants-10312017181359.html.

29 Peter Hartcher, "Saudi Arabian King Salman's Nine-Day Trip to Indonesia Is a Worry for Australia," *Sydney Morning Herald* (2017), https://www.smh.com.au/opinion/saudi-arabian-king-salmans-nineday-trip-to-indonesia-is-a-worry-for-australia-20170313-gux95l.html.

30 Margaret Scott, "Indonesia: The Saudis Are Coming," *New York Review of Books* (2016), http://www.nybooks.com/articles/2016/10/27/indonesia-the-saudis-are-coming/.

31 Boo Su-Lyn, "Marina Mahathir: Malaysia Undergoing 'Arab Colonialism,'" *MayalMailOnline* (2017), http://www.themalaymailonline.com/malaysia/article/marina-mahathir-malaysia-undergoing-arab-colonialism#FgeRTTZ QeLprTzMW.97.

32 Dennis Ignatius, "The Wahhabi Threat to Southeast Asia," *Malaysian Insider* (2016), http://www.themalaysianinsider.com/sideviews/article/the-wahhabi-threat-to-southeast-asia-dennis-ignatius#sthash.mLj9Q0n2.dpuf.

33 "Muslim World League and World Assembly of Muslim Youth," in *Muslim Networks and Movements in Western Europe* (Washington, DC: Pew Research Center: Religion & Public Life, 2010).

34 "Wahhabism Has No Place Here," *The Star Online* (2016), https://www.thestar.com.my/news/nation/2016/08/28/wahhabism-has-no-place-here/.

35 Abdar Rahman Koya, "'Wahhabisation' Greater Threat Than Arabisation, Says IRF Chief," *FMT News* (2017), http://www.freemalaysiatoday.com/category/nation/2017/12/01/wahhabisation-greater-threat-than-arabisation-says-irf-chief/.

36 Mohamad Sabu, "The Need to Stay at a Safe Distance from Saudi Arabia," *Malaysiakini* (2017), https://www.malaysiakini.com/news/404070.

37 Scott Shane, "Saudis and Extremism: Both the Arsonists and the Firefighters," *New York Times* (2017), https://www.nytimes.com/2016/08/26/world/middleeast/saudi-arabia-islam.html.

38 Daniel L. Byman, "The U.S.-Saudi Arabia Counterterrorism Relationship," *Testimony before the House Committee on Foreign Affairs. Subcommittee on Terrorism, Nonproliferation, and Trade* (2016), https://www.brookings.edu/testimonies/the-u-s-saudi-arabia-counterterrorism-relationship/, 1.

39 Lulwa Shalhoub, "Global Center to Combat Extremism Launched in Riyadh," *Arab News* (2017), http://www.arabnews.com/node/1103136/saudi-arabia.

40 Ibid.

Chapter 12

1   Portions of this chapter were first published as Lawrence Pintak, "ICYMI, Trump Has the U.S. Poised on the Edge of a Mideast Abyss," *Dailybeast. com* (2017), https://thebea.st/2jewfLZ.

2   "Watch & Read: Mohammed Bin Salman's Full Interview," *Al-Arabiya English* (2017), https://english.alarabiya.net/en/features/2017/05/03/Read-the-full-transcript-of-Mohammed-Bin-Salman-s-interview.html.

3   "Trump Gives Remarks with Pres. of Israel," *Bloomberg* (2017), https://www.youtube.com/watch?v=UaS633dA6Kc.

4   "Sheikh Tamim Denies Qatar Has Links to Terrorism," *Khaleej Times* (2017), https://www.khaleejtimes.com/region/qatar/sheikh-tamim-denies-qatar-has-links-to-terrorism.

5   Evan Perez and Shimon Prokupecz, "U.S. Suspects Russian Hackers Planted Fake News Behind Qatar Crisis," *CNN.com* (2017), https://edition.cnn.com/2017/06/06/politics/russian-hackers-planted-fake-news-qatar-crisis/index.html.

6   Zainab Fattah, "Gulf Spat Escalates as Saudi Arabia, U.A.E. Media Attack Qatar," *Bloomberg* (2017), https://www.bloomberg.com/news/articles/2017-05-30/gulf-spat-escalates-as-saudi-arabia-u-a-e-media-attack-qatar.

7   "The Kingdom Cuts Off Diplomatic and Consular Relations with the State of Qatar." News release, June 5, 2017, http://www.mofa.gov.sa/ServicesAndInformation/news/MinistryNews/Pages/ArticleID20176513029701.aspx.

8   Simeon Kerr and Laura Pitel, "Trump Offers Help to Resolve Gulf Diplomatic Crisis," *Financial Times* (2017), https://www.ft.com/content/5012668c-4b9e-11e7-a3f4-c742b9791d43.

9   Abdul Rahman al-Rashad, "This Is Not a Qatari Passing Cloud," *Asharq al-Awsat* (2017), https://eng-archive.aawsat.com/abdul-rahman-al-rashed/opinion/not-qatari-passing-cloud.

10 Associated Press, "Kuwait Ruler Meets with Qatari Leader amid Diplomatic Rift," *Khaleej Times* (2017), https://www.khaleejtimes.com/nation/dubai/kuwaits-emir-meets-with-qatari-leader-amid-diplomatic-rift-.

11 Ismail Sebugwaawo, "Strict Action against Anyone Showing Sympathy with Qatar: UAE," *Khaleej Times* (2017), 1.

12 "President Trump's Speech to the Arab Islamic American Summit."

13 Donald J. Trump, "Radical Ideology," *Twitter* (2017), https://twitter.com/realDonaldTrump/status/872062159789985792.

14 Dana Shell Smith, "Strong Partner," ibid., https://twitter.com/USEmbassyQatar/status/791170745175015424.

15 Karen DeYoung, Kareem Fahim and Sudarsan Raghavan, "Trump Jumps into Worsening Dispute between Qatar and Powerful Arab Bloc," *Washington Post* (2017), https://www.washingtonpost.com/ world/turkey-and-kuwait-move-to-mediate-middle-east-rift-over-qatar/2017/06/06/3fc3b070-4a8a-11e7-a186-60c031eab644_story. html?utm_term=.44368366777e.

16 Carla Babb, "U.S. Military: Qatar Regional Spat Has 'No Impact' on Operations," *VOA* (2017), https://www.voanews.com/a/us-military-qatar-regional-spat-no-impact-operations/3888041.html.

17 Donald J. Trump, "Hard Line on Funding," *Twitter* (2017).

18 Matt Shuham, "Trump Contradicts Tillerson Line on Blockade of Qatar within Hours," *Talkingpointsmemo.com* (2017), https://talkingpointsmemo. com/livewire/trump-contradicts-tillerson-qatar.

19 "Readout of President Donald J. Trump's Call with Amir Sheikh Tameem Bin Hamad Al Thani of Qatar." News release, June 7, 2017, https://www. whitehouse.gov/briefings-statements/readout-president-donald-j-trumps-call-amir-sheikh-tameem-bin-hamad-al-thani-qatar/.

20 Moniquet.

21 Ibid.

22 Erika Solomon, "The $1bn Hostage Deal That Enraged Qatar's Gulf Rivals," *Financial Times* (2017), https://www.ft.com/content/ dd033082-49e9-11e7-a3f4-c742b9791d43.

23 Wilson.

24 Javad Zarif, "Terror-Fighting Despots," (2017), https://twitter.com/JZarif/ status/872543822525464577.

25 Matthew Rosenberg and Adam Goldman, "C.I.A. Names the 'Dark Prince' to Run Iran Operations, Signaling a Tougher Stance," *New York Times* (2017), https://www.nytimes.com/2017/06/02/world/middleeast/cia-iran-dark-prince-michael-dandrea.html?_r=0.

Chapter 13

1 Portions of this chapter were first published as Lawrence Pintak, "Nuclear Pakistan Sees the Saudi Game against Qatar and Iran and Says, 'No, Thanks,'" *Dailybeast.com* (2017), https://thebea.st/2rcIP2T. And as 'Who Is Killing Pakistan's Educated Elite?', *PRI* (2015), https://bit.ly/2jfeT1E.

2 "Dangerous Alliance," *dawn.com* (2017), https://www.dawn.com/ news/1337285.

3 FE Online, "After India, Iran Warns Pakistan of 'Surgical Strikes': Is Islamabad Testing Patience of New Delhi, Tehran and Afghanistan?" *Financial Express* (2017), http://www.financialexpress.com/india-news/

after-india-iran-warns-pakistan-of-surgical-strikes-is-islamabad-testing-patience-of-new-delhi-tehran-and-afghanistan/660219/.

4 Kunwar Khuldune Shahid, "Why the Trump-Led Islamic Summit in Saudi Arabia Was a Disaster for Pakistan," *The Diplomat* (2017), https://thediplomat.com/2017/05/why-the-trump-led-islamic-summit-in-saudi-arabia-was-a-disaster-for-pakistan/.

5 "A Destabilizing Move," *Express Tribune* (2017), https://tribune.com.pk/story/1428060/a-destabilising-move/.

6 Kamran Yousaf, "Are You with Us or with Qatar, Saudis Ask Pakistan," ibid., https://tribune.com.pk/story/1434933/gulf-diplomatic-crisis-us-qatar-saudis-ask-pakistan/.

7 Donald J. Trump, "Pakistan," *Twitter* (2018), https://twitter.com/realdonaldtrump/status/947802588174577664?lang=en.

8 "PM Says No Distinction Now between Good and Bad Taliban," *dawn.com* (2014), https://www.dawn.com/news/1151397.

9 Haqqani.

10 Cyril Almeida, "For Nawaz, It's Not Over Till It's Over," *Dawn.com* (2018), https://www.dawn.com/news/1407192.

11 Ismail Khan, "'We Have Killed All the Children … What Do We Do Now?'," ibid. (2014), https://www.dawn.com/news/1151549.

12 News Desk, "490 Soldiers, 3,500 Militants Killed in Operation Zarb-E-Azb So Far: Dg Ispr," *Express Tribune* (2015), https://tribune.com.pk/story/1123356/1-dg-ispr-addresses-press-conference-afghanistan-pakistan-border-clashes/.

13 Ibid.

14 Saud Medhsud, "Pakistan's Most Hated Man: Volleyball Player, Child Killer," *Reuters* (2014), https://www.reuters.com/article/us-pakistan-school-commander/pakistans-most-hated-man-volleyball-player-child-killer-idUSKBN0JX1CX20141219.

15 "Freedom in a Realm of Fear," *The News* (2015), http://tn.thenews.com.pk/print/38469-freedom-in-a-realm-of-fear.

16 "Crl Appeal No 90 of 2011 and Capital Sentence Reference No 01 of 2011," ed. Islamabad High Court (Islamabad, 2015).

17 Faisal Siddiqi, "Supreme Court on Blasphemy," *Dawn.com* (2015), https://www.dawn.com/news/1217061/supreme-court-on-blasphemy.

18 Julia Boccagno, "Donald Trump Calls Pakistan a 'Fantastic Place of Fantastic People'," *CBSNews.com* (2016), https://www.cbsnews.com/news/donald-trump-calls-pakistan-a-fantastic-place-of-fantastic-people/.

19 Saeed Shah, "Pakistan Foreign Minister Says U.S. Has Undermined Countries' Ties," *Wall Street Journal* (2018), https://www.wsj.com/articles/pakistan-says-alliance-with-u-s-is-over-1515155860.

20 Donald J. Trump, "Remarks by President Trump on the Strategy in Afghanistan and South Asia." News release, August 21, 2017, https://www.whitehouse.gov/briefings-statements/remarks-president-trump-strategy-afghanistan-south-asia/.

21 Ibid.

Chapter 14

1 Khalil Kawtharani, "The Gates of the Gulf Are Opening Wide for a 'Cluster' Conflict," *Al-Akhbar* (2017), https://mideastwire.com/page/article.php?id=64230.

2 Alex Emmons, "Saudi Arabia Planned to Invade Qatar Last Summer. Rex Tillerson's Efforts to Stop It May Have Cost Him His Job," *The Intercept* (2018), https://theintercept.com/2018/08/01/rex-tillerson-qatar-saudi-uae/.

3 Reuters, "Saudi Prince Says Turkey Part of 'Triangle of Evil': Egyptian Media," (2018), https://www.reuters.com/article/us-saudi-turkey/saudi-prince-says-turkey-part-of-triangle-of-evil-egyptian-media-idUSKCN1GJ1WW.

4 "Saudi's Bin Salman Talks about Megacity Project in South Sinai, 'Triangle of Evil' during Egypt Visit," *Ahram Online* (2018), http://english.ahram.org.eg/NewsContent/1/64/292235/Egypt/Politics-/Saudis-Bin-Salman-talks-about-megacity-project-in-.aspx.

5 Farah Maraka, "Bin Salman Satanizes the Ottomans as a Message to Amman," *Rai al Youm (translated by Mideastwire.com)* (2018), https://mideastwire.com/page/article.php?id=66185.

6 Faisal Devji, "Will Saudi Arabia Cease to Be the Center of Islam?," *New York Times* (2018), https://www.nytimes.com/2018/09/07/opinion/saudi-arabia-islam-mbs.html?rref=collection%2Fsectioncollection%2Fopinion&action=click&contentCollection=opinion&region=rank&module=package&version=highlights&contentPlacement=7&pgtype=sectionfront.

7 Ibid.

8 "Turkish Republic Is Continuation of Ottomans: President Erdoğan," *Hurriyet Daily News* (2018), http://www.hurriyetdailynews.com/turkish-republic-is-continuation-of-ottomans-president-erdogan-127106.

9 Farah Maraka, "Bin Salman Satanizes the Ottomans as a Message to Amman," *Rai al Youm (translated by Mideastwire.com)* (2018), https://mideastwire.com/page/article.php?id=66185.

10 "Deal of the Century: Do the Arabs No Longer Need Palestine?" *Al-Quds al-Arabi* (2017), https://mideastwire.com/page/article.php?id=64234.

11 Anne Barnard, David M. Halbfinger and Peter Baker, "Talk of a Peace Plan That Snubs Palestinians Roils Middle East," *New York Times* (2017), https://

www.nytimes.com/2017/12/03/world/middleeast/palestinian-saudi-peace-plan.html.

12 "On Egypt's Reaction to Trump's Decision," *Al Ahram* (2017), https://mideastwire.com/page/article.php?id=65511.

13 David D. Kirkpatrick, "Tapes Reveal Egyptian Leaders' Tacit Acceptance of Jerusalem Move," *New York Times* (2018), https://www.nytimes.com/2018/01/06/world/middleeast/egypt-jerusalem-talk-shows.html.

14 "Israeli Message from President Erdogan: They Will Not Find a Tree to Hide Behind ..." *T24* (2017), http://t24.com.tr/video/cumhurbaskani-erdogandan-israil-mesaji-arkasina-saklanacak-agac-dahi-bulamayacaklar,10742.

15 "If the 'Islamic Army' Is Founded against Israel ..." *Yeni Safak* (2017), https://www.yenisafak.com/gundem/israile-karsi-islam-ordusu-kurulsa-2906245?utm_source=Subscribers&utm_campaign=cad3606efd-UA-5963141-2&utm_medium=email&utm_term=0_6e846e6217-cad3606efd-309922729.

16 "2017 Arab Youth Survey," (2018), http://arabyouthsurvey.com/index.html.

17 Muhammed Ahmed, " 'Finally, Who Is Mohammad Bin Salman?' " *AL Ahram* (2018), https://mideastwire.com/page/articleFree.php?id=66182.

18 Daniel Kilman and Abigail Grace, "China Smells Opportunity in the Middle East's Crisis," *ForeignPolicy.com* (2018), https://foreignpolicy.com/2018/06/14/china-smells-opportunity-in-the-middle-easts-crisis/?utm_source=PostUp&utm_medium=email&utm_campaign=Editors%20Picks%206/14/18%20-%20WTCA&utm_keyword=Editor.

19 "Arab Opinion Index 2017–2018" (Washington, DC: Arab Center, 2018).

20 Kamal Alam, "Pakistan's Army Reverses the Great Game: The Oxus Meets the Indus," *Newsbrief* (2018), https://rusi.org/regions/central-and-south-asia/pakistan.

Chapter 15

1 Peter Stubley, "Saudi Officials Apologise after Images of Scantily Clad Women Appear at Wrestling Event," *The Independent* (2018), https://ind.pn/2HGp0qw.

2 Staff Writer, "Saudi Crown Prince Pledges to Destroy Extremism, Return to Moderate Islam," *Al Arabiya* (2017), https://english.alarabiya.net/en/News/gulf/2017/10/24/Saudi-Arabia-Crown-Prince-pledges-to-destroy-extremism-urges-moderate-Islam.html.

3 Goldberg.

4   Thomas Friedman, "Saudi Arabia's Arab Spring, at Last," *New York Times* (2017), https://www.nytimes.com/2017/11/23/opinion/saudi-prince-mbs-arab-spring.html.

5   "Erdoğan Criticizes Saudi Crown Prince's 'Moderate Islam' Pledge," *Hurriyet Daily News* (2017), http://www.hurriyetdailynews.com/erdogan-criticizes-saudi-crown-princes-moderate-islam-pledge-122262.

6   Ben Hubbard et al., "Saudis Said to Use Coercion and Abuse to Seize Billions," *New York Times* (2018), https://www.nytimes.com/2018/03/11/world/middleeast/saudi-arabia-corruption-mohammed-bin-salman.html.

7   Anne Barnard and Maria Abi-Habib, "Why Saad Hariri Had That Strange Sojourn in Saudi Arabia," *The New York Times* (2017), https://www.nytimes.com/2017/12/24/world/middleeast/saudi-arabia-saad-hariri-mohammed-bin-salman-lebanon.html.

8   Norah O'Donnell, "Saudi Arabia's Heir to the Throne Talks to *60 Minutes*," *60 Minutes* (2018), https://www.cbsnews.com/news/saudi-crown-prince-talks-to-60-minutes/.

9   "Saudi Arabia Death Toll Reaches 100 as Authorities Carry Out Execution Spree," (London: Amesty International, 2017).

10 "Saudi Arabia Profile," in *Freedom in the World 2018* (New York: Freedom House, 2018).

11 John Paul Tasker, "Trudeau Rebuffs Saudi Call for an Apology as Diplomatic Spat Escalates," *CBC* (2018), https://www.cbc.ca/news/politics/canada-fix-big-mistake-saudi-foreign-minister-1.4777438.

12 Tristin Hopper, "'Canada Is the World's Worst Oppressor of Women': Saudi Arabia's Bizarre Propaganda Campaign," *The National* (2018), https://nationalpost.com/news/canada/saudi-arabias-bizarre-propaganda-campaign-against-canada.

13 Ali Al-Mujahed and Sudarsan Raghavan, "Airstrike by U.S.-Backed Saudi Coalition on Bus Kills Dozens of Yemeni Children," *Washington Post* (2018), https://www.washingtonpost.com/world/middle_east/airstrike-by-us-ally-on-bus-carrying-yemeni-children-kills-and-wounds-scores/2018/08/09/c047e55e-bbc6-42ff-a5db-4bd2e629f0b6_story.html?utm_term=.79fe62b832de.

14 Maggie Michael, Trish Wilson, and Lee Keath, "U.S. Allies, Al Qaeda Battle Rebels in Yemen," *Associated Press* (2018), http://www.foxnews.com/world/2018/08/07/unite-with-devil-yemen-war-binds-us-allies-al-qaida.html.

15 Abbas Al Lawati, "Saudi Arabia Crucifies Myanmar Man for Theft and Murder," *Bloomberg* (2018), https://www.bloomberg.com/news/articles/2018-08-08/saudi-arabia-carries-out-rare-crucifixion-for-murder-theft.

16 Sahih Bukhari, 1:365

17 "Urgent 'the Mark' Saleh Al-Lahaidan Calls the State to Torture and Discipline Sheikh Ahmed Al-Ghamdi," *YouTube* (2014), https://www.youtube.com/watch?v=mY35rIEFCO8&app=desktop.

Chapter 16

1 Portions of this chapter were first published as Lawrence Pintak, "An Idiot's Guide to Islam in America," *ForeignPolicy.com* (2016), https://bit.ly/2vUcfHJ.

2 Abigail Hauslohner, "A Virginia Imam Said Female Genital Mutilation Prevents 'Hypersexuality,' Leading to Calls for His Dismissal," *Washington Post* (2017), https://www.washingtonpost.com/news/acts-of-faith/wp/2017/06/05/virginia-mosque-embattled-after-imam-said-female-genital-mutilation-prevents-hypersexuality/?utm_term=.f6bf389b8e0d.

3 Jaafar Sheikh Idris, "A Reinterpreted Islam Is No Islam," (2005), http://www.jaafaridris.com/a-reinterpreted-islam-is-no-islam/.

4 Ihsan Bagby, "The American Mosque 2011" (The Hartford Institute for Religion Research (Hartford Seminary), The Council on American-Islamic Relations, 2012).

5 Ibid.

6 "La Raza Islamica: Prisons, Hip-Hop & Converting Converts," *Berkeley La Raza Law Journal* 22, no. 9 (2012), 186.

7 Subcommittee on Terrorism, Technology and Homeland Security. Senate Judiciary Committee, *Testimony of J. Michael Waller*, October 14, 2003.

8 Jennifer Hickey, "Ripe for Radicalization: Federal Prisons 'Breeding Ground' for Terrorists, Say Experts," *Foxnews.com* (2016), http://www.foxnews.com/us/2016/01/05/ripe-for-radicalization-federal-prisons-breeding-ground-for-terrorists-say-experts.html.

9 Useem Bert and Obie Clayton, "Radicalization of U.S. Prisoners," *Criminology & Public Policy* (2009).

10 Edward E. Curtis, *Muslims in America: A Short History*, Religion in American Life (Oxford; New York: Oxford University Press, 2009).

11 "Muslim Americans: No Signs of Growth in Alienation or Support for Extremism," (2011), http://www.people-press.org/2011/08/30/muslim-americans-no-signs-of-growth-in-alienation-or-support-for-extremism/.

12 "Converts and Conversions," in *The Cambridge Companion to American Islam*, ed. Omid Safi and Juliane Hammer, Cambridge Companions to Religion (Cambridge; New York: Cambridge University Press, 2013), Loc. 2506.

13 Sherman A. Jackson, *Islam and the Blackamerican: Looking toward the Third Resurrection*, Kindle ed/ (Oxford; New York: Oxford University Press, 2005), Loc. 53–60.

14 "Wahhabism," *Frontline* (2014), https://www.pbs.org/wgbh/pages/frontline/shows/saudi/analyses/wahhabism.html.

15 "Obama's Shariah Czar Mohamed Magid Hands Diversity Award to Jew-Hater Dawud Walid," *PJ Media* (2012), https://pjmedia.com/blog/obamas-shariah-czar-mohamed-magid-hands-diversity-award-to-jew-hater-dawud-walid/.

16 Jordan Schachtel, "NYT Profiles 'Counter Extremists' Who Are Actually Extremists," *Breitbart* (2015), http://www.breitbart.com/national-security/2015/02/21/nyt-profiles-counter-extremists-who-are-actually-extremists/.

17 "Recommendations of the Conference on Contemporary Dawah Issues in the West," (Assembly of Muslims Jurists of America, 2016).

18 Cleve Wootson Jr., "Parents Burned and Beat Their Teen Daughter after She Said No to 'Arranged' Marriage, Police Say," *Washington Post* (2018), https://www.washingtonpost.com/news/post-nation/wp/2018/03/25/a-teen-said-no-to-an-arranged-marriage-investigators-say-her-parents-threw-hot-oil-on-her/?utm_term=.38c4ad51d442.

19 Becheer Mohamed, "New Estimates Show U.S. Muslim Population Continues to Grow," Muslim population, *FactTank: News in the Numbers* (2018), http://www.pewresearch.org/fact-tank/2018/01/03/new-estimates-show-u-s-muslim-population-continues-to-grow/.

20 Bagby.

Chapter 17

1 David Horovitz, "Israel 'Our Indispensable Ally' in War on Islamic Terror, Says Paul Ryan on Visit to Jerusalem," *Times of Israel* (2016), http://www.timesofisrael.com/israel-our-indispensable-ally-in-war-on-islamic-terror-says-paul-ryan-on-visit-to-jerusalem/.

2 Portions of this chapter were first published as Lawrence Pintak, "Can Cartoons Save Pakistan's Children from Jihad?," *ForeignPolicy.com* (2016), https://bit.ly/2bpwjVI.

3 Editorial Board, "The Killing of Khurram Zaki," *Express Tribune* (2016), https://tribune.com.pk/story/1100021/the-killing-of-khurram-zaki/.

4 Raheem ul Haque, "Youth Radicalization in Pakistan" (Washington, DC: United States Institute of Peace, 2014).

5 Moeed Yusuf, "Radicalism among Youth in Pakistan: Human Development Gone Wrong?" (Islamabad: UNDP PAkistan and Jawan Pakistan, 2014).

6 "Jokowi: Alhamdulillah, Islam We Are Islam Nusantara," *jpnn.com* (2015), https://www.jpnn.com/news/jokowi-alhamdulillah-islam-kita-islam-nusantara?page=1.

7   Rikza Chamami, "The Irony of Failing to Understand the Islam of Nusantara," *Wahid Foundation* (2016), http://wahidfoundation.org/index.php/news/detail/The-Irony-of-Failing-to-Understand-the-Islam-of-Nusantara.

8   "Muslim Scholars: Suicide Attacks Violate Islamic Principles," *AP News* (2018), https://apnews.com/5295ee1c5f584122abd6a2267857cfc9.

Chapter 18

1   Jon Favreau, "El-Sayed," *Twitter* (2017), https://twitter.com/jonfavs/status/922856571771617280.

2   Talal Ansari, "A Republican Running for Governor in Michigan Is Using Unfounded Conspiracy Theories against a Muslim American Rival," *BuzzFeed* (2018), https://bzfd.it/2jg8W4s.

3   Dean Obeidallah, "Meet the Man Who Could Be America's First Muslim Governor," *Daily Beast* (2018), https://www.thedailybeast.com/meet-the-man-who-could-be-americas-first-muslim-governor.

4   Abigail Hauslohner, "The Blue Muslim Wave: American Muslims Launch Political Campaigns, Hope to Deliver 'Sweet Justice' to Trump," *Washington Post* (2018), https://wapo.st/2L7kxPN.

5   Laurie Roberts, "Roberts: Arizona Senate Candidate under Attack for Being Muslim," *Arizona Republic* (2017), https://www.azcentral.com/story/opinion/op-ed/laurieroberts/2017/07/18/senate-candidate-under-attack-being-muslim/489859001/.

6   Taylor Seely, "Here's What Senate Candidate Deedra Abboud Wants You to Know About Flood of Anti-Islamic Attacks," ibid., https://www.azcentral.com/story/news/politics/arizona/2017/08/01/senate-candidate-deedra-abboud-responds-fresh-ground-islamophobia/505805001/.

7   Hauslohner, "The Blue Muslim Wave: American Muslims Launch Political Campaigns, Hope to Deliver 'Sweet Justice' to Trump."

8   Josh Feldman, "Ingraham: 'America We Know and Love Doesn't Exist Anymore' in Some Places Because of 'Massive Demographic Changes,'" *Mediaite* (2018), https://www.mediaite.com/tv/ingraham-america-we-know-and-love-doesnt-exist-anymore-in-some-places-look-at-massive-demographic-changes/.

9   Andrew Kaczynski, Chris Massie and Nathan McDermott, "HHS Official Shared Post Saying 'Forefathers' Would Have 'Hung' Obama, Clinton for Treason," *KFile, CNN Politics* (2018), https://www.cnn.com/2018/04/13/politics/kfile-hhs-official-obama-clinton-treason/index.html.

10   Renae Reints, "UN Migration Agency Rejects Trump Nominee for Director-General," *Fortune.com* (2018), http://fortune.com/2018/06/29/iom-trump-nominee-un/.

11 Margot Patterson, "America's Anti-Islam Problem Didn't End with the Cancellation of 'Roseanne,'" *America: The Jesuit Review* (2018), https://www.americamagazine.org/politics-society/2018/06/25/americas-anti-islam-problem-didnt-end-cancellation-roseanne.

12 Mogahed and Chouhoud.

13 Rao, Shenkman and Buageila.

14 "Fierce," *Twitter* (2018), https://twitter.com/faiza_n_ali/status/978754563917434880.

15 Shaheen Pasha, "Shaheen Pasha: How Western Muslim Women Bear a Double Burden," *DallasNews* (2016), https://www.dallasnews.com/opinion/commentary/2016/04/11/shaheen-pasha-how-western-muslim-women-bear-a-double-burden.

16 Becheer Mohamed and Gregory A. Smith, "Muslims Concerned about Their Place in Society, But Continue to Believe in the American Dream" (Washington, DC: Pew Research Center, 2017).

17 "Discrimination against Muslim Women-Fact Sheet."

18 Tawfik Hamid, "A Strategic Plan to Defeat Radical Islam," in *Countering Violent Extremism: Scientific Methods & Strategies*, ed. Laurie Fenstermacher (Wright-Patterson Air Force Base, OH: U.S. Air Force Research Laboratory, 2015), 72.

19 Amani Al-Khatahtbeh, "A Letter to My Future Muslim Daughter," *Cosmopolitan* (2016), https://www.cosmopolitan.com/politics/a7557079/amani-al-khatahtbeh-muslim-girl-daughter-letter/?src=socialflowTW.

20 Shibley Telhami, "How Trump Changed American's View of Islam for the Better," *Washington Post* (2017), https://wapo.st/2GN4Fn2.

21 John Sides and Dalia Mogahed, "Muslims in America: Public Perceptions in the Trump Era" (Washington, DC: Voter Study Group, Democracy Fund, 2018).

22 "Man Arrested at Filthy New Mexico Compound Is Son of Imam Linked to 1993 Wtc Bombing," *WCBS Newsradio 880* (2018), https://wcbs880.radio.com/articles/news/man-arrested-filthy-new-mexico-compound-son-imam-linked-1993-wtc-bombing.

23 "Safe Spaces: An Updated Toolkit for Empowering Communities and Addressing Ideological Violence" (Los Angeles: Muslim Public Affairs Council, 2016), 8.

24 "North Carolina Resident Daniel Patrick Boyd Sentenced for Terrorism Violations." News release, August 24, 2012, https://archives.fbi.gov/archives/charlotte/press-releases/2012/north-carolina-resident-daniel-patrick-boyd-sentenced-for-terrorism-violations.

25 Author's Conversation with DHS Official Timothy Curry, February 17, 2017.

26 Alexander Meleagrou-Hitchens, Seamus Hughes and Bennett Clifford, "'The Travelers: American Jihadists in Syria and Iraq" (Washington, DC: Program on Extremism, George Washington University, 2018).

27 Esme Murphy, "German Expert: U.S. Way Behind in Terrorism De-Radicalization," *WCCO CBS Minnesota* (2016), http://minnesota. cbslocal.com/2016/09/21/deradicalization-expert/.

28 Camila Domonoske, "Suspect in New York City Truck Attack Accused of Terrorism in Federal Complaint," *The Two-Way* (2017), https://www.npr. org/sections/thetwo-way/2017/11/01/561304014/suspect-in-new-york-city-truck-attack-worked-as-commercial-truck-uber-driver.

29 Borzou Daragahi, "After the Black Flag of ISIS, Iraq Now Faces the White Flags," *BuzzFeed* (2018), https://www.buzzfeed.com/borzoudaragahi/isis-iraq-white-flags-syria-new-name?utm_term=.qc8zMVLR0#.jp0jEnAm3.

30 David Bier, "U.S. Approves Far Fewer Muslim Refugees, Immigrants, & Travelers" (Washington, DC: Cato Institute, 2018).

Postscript

1 "First Muslim Woman, the Daughter of Palestinian Immigrants, Bound for Congress," *Associated Press* (2018), https://www.nbcnews.com/politics/ elections/first-muslim-woman-daughter-palestinian-immigrants-bound-congress-n898836; ibid.

2 The author's own research.

3 Taylor Seely, "Here's What Senate Candidate Deedra Abboud Wants You to Know about the Flood of Anti-Islamic Rhetoric," *Arizona Republic* (2017), https://www.azcentral.com/story/news/politics/arizona/2017/08/01/senate-candidate-deedra-abboud-responds-fresh-ground-islamophobia/ 505805001/.

4 Poll carried out by the author.

5 Ryan Mauro, "Jihadi Cult Member Files to Run for Congress," (2018), https:// clarionproject.org/2nd-jihadi-cult-member-files-to-run-for-congress/.

6 Lloyd Billingsley, "The Terror-Reinforcing Primary," *Frontpagemag.com* (2018), https://www.frontpagemag.com/fpm/271684/terror-reinforcing-primary-lloyd-billingsley.

7 Linda Givetash, "Laura Loomer Banned from Twitter after Criticizing Ilhan Omar," *Daily Beast* (2018), https://www.nbcnews.com/tech/security/ laura-loomer-banned-twitter-after-criticizing-ilhan-omar-n939256.

8 @LauraLoomer, Nov. 28, 2018 https://twitter.com/KassyDillon/status/ 1065402204662755328/photo/1?ref_src=twsrc%5Etfw%7Ctwcamp% 5Etweetembed%7Ctwterm%5E1065402204662755328&ref_url= https%3A%2F%2Fwww.dailydot.com%2Flayer8%2Flaura-loomer-banned-twitter%2F

9   Nicky V., "Running on Hate Update: Anti-Muslim Candidates Underperform in Last Night's Elections," (Oakland, CA: Muslim Advocates, 2018).

10 "Details of Calls to Attack Trump by US 'Muslim Sisters' Allied to Brotherhood," *Al Arabiyah English* (2018), https://english.alarabiya.net/en/features/2018/12/08/Details-of-calls-by-US-Muslim-Sisters-of-Muslim-Brotherhood-to-attack-Trump-.html.

11 Nicholas Kristof, "If a Prince Murders a Journalist, That's Not a Hiccup," *New York Times* (2018), https://www.nytimes.com/2018/10/13/opinion/sunday/saudi-arabia-mbs-jamal-khashoggi.html.

12 Ola Salem, "Saudi Arabia Declares War on America's Muslim Congresswomen," *Foreign Policy* (2018), https://foreignpolicy.com/2018/12/11/saudi-arabia-declares-war-on-americas-muslim-congresswomen/.

13 Ibid.

14 Wesley Lowery, Kindy Kimberly and Andrew Ba Tran, "In the United States, Right-Wing Violence Is on the Rise," *Washington Post* (2018), https://www.washingtonpost.com/national/in-the-united-states-right-wing-violence-is-on-the-rise/2018/11/25/61f7f24a-deb4-11e8-85df-7a6b4d25cfbb_story.html?utm_term=.c37128969bb3.

15 "FBI Releases 2017 Hate Crime Statistics," (Washington, DC: Federal Bureau of Investigation, 2018).

16 Ilhan Omar, "Look Like America," *Twitter* (2018), https://twitter.com/IlhanMN/status/1070907694339502080?ref_src=twsrc%5Etfw%7Ctwcamp%5Etweetembed%7Ctwterm%5E1070907694339502080&ref_url=https%3A%2F%2Fwww.alaraby.co.uk%2Fenglish%2Fcomment%2F2018%2F12%2F13%2Fsaudi-disinformation-campaign-reveals-fear-of-progressive-muslim-congresswomen.

BIBLIOGRAPHY

"The 2015 Texas Hoax of the Year: Rumors about Sharia Courts." *Houston Chronicle* (2015). Published electronically December 23. https://www.chron.com/news/houston-texas/texas/article/The-2015-Texas-Hoax-of-the-Year-Rumors-about-6716157.php.

"2017 Arab Youth Survey" (2018). http://arabyouthsurvey.com/index.html.

"2017 Survey of U.S. Muslims." Washington, DC: Pew Research Center, 2017.

'Arabi, Ibn. "Garden among the Flames." Poem. http://www.ibnarabisociety.org/poetry/ibn-arabi-poetry-index.html.

Aburish, Said K. *Nasser: The Last Arab*. 1st ed. New York: St. Martin's Press/Thomas Dunne Books, 2004.

Abutaleb, Yasmeen, and Kristina Cooke. "A Teen's Turn to Radicalism and the U.S. Safety Net That Failed to Stop It." *Reuters Investigates* (2016). Published electronically June 6. https://www.reuters.com/investigates/special-report/usa-extremists-teen/.

Ackerman, Spencer. "FBI Fired Sebastian Gorka for Anti-Muslim Diatribes." *Daily Beast* (2017). Published electronically June 21. https://www.thedailybeast.com/fbi-fired-sebastian-gorka-for-anti-muslim-diatribes.

Acosta, Judge John V. "Arrest Warrant," edited by United States District Court for the District of Oregon. Vancouver, WA, 2010.

"Ahmadiyya Muslim Community." (2018). https://www.alislam.org/library/ahmadiyya-muslim-community/.

Ahmed, Muhammed. " 'Finally, Who Is Mohammad Bin Salman?' " *AL Ahram* (2018). Published electronically March 7. https://mideastwire.com/page/articleFree.php?id=66182.

Alam, Kamal. "Pakistan's Army Reverses the Great Game: The Oxus Meets the Indus." *Newsbrief* (2018). Published electronically September 7. https://rusi.org/regions/central-and-south-asia/pakistan.

Al-Khatahtbeh, Amani "A Letter to My Future Muslim Daughter." *Cosmopolitan* (2016). Published electronically October 27. https://www.cosmopolitan.com/politics/a7557079/amani-al-khatahtbeh-muslim-girl-daughter-letter/?src=socialflowTW.

Al-Mujahed, Ali, and Sudarsan Raghavan. "Airstrike by U.S.-Backed Saudi Coalition on Bus Kills Dozens of Yemeni Children." *Washington Post* (2018). Published electronically August 9. https://www.washingtonpost.com/world/middle_east/airstrike-by-us-ally-on-bus-carrying-yemeni-children-kills-and-

wounds-scores/2018/08/09/c047e55e-bbc6-42ff-a5db-4bd2e629f0b6_story.
html?utm_term=.79fe62b832de.

al-Munajjid, Muhammad Saalih. "A Brief Look at the Beliefs of the Druze." *Islam Question and Answer* (2003). Published electronically August 31 https://islamqa. info/en/26139.

al-Rashad, Abdul Rahman. "This Is Not a Qatari Passing Cloud." *Asharq al-Awsat* (2017). Published electronically June 7. https://eng-archive.aawsat.com/ abdul-rahman-al-rashed/opinion/not-qatari-passing-cloud.

Al Lawati, Abbas. "Saudi Arabia Crucifies Myanmar Man for Theft and Murder." *Bloomberg* (2018). Published electronically August 8. https://www.bloomberg.com/news/articles/2018-08-08/ saudi-arabia-carries-out-rare-crucifixion-for-murder-theft.

Allison, Robert J. *The Crescent Obscured: The United States and the Muslim World, 1776–1815*. New York: Oxford University Press, 1995.

Almeida, Cyril. "For Nawaz, It's Not Over Till It's Over." *Dawn.com* (2018). Published electronically May 12. https://www.dawn.com/news/1407192.

Almeida, Cyril. "Rally in Lahore Sends Alarm Bells Ringing." *Dawn.com* (2011). Published electronically December 21. https://bit.ly/2HPGOTL.

AlMuhaini, Mamdouh. "Why Arabs Hate Obama." *Al Arabiyah English* (2017). Published electronically January 6. https://english.alarabiya.net/en/views/news/ middle-east/2017/01/06/Why-Arabs-hate-Obama-.html.

Alter, Charlotte. "Transcript: Read the Full Text of the Fourth Republican Debate in Milwaukee." *Time.com* (2015). Published electronically November 11. http://time.com/4107636/transcript-read-the-full-text-of-the-fourth-republican-debate-in-milwaukee/.

Altschull, J. Herbert. "What Is News." *Mass Comm Review*, December (1974).

Amanullah, Shahed. "That Moment." Twitter, https://twitter.com/shahed/status/8659 20245105651712?lang=en.

Amir-Moezzi, Mohammad Ali. *The Divine Guide in Early Shi'ism: The Sources of Esotericism in Islam*. Albany: State University of New York Press, 1994.

Amry, Hend. "So True." *Twitter* (2016). Published electronically April 11. https:// twitter.com/LibyaLiberty/status/719551173766864897.

"Anderson Cooper Interviewed Trump, and It Was a Disgrace." *Slate.com* (2016). Published electronically March 9. http://www.slate.com/blogs/the_ slatest/2016/03/09/anderson_cooper_s_interview_with_donald_trump_was_a_ disgrace.html.

"Ann Coulter Explains How to Talk to a Liberal …" *Foxnews.com* (2004). Published electronically October 5. http://www.foxnews.com/story/2004/10/05/ann-coulter-explains-how-to-talk-to-liberal.html.

Ansari, Talal. "A Republican Running for Governor in Michigan Is Using Unfounded Conspiracy Theories against a Muslim American Rival." *Buzzfeed* (2018). Published electronically April 24. https://bzfd.it/2jg8W4s.

"Anti-Sharia Law Bills in the United States." Southern Poverty Law Center, https:// www.splcenter.org/hatewatch/2018/02/05/anti-sharia-law-bills-united-states.

Apuzzo, Matt. "Only Hard Choices for Parents Whose Children Flirt with Terror." *New York Times* (2016). Published electronically April 9. https://www.nytimes.

com/2016/04/10/us/parents-face-limited-options-to-keep-children-from-terrorism.html.

"Arab Opinion Index 2017–2018." Washington, DC: Arab Center, 2018.

Arango, Tim. "A Long-Awaited Apology for Shiites, But the Wounds Run Deep." *New York Times* (2011). Published electronically November 8. http://www.nytimes.com/2011/11/09/world/middleeast/iraqi-shiite-anger-at-united-states-remains-strong.html.

Arkin, Daniel, and Erik Ortiz. "Trump Calls Obama the 'Founder of Isis' over Anti-Terror Strategy." (2016). Published electronically August 11. https://www.nbcnews.com/politics/politics-news/trump-calls-obama-founder-isis-over-anti-terror-strategy-n628096.

Arshad, Owais, VarunSetlur and USAID Siddiqui. "Are Muslims Collectively Responsible?" 416Labs, 2015.

Associated Press. "Kuwait Ruler Meets with Qatari Leader Amid Diplomatic Rift." *Khaleej Times* (2017). Published electronically June 8. https://www.khaleejtimes.com/nation/dubai/kuwaits-emir-meets-with-qatari-leader-amid-diplomatic-rift-.

Atwan, Adel Bari. "Half an Apology Is Not Enough." *Al-Quds al-Arabi* (2005). Published electronically June 5. https://mideastwire.com/page/article.php?id=30107.

Author'sconversation with DHS official Timothy Curry, who spoke with the imam. February 17, 2017.

Author's email exchange with mediaQuant COO Mary Harris. April 3–4, 2018.

Awad, Abed. "The True Story of Sharia in American Courts." *The Nation* (2012). Published electronically June 14. https://www.thenation.com/article/true-story-sharia-american-courts/.

"Awad V. Ziriax et al." In *10–6273*, edited by US Court of Appeals for the Tenth Circuit. Denver, 2012.

Babb, Carla. "Us Military: Qatar Regional Spat Has 'No Impact' on Operations." *VOA* (2017). Published electronically June 5. https://www.voanews.com/a/us-military-qatar-regional-spat-no-impact-operations/3888041.html.

Bagby, Ihsan. "The American Mosque 2011." The Hartford Institute for Religion Research (Hartford Seminary), The Council on American-Islamic Relations, 2012.

Bajoria, Jayshree. "Pakistan's Education System and Links to Extremism." New York: Council on Foreign Relations, 2009.

Baker, Al, and Kate Taylor. "Bloomberg Defends Police's Monitoring of Muslim Students on Web." *New York Times* (2012). Published electronically February 12. https://www.nytimes.com/2012/02/22/nyregion/bloomberg-defends-polices-monitoring-of-muslim-student-web-sites.html.

"Bangladesh to Build Hundreds of Mosques with Saudi Cash." *The Star* (2017). Published electronically April 26. https://www.thestar.com.my/news/regional/2017/04/26/bangladesh-to-build-hundreds-of-mosques-with-saudi-cash/#tMggoEkgdIUSZHhI.99.

"Barbary Wars, 1801–1805 and 1815–1816." *Milestones: 1801–1829*. https://history.state.gov/milestones/1801–1829/barbary-wars.

Barnard, Anne, and Maria Abi-Habib. "Why Saad Hariri Had That Strange Sojourn in Saudi Arabia." *New York Times* (2017). Published electronically December

24. https://www.nytimes.com/2017/12/24/world/middleeast/saudi-arabia-saad-hariri-mohammed-bin-salman-lebanon.html.

Barnard, Anne, David M. Halbfinger and Peter Baker. "Talk of a Peace Plan That Snubs Palestinians Roils Middle East." *New York Times* (2017). Published electronically December 3. https://www.nytimes.com/2017/12/03/world/middleeast/palestinian-saudi-peace-plan.html.

Bassiouni, M. Cherif. "Islamic Law—the Sharia." (2012). Published electronically January 24. http://www.mei.edu/content/islamic-law-shariah.

Beck, Glenn. "Obama's Shocking Ties to the Muslim Brotherhood." *The Blaze* (Undated). http://www.glennbeck.com/2012/04/27/obama%e2%80%99s-shocking-ties-to-the-muslim-brotherhood/?utm_source=glennbeck&utm_medium=contentcopy_link.

Bellamy, Jann. "NY Federal Court Hands Triple Loss to Anti-Vaccination Ideology." *Science-Based Medicine* (2014). Published electronically June 26. https://sciencebasedmedicine.org/ny-federal-court-hands-triple-loss-to-anti-vaccination-ideology/.

Bert, Useem, and Obie Clayton. "Radicalization of U.S. Prisoners." *Criminology & Public Policy* (August 2009): 561–92.

Bier, David. "U.S. Approves Far Fewer Muslim Refugees, Immigrants, & Travelers." Washington, DC: Cato Institute, 2018.

Biesecker, Michael, Chad Day and Jeff Horowitz. "Private Clinton Speeches Leaked in Hacking Blamed on Russia." *AP News* (2016). Published electronically October 8. https://apnews.com/1fad9d4a8f004bcd99ead31e8509e437.

Bildt, Carl. "That's Ludicrous." (2017). Published electronically February 6. https://bit.ly/2JvnzvM.

Billingsley, Lloyd. "The Terror-Reinforcing Primary." *Frontpagemag.com* (2018). Published electronically October 19. https://www.frontpagemag.com/fpm/271684/terror-reinforcing-primary-lloyd-billingsley

bin Laden, Osama. "Declaration of Jihad against the Americans Occupying the Land of the Two Holiest Sites." Combating Terrorism Center at West Point: U.S. Military Academy, 1996.

bin Laden, Osama. "Declaration of War against the Americans Occupying the Land of the Two Holy Places." *al-Quds al-Arabi*, no. 15, April 2002 (1996). http://www.pbs.org/newshour/terrorism/international/fatwa_1996.html.

Blumenthal, Max. "How an American Right-Wing Conspiracy Traveled to Egypt and Has People Thinking Obama Is in Deep with the Muslim Brotherhood." *Alternet* (2013). Published electronically August 28. https://www.alternet.org/world/how-islamophobic-sleeper-cell-conspiracy-started-american-right-wingers-michele-bachmann-has.

Boccagno, Julia. "Donald Trump Calls Pakistan a 'Fantastic Place of Fantastic People.'" *CBSNews.com* (2016). Published electronically November 30. https://www.cbsnews.com/news/donald-trump-calls-pakistan-a-fantastic-place-of-fantastic-people/.

Bowe, Brian J., and Taj W. Makki. "Muslim Neighbors or an Islamic Threat? A Constructionist Framing Analysis of Newspaper Coverage of Mosque Controversies." *Media, Culture & Society* 38, no. 4 (2015): 540–58.

Bransten, Jeremy. "Middle East: Rice Calls for a 'New Middle East.'" *Radio Free Europe/Radio Liberty* (2006). Published electronically July 25. https://www.rferl.org/a/1070088.html.

Bronston, Sally. "McConnell on Trump Judge Comments: 'I Couldn't Disagree More.'" *Meet the Press* (2016). Published electronically June 5. http://www.nbcnews.com/meet-the-press/mcconnell-trump-judge-comments-i-couldn-t-disagree-more-n586056.

Brown, Jonathan. *Misquoting Muhammad: The Challenge and Choices of Interpreting the Prophet's Legacy*. Kindle ed. London: Oneworld, 2014.

Brown, Nathan. "Activist Calls for Action in Twin Falls before Muslims 'Take Over.'" *Times-News* (2016). Published electronically August 5. http://www.idahostatesman.com/news/state/idaho/article94057222.html.

Bruinessen, Martin van. *Contemporary Developments in Indonesian Islam: Explaining the "Conservative Turn."* Singapore: Institute of Southeast Asian Studies, 2013.

Bukhari, Muhammad Ibn Ishmail. *Sahih Al-Bukhari*, edited by Muhammed Muhsin Khan Alexandria, VA: Saadwai Publications, 1996.

Bump, Philip. "Why Did Sean Spicer Suggest That the Quebec Shooting Validated Trump's Policy Initiatives?" *Washington Post* (2017). Published electronically January 30. https://wapo.st/2vOCoro.

Bunt, Gary R. *IMuslims: Rewiring the House of Islam*. Islamic Civilization and Muslim Networks. Chapel Hill: University of North Carolina Press, 2009.

Bush, George, and Brent Scowcroft. *A World Transformed*. 1st ed. New York: Knopf, 1998.

Byman, Daniel L. "Hezbollah's Growing Threat against U.S. National Security Interests in the Middle East." Congressional Testimony, *Testimony before the House Committee on Foreign Affairs Subcommittee on the Middle East and North Africa* (2016). Published electronically March 22. https://www.brookings.edu/testimonies/hezbollahs-growing-threat-against-u-s-national-security-interests-in-the-middle-east/.

Byman, Daniel L. "The U.S.-Saudi Arabia Counterterrorism Relationship." Congressional Testimony, *Testimony before the House Committee on Foreign Affairs. Subcommittee on Terrorism, Nonproliferation, and Trade* (2016). Published electronically May 24. https://www.brookings.edu/testimonies/the-u-s-saudi-arabia-counterterrorism-relationship/.

Byrnes, Jesse. "Nikki Haley Denounces Trump's Muslim Ban Idea." *The Hill* (2015). Published electronically December 9. http://thehill.com/blogs/ballot-box/presidential-races/262589-nikki-haley-denounces-trumps-muslim-ban-idea.

Byrnes, Jesse. "Trump on Obama and Islam: 'There's Something Going On.'" *thehill.com* (2016). Published electronically June 13. http://thehill.com/blogs/blog-briefing-room/news/283246-trump-on-obama-and-islam-theres-something-going-on.

"CAIR Video Calls out Fox News' Faux 'Condemn Islamic Extremism' Challenge to Muslim Leaders." News release. November 13, 2014.

Caldwell, Leigh Ann, and Andrew Rafferty. "GOP Leaders Denounce Trump's Plan as Anti-American." *NBC News* (2016). Published electronically

December 8. https://www.nbcnews.com/politics/2016-election/
paul-ryan-denounces-donald-trumps-anti-muslim-plan-n476201.

"Capt. Joseph John: Muslim Brotherhood 'Fifth Column' Has Infiltrated U.S.
Government." *Breitbart News* (2016). Published electronically June 30. http://
www.breitbart.com/big-government/2016/06/30/capt-joseph-john-muslim-
brotherhood-fifth-column-infiltrated-u-s-government/.

Carr, Matthew. *Blood and Faith: The Purging of Muslim Spain*. Kindle ed. New York:
New Press, 2009.

Carter, Jimmy. "Relations with Islamic Nations Statement by the President." The
American Presidency Project, 1980.

Chamami, Rikza. "The Irony of Failing to Understand the Islam of Nusantara."
Wahid Foundation (2016). Published electronically September. http://
wahidfoundation.org/index.php/news/detail/The-Irony-of-Failing-to-
Understand-the-Islam-of-Nusantara.

"Chapter 1: Beliefs About Sharia." *The World's Muslims: Religion, Politics and Society*
(2013). Published electronically April 30. http://www.pewforum.org/2013/04/30/
the-worlds-muslims-religion-politics-society-beliefs-about-sharia/.

Charbel, Ghassan. "The Confusing Visitor." *Al-Hayat* (2009). Published electronically
June 5. https://mideastwire.com/page/article.php?id=30131.

Chatterjee, Soumya, and Haritha John. "Video of Kerala Islamic Leader Calling
Vaccination 'Work of Devil' Surfaces, Group Denies." (2015). Published
electronically October 22. http://www.thenewsminute.com/article/video-kerala-
islamic-leader-calling-vaccination-work-devil-surfaces-group-denies-35347.

Chellaney, Brahma. "How to Shut Down the 'Jihad Factories.'" *Toronto Globe and
Mail* (2016). Published electronically March 31. https://www.theglobeandmail.
com/opinion/how-to-shut-down-the-jihad-factories/article29452621/.

Chouhoud, Youssef, and Dalia Mogahed. "American Muslim Poll 2018." Dearborn,
MI: ISPU, 2018.

Christensen, Dan. "Saudi Arabia Cites FBI's Meese Commission in Asking Judge
to Toss 9/11 Victims' Lawsuit." *Florida Bulldog* (2017). Published electronically
August 8. http://www.floridabulldog.org/2017/08/saudi-arabia-cites-fbis-meese-
commission-in-asking-judge-to-toss-911-victims-lawsuit/.

Churchill, Col. Charles. *The Druzes and the Maronites*. London: Bernard
Quaritch, 1982.

Churchill, Winston, and Winston S. Churchill. *Never Give In! Winston
Churchill's Speeches*. Bloomsbury Revelations. Bloomsbury revelations ed.
London: Bloomsbury Academic, 2013.

"CIA Confirms Role in 1953 Iran Coup." *National Security Archive Electronic Briefing
Book No. 435* (2013). Published electronically August 19. https://nsarchive2.gwu.
edu/NSAEBB/NSAEBB435/.

Clinton, Hillary Rodham. "Terrorist Finance: Action Request for Senior Level
Engagement on Terrorism Finance." *The Guardian* (2010). Published
electronically December 5. https://www.theguardian.com/world/
us-embassy-cables-documents/242073.

CNN. "Transcript of Republican Debate in Miami, Full Text." Atlanta: CNN.
com, 2016.

Cole, David. "More Dangerous Than Trump." *New York Review of Books* (2017). Published electronically May 23. http://www.nybooks.com/daily/2017/05/23/more-dangerous-than-trump-jeff-sessions/.

Coll, Steve. *Ghost Wars: The Secret History of the Cia, Afghanistan, and Bin Laden, from the Soviet Invasion to September 10, 2001.* New York: Penguin Books, 2005.

Commins, David Dean. *The Wahhabi Mission and Saudi Arabia.* London; New York: I. B. Tauris, 2006. doi:9781845110802 (hbk.).

Committee on the Judiciary Subcommittee on the Constitution, Civil Rights and Human Rights. *Written Statement of the Council on American-Islamic Relations on Hate Crimes and the Threat of Domestic Extremism*, 2017.

"Complaint for Injunctive and Declaratory Relief," edited by Eastern District of Virginia United States District Court. Richmond, VA, 2017.

"Convert Straddles Worlds of Islam and Hip-Hop." *New York Times*, October 29, 2011, A16.

"Converts and Conversions." In *The Cambridge Companion to American Islam*, edited by Omid Safi and Juliane Hammer. Cambridge Companions to Religion. Cambridge; New York: Cambridge University Press, 2013.

"Country Reports on Terrorism 2016," edited by U.S. Department of State. Washington, DC, 2016.

"Crl Appeal No 90 of 2011 and Capital Sentence Reference No 01 of 2011," edited by Islamabad High Court. Islamabad, 2015.

"A Cry for Help: Millions Facing Famine in Yemen." Famine, *Al Jazeera English* (2017). Published electronically April 25. https://www.aljazeera.com/video/news/2017/04/raises-famine-alarm-yemen-170425075042281.html.

Curtis, Edward E. *Muslims in America: A Short History.* Religion in American Life. Oxford; New York: Oxford University Press, 2009.

Curtis, Mark. *Secret Affairs: Britain's Collusion with Radical Islam.* Kindle ed. London: Serpent's Tail, 2018.

"Dangerous Alliance." *dawn.com* (2017). Published electronically June 4. https://www.dawn.com/news/1337285.

Daragahi, Borzou. "After the Black Flag of ISIS, Iraq Now Faces the White Flags." *BuzzFeed* (2018). Published electronically April 1. https://www.buzzfeed.com/borzoudaragahi/isis-iraq-white-flags-syria-new-name?utm_term=.qc8zMVLR0#.jp0jEnAm3.

Davis, Aaron C. "The Day Terrorists Took DC Hostage." *Washington Post* (2017). Published electronically March 10. https://www.washingtonpost.com/local/dc-politics/the-day-muslim-terrorists-took-dc-hostage--and-there-was-a-happy-ending/2017/03/10/e7cf4918-0517-11e7-ad5b-d22680e18d10_story.html?utm_term=.5204aa06b519.

"Deal of the Century: Do the Arabs No Longer Need Palestine?." *Al-Quds al-Arabi* (2017). Published electronically July 6. https://mideastwire.com/page/article.php?id=64234.

"A Destabilizing Move." *Express Tribune* (2017). Published electronically June 6. https://tribune.com.pk/story/1428060/a-destabilising-move/.

"Details of Calls to Attack Trump by U.S. 'Muslim Sisters' Allied to Brotherhood." *Al Arabiyah English* (2018). Published electronically December 9. https://english.

alarabiya.net/en/features/2018/12/08/Details-of-calls-by-US-Muslim-Sisters-of-Muslim-Brotherhood-to-attack-Trump-.html

Detrow, Scott. "GOP Criticism Mounts as Trump Continues Attacks on Khan Family." *NPR* (2016). Published electronically August 1. https://www.npr.org/2016/08/01/488213964/gop-criticism-mounts-as-trump-continues-attacks-on-khan-family.

Devereaux, Ryan. "An Interview with Michael T. Flynn, the Ex-Pentagon Spy Who Supports Donald Trump." *The Intercept* (2016). Published electronically July 13. https://theintercept.com/2016/07/13/an-interview-with-lt-gen-michael-flynn/.

DeYoung, Karen DeYoung, Kareem Fahim and Sudarsan Raghavan. "Trump Jumps into Worsening Dispute between Qatar and Powerful Arab Bloc." *Washington Post* (2017). Published electronically June 6. https://www.washingtonpost.com/world/turkey-and-kuwait-move-to-mediate-middle-east-rift-over-qatar/2017/06/06/3fc3b070-4a8a-11e7-a186-60c031eab644_story.html?utm_term=.44368366777e.

Din, Wahid. "Nurturing Salafi Manhaj: A Study of Salafi Pesantren in Contemporary Indonesia." PhD dissertation, Utrecht University, 2014.

Diouf, Sylviane A. *Servants of Allah: African Muslims Enslaved in the Americas*. 15th anniversary ed. New York: New York University Press, 2013.

"Discrimination against Muslim Women—Fact Sheet." American Civil Liberties Union (New York: Undated), https://www.aclu.org/other/discrimination-against-muslim-women-fact-sheet.

"Disgraced Ex-FBI Agent John Guandolo Training Law Enforcement This Week in San Angelo, Texas." *Hate Watch* (2018). Published electronically May 2. https://www.splcenter.org/hatewatch/2018/05/02/disgraced-ex-fbi-agent-john-guandolo-training-law-enforcement-week-san-angelo-texas.

"Do American Muslims Need to Speak Out against Radical Islam?" *Foxnews.com* (2016). Published electronically December 27. http://www.foxnews.com/transcript/2016/12/27/amb-oren-israel-was-hurt-by-this-appalling-resolution-do-american-muslims-need.html.

"Does 20:130 Imply or Authorise 5 Salat?." *True Islam* (2010). http://www.quran-islam.org/main_topics/misinterpreted_verses/manipulation_of_20:130_(P1251).html.

Domonoske, Camila. "Suspect in New York City Truck Attack Accused of Terrorism in Federal Complaint." *The Two-Way* (2017). Published electronically November 1. https://www.npr.org/sections/thetwo-way/2017/11/01/561304014/suspect-in-new-york-city-truck-attack-worked-as-commercial-truck-uber-driver.

"Donald Trump Calls Pakistan Most Dangerous Country." *Reuters* (2015). Published electronically September 23. https://bit.ly/2Jtg1cR.

"Donald Trump Orlando Tweet." (2016). Published electronically June 12. https://twitter.com/realDonaldTrump/status/742096033207844864.

"Donald Trump Says May Seek India's Help on 'Unstable' Pakistan Nukes." *Press Trust of India* (2016). Published electronically April 28. https://bit.ly/2Jttstf.

Dorsey, James. "Creating Frankenstein: The Saudi Export of Wahhabism." *Straits-Times* (2016). Published electronically March 14. http://www.straitstimes.com/opinion/creating-frankenstein-the-saudi-export-of-wahhabism.

Dorsey, James. "The US-Saudi Plot for Iran That Spells Trouble for China's New Silk Road." *South China Morning Post* (2017). Published electronically May 27. http://www.scmp.com/week-asia/geopolitics/article/2095734/us-saudi-plot-iran-spells-trouble-chinas-new-silk-road.

Dreisbach, Daniel L., and Mark David Hall. *Faith and the Founders of the American Republic.* New York: Oxford University Press, 2014.

Duranni, Mariam. "A Portrait of Islamophobia?" *Religion Dispatches* (2015). Published electronically December 15. http://religiondispatches.org/a-portrait-of-islamophobia/.

Eban, A. *The Beirut Massacre: The Complete Kahan Commission Report.* Princeton; New York: Karz-Cohl Publishing, 1983.

Editorial Board. "The Killing of Khurram Zaki." *Express Tribune* (2016). Published electronically May 9. https://tribune.com.pk/story/1100021/the-killing-of-khurram-zaki/.

Editorial Board . "Mr. Trump's Applause Lies." *New York Times* (2015). Published electronically November 24. https://www.nytimes.com/2015/11/24/opinion/mr-trumps-applause-lies.html.

Editorial Board. "Truth and Lies in the Age of Trump." *New York Times* (2016). Published electronically December 10. https://www.nytimes.com/2016/12/10/opinion/truth-and-lies-in-the-age-of-trump.html.

Edwards, Jonathan, and Jonathan Edwards. *Apocalyptic Writings. The Works of Jonathan Edwards*, vol. 5. New Haven: Yale University Press, 1977.

Ehrenfreund, Max. "The Four Cryptic Words Donald Trump Can't Stop Saying." *Washingtonpost.com* (2016). Published electronically June 13. https://www.washingtonpost.com/news/wonk/wp/2016/06/13/the-four-cryptic-words-donald-trump-cant-stop-saying/?utm_term=.cf5bf1efa4b3.

Eilperin, Juliet, and Sandhya Somashekhar. "Trump Considering Order on Religious Freedom That Critics Warn Could Lead to Discrimination." *Sltrib.com* (2017). http://www.sltrib.com/home/4899090-155/trump-considering-order-on-religious-freedom.

El-Haddad, Gehad. "I Am a Member of the Muslim Brotherhood, Not a Terrorist." *New York Times* (2017). Published electronically February 22. https://mobile.nytimes.com/2017/02/22/opinion/i-am-a-member-of-the-muslim-brotherhood-not-a-terrorist.html.

Elliott, Andrea. "The Man Behind the Anti-Shariah Movement." *New York Times* (2011). Published electronically July 30. https://www.nytimes.com/2011/07/31/us/31shariah.html.

Elving, Ron. "What Trump Really Meant When He Said Obama Has 'Something Else in Mind'." *NPR* (2016). Published electronically June 13. https://n.pr/2HwvlJm.

Emmons, Alex. "Saudi Arabia Planned to Invade Qatar Last Summer. Rex Tillerson's Efforts to Stop It May Have Cost Him His Job." *The Intercept* (2018). Published electronically August 1. https://theintercept.com/2018/08/01/rex-tillerson-qatar-saudi-uae/.

Engel, Pamela. "Donald Trump: 'I Would Bomb the S--- out of' ISIS." *Businessinsider.com* (2015). Published electronically November 13. http://www.businessinsider.com/donald-trump-bomb-isis-2015-11.

Engel, Pamela. "Fox News Hosts Grill Donald Trump in Tense Interview about His George W. Bush Criticism." *Businessinsider.com* (2016). Published electronically February 15. http://www.businessinsider.com/ donald-trump-fox-news-george-w-bush-9-11-iraq-2016-2.

"Erdoğan Criticizes Saudi Crown Prince's 'Moderate Islam' Pledge." *Hurriyet Daily News* (2017). Published electronically November 10. http://www.hurriyetdailynews.com/ erdogan-criticizes-saudi-crown-princes-moderate-islam-pledge-122262.

Esfandiari, Golnaz. "Iranian Ex-President Says U.S. Seeks Arrest of Hidden Imam." *Radio Free Europe/Radio Liberty* (2015). Published electronically June 22. https:// www.rferl.org/a/iran-ahmadinejad-hidden-imam-us/27086798.html.

Eustachewitz, Lia. "Obama Honors 9/11 Hero Behind 'the Red Bandanna.'" (2014). Published electronically May 16. https://nypost.com/2014/05/16/ obama-honors-911-hero-behind-the-red-bandanna/.

"An Exceptional Summit and a Historic Speech." *Al Ahram* (2009). Published electronically June 5. https://mideastwire.com/page/article.php?id=30118.

"Extremist Recruitment on the Rise in Southern Punjab," Bureau of Security and Consular Affairs, Bureau of South and Central Asian Affairs. *Wikileaks* (2008). Published electronically November 13. https://www.wikileaks.org/plusd/ cables/08LAHORE302_a.html.

Ezzat, Amr, and Islam Barakat. "State's Islam and Forbidden Diversity." Cairo: Egypt Initiative for Personal Rights, 2016.

Faisal, Saud al. "The Fight against Extremism and the Search for Peace." New York: Council on Foreign Relations, 2005.

Faisal, Saud al. "Saudi Arabia and the International Oil Markets." Houston: James A. Baker III Institute for Public Policy, Rice University, 2005.

Fattah, Zainab. "Gulf Spat Escalates as Saudi Arabia, U.A.E. Media Attack Qatar." *Bloomberg* (2017). Published electronically May 30. https://www.bloomberg.com/news/articles/2017-05-30/ gulf-spat-escalates-as-saudi-arabia-u-a-e-media-attack-qatar.

Favreau, Jon. "El-Sayed." *Twitter* (2017). Published electronically October 24. https:// twitter.com/jonfavs/status/922856571771617280.

"FBI Releases 2017 Hate Crime Statistics." Washington, DC: Federal Bureau of Investigation, 2018. https://www.fbi.gov/news/pressrel/press-releases/ fbi-releases-2017-hate-crime-statistics.

FE Online. "After India, Iran Warns Pakistan of 'Surgical Strikes': Is Islamabad Testing Patience of New Delhi, Tehran and Afghanistan?" *Financial Express* (2017). Published electronically May 9. http://www.financialexpress.com/india-news/after-india-iran-warns-pakistan-of-surgical-strikes-is-islamabad-testing-patience-of-new-delhi-tehran-and-afghanistan/660219/.

Feldman, Josh. "CBS' Scott Pelley: 'It Has Been a Busy Day for Presidential Statements Divorced from Reality.'" *Mediaite* (2017). Published electronically February 6. https://bit.ly/2Hy2FeU.

Feldman, Josh. "Ingraham: 'America We Know and Love Doesn't Exist Anymore' in Some Places Because of 'Massive Demographic Changes.'" *Mediaite* (2018). Published electronically August 8. https://www.mediaite.com/tv/

ingraham-america-we-know-and-love-doesnt-exist-anymore-in-some-places-look-at-massive-demographic-changes/.

"Fierce." *Twitter* (2018). Published electronically March 27. https://twitter.com/faiza_n_ali/status/978754563917434880.

"First Muslim Woman, the Daughter of Palestinian Immigrants, Bound for Congress." *Associated Press* (2018). Published electronically August 8. https://www.nbcnews.com/politics/elections/first-muslim-woman-daughter-palestinian-immigrants-bound-congress-n898836.

Fisher, Max. "It's Not Just Fox News: Islamophobia on Cable News Is out of Control." *Vox.com* (2015). Published electronically January 13. https://www.vox.com/2014/10/8/6918485/the-overt-islamophobia-on-american-tv-news-is-out-of-control.

Fisk, Robert. "Why We Reject the West—by the Saudis' Fiercest Arab Critic." *The Independent*, July 10, 1996, 14.

Flynn, Lt. Gen. Michael T. "'I Dare.'" *Twitter* (2016). Published electronically July 14. https://twitter.com/genflynn/status/753772080471179264?lang=en.

"Francis Scott Key." *Strangers to Us All: Lawyers and Poetry* (2001). Published electronically December 2. http://myweb.wvnet.edu/~jelkins/lp-2001/key.html.

Fraser, T. G., Andrew Mango and Robert McNamara. *Making the Modern Middle East*. Rev. and updated paperback ed. London: Gingko Library, 2017.

"Freedom in a Realm of Fear." *The News* (2015). Published electronically May 3. http://tn.thenews.com.pk/print/38469-freedom-in-a-realm-of-fear.

Friedman, Thomas. "Saudi Arabia's Arab Spring, at Last." *New York Times* (2017). Published electronically November 23. https://www.nytimes.com/2017/11/23/opinion/saudi-prince-mbs-arab-spring.html.

Friedman, Yaron. *The NuṣAyrī-ʿalawīS: An Introduction to the Religion, History, and Identity of the Leading Minority in Syria*. Islamic History and Civilization. Leiden; Boston: Brill, 2010.

"From the MEMRI Archives: Reports on Pakistani School, Radical Mosque That Played a Role in Ca Jihadi Tashfeen Malik's Radicalization." *MEMRI* (2016). Published electronically December 16. https://bit.ly/2HSKN1z.

Gabriel, Brigitte. "Brigitte Gabriel Twin Falls Idaho." (2016). Published electronically August 14. https://www.youtube.com/watch?v=YFL7LQ7TKiM.

Gabriel, Brigitte. "Personal Message from Brigitte." (2016). Published electronically undated. http://www.actforamerica.org/bgeoy.

Gabriel, Brigitte. "A Survivor of Islamic Terror Warns America." *Frontpage Mag* (2006). Published electronically February 20. http://archive.frontpagemag.com/Printable.aspx?ArtId=5480.

Gajanan, Mahita. "President Trump Says Media 'Doesn't Want to Report' on Terror Attacks." *Time.com* (2017). Published electronically February 6. http://time.com/4661625/president-trump-media-report-terrorism/.

Gaouette, Nicole, and Barbara Starr. "Trump Is Calling for 30,000 Troops. Would That Defeat ISIS?" *CNN.com* (2016). Published electronically March 11. https://www.cnn.com/2016/03/11/politics/donald-trump-30000-troops-isis/.

Gass, Nick. "Trump Ally: Clinton Aide Could Be 'Terrorist Agent.'" *Politico.com* (2016). Published electronically June 13. https://www.politico.com/story/2016/06/roger-stone-huma-abedin-terrorist-agent-224261.

Gawad, Maha Abdul. "My First Racist Encounter." Facebook, https://www.facebook.com/shaunking/photos/a.799605230078397.1073741828.799539910084929/1194283823943867/?type=3.

Geller, Pam. "Pamela Geller: How Muslim Migrants Devastate a Community." *Breitbart* (2016). Published electronically July 26. http://www.breitbart.com/immigration/2016/07/26/geller-muslim-migrants-devastate-community/.

Geraghty, Jim. "Attention Marvel Heros." *Twitter* (2017). Published electronically May 21. https://bit.ly/2Fk86MG.

Gertz, Matt. "Here Come the Anti-Muslim Attacks on Keith Ellison." *Media Matters for America* (2016). Published electronically November 16. https://www.mediamatters.org/blog/2016/11/16/here-come-anti-muslim-attacks-keith-ellison/214496.

GhaneaBassiri, Kambiz. *A History of Islam in America: From the New World to the New World Order*. New York: Cambridge University Press, 2010.

Ghareeb, Edmund. *Split Vision: The Portrayal of Arabs in the American Media*. Rev. and expanded ed. Washington, DC: American-Arab Affairs Council, 1983.

Givetash, Linda. "Laura Loomer Banned from Twitter after Criticizing Ilhan Omar." *Daily Beast* (2018). Published electronically November 22. https://www.nbcnews.com/tech/security/laura-loomer-banned-twitter-after-criticizing-ilhan-omar-n939256

Glassé, Cyril. *The Concise Encyclopædia of Islam*. London: Stacey International, 1989.

Glubb, John Bagot. "Ibn Saʿūd: King of Saudi Arabia." *Britannica.com*.

Glubb, John Bagot. *War in the Desert, an R.A.F. Frontier Campaign*. 1st American ed. New York: Norton, 1961.

"The Godfather." *Intelligence Report* (2014). Published electronically May 24. https://www.splcenter.org/fighting-hate/intelligence-report/2014/godfather.

Gold, Matea. "Bannon Film Outline Warned U.S. Could Turn into 'Islamic States of America.'" *Washington Post* (2017). Published electronically February 3. https://www.washingtonpost.com/politics/bannon-film-outline-warned-us-could-turn-into-islamic-states-of-america/2017/02/03/f73832f4-e8be-11e6-b82f-687d6e6a3e7c_story.html?utm_term=.dffe65ed5df4.

Goldberg, Jeffrey. "Saudi Crown Prince: Iran's Supreme Leader 'Makes Hitler Look Good.'" *The Atlantic* (2018). Published electronically April 2. https://www.theatlantic.com/international/archive/2018/04/mohammed-bin-salman-iran-israel/557036/.

Gomez, Michael A. "Muslims in Early America." *Journal of Southern History* 60, no. 4 (1994): 671–710.

Gonzales, Alberto. "Countering the Islamic State's Message." *Journal of International Security Affairs* 30 (Winter 2016).

"Government Letter to Sherif of Mecca, November 1914, (Pro), Fo141/710/9." Cited in *Secret Affairs: Britain's Collusion with Radical Islam*, p. 7, edited by Mark Curtis. London: Serpent's Tail, 2018.

Graham, Bob, Porter Gross, Richard Shelby and Nancy Pelosi. "Part Four: Finding, Discussion and Narrative Regarding Certain Sensitive National Security Matters; Report of the U.S. Senate Select Committee on Intelligence and U.S. House Permanent Select Committee on Intelligence." Washington, DC: U.S. Congress, 2002.

Greenwald, Glenn, and Murtaza Hussain. "Meet the Muslim-American Leaders the FBI and NSA Have Been Spying On." *The Intercept* (2014). Published electronically July 9. https://theintercept.com/2014/07/09/under-surveillance/.

Gregg, Christina. "Why Us Veterans Voted 2-to-1 for Donald Trump." *AOL.com* (2016). Published electronically November 11. https://www.aol.com/article/news/2016/11/11/why-veterans-voted-donald-trump-swing-states/21603486/.

Gritz, Jennie Rothenberg. "When Dr. Seuss Took on Adolf Hitler." *theatlantic.com* (2013). Published electronically January 15. https://www.theatlantic.com/national/archive/2013/01/when-dr-seuss-took-on-adolf-hitler/267151/.

Groening, Chad. "Muslim Brotherhood Embedded in National Security." *OneNewsNow.com* (2018). Published electronically July 19. https://www.onenewsnow.com/national-security/2018/07/19/muslim-brotherhood-embedded-in-national-security.

Haberman, Maggie. "Donald Trump Calls for Surveillance of 'Certain Mosques' and a Syrian Refugee Database." *Newyorktimes.com* (2015). Published electronically November 21. https://www.nytimes.com/2015/11/22/us/politics/donald-trump-syrian-muslims-surveillance.html.

Hamid, Tawfik. "A Strategic Plan to Defeat Radical Islam." In *Countering Violent Extremism: Scientific Methods & Strategies*, edited by Laurie Fenstermacher, 72–7. Wright-Patterson Air Force Base, OH: U.S. Air Force Research Laboratory, 2015.

Haqqani, Husain. "Islamism and the Pakistani State." In *Current Trends in Islamist Ideology*. Washington, DC: Hudson Institute, 2013.

Haque, Raheem ul. "Youth Radicalization in Pakistan." Washington, DC: United States Institute of Peace, 2014.

Hare, Shawn Scott. "Affidavit in Support." United States of America v. Erick Jamal Hendricks, United States District Court for the Northern District of Ohio. (Cleveland: 2016).

Harris, Mary. "A Media Post-Mortem on the 2016 Presidential Election." Portland, OR: mediaQuant, 2016.

Hartcher, Peter. "Saudi Arabian King Salman's Nine-Day Trip to Indonesia Is a Worry for Australia." *Sydney Morning Herald* (2017). Published electronically March 14. https://www.smh.com.au/opinion/saudi-arabian-king-salmans-nineday-trip-to-indonesia-is-a-worry-for-australia-20170313-gux95l.html.

Hasan, Noorhaidi. *Laskar Jihad: Islam, Militancy, and the Quest for Identity in Post-New Order Indonesia*. Studies on Southeast Asia. Ithaca, NY: Southeast Asia Program Publications, Southeast Asia Program, Cornell University, 2006.

Hasan, Noorhaidi. "Laskar Jihad: Islam, Militancy, and the Quest for Identity in Post-New Order Indonesia." In *Southeast Asia Program Publications*. Ithaca, NY: Cornell University, 2006.

Hauslohner, Abigail. "The Blue Muslim Wave: American Muslims Launch Political Campaigns, Hope to Deliver 'Sweet Justice' to Trump." *Washington Post* (2018). Published electronically April 15. https://wapo.st/2L7kxPN.

Hauslohner, Abigail. "A Virginia Imam Said Female Genital Mutilation Prevents 'Hypersexuality', Leading to Calls for His Dismissal." *Washington Post* (2017). Published electronically June 5. https://www.washingtonpost.com/news/acts-of-faith/wp/2017/06/05/virginia-mosque-embattled-after-imam-said-female-genital-mutilation-prevents-hypersexuality/?utm_term=.f6bf389b8e0d.

Hazleton, Lesley. *After the Prophet: The Epic Story of the Shia-Sunni Split in Islam.* 1st ed. New York: Doubleday, 2009.

Hefner, Robert W., and Barbara Watson Andaya. *Routledge Handbook of Contemporary Indonesia.* New York: Routledge, 2018.

Hegghammer, Thomas, and StéphaneLacroix. "Rejectionist Islamism in Saudi Arabia: The Story of Juhayman Al-'Utaybi Revisited." *International Journal of Middle East Studies* 39, no. 1 (2007): 122b–22b.

Hersh, Seymour. "U.S. Secretly Gave Aid to Iraq Early in Its War against Iran." *New York Times* (1992). Published electronically January 26. https://www.nytimes.com/1992/01/26/world/us-secretly-gave-aid-to-iraq-early-in-its-war-against-iran.html.

Hickey, Jennifer. "Ripe for Radicalization: Federal Prisons 'Breeding Ground' for Terrorists, Say Experts." *Foxnews.com* (2016). Published electronically January 5. http://www.foxnews.com/us/2016/01/05/ripe-for-radicalization-federal-prisons-breeding-ground-for-terrorists-say-experts.html.

Hof, Frederick. "Leaving." *Syria Source* (2018). Published electronically March 28. http://www.atlanticcouncil.org/blogs/syriasource/leaving?tmpl=component&print=1.

Hohmann, Leo. "Keith Ellison Is 'Muslim Brotherhood Operative'." *WND* (2016). Published electronically December 25. http://www.wnd.com/2016/12/keith-ellison-is-muslim-brotherhood-operative/.

Hoodbhoy, Pervez. "Can Pakistan Work? A Country in Search of Itself." *Foreign Affairs* (2004).

Hopper, Tristin. " 'Canada Is the World's Worst Oppressor of Women': Saudi Arabia's Bizarre Propaganda Campaign." *The National* (2018). Published electronically August 10. https://nationalpost.com/news/canada/saudi-arabias-bizarre-propaganda-campaign-against-canada.

Horovitz, David. "Israel 'Our Indispensable Ally' in War on Islamic Terror, Says Paul Ryan on Visit to Jerusalem." *Times of Israel* (2016). Published electronically April 4. http://www.timesofisrael.com/israel-our-indispensable-ally-in-war-on-islamic-terror-says-paul-ryan-on-visit-to-jerusalem/.

House, Karen Elliott. *On Saudi Arabia: Its People, Past, Religion, Fault Lines—and Future.* 1st ed. New York: Alfred A. Knopf, 2012.

Howell, Julia Day. "Indonesia's Salafist Sufis." *Modern Asian Studies* 44, no. 5 (2009): 1029–51.

Hubbard, Ben, David D. Kirkpatrick, Kate Kelly and Mark Mazzetti. "Saudis Said to Use Coercion and Abuse to Seize Billions." *New York Times* (2018).

Published electronically March 11. https://www.nytimes.com/2018/03/11/world/
middleeast/saudi-arabia-corruption-mohammed-bin-salman.html.

Huntington, Samuel P. *The Clash of Civilizations and the Remaking of World Order.*
New York: Simon & Schuster, 1996.

Idris, Jaafar Sheikh. "A Reinterpreted Islam Is No Islam" (2005). Published
electronically February 12. http://www.jaafaridris.com/a-reinterpreted-islam-is-
no-islam/.

"If the 'Islamic Army' Is Founded against Israel …". *Yeni Safak* (2017). Published
electronically December 12. https://www.yenisafak.com/gundem/israile-karsi-
islam-ordusu-kurulsa-2906245?utm_source=Subscribers&utm_campaign=
cad3606efd-UA-5963141-2&utm_medium=email&utm_term=0_6e846e6217-
cad3606efd-309922729.

Ignatius, Dennis. "The Wahhabi Threat to Southeast Asia." *Malaysian Insider* (2016).
Published electronically February 11. http://www.themalaysianinsider.com/
sideviews/article/the-wahhabi-threat-to-southeast-asia-dennis-ignatius#sthash.
mLj9Q0n2.dpuf.

"Iran." In *Amnesty International Briefing.* London: Amnesty International, 1976.

"Islamic Radicalism: Its Wahhabi Roots and Current Representation." https://bit.
ly/1E1YEKQ.

"Israeli Message from President Erdogan: They Will Not Find a Tree to Hide Behind
…". *T24* (2017). Published electronically December 12. http://t24.com.tr/video/
cumhurbaskani-erdogandan-israil-mesaji-arkasina-saklanacak-agac-dahi-
bulamayacaklar,10742.

"Jabhat Al-Nusra Commander Abu Muhammad Al-Jourlani: The Muslim
Brotherhood Should Bear Arms and Wage Jihad." *MEMRI* (2015). Published
electronically June 3. https://www.memri.org/tv/jabhat-al-nusra-commander-
abu-muhammad-al-joulani-muslim-brotherhood-should-bear-arms-and-wage.

Jackson, Sherman A. *Islam and the Blackamerican: Looking toward the Third
Resurrection.* Kindle ed. Oxford; New York: Oxford University Press, 2005.

Jaffe, Greg. "For a Trump Adviser, an Odyssey from the Fringes of Washington
to the Center of Power." *Washington Post* (2017). Published electronically
February 20. https://www.washingtonpost.com/world/national-security/
for-a-trump-adviser-an-odyssey-from-the-fringes-of-washington-to-the-
center-of-power/2017/02/20/0a326260-f2cb-11e6-b9c9-e83fce42fb61_story.
html?utm_term=.5477516b0d20.

"Je Suis Charlie." *Real Time with Bill Maher* (2015). Published electronically
January 9. http://www.real-time-with-bill-maher-blog.com/index/2015/1/10/
je-suis-charlie-january-9-2015.

"Jemaah Islamiyah in South East Asia: Damaged but Still Dangerous." Jakarta/
Brussels: International Crisis Group, 2003.

"Jimmy Carter Toasting with the Shah." YouTube, https://www.youtube.com/
watch?v=DqrHQpRHwws.

Johnson, Jenna. "Donald Trump Says He 'Absolutely' Wants a Database of Syrian
Refugees." *Washington Post* (2015). Published electronically November
21. https://www.washingtonpost.com/news/post-politics/wp/2015/11/21/

donald-trump-says-he-absolutely-wants-a-database-of-syrian-refugees/?utm_
term=.fe5393caa3eb.

Johnson, Jenna. "Trump Calls for 'Total and Complete Shutdown of Muslims
Entering the United States." *Washington Post* (2015). Published electronically
December 7. https://www.washingtonpost.com/news/post-politics/
wp/2015/12/07/donald-trump-calls-for-total-and-complete-shutdown-of-
muslims-entering-the-united-states/?utm_term=.5faf050567b5.

Johnson, Timothy J. *Franciscans and Preaching: Every Miracle from the Beginning
of the World Came about through Words.* The Medieval Franciscans. Leiden;
Boston: Brill, 2012.

Johnson, Toni, and Mohammed Aly Sergie. "Islam: Governing under Sharia."
(2014). Published electronically July 25. https://www.cfr.org/backgrounder/
islam-governing-under-sharia.

"A Joint Muslim Statement on the Carnage in Orlando." http://orlandostatement.com/.

"Jokowi: Alhamdulillah, Islam We Are Islam Nusantara." *jpnn.com*
(2015). Published electronically June 14. https://www.jpnn.com/news/
jokowi-alhamdulillah-islam-kita-islam-nusantara?page=1.

Jones, Alex. "Infowars 'Migrant Rapists' Tweet." *InfoWars* (2017).
Published electronically April 11. https://twitter.com/PrisonPlanetTV/
status/851850584508567552.

Jorgic, Drazen. "Army Chief Says Pakistan Should 'Revisit' Islamic Madrassa
Schools." *Reuters* (2017). Published electronically December 7. https://www.
reuters.com/article/us-pakistan-religion-army/army-chief-says-pakistan-should-
revisit-islamic-madrassa-schools-idUSKBN1E12F6.

Joscelyn, Thomas. "Zawahiri Compares Members of the Muslim Brotherhood to
Chickens." *Long War Journal* (2016). Published electronically August 14. https://
www.longwarjournal.org/archives/2016/08/zawahiri-compares-members-
of-muslim-brotherhood-to-chickens.php?utm_source=feedburner&utm_
medium=email&utm_campaign=Feed%3A+LongWarJournalSiteWide+%28The
+Long+War+Journal+%28Site-Wide%29%29.

Kaczynski, Andrew. "On Twitter, Michael Flynn Interacted with Alt-Right, Made
Controversial Comments on Muslims, Shared Fake News." Flynn on Twitter,
(2016). Published electronically November 18. http://www.cnn.com/2016/11/18/
politics/kfile-flynn-tweets/.

Kaczynski, Andrew, Chris Massie and Nathan McDermott. "HHS Official Shared
Post Saying 'Forefathers' Would Have 'Hung' Obama, Clinton for Treason."
KFile, CNN Politics (2018). Published electronically April 13. https://www.cnn.
com/2018/04/13/politics/kfile-hhs-official-obama-clinton-treason/index.html.

Kawtharani, Khalil "The Gates of the Gulf Are Opening Wide for a 'Cluster'
Conflict." *Al-Akhbar* (2017). Published electronically July 6. https://mideastwire.
com/page/article.php?id=64230.

Kedar, Mordechai, and David Yerushalmi. "Shari'a and Violence in American
Mosques." *Middle East Quarterly* 18, no. 3 (2011).

Kedourie, Elie. *In the Anglo-Arab Labyrinth: The McMahon-Husayn Correspondence
and Its Interpretations, 1914–1939.* Cambridge Studies in the History and Theory
of Politics. Cambridge; New York: Cambridge University Press, 1976.

Kenobi, Obi-Sean. "Spacejam." *Twitter* (2017). Published electronically May 21. https://bit.ly/2JxBTUx.

Kepel, Gilles. *Jihad: The Trail of Political Islam.* Cambridge, MA: Harvard University Press, 2002.

Kerr, Simeon, and Laura Pitel. "Trump Offers Help to Resolve Gulf Diplomatic Crisis." *Financial Times* (2017). https://www.ft.com/content/5012668c-4b9e-11e7-a3f4-c742b9791d43.

Khan, Ismail. "'We Have Killed All the Children … What Do We Do Now?'" *Dawn.com* (2014). Published electronically December 17. https://www.dawn.com/news/1151549.

Khan, Khizr. "Khizr Khan's DNC 2016 Speech." *The Independent.* Published electronically July 29. https://www.independent.co.uk/news/world/americas/dnc-2016-khizr-khan-donald-trump-read-full-transcript-father-muslim-soldier-a7161616.html.

Khan, Miriam. "Donald Trump National Security Adviser Mike Flynn Has Called Islam 'a Cancer.'" *ABC News* (2016). Published electronically November 18. http://abcnews.go.com/Politics/donald-trump-national-security-adviser-mike-flynn-called/story?id=43575658.

Khan, Ruqayya Yasmine. "Did a Woman Edit the Qur'an?: Ḥafṣa and Her Famed 'Codex.'" *Journal of the American Academy of Religion* 82, no. 1 (2014): 174–216.

Khan, Tahir. "Remarks by Pakistani Cleric Spark Controversy, Stir up Pak-Afghan Tension." *Express Tribune* (2013). Published electronically March 19. https://bit.ly/2qZUIZI.

Khuri, Rafiq. "An American Speech with an Islamic and Universal Taste." *Al-Anwar* (2009). Published electronically June 5. https://mideastwire.com/page/article.php?id=30119.

Kidd, Thomas S. *American Christians and Islam: Evangelical Culture and Muslims from the Colonial Period to the Age of Terrorism.* Princeton, NJ: Princeton University Press, 2009.

"Kill the Imams of Kufr in the West." *Dabiq,* no. 14, 1437 Rajab (2016): 8–17. Published electronically April. https://clarionproject.org/docs/Dabiq-Issue-14.pdf.

"The Killing of Ismaili Starts from Fatwa of Mufti Naeem Madarsa." *Jhang TV* (2015). Published electronically May 15. http://jhangtv.com/the-killing-of-ismaili-started-from-the-fatwa-of-mufti-naeem-madarsas-must-watch/.

Kilman, Daniel, and Abigail Grace. "China Smells Opportunity in the Middle East's Crisis." *ForeignPolicy.com* (2018). Published electronically June 14. https://foreignpolicy.com/2018/06/14/china-smells-opportunity-in-the-middle-easts-crisis/?utm_source=PostUp&utm_medium=email&utm_campaign=Editors%20Picks%206/14/18%20-%20WTCA&utm_keyword=Editor.

"The Kingdom Cuts Off Diplomatic and Consular Relations with the State of Qatar." News release. June 5, 2017, http://www.mofa.gov.sa/ServicesAndInformation/news/MinistryNews/Pages/ArticleID20176513029701.aspx.

Kirkpatrick, David D. "Tapes Reveal Egyptian Leaders' Tacit Acceptance of Jerusalem Move." *New York Times* (2018). Published electronically January 6. https://www.nytimes.com/2018/01/06/world/middleeast/egypt-jerusalem-talk-shows.html.

Knight, Muhammad Michael. *Why I Am a Salafi*. Kindle ed. Berkeley, CA: Soft Skull Press, 2015.

Koya, Abdar Rahman. "'Wahhabisation' Greater Threat Than Arabisation, Says IRF Chief." *FMT News* (2017). Published electronically December 1. http://www.freemalaysiatoday.com/category/nation/2017/12/01/wahhabisation-greater-threat-than-arabisation-says-irf-chief/.

Kristof, Nicholas. "If a Prince Murders a Journalist, That's Not a Hiccup." *New York Times* (2018). Published electronically October 14. https://www.nytimes.com/2018/10/13/opinion/sunday/saudi-arabia-mbs-jamal-khashoggi.html.

Kurzman, Charles. "Death Tolls of the Iran-Iraq War." (2013). Published electronically October 31. http://kurzman.unc.edu/death-tolls-of-the-iran-iraq-war/.

"La Raza Islamica: Prisons, Hip-Hop & Converting Converts." *Berkeley La Raza Law Journal* 22, no. 9 (2012): 175–202.

LaCapria, Kim. "Horton Hears a Hitler." *Snopes.com* (2015). Published electronically November 23. http://www.snopes.com/dr-seuss-adolf-wolf/.

Lacey, Robert. *The Kingdom*. 1st American ed. New York: Harcourt Brace Jovanovich, 1982.

Lambert, Malcolm. *Crusade and Jihad*. London: Profile Books Ltd., 2016.

Landler, Mark. "The Afghan War and the Evolution of Obama." *New York Times* (2017). Published electronically January 1. https://www.nytimes.com/2017/01/01/world/asia/obama-afghanistan-war.html.

Larison, Daniel. "The Power of Riyadh." *Twitter* (2017). Published electronically May 21. https://bit.ly/2KkjdZs.

Laub, Zachary. "International Sanctions on Iran." New York: Council on Foreign Relations, 2015.

Leahy, Michael Patrick. "TB Spiked 500 Percent in Twin Falls during 2012, as Chobani Yogurt Opened Plant." *Breitbart* (2016). Published electronically August 26. http://www.breitbart.com/big-government/2016/08/26/tb-spiked-500-percent-twin-falls-2012-year-chobani-opened-local-plant/.

Leatherdale, Clive. *Britain and Saudi Arabia, 1925–1939: The Imperial Oasis*. London; Totowa, NJ: F. Cass, 1983.

Levy, Pema. "Long before Trump, Kellyanne Conway Worked for Anti-Muslim and Anti-Immigrant Extremists." *Mother Jones* (2016). Published electronically December 9. https://www.motherjones.com/politics/2016/12/kellyanne-conway-immigration-islam-bannon-trump/.

Lord, Jeffrey. "Hannity, Cleric Fight over Muslim Brotherhood's Nazi Link." *American Spectator* (2011). Published electronically February 3. https://spectator.org/24993_hannity-cleric-fight-over-muslim-brotherhoods-nazi-link/.

Lowery, Wesley, Kindy Kimberly and Andrew Ba Tran. "In the United States, Right-Wing Violence Is on the Rise." *Washington Post* (2018). Published electronically November 25. https://www.washingtonpost.com/national/in-the-united-states-right-wing-violence-is-on-the-rise/2018/11/25/61f7f24a-deb4-11e8-85df-7a6b4d25cfbb_story.html?utm_term=.c37128969bb3

Lynch, Marc. "Is the Muslim Brotherhood a Terrorist Organization or a Firewall against Violent Extremism?" *Washington Post* (2016). Published electronically

March 7. https://www.washingtonpost.com/news/monkey-cage/wp/2016/03/07/is-the-muslim-brotherhood-a-terrorist-organization-or-a-firewall-against-violent-extremism/?utm_term=.3c743eb24922.

Lynfield, Ben. "Who Is Walid Phares, Trump's Mideast Adviser?" *Jerusalem Post* (2016). Published electronically November 16. http://www.jpost.com/Us-Elections/Who-is-Walid-Phares-Trumps-Mideast-adviser-472741.

Macguire, Robert. "Exclusive: Robert Mercer Backed a Secretive Group That Worked with Facebook, Google to Target Anti-Muslim Ads at Swing Voters." *OpenSecrets,org* (2018). Published electronically, April 5. https://www.opensecrets.org/news/2018/04/exclusive-robert-mercer-backed-a-secretive-group-that-worked-with-facebook-google-to-target-anti-muslim-ads-at-swing-voters/.

Madelung, Wilferd. *The Succession to Muhammad: A Study of the Early Caliphate.* Kindle ed. Cambridge; New York: Cambridge University Press, 1997.

Mahler, Jonathan. "CNN Had a Problem. Donald Trump Solved It." *New York Times Magazine* (2017). Published electronically April 4. https://www.nytimes.com/2017/04/04/magazine/cnn-had-a-problem-donald-trump-solved-it.html.

"Man Arrested at Filthy New Mexico Compound Is Son of Imam Linked to 1993 WTC Bombing." *WCBS Newsradio 880* (2018). Published electronically August 9. https://wcbs880.radio.com/articles/news/man-arrested-filthy-new-mexico-compound-son-imam-linked-1993-wtc-bombing.

Maraka, Farah. "Bin Salman Satanizes the Ottomans as a Message to Amman." *Rai al Youm* (translated by Mideastwire.com) (2018). Published electronically March 7. https://mideastwire.com/page/article.php?id=66185.

March, Andrew. "Designating the Muslim Brotherhood a 'Terrorist Organization' Puts Academic Researchers at Risk." *Washington Post* (2017). Published electronically January 25. https://www.washingtonpost.com/news/monkey-cage/wp/2017/01/25/how-the-courts-have-put-middle-east-researchers-at-risk/?utm_term=.b1fbad38b993.

Marr, Timothy. *The Cultural Roots of American Islamicism.* Cambridge; New York: Cambridge University Press, 2006.

Mascaro, Lisa. "Speaker Paul Ryan Defends Trump's Immigrant and Refugee Ban, as Congress Grumbles about Being Left Out." *LATimes.com* (2017). Published electronically January 31. http://www.latimes.com/politics/washington/la-na-trailguide-updates-speaker-paul-ryan-stands-behind-trump-s-1485881647-htmlstory.html.

Mathis-Lilley, Ben. "Longtime Trump Adviser Claims Khizr Khan Is a Terrorist Agent." *Slate* (2016). Published electronically August 1. http://www.slate.com/blogs/the_slatest/2016/08/01/roger_stone_says_khizr_khan_is_a_muslim_brotherhood_saboteur.html.

Mauro, Ryan. "Jihadi Cult Member Files to Run for Congress." (2018). Published electronically May 16. https://clarionproject.org/2nd-jihadi-cult-member-files-to-run-for-congress/.

McLeary, Paul, and Dan De Luce. "Trump's Possible VP Believes ISIS Could Conquer the U.S. and Drink Americans' Blood." *Foreignpolicy.com* (2016). Published electronically July 12. http://foreignpolicy.com/2016/07/12/

trumps-possible-vp-believes-isis-could-conquer-the-u-s-and-drink-americans-blood/.

Medhsud, Saud. "Pakistan's Most Hated Man: Volleyball Player, Child Killer." *Reuters* (2014). Published electronically December 19. https://www.reuters.com/article/us-pakistan-school-commander/pakistans-most-hated-man-volleyball-player-child-killer-idUSKBN0JX1CX20141219.

"Meet the Press Transcript." (2015). Published electronically August 16. https://www.nbcnews.com/meet-the-press/meet-press-transcript-august-16-2015-n412636.

Meleagrou-Hitchens, Alexander. "As American as Apple Pie: How Anwar Al-Awlaki Became the Face of Western Jihad." London: ICSR, King's College, 2011.

Meleagrou-Hitchens, Alexander, Seamus Hughes and Bennett Clifford. "The Travelers: American Jihadists in Syria and Iraq." Washington, DC: Program on Extremism, George Washington University, 2018.

Menocal, Maria Rosa. *The Ornament of the World: How Muslims, Jews, and Christians Created a Culture of Tolerance in Medieval Spain.* Kindle ed. Boston: Little, Brown, 2002.

Merica, Dan. "Trump: Frederick Douglass 'Is Being Recognized More and More.'" *CNN.com* (2017). Published electronically February 2. https://cnn.it/2vK8Yum.

Michael, Maggie, Trish Wilson and Lee Keath. "U.S. Allies, Al Qaeda Battle Rebels in Yemen." *Associated Press* (2018). Published electronically August 9. http://www.foxnews.com/world/2018/08/07/unite-with-devil-yemen-war-binds-us-allies-al-qaida.html.

Miller, Erin, and Michael Jensen. "American Deaths in Terrorist Attacks, 1995–2016." College Park, MD: The National Consortium for the Study of Terrorism and Responses to Terrorism (START), 2017.

Miller, S. A. "Speaker Paul Ryan Blasts Trump's Muslim Ban: 'This Is Not Conservatism.'" *Washingtontimes.com* (2015). Published electronically December 8. http://www.washingtontimes.com/news/2015/dec/8/paul-ryan-blasts-trump-muslim-ban-not-conservatism/.

Mogahed, Dalia, and Youssef Chouhoud. "American Muslim Poll." Dearborn, MI: ISPU, 2017.

Mohajer, Shaya Tafeye. "Q&A: Hannah Allam on Covering Muslim Life in America for BuzzFeed." *Columbia Journalism Review* (2017). Published electronically July 24. https://www.cjr.org/q_and_a/qa-hannah-allam-on-covering-muslim-life-in-america-for-buzzfeed.php.

Mohamed, Becheer. "New Estimates Show U.S. Muslim Population Continues to Grow." Muslim Population, *FactTank: News in the Numbers* (2018). Published electronically January 3. http://www.pewresearch.org/fact-tank/2018/01/03/new-estimates-show-u-s-muslim-population-continues-to-grow/.

Mohamed, Becheer, and Gregory A. Smith. "Muslims Concerned about Their Place in Society, But Continue to Believe in the American Dream." Washington, DC: Pew Research Center, 2017.

Moniquet, Claude. "The Involvement of Salafism/Wahabbism in the Support and Supply of Arms to Rebel Groups around the World." Brussels: Directorate-General for External Policies, Directorate B, European Parliament, 2013.

Morgan, Matthew J. "The Origins of the New Terrorism." *Parameters* 34, no. 1 (Spring 2004): 29.

Morlin, Bill. "Experts Seeing Spike in Possible Anti-Muslim Hate Crimes." Atlanta: Southern Poverty Law Center, 2016.

Morris, Loveday, Karen DeYoung and Missy Ryan. "U.S. Forces Begin Airstrikes in Tikrit, Where Iran-Backed Militias Are in Lead." *Washington Post* (2015). Published electronically March 25. https://www.washingtonpost.com/world/middle_east/us-providing-surveillance-to-iraqi-forces-fighting-islamic-state-in-tikrit/2015/03/25/1851a070-d236-11e4-8b1e-274d670aa9c9_story.html?utm_term=.2ff369d790a2.

Mosalli, Irene. "Brigitte Gabriel et sa 'Marche contre la charia.'" *L'Orient du Jour* (2017). Published electronically June 15. https://www.lorientlejour.com/article/1057222/brigitte-gabriel-et-sa-marche-contre-la-charia-.html.

Muir, William. *The Life of Mahomet and History of Islam, to the Era of the Hegira.* 4 vols. n. p.: n. pub., 1858.

Murdoch, Rupert. "Maybe Most Moslems." *Twitter* (2015). Published electronically January 9. https://twitter.com/rupertmurdoch/status/553734788881076225?lang=en.

Murphy, Esme. "German Expert: U.S. Way Behind in Terrorism De-Radicalization." *WCCO CBS Minnesota* (2016). Published electronically September 21. http://minnesota.cbslocal.com/2016/09/21/deradicalization-expert/.

"Muslim Americans: No Signs of Growth in Alienation or Support for Extremism." (2011). Published electronically August 30. http://www.people-press.org/2011/08/30/muslim-americans-no-signs-of-growth-in-alienation-or-support-for-extremism/.

"The Muslim Brotherhood Infiltrates Obama Administration." *Frontpage Mag* (2013). Published electronically March 28. https://www.frontpagemag.com/fpm/183352/muslim-brotherhood-infiltrates-obama-frontpagemagcom.

"Muslim Brotherhood Review: Main Findings." London: House of Commons, 2015.

"Muslim Scholars: Suicide Attacks Violate Islamic Principles." *AP News* (2018). Published electronically May 11. https://apnews.com/5295ee1c5f584122abd6a22 67857cfc9.

"Muslim World League and World Assembly of Muslim Youth." In *Muslim Networks and Movements in Western Europe.* Washington, DC: Pew Research Center: Religion & Public Life, 2010.

Mustafa-Hakima, Ahmad. *History of Eastern Arabia 1750–1800: The Rise and Development of Bahrain, Kuwait and Wahhabi Saudi Arabia.* 2nd ed. London: Probsthain, 1988.

Naji, Kasra. *Ahmadinejad: The Secret History of Iran's Radical Leader.* Berkeley: University of California Press, 2008.

Nasr, Seyyed Hossein. *The Study Quran : A New Translation and Commentary.* 1st ed. New York: HarperOne, an imprint of Collins Publishers, 2015.

Nawaz, Maajid. "My Open Letter to a Jailed Muslim Brotherhood Leader." *Daily Beast* (2017). Published electronically March 5. https://www.thedailybeast.com/my-open-letter-to-a-jailed-muslim-brotherhood-leader.

Neuwirth, Angelika. "Two Faces of the Qur'an: Qur'an and Mushaf." *Oral Traditions* 25, no. 1 (2010).

News Desk. "490 Soldiers, 3,500 Militants Killed in Operation Zarb-E-Azb So Far: DG ISPR." *Express Tribune* (2015). Published electronically June 15. https://tribune.com.pk/story/1123356/1-dg-ispr-addresses-press-conference-afghanistan-pakistan-border-clashes/.

"Newt Gingrich: Deport Every Muslim Who Believes in Sharia." *Foxnews.com* (2016). Published electronically July 14. http://video.foxnews.com/v/5036444136001/?#sp=show-clips.

"North Carolina Resident Daniel Patrick Boyd Sentenced for Terrorism Violations." News release. August 24, 2012, https://archives.fbi.gov/archives/charlotte/press-releases/2012/north-carolina-resident-daniel-patrick-boyd-sentenced-for-terrorism-violations.

Norton, Ben. "Leaked Hillary Clinton Emails Show U.S. Allies Saudi Arabia and Qatar Supported ISIS." *Salon.com* (2016). Published electronically October 11. https://www.salon.com/2016/10/11/leaked-hillary-clinton-emails-show-u-s-allies-saudi-arabia-and-qatar-supported-isis/.

Nossiter, Adam. " 'Let Them Call You Racists': Bannon's Pep Talk to National Front." *New York Times* (2018). Published electronically March 10. https://www.nytimes.com/2018/03/10/world/europe/steve-bannon-france-national-front.html?module=WatchingPortal&region=c-column-middle-span-region&pgType=Homepage&action=click&mediaId=thumb_square&state=standard&contentPlacement=7&version=internal&contentCollection=www.nytimes.com&contentId=https%3A%2F%2Fwww.nytimes.com%2F2018%2F03%2F10%2Fworld%2Feurope%2Fsteve-bannon-france-national-front.html&eventName=Watching-article-click.

Nossiter, Adam. "Too Radical for France, a Muslim Clergyman Faces Deportation." *New York Times* (2018). Published electronically April 5. https://nyti.ms/2qay13W.

Notezai, Muhammad Akhbar. "The Rise of Religious Extremism in Balochistan." *The Diplomat* (2017). Published electronically January 9. https://thediplomat.com/2017/01/the-rise-of-religious-extremism-in-balochistan/.

Nowrasteh, Alex. "Terrorism and Immigration: A Risk Analysis." In *Policy Analysis*. Washington, DC: Cato Institute, 2016.

Nuraniyah, Nava. "Mothers to Bombers: The Evolution of Indonesian Women Extremists." Jakarta: Institute for Policy Analysis of Conflict, 2017.

Nyrop, Richard F. *Saudi Arabia, a Country Study.* Area Handbook Series. 4th ed. Washington, DC: Foreign Area Studies, For sale by the Supt. of Docs., U.S. G.P.O., 1984.

O'Donnell, Norah. "Saudi Arabia's Heir to the Throne Talks to 60 Minutes." *60 Minutes* (2018). Published electronically March 19. https://www.cbsnews.com/news/saudi-crown-prince-talks-to-60-minutes/.

"Obama's Shariah Czar Mohamed Magid Hands Diversity Award to Jew-Hater Dawud Walid." *PJ Media* (2012). Published electronically July 5. https://pjmedia.com/blog/obamas-shariah-czar-mohamed-magid-hands-diversity-award-to-jew-hater-dawud-walid/.

Obama, Barack. "Remarks by the President on a New Beginning," edited by The White House. Cairo: The White House, 2009.

Obeidallah, Dean. "Meet the Man Who Could Be America's First Muslim Governor." *Daily Beast* (2018). Published electronically, February 8. https://www.thedailybeast.com/meet-the-man-who-could-be-americas-first-muslim-governor.

Obeidallah, Dean. "The Terror Trial We're Really Ignoring." *dailybeast.com* (2017). Published electronically February 6. http://www.thedailybeast.com/articles/2017/02/07/mr-president-a-terrorist-is-on-trial-right-now-but-he-s-christian.html.

Office of the Inspector General. "A Review of the FBI's Handling of the Brandon Mayfield Case." Washington, DC: Department of Justice, 2006.

"An Official Proclamation from the Government of Great Britain to the Natives of Arabia and Arab Provinces, Public Record Office, 1914 (Pro), Fo141/710/9." Cited in *Secret Affairs: Britain's Collusion with Radical Islam*, p. 6, edited by Mark Curtis. London: Serpent's Tail, 2018.

Omar, Ilhan. "Look Like America." *Twitter* (2018). Published electronically December 6. https://twitter.com/IlhanMN/status/1070907694339502080?ref_src=twsrc%5Etfw%7Ctwcamp%5Etweetembed%7Ctwterm%5E10709076943395 02080&ref_url=https%3A%2F%2Fwww.alaraby.co.uk%2Fenglish%2Fcomment%2F2018%2F12%2F13%2Fsaudi-disinformation-campaign-reveals-fear-of-progressive-muslim-congresswomen

"On Egypt's Reaction to Trump's Decision." *Al Ahram* (2017). Published electronically December 13. https://mideastwire.com/page/article.php?id=65511.

Owens, John B. "United States of America v. Mohamed Osman Mahomud," edited by Ninth Circuit United States Court of Appeals. San Francisco, 2016.

Pandith, Farah. "The World Needs a Long-Term Strategy for Defeating Extremism." *New York Times* (2015). Published electronically December 8. https://www.nytimes.com/roomfordebate/2015/12/08/is-saudi-arabia-a-unique-generator-of-extremism/the-world-needs-a- long-term-strategy-for-defeating-extremism.

Pargeter, Alison. *The New Frontiers of Jihad: Radical Islam in Europe.* Philadelphia: University of Pennsylvania Press, 2008.

Parlapiano, Alicia. "A Final Count of Candidate Speaking Time." *New York Times* (2015). Published electronically August 6. https://www.nytimes.com/live/republican-debate-election-2016-cleveland/a-final-count-of-candidate-speaking-time/.

Pasha, Shaheen. "Donald Trump Is My Son's Bogeyman," *usatoday.com* (2015). Published electronically December 10. http://www.usatoday.com/story/opinion/voices/2015/12/10/voices-donald-trump-my-sons-bogeyman/77088272/.

Pasha, Shaheen. "Shaheen Pasha: How Western Muslim Women Bear a Double Burden." *Dallas News* (2016). Published electronically April 11. https://www.dallasnews.com/opinion/commentary/2016/04/11/shaheen-pasha-how-western-muslim-women-bear-a-double-burden.

"Pat Robertson Praises 'Mideast Beast' on 'the 700 Club." *endureinstrength.org.* http://www.endureinstrength.org/pages.asp?pageid=119412.

Patterson, Margot. "America's Anti-Islam Problem Didn't End with the Cancellation of 'Roseanne.'" *America: The Jesuit Review* (2018). Published electronically June 25. https://www.americamagazine.org/politics-society/2018/06/25/ americas-anti-islam-problem-didnt-end-cancellation-roseanne.

Perez, Evan, and Shimon Prokupecz. "U.S. Suspects Russian Hackers Planted Fake News Behind Qatar Crisis." *CNN.com* (2017). Published electronically June 7. https://edition.cnn.com/2017/06/06/politics/russian-hackers-planted-fake-news-qatar-crisis/index.html.

Phillips, Kristine. "In the Latest JFK Files: The FBI's Ugly Analysis on Martin Luther King Jr., Filled with Falsehoods." *Washington Post*, November 12 (2017). Published electronically 4 November. https://wapo.st/2qgJijY.

Pillar, Paul R. "Ideological Warfare against Nonviolent Political Islam." *National Interest* (2017). Published electronically January 14. http://nationalinterest.org/blog/paul-pillar/ ideological-warfare-against-nonviolent-political-islam-19068?page=2.

Pintak, Lawrence. "Black and White and Trump All Over." *ForeignPolicy.com* (2016). Published electronically September 1. https://bit.ly/2r6we12.

Pintak, Lawrence. "Can Cartoons Save Pakistan's Children from Jihad?" *ForeignPolicy.com* (2016). Published electronically August 19. https://bit. ly/2bpwjVI.

Pintak, Lawrence. "For Muslim Americans, Fear and Shock at a Trump Presidency." *ForeignPolicy.com* (2016). Published electronically November 10. https://bit. ly/2eWMQQG.

Pintak, Lawrence. "ICYMI, Trump Has the U.S. Poised on the Edge of a Mideast Abyss." *Dailybeast.com* (2017). Published electronically June 9. https://thebea. st/2jewfLZ.

Pintak, Lawrence. "An Idiot's Guide to Islam in America." *ForeignPolicy.com* (2016). Published electronically December 4. https://bit.ly/2vUcfHJ.

Pintak, Lawrence. "The Muslims Are Coming! The Muslims Are Coming!" *ForeignPolicy.com* (2016). Published electronically June 14. https://bit. ly/1WN6XDS.

Pintak, Lawrence. "Not All Islamists Are Out to Kill Us." *ForeignPolicy.com* (2016). Published electronically July 19. https://bit.ly/2HFI9Ja.

Pintak, Lawrence. "Nuclear Pakistan Sees the Saudi Game against Qatar and Iran and Says, 'No, Thanks.'" *Dailybeast.com* (2017). Published electronically June 6. https://thebea.st/2rcIP2T.

Pintak, Lawrence. "Portland Is the Most Livable City in America—Except If You're Muslim." *ForeignPolicy.com* (2016). Published electronically April 8. https://bit. ly/1VFldfK.

Pintak, Lawrence. *Reflections in a Bloodshot Lens: America, Islam and the War of Ideas*. London; Ann Arbor, MI: Pluto, 2006.

Pintak, Lawrence. "'The Rise of the American Taliban.'" *ForeignPolicy.com* (2016). Published electronically February 4. https://bit.ly/2FqfCFz.

Pintak, Lawrence. *Seeds of Hate: How America's Flawed Lebanon Policy Ignited the Jihad*. Sterling, VA: Pluto Press, 2003.

Pintak, Lawrence. "Translating Spirituality into Real Life." *Beliefnet.net* (2000). https://bit.ly/2vKIoRQ.

Pintak, Lawrence. "The Trump Administration's Islamophobic Holy Grail." *ForeignPolicy.com* (2017). Published electronically February 2. https://bit.ly/2I0iE98.

Pintak, Lawrence. "Who Is Killing Pakistan's Educated Elite?" *PRI* (2015). Published electronically 28 May. https://bit.ly/2jfeT1E.

Pintak, Lawrence, and Syed Javid Nazir. "Inside the (Muslim) Journalist's Mind." *New York Times*, February 12, 2011.

"PM Says No Distinction Now between Good and Bad Taliban." *dawn.com* (2014). Published electronically December 17. https://www.dawn.com/news/1151397.

"Portland Passes Resolution for Welcoming Muslims." *KGW.com* (2016). Published electronically December 16. https://bit.ly/2JuliRq.

Poushter, Jacob. "The Divide over Islam and National Laws in the Muslim World." Washington, DC: Pew Research Center, 2016.

Powell, Colin L., and Joseph E. Persico. *My American Journey.* 1st Ballantine Books rev. ed. New York: Ballantine Books, 2003.

"PPP Demands Probe Based on Benazir's Letter." *dawn.com* (2007). Published electronically December 30. https://www.dawn.com/news/282349.

"President Trump's Speech to the Arab Islamic American Summit," edited by The White House. Washington, DC, May 21, 2017.

Price, Michael. "Community Outreach or Intelligence Gathering?" Brennan Center for Justice at New York University School of Law, 2015.

"Prince Saud Al-Faisal / Speech /the Council on Foreign Relations New York 20/-09-2005." News release. 2005, http://www.mofa.gov.sa/sites/mofaen/Minister/MinisterMedia/OfficialSpeeches/Pages/NewsArticleID39973.aspx.

Procházka-Eisl, Gisela, and Stephan Procházka. *The Plain of Saints and Prophets: The Nusayri-Alawi Community of Cilicia (Southern Turkey) and Its Sacred Places.* Wiesbaden: Harrassowitz Verlag, 2010.

Qadhi, Yusuf. "On Salafi Islam." (2014). https://muslimmatters.org/2014/04/22/on-salafi-islam-dr-yasir-qadhi/.

"Quran: All You Need for Salvation." *True Islam* (2010). http://www.quran-islam.org/main_topics/quran/new_information/quran_is_all_we_need_(P1253).html.

Rachidi, Ilhem. "Morocco Struggles to Tamp Down Radical Islam." *Christian Science Monitor* (2003). Published electronically December 15. https://www.csmonitor.com/2003/1215/p07s01-woaf.html.

Rakowski, Stephen. "How the 1979 Siege of Mecca Haunts the House of Saud." *Worldview* (2017). Published electronically, July 2. https://worldview.stratfor.com/article/how-1979-siege-mecca-haunts-house-saud.

Rao, Kumar, Carey Shenkman and Sarrah Buageila. "Equal Treatment? Measuring the Legal and Media Responses to Ideologically Motivated Violence in the United States," edited by Dalia Mogahed. Washington, DC; Dearborn, MI: Institute for Social Policy and Understanding, 2018.

Rashid, Ahmed. *Taliban: Militant Islam, Oil and Fundamentalism in Central Asia.* 2nd ed. New Haven: Yale University Press, 2010.

Raza, Shahzad. "A Religious Edict against Pakistan's Information Minister Is a Worrying Sign." *Friday Times* (2015). Published electronically May 22. http://www.thefridaytimes.com/tft/fatwa-fears/.

"Readout of President Donald J. Trump's Call with Amir Sheikh Tameem Bin Hamad Al Thani of Qatar." News release. June 7, 2017, https://www.whitehouse.gov/briefings-statements/readout-president-donald-j-trumps-call-amir-sheikh-tameem-bin-hamad-al-thani-qatar/.

Reagan, Ronald. "Remarks at the Annual Dinner of the Conservative Political Action Conference." In *The American Presidency Project*. Santa Barbara: University of California, Santa Barbara, 1985.

Reagan, Ronald. "Statement on the Third Anniversary of the Soviet Invasion of Afghanistan," edited by The White House. Washington, DC: Ronald Reagan Presidential Library & Museum, 1982.

"Recommendations of the Conference on Contemporary Dawah Issues in the West." Assembly of Muslims Jurists of America, 2016.

Reints, Renae. "UN Migration Agency Rejects Trump Nominee for Director-General." *Fortune.com* (2018). Published electronically June 29. http://fortune.com/2018/06/29/iom-trump-nominee-un/.

"A Resolution to Declare Support for the Muslim Community and Reaffirm Beaverton as a Welcoming City." Beaverton, OR: City Council, 2017.

Reuters. "Islamic State Beheads Two for 'Sorcery' in Egypt's Sinai." (2017). Published electronically March 29. https://www.reuters.com/article/uk-egypt-insurgency/islamic-state-beheads-two-for-sorcery-in-egypts-sinai-idUSKBN16Z2PX.

Reuters. "Saudi Prince Says Turkey Part of 'Triangle of Evil': Egyptian Media." (2018). Published electronically March 7. https://www.reuters.com/article/us-saudi-turkey/saudi-prince-says-turkey-part-of-triangle-of-evil-egyptian-media-idUSKCN1GJ1WW.

Reuters. "War in the Gulf: Bush Statement; Excerpts from 2 Statements by Bush on Iraq's Proposal for Ending Conflict." *New York Times* (1991). Published electronically February 16. https://www.nytimes.com/1991/02/16/world/war-gulf-bush-statement-excerpts-2-statements-bush-iraq-s-proposal-for-ending.html.

Riedel, Bruce. "Captured: Mastermind behind the 1996 Khobar Towers Attack." (2015). Published electronically August 26. https://www.brookings.edu/blog/markaz/2015/08/26/captured-mastermind-behind-the-1996-khobar-towers-attack/.

Riedel, Bruce. "Saudi Arabia Uses Aggression Abroad to Calm Clerics at Home." (2018). Published electronically January 31. http://www.crpme.gr/analysis/saudi-arabia/saudi-arabia-uses-aggression-abroad-to-calm-clerics-at-home.

Risen, James. "The C.I.A. In Iran." *New York Times* (2000). https://archive.nytimes.com/www.nytimes.com/library/world/mideast/041600iran-cia-chapter4.html.

Roberts, Laurie. "Roberts: Arizona Senate Candidate under Attack for Being Muslim." *Arizona Republic* (2017). Published electronically July 18. https://www.azcentral.com/story/opinion/op-ed/laurieroberts/2017/07/18/senate-candidate-under-attack-being-muslim/489859001/.

Rodda, Chris. "Maher Season Premiere Includes Islamophobe Who Said Muslim-Americans Shouldn't Be Allowed to Hold Public Office." *Huffington Post* (2017). Published electronically December 6. https://www.huffingtonpost.com/chris-rodda/maher-season-premiere-inc_b_168972.html.

Rosenberg, Eli, and Abigail Hauslohner. "Children Were Brought to New Mexico Compound for Weapons Training, Officials Said." *Washington Post* (2018). Published electronically August 8. https://www.washingtonpost.com/news/post-nation/wp/2018/08/08/children-were-being-trained-to-commit-school-shootings-by-man-arrested-at-new-mexico-compound/?utm_term=.779d02361366.

Rosenberg, Matthew, and Adam Goldman. "C.I.A. Names the 'Dark Prince' to Run Iran Operations, Signaling a Tougher Stance." *New York Times* (2017). Published electronically June 2. https://www.nytimes.com/2017/06/02/world/middleeast/cia-iran-dark-prince-michael-dandrea.html?_r=0.

Roth, John, Douglas Greenburg and Serena Wille. "Monograph on Terrorist Financing: Staff Report to the Commission." National Commission on Terrorist Attacks upon the United States, 2004.

Roy, Olivier, and Cynthia Schoch. *Jihad and Death: The Global Appeal of Islamic State*. New York: Oxford University Press, 2017.

Rubin, Barnett R. *The Fragmentation of Afghanistan: State Formation and Collapse in the International System*. 2nd ed. New Haven: Yale University Press, 2002.

"Rubio: Senate Dems Will Back Bill to Pause Refugee Program." *The Kelly File* (2015). Published electronically November 19. http://video.foxnews.com/v/4622536839001/?playlist_id=2694949842001#sp=show-clips.

Russell, Betsy K. "False Story on Social Media Charges Syrian Refugees Raped Idaho Girl." *Spokesman-Review* (2016). Published electronically June 20. http://www.spokesman.com/stories/2016/jun/20/false-story-social-media-charges-syrian-refugees-r/.

Sabu, Mohamad. "The Need to Stay at a Safe Distance from Saudi Arabia." *Malaysiakini* (2017). Published electronically December 7. https://www.malaysiakini.com/news/404070.

"Safe Spaces: An Updated Toolkit for Empowering Communities and Addressing Ideological Violence." Los Angeles: Muslim Public Affairs Council, 2016.

Said, Edward W. *Covering Islam: How the Media and the Experts Determine How We See the Rest of the World*. New York: Vintage Books, 1997.

Salem, Ola. "Saudi Arabia Declares War on America's Muslim Congresswomen." *Foreign Policy* (2018). Published electronically December 11. https://foreignpolicy.com/2018/12/11/saudi-arabia-declares-war-on-americas-muslim-congresswomen/

"Saudi Arabia Death Toll Reaches 100 as Authorities Carry out Execution Spree." London: Amnesty International, 2017.

"Saudi Arabia Profile." In *Freedom in the World 2018*. New York: Freedom House, 2018.

"Saudi Arabia Turns against Political Islam." *The Economist* (2018). Published electronically June 23. https://www.economist.com/special-report/2018/06/23/saudi-arabia-turns-against-political-islam?frsc=dg%7Ce.

"Saudi Influence and Islamic Radicalization in Indonesia." *Lausanne Global Analysis* 6, no. 5 (September 2017).

"Saudi Invasion of Al-Mahrah: A Salafist 'Princedom' on Oman's Borders?" *Al-Akhbar* (2018). Published electronically January 11.

"Saudi Politics Entangle Hajj Pilgrimage." *Associated Press* (2017). Published electronically August 29. https://www.cbsnews.com/news/hajj-pilgrimage-entangled-in-web-of-saudi-politics/.

"Saudi Prince Sees Trump as 'True Friend' to Muslims (Full Text)." *Bloomberg* (2017). Published electronically March 14. https://www.bloomberg.com/news/articles/2017-03-15/saudi-prince-sees-trump-as-true-friend-to-muslims-full-text.

"Saudi TV Host Abdullellah Al-Dosari Celebrates Death of Iranian Pilgrims in Hajj Stampede in Mecca." *Clip #5134* (2015). Published electronically October 3. https://www.memri.org/tv/saudi-tv-host-abdulellah-al-dosari-celebrates-death-iranian-pilgrims-hajj-stampede-mecca.

"Saudi's Bin Salman Talks about Megacity Project in South Sinai, 'Triangle of Evil' during Egypt Visit." *Ahram Online* (2018). Published electronically March 6. http://english.ahram.org.eg/NewsContent/1/64/292235/Egypt/Politics-/Saudis-Bin-Salman-talks-about-megacity-project-in-.aspx.

Savransky, Rebecca. "Giuliani: Trump Asked Me How to Do a Muslim Ban 'Legally.'" *thehill.com* (2017). Published electronically January 29. http://thehill.com/homenews/administration/316726-giuliani-trump-asked-me-how-to-do-a-muslim-ban-legally.

Scahill, Jeremy. "Blackwater Founder Erik Prince Implicated in Murder." *The Nation* (2018). Published electronically August 4. https://thenation.com/article/blackwarer-founder-implicated-murder/.

Scarborough, Joe. "Trump: 'Something Going on' with Islam and Violence" (2015). Published electronically November 30. http://www.msnbc.com/morning-joe/watch/trump--something-going-on-with-islam-and-violence-576200259724.

Scarborough, Rowan. "Saudi Government Funded Extremism in U.S. Mosques and Charities: Report." *Washington Times* (2016). Published electronically July 19. https://www.washingtontimes.com/news/2016/jul/19/911-report-details-saudi-arabia-funding-of-muslim-/.

Schachtel, Jordan. "NYT Profiles 'Counter Extremists' Who Are Actually Extremists." *Breitbart* (2015). Published electronically February 21. http://www.breitbart.com/national-security/2015/02/21/nyt-profiles-counter-extremists-who-are-actually-extremists/.

Schleifer, Theodore. "Donald Trump: 'I Think Islam Hates Us.'" (2016). Published electronically March 10. https://www.cnn.com/2016/03/09/politics/donald-trump-islam-hates-us/.

Scott, Eugene. "Ted Cruz: Program Patrolling Muslim Neighborhoods Was a Success." *CNN.com* (2016). Published electronically March 30. https://cnn.it/2vRNhJ3.

Scott, Margaret. "Indonesia: The Saudis Are Coming." *New York Review of Books* (2016). Published electronically October 26. http://www.nybooks.com/articles/2016/10/27/indonesia-the-saudis-are-coming/.

Sebugwaawo, Ismail. "Strict Action against Anyone Showing Sympathy with Qatar: UAE." *Khaleej Times* (2017). Published electronically June 8.

Seely, Taylor. "Here's What Senate Candidate Deedra Abboud Wants You to Know About Flood of Anti-Islamic Attacks." *Arizona Republic* (2017). Published electronically July 31. https://www.azcentral.com/story/news/politics/arizona/2017/08/01/senate-candidate-deedra-abboud-responds-fresh-ground-islamophobia/505805001/.

Seunagal, Gabrielle. "No Islam in America." Twitter, https://twitter.com/ClassySnobbb/status/796224917905833984?lang=en].

Sexton, Nick Kim. "GOP Hopeful Carly Fiorina under Fire for 'Praising Muslims.'" *MSNBC.com* (2015). Published electronically August 17. https://nbcnews.to/2vLnyle.

Shah, Saeed. "Pakistan Foreign Minister Says U.S. Has Undermined Countries' Ties." *Wall Street Journal* (2018). Published electronically January 5. https://www.wsj.com/articles/pakistan-says-alliance-with-u-s-is-over-1515155860.

Shahid, Kunwar Khuldune. "Why the Trump-Led Islamic Summit in Saudi Arabia Was a Disaster for Pakistan." *The Diplomat* (2017). Published electronically May 23. https://thediplomat.com/2017/05/why-the-trump-led-islamic-summit-in-saudi-arabia-was-a-disaster-for-pakistan/.

Shalhoub, Lulwa. "Global Center to Combat Extremism Launched in Riyadh." *Arab News* (2017). Published electronically May 22. http://www.arabnews.com/node/1103136/saudi-arabia.

Shane, Scott. "Moussaoui Calls Saudi Princes Patrons of Al Qaeda." *New York Times* (2015). Published electronically February 3. https://www.nytimes.com/2015/02/04/us/zacarias-moussaoui-calls-saudi-princes-patrons-of-al-qaeda.html?_r=0&mtrref=undefined&assetType=nyt_now.

Shane, Scott. "Saudis and Extremism: Both the Arsonists and the Firefighters." *New York Times* (2017). Published electronically August 25. https://www.nytimes.com/2016/08/26/world/middleeast/saudi-arabia-islam.html.

Shapiro, Nina. "CEO Makes Fiery Emails about Muslims Part of the Workday." *Seattle Times*, April 29, 2016.

Shawky, Ahmed. "A Man and Brothers in the White House." *Rose al-Yusuf* (2012). Published electronically December 22. https://bit.ly/2uC6CND.

Shea, Nina. "Saudi Publications on Hate Ideology Invade American Mosques." New York: Center for Religious Freedom, Freedom House, 2005.

"Sheikh Tamim Denies Qatar Has Links to Terrorism." *Khaleej Times* (2017). Published electronically May 25. https://www.khaleejtimes.com/region/qatar/sheikh-tamim-denies-qatar-has-links-to-terrorism.

Sherfinski, David. "Donald Trump: We Will 'Eradicate' 'Radical Islamic Terrorism' 'from the Face of the Earth.'" *washingtontimes.com* (2017). Published electronically January 20. http://www.washingtontimes.com/news/2017/jan/20/donald-trump-we-will-eradicate-radical-islamic-ter/.

Shuham, Matt. "Trump Contradicts Tillerson Line on Blockade of Qatar within Hours." *Talkingpointsmemo.com* (2017). Published electronically June 9. https://talkingpointsmemo.com/livewire/trump-contradicts-tillerson-qatar.

Siddiqi, Faisal. "Supreme Court on Blasphemy." *Dawn.com* (2015). Published electronically November 3. https://www.dawn.com/news/1217061/supreme-court-on-blasphemy.

Sides, John, and Dalia Mogahed. "Muslims in America: Public Perceptions in the Trump Era." Washington, DC: Voter Study Group, Democracy Fund, 2018.

Simon, Steven, and Daniel Benjamin. "The Islamophobic Huckster in the White House." *New York Times* (2017). Published electronically February 24. https://nyti.ms/2lF12C2.

Smietana, Bob. "Covering the Anti-Islam Movement." In *Islam for Journalists (and Everyone Else)*, edited by Lawrence Pintak and Stephen Franklin, Loc. 887–919. Columbia, MO: Donald W. Reynolds Journalism Institute, 2017.

Smith, Dana Shell. "Strong Partner." *Twitter* (2017). Published electronically May 31. https://twitter.com/USEmbassyQatar/status/791170745175015424.

Smith, Oli. "Video Shows Trump's New National Security Advisor Brand Islam a 'Malignant Cancer'." *Express.com.uk* (2016). Published electronically November 20. http://www.express.co.uk/news/world/734285/Michael-Flynn-Donald-Trump-National-Security-Advisor-Islam.

Solomon, Erika. "The $1bn Hostage Deal That Enraged Qatar's Gulf Rivals." *Financial Times* (2017). Published electronically June 5. https://www.ft.com/content/dd033082-49e9-11e7-a3f4-c742b9791d43.

Sommerfeldt, Chris. "Texas Pastor Who Calls Islam 'Evil', Homosexuals 'Filthy' to Give Donald Trump Private Inauguration Sermon." *nydailynews.com* (2017). Published electronically January 20. http://www.nydailynews.com/news/politics/trump-inauguration-sermon-rev-calls-islam-evil-article-1.2951078.

Spellberg, Denise A. *Thomas Jefferson's Qur'an: Islam and the Founders*. 1st ed. New York: Alfred A. Knopf, 2013.

Sprunt, Barbara, and Ally Mutnick. "On the Clock: Trump Gets Most Time in GOP Debate." *It's All Politics* (2015). Published electronically September 16. https://www.npr.org/sections/itsallpolitics/2015/09/16/440827414/on-the-clock-who-spoke-the-longest.

Stableford, Dylan. "Marco Rubio Bought a Gun to Be 'Last Line of Defense between ISIS and My Family'." *Yahoo!* (2016). Published electronically January 17. https://www.yahoo.com/news/rubio-bought-gun-isis-174728777.html.

Stone, Meighan. "Snake and Stranger: Media Coverage of Muslims and Refugee Policy." Cambridge, MA: Joan Shorenstein Center on Media, Politics, and Public Policy; Kennedy School; Harvard University, 2017.

Stranahan, Lee. "Twin Falls Refugee Rape Special Report: Why Are the Refugees Moving in?" *Breitbart* (2016). Published electronically August 10. http://www.breitbart.com/big-government/2016/08/10/twin-falls-refugee-rape-special-report-refugees/.

Stratton, Jordan. "Art of the Deal." *Twitter* (2017). Published electronically May 21. https://bit.ly/2FkkkVr.

Stubley, Peter. "Saudi Officials Apologise after Images of Scantily Clad Women Appear at Wrestling Event." *The Independent* (2018). Published electronically April 28. https://ind.pn/2HGp0qw.

Su-Lyn, Boo. "Marina Mahathir: Malaysia Undergoing 'Arab Colonialism.'" *MayalMailOnline* (2017). Published electronically May 23. http://www.themalaymailonline.com/malaysia/article/marina-mahathir-malaysia-undergoing-arab-colonialism#FgeRTTZQeLprT zMW.97.

Subcommittee on Terrorism, Technology and Homeland Security. Senate Judiciary Committee. *Testimony of J. Michael Waller*, October14, 2003.

"Suicide Attacks in Afghanistan (2001–2007)." Kabul: UN Assistance Mission to Afghanistan, 2008.

Suleiman, Omar. "Exploring the Faith and Identity Crisis of American Muslim Youth." Yaqueen Institute for Islamic Research, 2017.

Super User. "Anti-Pakistan Mufti Naeem Declares Quaid-E-Azam Was an Infidel." (2015). Published electronically May 9. http://www.shiitenews.org/index.php/pakistan/item/15936-anti-pakistan-mufti-naeem-declares-quaid-e-azam-was-an-infidel/15936-anti-pakistan-mufti-naeem-declares-quaid-e-azam-was-an-infidel.

Swayd, Samy S. *Historical Dictionary of the Druzes*. Historical Dictionaries of Peoples and Cultures. 2nd ed. Lanham, MD: Rowman & Littlefield, 2015.

Tabatabai, Ariane, and Dina Esfandiary. "Partnering with Iran to Counter ISIS?" *Lawfare Blog* (2016). Published electronically August 14. https://www.lawfareblog.com/partnering-iran-counter-isis.

Talhamy, Yvette. "The Fatwas and the Nusayri/Alawis of Syria." *Middle Eastern Studies* 46, no. 2 (2010): 175–94.

Tapson, Mark. "Harry Reid Endorses Muslim Brotherhood Shill Keith Ellison for DNC Chairman." *Truth Revolt* (2016). Published electronically November 14. https://www.truthrevolt.org/news/harry-reid-endorses-muslim-brotherhood-shill-keith-ellison-dnc-chairman.

Tasker, John Paul. "Trudeau Rebuffs Saudi Call for an Apology as Diplomatic Spat Escalates." *CBC* (2018). Published electronically August 8. https://www.cbc.ca/news/politics/canada-fix-big-mistake-saudi-foreign-minister-1.4777438.

Tatum, Sophie. "France Attack Highlights Differences in Trump, Clinton Terror Responses." *CNN.com* (2016). Published electronically July 15. https://cnn.it/2FjI77O.

Tazamal, Mobashra "Robert Mercer's Financing of Islamophobia" (2018). Published electronically March 20. http://bridge.georgetown.edu/robert-mercers-financing-islamophobia/.

Telhami, Shibley. "How Trump Changed American's View of Islam for the Better." *Washington Post* (2017). Published electronically January 25. https://wapo.st/2GN4Fn2.

"Terminology to Define the Terrorists: Recommendations from American Muslims." Washington, DC: Department of Homeland Security, 2008.

"'This Week' Transcript: Donald Trump and Ben Carson." *This Week* (2015). Published electronically November 21. http://abcnews.go.com/Politics/week-transcript-donald-trump-ben-carson/story?id=35336008.

Tiba, Zahara. "Concept of Islamic Caliphate Grows More Popular among Indonesian Students: Survey." *BenarNews* (2017). Published electronically

October 31. https://www.benarnews.org/english/news/indonesian/indonesia-militants-10312017181359.html.

"Transcript: Donald Trump's Full Immigration Speech, Annotated." *Los Angeles Times* (2016). Published electronically August 31. https://lat.ms/2bEhguL.

"Transcript: Donald Trump's Victory Speech." *New York Times* (2017). Published electronically November 9. https://www.nytimes.com/2016/11/10/us/politics/trump-speech-transcript.html.

Trofimov, Yaroslav. *The Siege of Mecca: The Forgotten Uprising in Islam's Holiest Shrine and the Birth of Al Qaeda.* 1st ed. New York: Doubleday, 2007.

Trump, Donald J. "Call It What You Will." *Twitter* (2017). Published electronically February 1. https://bit.ly/2r4TDPt.

Trump, Donald J. "Extraordinary Influx." *Twitter* (2015). Published electronically December 15. https://bit.ly/2FhOfO8.

Trump, Donald J. "Hard Line on Funding." *Twitter* (2017). Published electronically June 6.

Trump, Donald J. "Pakistan." *Twitter* (2018). Published electronically January 1. https://twitter.com/realdonaldtrump/status/947802588174577664?lang=en.

Trump, Donald J. "Pouring In." *Twitter* (2015). Published electronically November 17. https://bit.ly/2pJl3ZW.

Trump, Donald J. "Presidential Announcement Speech." *time.com* (2015). Published electronically June 16. http://time.com/3923128/donald-trump-announcement-speech/.

Trump, Donald J. "Radical Ideology." *Twitter* (2017). Published electronically June 6. https://twitter.com/realDonaldTrump/status/872062159789985792.

Trump, Donald J. "Remarks by President Trump on the Strategy in Afghanistan and South Asia." News release. August 21, 2017, https://www.whitehouse.gov/briefings-statements/remarks-president-trump-strategy-afghanistan-south-asia/.

Trump, Donald J. "Statement on Preventing Muslim Immigration." News release. December 7, 2015, https://www.donaldjtrump.com/press-releases/donald-j.-trump-statement-on-preventing-muslim-immigration.

"Trump Gives Remarks with Pres. of Israel." *Bloomberg* (2017). Published electronically May 22. https://www.youtube.com/watch?v=UaS633dA6Kc.

"Trump Tweet: Right on Radical Islam." (2017). Published electronically June 12. https://twitter.com/realdonaldtrump/status/742034549232766976?lang=en.

"Turkish Republic Is Continuation of Ottomans: President Erdoğan." *Hurriyet Daily News* (2018). Published electronically February 10. http://www.hurriyetdailynews.com/turkish-republic-is-continuation-of-ottomans-president-erdogan-127106.

Turnham, Steve. "Donald Trump to Father of Fallen Soldier: 'I've Made a Lot of Sacrifices.'" *ABC News* (2016). Published electronically July 30. http://abcnews.go.com/Politics/donald-trump-father-fallen-soldier-ive-made-lot/story?id=41015051.

"United States of America v. Justin Nojan Sullivan a/K/a 'the Mujahid.' Bill of Indictment," edited by Asheville Division United States District Court for the Western District of North Carolina. Asheville, NC, 2016.

"University of Terror: The Jihadi School on Australia's Doorstep Funded by Donald Trump's Friend Saudi Arabia." *News.com.au.* Published electronically June 14.

http://www.news.com.au/world/asia/university-of-terror-the-jihadi-school-on-australias-doorstep-funded-by-donald-trumps-friend-saudi-arabia/news-story/2 67fcd2904925182cc3092833efff0f2.

"Urgent 'the Mark' Saleh Al-Lahaidan Calls the State to Torture and Discipline Sheikh Ahmed Al-Ghamdi." *YouTube* (2014). Published electronically December 16. https://www.youtube.com/watch?v=mY35rIEFCO8&app=desktop.

"U.S. TV Primetime News Prefer Stereotypes: Muslims Framed Mostly as Criminals." London: Media Tenor, 2013.

V., Nicky. "Running on Hate Update: Anti-Muslim Candidates Underperform in Last Night's Elections." Oakland, CA: Muslim Advocates, 2018.

"Vaccination for Smallpox? The Paper War during Boston's Smallpox Epidemic of 1721." *National Humanities Center Resource Toolbox* http://nationalhumanitiescenter.org/pds/becomingamer/ideas/text5/smallpoxvaccination.pdf.

Versteegh, C. H. M. *Arabic Grammar and Qur'anic Exegesis in Early Islam*. Studies in Semitic Languages and Linguistics. Leiden; New York: E. J. Brill, 1993.

Veteran Intelligence Professionals for Sanity. "Intel Vets Tell Trump Iran Is Not Top Terror Sponsor." (2017). Published electronically December 26. http://www.ronpaulinstitute.org/archives/featured-articles/2017/december/26/intel-vets-tell-trump-iran-is-not-top-terror-sponsor/.

Visser, Nick. "CBS Chief Les Moonves Says Trump's 'Good' for Business." *Huffington Post Media* (2016). Published electronically March 1. https://www.huffingtonpost.com/entry/les-moonves-donald-trump_us_56d52ce8e4b03260bf780275.

Voltaire, James Miller, John Hoadly and David Garrick. *Mahomet, the Imposter*. London: C. Bathurst etc., 1777.

"Wahhabism." *Frontline* (2014). https://www.pbs.org/wgbh/pages/frontline/shows/saudi/analyses/wahhabism.html.

"Wahhabism Has No Place Here." *The Star Online* (2016). Published electronically August 28. https://www.thestar.com.my/news/nation/2016/08/28/wahhabism-has-no-place-here/.

Wang, Amy B. "Trump Lashes Out at 'So-Called Judge' Who Temporarily Blocked Travel Ban." *Washington Post* (2017). Published electronically February 4. https://wapo.st/2vLbXCI.

Warrick, Joby. *Black Flags: The Rise of Isis*. 1st ed. New York: Doubleday 2015.

"Watch & Read: Mohammed Bin Salman's Full Interview." *Al-Arabiya English* (2017). Published electronically May 3. https://english.alarabiya.net/en/features/2017/05/03/Read-the-full-transcript-of-Mohammed-Bin-Salman-s-interview.html.

Weiner, Rachel, and Justin Jouvenal. "Government Reveals More Than 100,000 Visas Revoked Due to Travel Ban." *washingtonpost.com* (2017). Published electronically February 3. https://www.washingtonpost.com/local/public-safety/government-reveals-over-100000-visas-revoked-due-to-travel-ban/2017/02/03/7d529eec-ea2c-11e6-b82f-687d6e6a3e7c_story.html?hpid=hp_hp-top-table-main_visas-1246pm%3Ahomepage%2Fstory&utm_term=.7277cc050267.

Whelan, Estelle. "Forgotten Witness: Evidence for the Early Codification of the Qur'an." *Journal of the American Oriental Society* 118 (1998).

"When Is It 'Terrorism'? How the Media Cover Attacks by Muslim Perpetrators." *The Hidden Brain* (2017). Published electronically June 19. https://www.npr.org/2017/06/19/532963059/ when-is-it-terrorism-how-the-media-covers-attacks-by-muslim-perpetrators.

"Who We Are." Muslim Students Association, http://msanational.org/about-us/ who-we-are/.

"Wikileaks: Saudi Arabia and Azhar on the 'Shia Encroachment' in Egypt." *Mada Masr* (2015). Published electronically July 9. https://www.madamasr.com/en/2015/07/09/feature/politics/ wikileaks-saudi-arabia-and-azhar-on-the-shia-encroachment-in-egypt/.

Williams, Thomas. *The American Spirit: The Story of Commodore William Phillip Bainbridge*. Kindle ed. AuthorHouse, 2010.

Wilson, Tom. "Foreign Funded Islamist Extremism in the UK." London: Centre for the Response to Radicalisation and Terrorism, 2017.

Wilstein, Mark. "Bobby Jindal on Muslim Americans: 'That's Not Immigration', It's 'Invasion.'" *Mediaite* (2015). Published electronically January 27. https://www.mediaite.com/online/ bobby-jindal-on-muslim-americans-thats-not-immigration-its-invasion/.

Woodward, Bob. *The War Within: A Secret White House History, 2006–2008*. 1st Simon & Schuster trade pbk. ed. New York: Simon & Schuster Paperbacks, 2009.

Wootson Jr., Cleve. "Parents Burned and Beat Their Teen Daughter after She Said No to 'Arranged' Marriage, Police Say." *Washington Post* (2018). Published electronically March 26. https://www.washingtonpost.com/news/post-nation/ wp/2018/03/25/a-teen-said-no-to-an-arranged-marriage-investigators-say-her-parents-threw-hot-oil-on-her/?utm_term=.38c4ad51d442.

Wright, Robin, and Peter Baker. "Iraq, Jordan See Threat to Election from Iran." *Washington Post*, December 8, 2004, A01.

Writer, Staff. "Saudi Crown Prince Pledges to Destroy Extremism, Return to Moderate Islam." *Al Arabiya* (2017). Published electronically October 24. https:// english.alarabiya.net/en/News/gulf/2017/10/24/Saudi-Arabia-Crown-Prince-pledges-to-destroy-extremism-urges-moderate-Islam.html.

"Yemen: Events of 2016." *World Report 2017* (2017). https://www.hrw.org/ world-report/2017/country-chapters/yemen.

Young, Michael. "The Dark Angel Gabriel." *Now Lebanon* (2011). Published electronically March 11. http://michaelyoungscolumns.blogspot.com/2011/03/ dark-angel-gabriel.html.

Yousaf, Kamran. "Are You with Us or with Qatar, Saudis Ask Pakistan." *Express Tribune* (2017). Published electronically June 14. https://tribune.com.pk/ story/1434933/gulf-diplomatic-crisis-us-qatar-saudis-ask-pakistan/.

Yusuf, Moeed. "Radicalism among Youth in Pakistan: Human Development Gone Wrong?." Islamabad: UNDP Pakistan and Jawan Pakistan, 2014.

Zarif, Javad. "Terror-Fighting Despots" (2017). Published electronically June 7. https://twitter.com/JZarif/status/872543822525464577.

Zernike, Kate, and Michael T. Kaufman. "The Most Wanted Face of Terrorism."
New York Times (2011). Published electronically May 2. http://www.nytimes.
com/2011/05/02/world/02osama-bin-laden-obituary.html?hp=&pagewanted=all.
Zogby, James. "Saudis Reject Bin Laden and Terrorism" (2003). Published
electronically August 1. http://www.aaiusa.org/w081103.
Zuhur, Sherifa. *Saudi Arabia*. Middle East in Focus. Santa Barbara,
CA: ABC-CLIO, 2011.

INDEX